MEDIEVAL HISTORY

Selected Reading Lists and Course Outlines from
American Colleges and Universities

MEDIEVAL HISTORY

edited by Penelope D. Johnson
New York University

Third updated and expanded edition, 1988

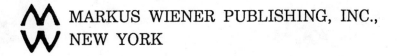 MARKUS WIENER PUBLISHING, INC.,
NEW YORK

First M. Wiener Publishing Inc. Edition 1983
Second Edition 1985
Third Edition 1988/9

Medieval history / edited by Penelope D. Johnson.—3rd updated and expanded ed.
    p. cm.—(Selected reading lists and course outlines from American
colleges and universities)
  Includes bibliographies.
  ISBN 0-910129-92-4: $14.50
  1. Middle Ages—History—Outlines, syllabi, etc. 2. Middle Ages—History—
Bibliography. I. Johnson, Penelope D. (Penelope Delafield), 1938- . II. Series.
D118.M39 1989
909.07'07'1173—dc19   88-26104
                                              CIP

Printed in America

Table of Contents

VIII. Institutional History

IX. History of Women

X. History of Jews

XI. Teaching Students to Explore and do Research in Medieval History

Introduction

This volume of course outlines and reading lists represents the third edition of syllabi in medieval history. When I gathered syllabi for the original volume in the spring of 1983, the range and creativity of the submissions struck me as exciting and provocative. Now, five years later, the collection has changed substantially with twenty-four new and ten revised syllabi, and continues, I believe, to offer a stimulating collection of medieval history teaching outlines.

In selecting course materials for this edition, I looked for either elegantly classic courses or particularly innovative syllabi which present material in fresh ways. Some of the courses are organized around a re-conceptualization of the material, others offer unusual examples of assignments, exam formats, reading lists, or out-of-class activities. For instance, Barbara Hanawalt structures her survey by formulating specific objectives for each lecture and assignment, and John Nichols personalizes the Middle Ages with a series of unusual assignments. Some of the outlines I particularly liked cannot properly be classified as history or as exclusively medieval; but having decided that the prime purpose of this volume is to encourage pedagogic creativity, I decided to include some courses that do not fit exactly within the framework of medieval chronology, such as Jeremy Adams' "France from the Stone Age to Joan of Arc" and Emily Tabuteau's "Magna Carta Through the Ages," or that lie outside the discipline of history, such as Elizabeth Petroff's "Medieval Women Writers."

Scholars drawn to the study of the Middle Ages seem to enjoy the challenge of constructing innovative courses, which led to my receiving much more good material that I could use. But the continuing concentration on social history and the focus of American scholars on northwestern Europe made it difficult to find syllabi in all fields. Courses in women's history and legal history heavily outweighed those in intellectual and institutional history, and very few scholars seem to be teaching straight economic history. Also, this time around, my colleagues seem to be emphasizing the early Middle Ages, while the later medieval period would appear to be out of vogue.

The organization of this collection is admittedly arbitrary and the categorization of each course reflects my judgment and not necessarily that of the instructor. Many courses can logically and appropriately fit into more than one niche. Thus, for example, John Carter's course "Concepts of Eve and Mary" is a cultural history course, although I chose to categorize it as women's history. Equally, it has been my choice to include in this volume courses intended for graduate as well as undergraduate students on the assumption that an instructor can amend a syllabus to the appropriate level of a class, and that advanced undergraduates are often working on the same material as are first-year graduate students. The comparison of two courses in Church history—one for undergraduate and the other for graduate students—suggests some ways in which material can be presented at different levels. I excluded highly specialized graduate seminars, since they generally rely on personalized reading lists and individual meetings with the instructor so that they were not amenable to the purposes of this collection. Finally, I have chosen more than one syllabus for a subject when the duplication offered a useful comparison of differing methods and approaches. For instance, I included two courses on monasticism, since the dramatically different reading lists show how two scholars can approach the same subject with entirely different conceptualizations of the material.

It has been a pleasure to have had contact with so many exciting and creative teachers from all over the country, and gratifying that so many responded generously to contribute their materials. My thanks go to all who shared syllabi, and I regret that only a small percentage could actually be printed.

This collection of syllabi is offered to the graduate student in medieval history who is examining options in preparation for future employment; to the new teacher, who happily installed in a brand new academic job finds himself/herself facing the daunting prospect of creating a clutch of courses with little time to spare; to the established academic who is intrigued by the possibility of experimenting with the team-teaching approach, new methods, or new subject matter; and to all inveterate collectors of syllabi in medieval studies.

Penelope D. Johnson
New York University

BARBARA A. HANAWALT, DEPARTMENT OF HISTORY, UNIVERSITY OF MINNESOTA

1101 Survey of Medieval History

Fall 1987   B. Hanawalt
And Hall 250   Office: Soc. Sci 578
MWF 9:15-10:00   Phone: 624-4834
                                             Office Hours: MW 10:30-12:00

BOOKS FOR THE COURSE
    C. Warren Hollister, MEDIEVAL EUROPE: A SHORT HISTORY
    David Herlihy, ed., MEDIEVAL CULTURE AND SOCIETY
    Eileen Power, MEDIEVAL PEOPLE

COURSE DESCRIPTION
    The course surveys the history and culture of Europe, 300-1453. It
is divided into five basic parts. We look first at the breakdown of
Roman authority in response to barbarian invasions and the rise of
Christian institutions. The second part centers on the social
institutions of Europe: feudalism, manorialism, urban life. The third
theme is the economic recovery of Europe and the consequent development
of monarchies and of papal power. The fourth part looks at political
violence in Europe as the monarchy and papacy clash, barons try to limit
the power of kings, and peasants rise in revolt. The final section is on
the culture of Europe. Throughout the basic narrative of events and
broader political and economic change, the course emphasizes the
experience of people from all levels of society as they are influenced by
events or as they carry on their daily life oblivious to the flow of
history.

COURSE REQUIREMENTS
    Students are required to take two midterms and a final examination.
A brief paper will be required. There will be quizzes during the
section meetings.

LECTURES AND ASSIGNMENTS
    *Note that the major points of the lectures are entered under each
lecture topic here. In addition you will be given a time line and a
brief lecture outline for each class.* Use these to study for exams with
lecture notes and readings for the course.

Sept. 28   INTRODUCTION
           This class period has 3 objectives. One is to establish the
           class assignments and expectations for performance for the
           course. My expectations are that you will learn about the
           Middle Ages by attending lectures, reading the texts,
           participating in discussion groups, and asking questions when
           you are puzzled or want more information. Second, I use the
           class to get to know you better and know what you want from the
           course. Third, I will summarize the conditions in Europe on
           the verge of the Middle Ages so that we all start at the same
           point in our knowledge.   This will be a brief lecture on the
           decline of Rome.

Reading: Power, "The Precursors"

Discussion sections: Discuss the readings on the Church from
the Herlihy book (Sept. 30 assignment).

I. FOUNDATIONS OF MEDIEVAL CULTURE

Sept. 30   CONTRIBUTIONS OF CHRISTIANITY TO MEDIEVAL CULTURE

Readings: Hollister: chs. 1,4
Herlihy: pp. 56-117

Performance Objectives: Readings
Concentrate on how Christianity spread, what its functions
were in society, what institutions it developed. What were
Benedict's rules for monks like? What types of literature did
Christianity produce? What values did the literature emphasize?

Performance Objectives: Lecture
The lecture will cover the early formation of church dogma and
the early organization of the church. It will also discuss the
role of the Church in bringing both Christian and Roman values to
the barbarian tribes. Monasticism will be an important theme
of the lecture

Oct. 2   GERMANIC TRIBES AND THE SETTLEMENT OF EUROPE
Readings: Hollister, Chapters 2,3
Herlihy: 20-33, 118-153

Performance Objectives: Readings.
Medieval culture is formed from three major cultural traditions
coming together in western Europe: Roman, Germanic, and
Christian. In this reading and the next, look carefully at the
contributions of the three cultures. In the Herlihy reading
note how a Roman describes the Germanic culture. What does he
find positive about it? How is German society organized? What
values does the poetry show that the barbarians held?

Performance Objectives: Lecture
The lecture will investigate invasions of the Germanic tribes
in the 4th and 5th centuries. We will be interested in where
the different tribes settled, what types of governments they
set up, and what happened to Romans and their culture.

Oct. 5   THE FRANKS AND CAROLINGIAN EUROPE

Readings: Hollister, ch. 6

Performance Ojbectives: Readings and Lecture
Concentrate on the synthesis of the Germanic, Christian, and
Roman traditions that the Carolingians gave to Europe both
politically and intellectually.

Discussion Sections: Discuss the Germanic tribes as portrayed in the readings from Herlihy for Oct. 2.

Oct. 7   CHARLEMAGNE AND THE DECLINE OF THE CAROLINGIAN EMPIRE

Performance Objectives: Lecture
What were the strengths of Charlemagne as a leader? What
were the real weaknesses of the Carolingian Empire? How was
the empire divided? What long range consequences did the
division have for European history?

Oct. 9   VIKINGS AND CONDITIONS LEADING TO FEUDALISM

Reading: Hollister, ch. 7

Performance Objectives: Reading
Who were the new invaders of Eusrope? Did the Carolingians
manage to defend themselves against the invasion? Why were
the invasions so destructive? Where did the Vikings finally
settle?

Performance Objectives: Lecture
The lecture will discuss the Vikings and their invasion of
Europe. It will emphasize the reasons that these new
invasions encouraged people to look for local leadership
rather than place their confidence in kings. It is this
system of personal ties with a local strongman that led to the
institution of feudalism.

II. THE SOCIAL AND ECONOMIC STRUCTURE OF MEDIEVAL EUROPE

Oct. 12   THE FEUDAL STRUCTURE

Reading: Hollister ch. 8
Herlihy, 229-281

Performance Objectives: Reading
What is the nature of the feudal contract? What are the
obligations and privileges of the lord; what are the
obligations of the vassal? Be able to define a fief, homage
and fealty, and vassalage. By the twelfth century how were
nobles supposed to behave? Do you think that they really did
act this way? Note the differences between the SONG OF
ROLAND and the ROMANCE OF TRISTAN AND ISEULT.

Performance Objectives: Lecture
The lecture will cover the origins of feudalism and review
the feudal contract. Note in particular that we are
discussing only the ruling elite of the society or about 5%
of the population. Pay very close attention to this lecture
because it will form the basis for understanding much of the
rest of the course material.

Discussion sessions: Discussions will be based on the Herlihy
readings on feudal society. The object is to understand the

values and attitudes of medieval nobility.

Oct. 14   THE IMPLICATIONS OF FEUDALISM

Performance Objectives: Lecture
The feudal structure led to a distinct social class whose
membership was protected by hereditary entrance into the
class. The class developed distinctive methods of warfare
and social behavior. The government under feudalism also had
distinctive characteristics.

OAt. 16   THE CASTLE

Oct. 19   MANORIALISM

Reading: Power, "The Peasant Bodo"
         Herlihy, 33-55

Performance Objective: Reading
What were the duties of manorial officials? What could one
find on a manor in the way of products? What were the
possible statuses of people on the manor? How well did the
peasants understand Christianity? In "The Peasant Bodo"
what was the life of peasant Bodo like on a Carolingian
manor? What did he and his family do for a living and for
entertainment? Identify not only his work but also that of
his wife and children.

Performance Objective: Lecture
We will be talking about the majority of the population for
the next two lectdures: 90% of the population were peasants
living on manors. The lecture will define a manor, discuss
the economic organization of the manor and the administration
of the manor. The work of the peasants on the manor
supported the comfortable lifestyle of the nobility who held
the manors as fiefs. This is a fundamental lecture to
understand. Take good notes.

Discussion Sections: Discussion will center on the life of
the peasantry based on the readings from Herlihy and Power.

Oct. 21   PEASANTRY

Performance Objective: Lecture
We will investigate the status differences within the peasant
community and the daily life of the peasants. We will also
look at the improved condition of the peasants in the 12th
century.

Oct. 23   ECONOMIC REVIVAL AND TRADE

Reading: Hollister, ch. 9
         Herlihy, pp. 176-189

Performance Objective: Reading
In Hollister, know the reasons for the expansion of the
European economy after 1050 and the causes of the rise of towns.
The documents in Herlihy illustrate the *Drang Nach Osten* and
the establishment of independent rights for villages and
towns. What rights did peasants and townsmen procure from
their lords?

Performance Objective: Lecture
The lecture will deal with the expansion of the European
economy after 1050. It will discuss instruments of trade,
such as banking, joint stock companies, and usury. This is a
foundation lecture for the course and will help you to
to understand the other lectures better.

Oct. 26   RISE OF TOWNS

Reading: Power: "The Menagier's Wife"
·Herlihy: pp. 282-291

Performance Objective: Reading
What type of literature did townspeople enjoy? Note the
pleasure in grossness and turning the tables on characters.
What was the age of the menagier's wife compared to that
of her husband? Be able to describe her daily life.

Performance Objective: Lecture
The lecture will discuss the organization of medieval
industry, gilds, and town government.

Discussion section: discussion of the bourgeois life based on
the readings in Power and Herlihy

Oct. 27   EXPANSION OF EUORPE: THE CRUSADES

Reading: Hollister: ch. 5, 10
Power: "Marco Polo"

Performance Objective: Reading
Chapter 5 is background reading for the lecture. This
material will not be covered in class so that you are
expected to come to class with this knowledge. Chapter 10
will provide a description of the crusades and the reasons
for them. The "Marco Polo" provides a good description
of a merchant's reaction to the orient and the nature of
trade wars.

Performance Objective: Lecture
The lecture will discuss the motivations for the crusades
including those of the pope, the Byzantine Emperor, the
nobility and the peasants. It will give a narrative of the
first crusade.

Oct. 30   MIDTERM EXAMINATION: ALL STUDENTS MUST TAKE THE EXAMINATION

III. THE FORCES OF CENTRALIZATION IN EUROPE

Nov. 2   THE PAPACY

Reading: Hollister: ch. 12

Performance Objective: Reading
Note how the papacy became a dominant political power in
Europe. Know what the College of Cardinals is and the papal
curia. What political ambitions did the papacy have.

Performance Objective: Lecture
The lecture will discuss the papal claims of political
dominance. It will describe the papal bureaucracy and the
ways in which the popes became politically prominent.

Discussion section: Discussion of the political and worldly
nature of the medieval papacy. Compare the papal government
with that of the monarchies of Europe

Nov. 4   MONARCHY IN ENGLAND

Reading: Hollister: ch. 13

Performance Objective: Reading
Read the first part of the chapter. What were the
institutions of government that the Normans established
under William and Henry I and Henry II?

Performance Objective: Lecture
We will look at the way that the English monarchy functioned
and in particular at the establishment of the English
judicial system

Nov. 6   MONARCHY ON THE CONTINENT: FRANCE

Reading: Hollister: ch. 13

Performance Objective: Reading and lecture
What system did the French develop for government? How did
conditions in France differ from those in England?

Nov. 9   CLASH BETWEEN CHURCH AND STATE: PAPACY AND GERMAN EMPEROR

Reading: Hollister: ch. 12

Performance Objective: Reading
Over what issues did the church and monarchies of Europe come
into conflict? What weapond did they have at their disposal
in fighting each other? Did either side win?

Performance Objective: Lecture
The lecture will discuss the reasons for the conflict between

the pope and the German emperors. It will cover both the narrative of the struggles and the issues over which they fought.

Discussion sections: Discussion of the readings listed in Nov. 11.

IV. MEDIEVAL POLITICAL AND RELIGIOUS CONFLICT

Nov. 11   REVOLT AGAINST THE CHURCH

Reading: Hollister: ch. 11
         Herlihy: pp. 289-314
         Power: "Madame Eglentyne"

Performance Objective: How corrupt was the church? Was some corruption more serious than others? Was Madame Egletyne one of the seriously corrupt? What did Francis and Dominic offer the Church and the laity; what was their appeal?

Performance Objective: Problems of the worldly Church including heresy and lay criticism. The spiritual remedies of the two mendicant monastic orders: the Franciscans and Dominicans.

Nov. 13   BARONS AGAINST KINGS

Reading: review Hollister, ch. 13

Performance Objective: Lecture
The lecture will cover the conflict between the English monarch and the barons. Magna Carta and the origins of Parliament will be discussed. The English barons clearly established that the king of England would be subject to the law of the land and not above it.

Nov. 16   KINGS AGAINST KINGS: THE HUNDRED YEARS' WAR

Reading: Hollister, ch. 15
         Herlihy, pp. 385-393
         Power: "Thomas Betson"

Performance Objective: Reading
What were the causes of the Hundred Years' War? Who won the battles? Who won the war? What was a merchant of the staple? What was Betson's life like?

Performance Objective: Lecture
We will discuss the nature of the war and the major campaigns and battles.

Discussion Section: Discussion of Betson's life as a merchant of the Staple.

Nov. 18   FAMINE AND DISEASE

               Reading: Herlihy, pp. 342-361

               Performance Objective: What are the symptoms of the Black
               Death? How many died in Florence? What social disruptions
               did it cause? How did England respond to effects of
               decreased labor and increased wages?

               Performance Objective: Lecture
               Fourteenth century famines. The nature of the bubonic plague
               and its reoccurrence. Social and economic effects.

Nov. 20   THE PEASANT REVOLTS

               Performance Ojective: Lecture
               Reasons for the peasant revolts in Europe in the late
               fourteenth century. The response of peasants and land lords
               to depopulation from plague and other diseases.

Nov. 23   MIDTERM EXAMINATION: ALL STUDENTS MUST TAKE THIS EXAMINATION

           V. MEDIEVAL CULTURE AND THE CLOSE OF THE MIDDLE AGES

Nov. 25   MEDIEVAL UNIVERSITIES

               Reading: Hollister, ch. 14
                        Herlihy, pp. 209-220

               Performance Objective: Readings
               Note the organization of the universities and the
               curriculum. What were the concerns covered in the charters
               for the University of Paris? Why did they need a charter?
               What did students sing about?

               Performance Objective: Lecture
               The lecture will cover the origins of universities and the
               difference between student run universities and the
               professor run universities. We will also discuss the
               curriculum. It is important to know the material of the
               lecture because you attend an institution of higher
               education that is directly descended from the medieval
               university.

               Discussion section: discussion of student life at
               university

Nov. 27   Thanksgiving holiday

Nov. 30   SCHOLASTICISM

               Reading: Herlihy, pp.190-206, 220-228

               Performance Objective: Reading

What were Peter Abelard's misfortunes? What was so radical about SIC ET NON? Can you follow Aquinas' proof for the existance of God?

Performance Objective: Lecture
The lecture will discuss medieval philosophy and explain what scholasticism is. The Aristotelean influence on European philosophy is one of the important points to get from the lecture.

Discussion Section: Discussion of the Herlihy reading for Nov. 30 and Dec. 3

Dec. 1   MEDIEVAL ART AND LITERATURE

Performance Objectives: Lecture
You will learn how medieval art was unique. We will concentrate on distinguishing the Romanesque from the Gothic architectural styles. You should learn the parts of a cathedral.

Dec. 3   A SUMMING UP: 1453

Reading: Hollister, ch. 16
         Herlihy, pp. 314-341, 361-384,394-410

Performance Objective: Reading
Who comprised society according to Chaucer? Note the emphasis on the middle class. What is a beatific vision according to Dante? What is the message of Meister Eckhart?

Performance Objective: Lecture
The lecture will discuss what happens to the monarchies and the Church at the end of the Middle Ages. 1453 is significant because it marks the end of the Hundred Years' War, the fall of Constantinople, and the invention of the printing press.

Dec. 5   MENTAL ATTITUDES AT THE END OF THE MIDDLE AGES

Reading: Power, "Thomas Paycocke of Coggeshall"

Performance Objective: Reading
What were the goals of Paycocke? What were his religious attitudes? How different is he from the earlier personalities that you have read about in the Power book?

Performance Objective: Lecture
The lecture will concentrate on how society changed in response to the Hundred Years' War, the plague, and the corruption of the Church. It will look at the social attitudes of people at the end of the middle ages.

ALL STUDENTS MUST TAKE THE FINAL EXAMINATION AS SCHEDULED

Mount Holyoke College

Carole Straw
Undergraduate Level Course; two 75 minute classes per week

Classical and Christian Worlds

Moderation, discipline and self-control are virtues prized in classical and Christian traditions. We shall examine how Christian writers have adapted or diverged from classical ideas, focusing on the definition of body and soul and the relationship of humanity with the divine. To what extent is the body the soul's friend or enemy? What kinds of pleasure are permissible? What forms of self-control or ascetic practices are considered salutary? These questions will lead us to consider private and public realms of behavior, appropriate roles of men and women, and the emotional ties permitted in man's quest for God.

Books to be purchased

Epictetus, The Enchiridion
Irwin Edman, ed. The Works of Plato (Modern Library)
Moses Hadas, ed. The Stoic Philosophy of Seneca (Norton)
Petronius, The Satyricon (Penguin)
Evagrius of Pontus, On Prayer (Cistercian Studies)
Helen Waddell, The Desert Fathers (Ann Arbor)
Xerox packet

On reserve

1. Armstrong, A. H., ed. The Cambridge History of Later Greek and Early Medieval Philosophy. Cambridge: At the University Press, 1970.
2. Foucault, Michel. The History of Sexuality. 3 vols. New York: Pantheon Press, 1984-6.
3. Veyne, Paul, ed. A History of Private Life: From Pagan Rome to Byzantium, tr. Arthur Goldhammer. Vol. 1 of Philipp Ariès and Georges Duby, A History of Private Life. Cambridge, Mass. and London: Harvard University Press, 1987.
4. Gosling, J.C.B. and Taylor,C.C.W., The Greeks on Pleasure. Oxford: Clarendon Press, 1982.
5. Hadot, Pierre. Exercises spirituels et philosophie antique. Paris, 1981.
6. Rist, J. M. Stoic Philosophy. Cambridge: At the University Press, 1969.
7. Long, Hellenistic Philosophy: Stoics, Epicureans, Sceptics. Berkeley and Los Angeles: University of California Press, 1986.
8. Fox, Robin Lane. Pagans and Christians. New York: Knopf, 1987.
9. North, Helen. Sophrosyne: Self-Knowledge and Self-Restraint in Greek Literature. Cornell Studies in Classical Philology 35. Ithaca: Cornell University Press, 1966.
10. Colish, Marcia. The Stoic Tradition From Antiquity to the Middle Ages. 2 vols. Studies in the History of Christian Thought 34 and 35. Leiden: E. J. Brill, 1985.

Course Requirements

1. Active participation in class discussions.
2. A short oral report on a primary or secondary source.
3. One take-home midterm, a five to seven page essay. One final paper, a ten to fifteen page essay on a subject of your choice.

Schedule of Class Meetings

Week 1
    Introduction
    Plato, The Symposium

Week 2
    Plato, Phaedo
    Plato, The Apology

WeeK 3
    Aristotle, Ethics, book 5
    Aristotle, Ethics, books 4 and 7

Week 4
    Xenophon, Oeconomicus
    Aeschines, "Against Timarchus"

Week 5
    Sexual politics in Greek Art: Classical and Hellenistic examples
    Selections from the Hippocratic Corpus

Week 6
    Cicero, Selections from The Tusculan Disputations; and from his Letters

Week 7
    Lucretius, On the Nature of the Universe, book 4 (xerox packet)
    Petronius, The Satyricon

Week 8
    Epictetus, The Enchridion
    Seneca, On Tranqillity, Letters, Maxims

Week 9
    Seneca, On Providence, Consolation of Helvetia
    Plutarch, On Marriage; A Letter of Consolation to his Wife on the Death of an Infant Daughter

Week 10
    Plotinus, Selections from the Enneads

Week 11
  Origen, An Exhortation to Martyrdom (xerox packet)
  Evagrius of Pontus, On Prayer

Week 12
  Helen Waddell, The Desert Fathers
  Cassian, Selections from the Institutes and Conferences

Week 13
  Gregory of Nyssa, On Virginity
  Jerome, Selections from his Letters to women; and from Against Jovinian

Week 14
  Augustine, On the Good of Marriage, Letter 211 (xerox packet)
  Prudentius, Psychomachia, book 4; Paulinus of Nola, Selection from his
Poems

Geoffrey Koziol
Harvard University

History 1127
Europe in the Early Middle Ages

Books to be purchased:

Either R.H.C. Davis, _History of Medieval Europe_
  or R. Hoyt and S. Chodorow, _Europe in the Middle Ages_ [= HC]
Peter Brown, _The Cult of the Saints_
Political Writings of St. Augustine
Gregory of Tours, _History of the Franks_
Bede, _The Ecclesiastical History_
Pierre Riche, _Daily Life in the World of Charlemagne_
Hodges & Whitehouse, _Mohammed, Charlemagne, and the Origins of
  Europe_
Njal's Saga, trans. Magnusson and Palsson
E.E. Emerton, _The Correspondence of Pope Gregory VII_

Requirements: A midterm and a final, both modified take-home
exams (i.e., a list of possible questions will be handed out
before the exam, which will be written in class or during the
scheduled period.) There will also be a 12-15 page paper, due
January 11, one week before the final exam, at 5 p.m. **N.B.**
Begin preparing this paper well in advance of its due date; and
leave enough time to revise and proofread it. Although you may
choose your own topic, you should clear it with me first. (If
you have difficulty creating a topic I'll help.)

LIST OF CLASSES AND READINGS

An [R] after a work means that it is on reserve at Lamont and
Hilles, [RH] on reserve in the History Department library. Where
more than one reading is assigned (apart from the textbook),
those marked with an asterisk [*] will be the ones focused on in
discussions.

I. The Roman Prelude

9/21   Introduction
W   The third-century crisis: did Rome fall?
F   . Discussion: Brown, _Cult of Saints_; Davis, 3-20; HC, 1-27

9/28   Religion in late antiquity: Constantine's conversion
W   The meaning of the "church" in late antiquity: Donatism
F   Discussion: _Political Writings of St. Augustine_, 1-19,
       28-48, 53-8, 84-94, 102-3, 108-10, 118-19, 125-31, 133-4,
       137-8, 141-53, 184-219, 226-37, 252-62, 265-76, 282-91,
       305-12, 314-7; Davis, 68-74; HC, 28-54

II. The Frankish Kingdoms

10/5   The Germanic invasions: were they?
W   The making of Frankish kingship
F   Discussion: Gregory of Tours, History of the Franks

> Introduction, 7-23 (skim the rest if you have the time; it's quite good); Preface; I.pref.-4; II.pref.-2, 6-7, 9-12, 16-24, 27-33, 35-43; III.pref.-1, 5-15, 18-37; IV.1-7, 9-31, 34, 39, 42, 44-5, 47-51; V.pref.-4, 11-14, 17-18, 29-32, 34-6, 38-9, 42, 44, 47-50; VI.1-5, 8, 11-14, 17, 19-27, 31-5, 37-8, 41, 45-6; VII.2, 4-15, 18-39, 45-7; VIII.1-11, 18, 29-31, 36, 41-4; IX.6, 8-12, 19-21, 30-34; X.25, 27, 31 (pp. 593, 601-4); Davis, 21-67, 109-20; HC, 55-83

10/12   Columbus Day
W   Murder, mayhem, and the decline of the Merovingians
F   Discussion: Bede, The Ecclesiastical History, Introduction (pp. 15-21, skim), 66-192, 198-207, 214-18, 226-43, 250-3, 257-69, 282-300; Davis, 79-88; HC, 85-111

III. The Carolingians

10/19   Techniques of Carolingian government
W   Poor Louis the Pious
F   Discussion: Pierre Riché, Daily Life; Davis, 89-107, 120-53; HC, 123-79

10/26   The endemic crisis of tenth-century Europe

> Discussion: Hodges and Whitehouse, Mohammed, Charlemagne, and the Origins of Europe; Davis, 154-99; HC, 181-94

F   Midterm

IV. Images and Forces of Order

11/2   Kinship and lordship
W   Gender roles
F   Discussion: Njal's Saga

11/9   Law and order
W   Veterans' Day
F   Discussion: Rebecca Coleman, "Reason and Unreason in Early Medieval Society," J. Interdisc. Hist. 4 (1974), 571-91 [R, RH]; Patrick Geary, "Living with Conflict in Stateless France," Annales 41 (1986), 1107-33 [RH, English version of French]; Pauline Stafford, "Sons and Mothers: Family Politics in the Early Middle Ages,"

Medieval Women, ed. Derek Baker [R, RH]; David
Herlihy, Medieval Households, 29-78 [R]; Marc Bloch,
Feudal Society, vol. 1, 123-75 [R]; HC, 202-250

11/16   Monasticism I
W   Monasticism II
F   Discussion: David Knowles, The Constitutions of Lanfranc,
         vii-xxi, xxxv-xxxvii, 17-20, 22-48, 55-9, 72-95,
         98-103, 104-118, 123-31* [R, xerox RH]; C.H. Lawrence,
         Medieval Monasticism, (pages to be assigned) [R];
         Davis, 74-9, 260-66

11/23   The ideal of kingship on the eve of the Investiture Contest
W   The reality: how kings governed
F   Discussion: J.M. Wallace-Hadrill, "The Via Regia of the
         Carolingian Age," Trends in Medieval Political Thought,
         ed. Beryl Smalley, 22-41* [R]; Koziol, Sources on
         Kingship* [R]; Karl Leyser, "Ottonian Government," in
         either idem, Medieval Germany and its Neighbours [R] or
         Engl. Hist. Rev. 381 (1981): 721-53* [R]; Vita
         Chuonradi, trans. Mommsen and Morrison, Imperial Lives
         and Letters, pp. 52-3 and chs. i-iii, v-vi, x,
         xix-xxi, xxv, xxvii-xxviii [R]; Davis, 203-31

                    V.   The Crucible

11/30   The economic transformation of Western Europe: commerce
         and industry
W   The economic transformation of Western Europe: the
         agrarian regime
F   Discussion: Georges Duby, The Early Growth of the European
         Economy, 112-57, 168-80, 186-208* [R]; Lynn White, Jr.,
         Medieval Technology and Social Change, 39-79* [R];
         Davis, 176-99; HC, 251-71 Recommended: David Herlihy,
         "Economical Conditions and Demographic Change," One
         Thousand Years, ed. Richard L. De Molen, 3-33 only [R]

12/7   The desire for peace
W   The Investiture Contest
F   Discussion: Koziol, Sources on the Peace of God [RH];
         H.E.J. Cowdrey, "The Peace and the Truce of God in
         Eleventh-Century France," Past and Present 46 (1970):
         42-67 [R]; one of the following: either R.I. Moore,
         The Birth of Popular Heresy, 10-15 (I.2), 19-21 (I.4),
         24-6 (I.6-7) [R] or W.L. Wakefield and A.P. Evans,
         Heresies of the High Middle Ages, 74-81, 86-9, 95-6 [R]

12/14   Gregory VII and Romana Ecclesia
W   An overview of the course
F   Discussion: The Correspondence of Pope Gregory VII, pp.
         1-4, 6-9, 11-12, 15-16, 17-19, 25-26, 26-27, 29, 30-32,
         35-36, 42-45, 58-59, 51-58, 60-61, 62-65, 67-70, 80-91,
         96-109, 110-16, 121-23, 128-30, 133-34, 138-39, 146-56,

158-60, 161-64, 165-86, 188-89, 192-95*; J.P.Whitney,
"Milan," <u>Hildebrandine Essays</u>, 143-57; Davis, 232-59;
HC, 279-302

Comments: I have also used J.N. Hillgarth's <u>The Conversion of
Europe</u>, an excellent and inexpensive selection of sources, but
using it requires omitting Brown and Bede. When Emerton is (as
now) out of print I use Tierney's <u>Crisis of Church and State</u>,
scattering readings from it throughout the semester and for the
week on the Investiture Contest supplementing it with Robert
Benson, "The Gelasian Doctrine: Uses and Transformations," <u>La
notion d'autorite au moyen age</u>, ed. George Makdisi (Paris, 1982),
13-44. I tend to assign a different saga every year, primarily
to give me a chance to read them. It's anachronistic (as at
least one graduate student zealously points out each year), but
that allows an interesting discussion on the appropriate use of
sources, and besides, the students like them better than <u>Beowulf</u>.
(<u>Laxdaela Saga</u> works even better than <u>Njal's</u>, since it's shorter;
but it is even more obviously part of 13th-century culture,
though the students don't notice unless you tell them.)

Wallace-Hadrill's article is excellent, but has perhaps too many
Latin citations for most students' tastes. Two other
alternatives are the passages pertaining to kingship in Johann
Chydenius, <u>Medieval Institutions and the Old Testament</u>, or Janet
Nelson, "The Lord's Anointed and the People's Choice," <u>Rituals of
Royalty</u>, ed. David Cannadine (Cambridge, 1987). <u>Sources on
Kingship</u> includes Widukind's account of Otto I's coronation as
translated in Brian Pullan, <u>Sources for the History of Medieval
Europe</u>; Liudprand's account of Otto's deposition of John XII in
A.R. Lewis, <u>The High Middle Ages</u>; and my own translations of the
<u>laudes regiae</u> (ed. Kantorowicz) and the coronation order from
the Pontifical of Mainz (for which I used Schramm's edition in
<u>Konige, Kaiser u. Papste</u>, since it was most convenient).
<u>Sources on the Peace of God</u> include Orderic Vitalis' account of
the Council of Lillebonne; the canons of Charroux and Poitiers in
Brian Tierney, ed., <u>The Middle Ages</u>, vol. 1, <u>Sources</u>; my
translation of the statutes of Le Puy (c. 994) edited by
Magnou-Nortier in <u>Melanges Jean Dauviller</u>; and David Herlihy's
translation of Raoul Glaber's description of the movement in
<u>Feudalism</u>. I have also assigned, and still recommend, Georges
Duby, "Laity and the Peace of God," in <u>The Chivalrous Society</u>;
Janet Nelson, "Society, theodicy, and the origins of heresy,"
<u>Studies in Church History</u> 9 (1972), 65-78; and R.I. Moore,
"Family, community and cult on the eve of the Gregorian Reform,"
<u>TRHS</u>, 5th series, 30 (1980), 49-69.

I owe the English version of "Vivre en conflit" to Patrick Geary.

History 311   Prof. McNamara
The Early Middle Ages   Room 507W
T. 5:40-7:00; TH 5:40-7:05

Textbook, C. Warren Hollister, _Europe in the Middle Ages._
Midterm examination: October 23

Final Examination: December 18, 5:30.

A research paper 15-20 pages in length is required following the
attached instructions. The paper is due on December 11.

Attribution of all material in the term paper is to be footnoted in
accordance with accepted forms. To avoid plagiarism and guide your
reader, you must supply notes for all statements quoting or
paraphrasing the opinions of others, including class notes and oral
presentations. For the correct forms for footnotes and bibliography
please consult the _MLA Handbook for Writers of Research Papers,
Theses and Dissertations_, available in the bookstore.

Grades for all essays will be scaled to content and to style (grammar
and spelling included). Errors in the latter will reduce your grade
by half a point (from A to A-, etc.).

To get a start on gathering bibliography for your research paper, you
should consult the most recent book on the subject of your choice.
This is usually found by looking through the review and "books
received" section of the appropriate journals. For medieval history,
the most comprehensive journal in English is _Speculum_. For articles
and shorter pieces, the _International Medieval Bibliography_ gives
thorough coverage on an annual basis (though it is generally a year
or two behind).

Historiography paper for History 311.

Historiography is the study of history, its writing, its methods and its conclusions as they vary in accordance with changing cultural fashions. Every historian begins with a limited amount of primary source material pertinent to the subject of study. Primary sources are the most direct evidence from eye witnesses or contemporary artifacts and documents. All knowledge of the past depends on a conscientious use of such sources. However, historians are constantly looking for new ways to use their sources to answer new questions or support new interpretations of the evidence. Your paper will focus on these methods and conflicting interpretations of a single problem.

Choose a problem that interests you from the history of medieval Europe, 400-1050, or thereabouts. Think small: the more limited the subject the better your chances are of covering the available literature. Think carefully: the success of your paper depends upon choice of a topic for which there is an adequate literature available to you and in a language you can read.

Describe the problem as fully as possible. Include:
a discussion of its historical context: chronological, geographical, social, cultural, and economic.
a consideration of particular questions raised by the problem.

Survey the available evidence:
list all available primary sources (whether or not you can read them or see them). Include archeological or pictorial material as well as literary.
discuss the information the sources yield and the gaps in the information which have never been filled.
analyze the primary sources available to you and relate them to your problem.
Note. You must use at least one and preferable more than one primary source in the composition of your paper.

Collect an annotated bibliography of secondary sources pertinent to your problem:
discuss the recent books and articles relevant to your problem and show how they differ in their contributions to an answer.
if possible, include material in foreign languages. If you cannot read them directly, refer to reviews and illuminating notes and discussions in English speaking authors.
summarize the opinions of historians about the problem itself and about the evidence available for its solution.

Conclude with a summary of the status of modern scholarship regarding your problem and, if you like, an expression of any opinion you have formed in the course of your research.

I. The Making of the West.
    1. The Christian Mediterranean
    2. The Barbarian North
    3. The Germanic Invasions.
    4. The Division of the Mediterranean
    5. Byzantium and the Roman Heritage
    6. Islam and the Isolation of the West
    7. The Germanic Kingdoms.
    8. Monasticism and the Conversion of the West.

Primary Sources:

Ammianus Marcellinus, <u>History.</u>
Ante-Nicene Fathers: translations of Christian writers before 300 AD
Augustine, <u>The Confessions</u>
Augustine, <u>The City of God</u>
Egeria (sometimes called Etheria), <u>Travels to the Holy Land.</u>
Jerome, <u>Letters</u>
Jordanes Gothicus, <u>History of the Goths</u>.
Procopius, <u>Secret History</u>
Nicene and Post-Nicene Fathers: translations of Christian writers
    after 300 AD

Secondary Sources:

Baker, G.P., <u>Constantine the Great and the Christian Revolution.</u>
Brown, Peter, <u>The Cult of the Saints.</u>
Brown, Peter, <u>Religion and Society in the Age of Saint Augustine</u>
Bullough, V L. and Brundage, J A., <u>Sexual Practices and the</u>
    <u>Medieval Church.</u>
Burns, C.D., <u>The First Europe</u>
Chadwick, N., <u>The Celts</u>.
Clark, Elizabeth A., <u>Jerome, Chrysostom and Friends.</u>
Dill, S., <u>Roman Society in the Last Century of the Roman Empire</u>
Dopsch, A., <u>The economic and Social Foundations of Europe</u>
Gibbon, E., <u>The Decline and Fall of the Roman Empire</u>
Gordon, C.D., <u>The Age of Attila</u>
Holum, Kenneth, <u>Theodosian Empresses.</u>
Kelly, JD., <u>Jerome, His Life, Writings and Controversies</u>
Lopez, R. S., <u>The Birth of Europe.</u>
Lot, F., <u>The End of the Ancient World</u>
Matthews, John, <u>Western Aristocracies and Imperial Court.</u> Momigliano,
Arnaldo, <u>The conflict between Paganism and Christianity in the Fourth</u>
    <u>Century.</u>
Oost, Steward I., <u>Galla Placidia Augusta.</u>
Pirenne, H., <u>Mohammed and Charlemagne.</u>
Taylor, H.O., <u>The Emergence of Christian Culture in the West.</u>

II. The First Europe
1. The papacy and the creation of christendom
2. The Frankish spate
3. The Anglo-Saxon monarchy
4. Charlemagne and his Empire
5. Land and loot
6. The Viking invasions.
7. Warriors and Peasants

Primary Sources:
Anglo-Saxon Chronicle, G.N. Garmonsway, trans.
Asser, The Life of Alfred the Great
Bede, History of the English Church and People.
The Benedictine Rule
Cabaniss, Allen,ed. Charlemagne's Cousins
Cabaniss, Allen, Son of Charlemagne
Cassiodorus, Letters, Thomas Hodgkij trans.
Drew, K.F., ed. The Lombard Laws
Drew, K.F., ed., The Burgundian Laws
Einhard, The Life of Charlemagne.
Emerton, E., ed. and trans., Letters of Saint Boniface.
Gregory the Great, Letters
Gregory of Tours, History of the Franks.
Hillgarth, Joyce N., The Conversion of Western Europe, 350-750.
Hoare, F.R., The Western Fathers.
Isidore of Seville, Letters
McNeill, J T. and Gamer, H M., Medieval Handbooks of Penance
Notker the Stammerer,   Life of Charlemagne
Rivers, Theodore, J., trans., Laws of the Alamans and Bavarians.
Scholz, Berhard, ed. and trans., Carolingian Chronicles
Talbot, C.H., The Anglo-Saxon Missionaries in Germany

Secondary Sources:
Bachrach, B S, Early Medieval Jewish Policy in Western Europe
Chadwick, Nora K., Poetry and Letters in Merovingian Gaul.
Duby, Georges, The Early Growth of the European Economy
Eckenstein, Lina, Women under Monasticism, 500-1500.
Geary, Patrick L., Before France and Germany
Hodges, R, Dark Age Economics: the origin of towns and trade
James, E, The Origins of France: from Clovis to the Capetians.
James, Edward, ed., Visigothic Spain: new approaches.
Levison, W, England and the Continent in the Eighth Century
Marnell, William H., Light from the West: The Irish Mission
McKitterick, R, The Frankish Church and the Carolingian Reforms
McNeill, John T., The Celtic Churches:A History, AD 200-1200.
Morris, John, The Age of Arthur
Peters, Edward, ed., Monks, Bishops and Pagans.
Riche, Pierre, Daily Life in the World of Charlemagne.
Richards, Jeffrey,   Consul of God: Life and Times of Gregory I
Stafford, Pauline, Queens, Concubines and Dowagers.
Stenton, Frank M., Anglo Saxon England.
Wemple, Suzanne F., Women in Frankish Society

III. A New Beginning
      1. The German Empire
      2. The French Monarchy
      3. The Unification of England
      4. The Seigneurial System
      5. The Rise of Towns
      6. The Proprietary Church
      7. The Gregorian Revolution

Primary Sources:
Adam of Bremen, History of the Archbishops of Hamburg-Bremen
Domesday Book, county by county series
Duby, G, Rural economy and country life in the Medieval West
Florence of Worcester, Chronicle.
Harmer, Florence A., Anglo-Saxon Writs
Hill, Boyd H., Medieval Monarchy in Action.
Hroswitha, The Non-dramatic Works of Hroswitha.
Hroswitha, Plays.
Liudprand of Cremona, Works.
Momsen, T. E. and Morrison, K. F, Imperial Lives and Letters.
Robertson, ed. Anglo Saxon Charters
Saxo Grammaticus, History of the Danes.
Roger of Wendover, Flowers of History.

Secondary sources:
Barraclough, G., Medieval Germany
Bates, David, Normandy Before 1066
Blair, P., Anglo-Saxon England
Bloch, M., The Feudal Society
Brooks, Nicholas, "Anglo Saxon Charters: the work of the last 20
     years," Anglo-Saxon England 3, (1974) 211-231.
Duckett, Eleanor, Death and Life in the Tenth Century,
Evans, J., Monastic Life and Cluny
Finberg, H.P., The Agrarian History of England and Wales
Fleckenstein, Josef, Early Medieval Germany
Hunt, Noreen, Cluniac Monasticism of the Central Middle Ages.
Kendrick, T.D., History of the Vikings
Lewis, A R., The Development of Southern French and Catalan
     Society
Leyser,K.J., Rule and Conflict in an Early Medieval Society
Pirenne, H., Medieval Cities
Rosenwein, B, Rhinoceros Bound: Cluny in the Tenth Century
Stuard, S., Women in Medieval Society
White, L., Medieval Technology and Social Change
Wickham, Chris, Early Medieval Italy, 400-1000.
Wilson, David M., ed., The Northern World

Brigham Young University

History 311
The High Middle Ages

Spring Term 1987
Instructor: P.B. Pixton

4:00 - 6:30 p.m. T, Th
Office: 413 KMB; x. 3335
Office Hours: by appointment only

Description and Rationale

This course will focus on the five centuries from ca. 900 to 1400 A.D. which
constitute what historians generally term the High Middle Ages. It will address the
major social, cultural and intellectual developments of the period within their
political and economic framework; perhaps we should pervert that a bit and say that it
will also look at political and economic developments within the
intellectual/cultural/religious context of the times.

The five centuries under consideration are those which demonstrate the vitality,
diversity and originality of the European Middle Ages no longer overshadowed by
classical antiquity and not yet anticipating the Renaissance and the Early-Modern
period.

The course has as its purposes the following: the introduction of the main themes of
European history during this significant age; the presentation of the major
interpretations of the period by major modern historians; the development of a better
understanding and appreciation of the challenges, failures and accomplishments of
those men and women who lived during this epoch; the development of historical
thinking and analysis; the disabusement of commonly-held notions about "the Dark
Ages;" and enjoyment in a humanistic enterprise.

Texts

> Richard W. Southern, The Making of the Middle Ages
> Jean Gimpel, The Medieval Machine
> Umberto Eco, The Name of the Rose

In addition, there will be several items distributed in class for which all will be
responsible. Although the contact hours in class are roughly equivalent to those of a
regular semester, there are only half the normal hours for study time: the solution,
get at it now!

Tests and Papers

There will be no mid-term exam. The final exam will consist of two comprehensive
essays which you will write the last day of class. In between you will be required to
write four papers, 4-5 pages in length each, in which you discuss in a critical way
issues raised by questions found in the syllabus and elucidated in the readings and
lectures. The papers are due when stipulated and no late papers will be accepted.
All papers are to be typewritten and to employ some scholarly apparatus (at the barest
minimum footnotes or endnotes).

Course Grade

Grades will be determined on the basis of scores achieved on the four papers (50 points each) and the final exam (200 points). Attendance and classroom participation will also be considered (50 points). The grade will be calculated at percentages of the total: 406 and better = A-, A; 361 and better = B-, B, B+; 316 and better = C-, C, C+; etc.

Lecture Topics and Reading Schedule

1st week: April 28   Introduction to the Course
The Tenth Century
The Geopolitical Setting

    Reading: Strayer, "The Future of Medieval History"
Robinson, "Medieval: The Middle Ages"
Southern, Intro and Ch. 1 (15-73)

    April 30   The Dynamics of Medieval Society: Agricultural Economy
Life on a Medieval Manor
Women and Family in Medieval Agrarian Society

    Reading: Southern, Ch. 2 (74-117)
Marsh, "The End of Serfdom" (handout)
Gimpel, The Medieval Machine, vii-58
Power, Medieval Women 7-34

2nd week: May 5   Feudalism: The Scholarly Debate
Life on a Medieval Barony
Women and Family in the Feudal World

    Reading: Strayer et al, "Feudalism"
McCash, "Eleanor of Aquitaine and Marie de Champaigne"
Power, 35-52

First Paper is Due by Tomorrow Morning at 8:00

Questions:

1. Southern assigns to medieval women the important task of "[bringing] new influences from distant parts and [establishing] bonds between men of little or no identity of purpose or of interest."

Discuss this important role in as broad a context as possible.

2. One of the basic forces of social cohesion in the Middle Ages was the personal bond which joined men and women in various types pf relationships.

Discuss the nature of those relationships, noting the differences between those of the nobility and those binding peasants to landlords.

3. The term "Dark Ages" is frequently used with reference to the medieval period in general. Scholars tend to agree that only the period from about 850 until 950/1000 in any way deserves that designation.

Discuss the general tenor of that age, noting what aspects of it warrant its being called the "Dark Ages," and what features tended to point toward a new age for European civilization.

4. To comprehend the Middle Ages, one must imagine a world without modern machines, yet certainly not one which lacked technology, even at the agrarian level.

Discuss the relationship of technology to peasant life, construing the former in as broad terms as possible.

	May 7	The Medieval Political World: Kings vs. Subjects
		: The Empire and Its Neighb
		: England and France

> Reading: McGurk, "Henry II and the Revolts of 1173"
> Bloch, "The Empire and the Idea of Empire Under the Hohenstaufen"

| 3rd week: | May 12 | The Dynamics of Medieval Society: The Church Militant Cluny, Hirsau etc The Crusades |

> Reading: Southern, Ch. 3 (118-169)

| | May 14 | The Dynamics of Medieval Society: Sacerdotium vs. Imperium |

> Reading: Carlyle, "The Dualism of Medieval Society"
> Ullmann, "The Hierocratic Doctrine"
> Morrison, "Canossa - A Revision"

| 4th week: | May 19 | Life in the Medieval Religious World |

> Reading: Bernard Guy, "Manual of the Inquisitor"

Second Paper is Due by Tomorrow Morning at 8:00

Questions

1. Although the Investiture Controversy is most commonly associated with Germany (Holy Roman Empire), it did in fact touch all of the Western monarchies to some degree.

What was at bottom in this dispute? Why did the antagonists consider it such a major issue? How effectively was the dispute settled?

2. Ca. 950 A.D., the monarchy of Germany was just entering its greatest era, while that of France was powerless. Three centuries later, France was being ruled by one of

its greatest and most effective monarchs (Louis IX) and the German monarchy had gone into eclipse.

What factors contributed to the rise of the French monarchy from such hopeless conditions in the mid-10th century? What factors produced just the opposite effect for the German monarchy? Could the latter's collapse have been averted?

3. The role of religion and of the Church was vital and predominant in the lives of most medieval men and women. Some entered the ranks of the clergy, while others benefitted from the service of the religious.

Discuss this role, noting how religion affected political, social and economic activities as well.

May 21   The Dynamics of Medieval Society: Merchant Economy
Life in a Medieval City
Women and Family in Medieval Urban Life

Reading: Power, 53-75
Gimpel, 59-170

5th week: May 26   The Dynamics of Medieval Society: The World of the Mind

Reading: The Song of Songs
Gimpel, 171-198
Southern, Ch. 4 (170-218)
Eco, The Name of the Rose, Intro and 1-50
Power, 76-99

May 28   The Dynamics of Medieval Society: The Artistic World

Reading: Southern, Ch. 5 (219-257)
Moller, "The Social Causation of the Courtly-Love
     Complex"
Eco, 51-110

6th week: June 2   The Closing of the Medieval Frontier: Europe ca. 1270

Reading: Lewis, "The Closing of the Medieval Frontier"
Eco, 113-207

Third Paper is Due by Tomorrow Morning at 8:00

Questions:

1. Despite their small size by any modern standards, the towns of the Middle Ages played an enormous role and had an impact upon the lives of peasants, nobility and burghers alike.

Explain the basic character of a medieval town, noting the fundamental differences from other types of settlement. Then, account for the numerous changes which towns wrought in medieval society between ca. 950 and 1350.

2. How effective an explanation of the period 1250-1350 is Archibald Lewis' essay on "The Closing of the Medieval Frontier?"

3. Literature and art are frequently commentaries on the age which produced them.

Using Epic and Romance literature, Romanesque and Gothic architecture, demonstrate the validity of the above statement. Account for the shift from the earlier style to the later one in each case, relating this shift to broader issues wherever possible.

4. "So long as knowledge was limited to the seven liberal arts of the Early Middle Ages, there could be no universities, for there was nothing to teach beyond the bare elements of grammar, rhetoric, logic, and the still barer notions of arithmetic, astronomy, geometry, and music, . . ." [Haskins, The Rise of Universities 4]

Discuss the change which occurred in the amount of knowledge available to western students after 1100, noting its origin, nature, and impact.

5. In what fundamental ways did technology transform medieval European society far beyond that of its classical predecessors? Show where possible evidence of cause and effect.

	June 4	The Failure of the Church
		Reading: Strayer, "Laicization of French and English Society in the 13th Century" Boniface VIII, Selected bulls Marsilius of Padua, Defensor Pacis (excerpts) Eco, 211-305
7th week:	June 9	The Failure of the State
		Reading: Cuttino, "The Causes of the Hundred Years War" Eco, 309-400 Born, "The Perfect Prince" (handout)
	June 11	Intellectual Uncertainty
		Reading: Eco, 403-493 Gimpel, 199-252
8th week:	June 16	The Waning of the Middle Ages
		Reading: Eco, 497-611

Fourth Paper is Due by Tomorrow Morning at 8:00

Questions:

1. Strayer argues that a fundamental shift occurred in the thirteenth century which explains the inability of the Church to mount opposition to the growing power of the monarchies.

What evidence can you marshal to argue that prior to this shift medieval society was dominated by religious/ecclesiastical influences and that thereafter it tended to be dominated by more secular ones?

2. Two types of Christians are juxtaposed in The Rose, Adso the sinful monk who depends on the Sacraments of the Church for the hope of salvation, and the mystic Ubertino for whom the institutional Church has become all but superfluus.

Compare and contrast these two types, noting the inherent dangers or problems with each approach. Which type seemed more typical of the 10th century? which more typical of the 14th? Why?

3. By general agreement among historians the twelfth century is the most characteristic of the High Middle Ages; already by the 13th the winds of change had begun to blow, and by the 14th a very different world was emerging.

Discuss the nature of those changes, noting both the major causes and the evidence we have of their reality.

4. "But now tell me," William was saying, "why? Why did you want to shield this book more than so many others? Why did you hide -- though not at the price of crime -- treatises on necromancy, pages that may have blasphemed against the name of God, while for these pages you damned your brothers and have damned yourself? Thare are many other books that speak of comedy, many others that praise laughter. Why did this one fill you with such fear?"

"Because it was by the Philosopher. Every book by that man has destroyed a part of the learning that Christianity had accumulated over the centuries. The fathers had said everything that needed to be known about the power of the Word, but then Boethius had only to gloss the Philosopher and the divine mystery of the Word was transformed into a human parody of categories and syllogism. The book of Genesis says what has to be known about the composition of the cosmos, but it sufficed to rediscover the Physics of the Philosopher to have the universe reconceived in terms of dull and slimy matter, and the Arab Averroes almost convinced everyone of the eternity of the world. We knew everything about the divine names, and the Dominican buried by Abo -- seduced by the Philosopher -- renamed them, following the proud paths of natural reason. And so the cosmos, which for the Areopagite (St. John) revealed itself to those who knew how to look up at the luminous cascade of the exemplary first cause, has become a perverse of terrestrial evidence for which they refer to an abstract agent. Before, we used to look to heaven; now we look to the earth, and we believe in the heavens because of earthly testimony. Every word of the Philosopher, by whom now even the saints and prophets swear, has overturned the image of the world."

Discuss in detail the issue involved in this passage within the larger context of the High Middle Ages.

June 18   Final Exam

Review Questions for the Final

1. While medieval society was clearly male-dominated, women could and did occupy significant roles.

Discuss the various roles into which women were placed or freely entered, giving attention to the breadth of society. Cite examples where women made contributions beyond their roles as bearers of children and workers in the labor market.

2. The Middle Ages have often suffered in the popular mind from the stereotype of being backward, uncreative, unchanging, narrow-minded, etc. This attitude reveals itself in the language of those who seek to describe a situation, system or idea by using epithets as "medieval" or "feudal."

Comment on this stereotyped view, either supporting or correcting it.

3. Apocalypticism forms a major theme in Eco's book, The Name of the Rose.

Why was it essential to the historicity of that novel to place the story within the 14th century, rather than within the 12th or 13th? What relationship existed between secular events of the High Middle Ages and religious movements or aberrations?

History 434   W. A. Ernest
Spring Semester, 1988   University of Hawaii at Manoa

THE HIGH MIDDLE AGES

N.B.   In accordance with University policy, the taping of lectures is not permitted. Exceptions will be made only for physically handicapped students having the instructor's written permission.

TEXTS: N. F. Cantor, Medieval History: The Life and Death of a Civilization. (Second Edition, 1969)
        The Crisis of Church and State, 1050-1300, ed. B. Tierney   (Prentice-Hall, 1964)
        The Twelfth-Century Renaissance, ed. C. W. Hollister   (Available from Dittos Copies.)
        J. Gimpel, The Medieval Machine: The Industrial Revolution of the Middle Ages.
        (Penguin, 1976)

There follows a proposed schedule of lectures and readings. With the exception of the texts listed above, all of the books will be found in the Reserve Room in Sinclair Library. If you desire bibliographical suggestions for further reading, you have only to ask!

You are expected to pursue a research project throughout the greater part of the semester, dealing with a topic or problem of your choice (which must, however, have the instructor's approval). Submission of your topic (29 January, on a form which will be provided) ipso facto will constitute affirmation of the fact that you have checked out the library holdings to determine the feasibility of the project and that the requisite primary sources, monographic literature and periodical material all are available in languages in which you are competent. A first draft of the paper, as nearly as possible in final form and complete with scholarly apparatus, is to be submitted for comment and criticism by 28 March. The final version, impeccable in style, form, and content, and representing so far as possible a significant original contribution to the sum total of human knowledge, will be turned in on or before 2 May.

I will gladly furnish advice and a reasonable degree of assistance, both with the paper and with the course. My office is Sakamaki Hall A408.   See me MWF 7:00 - 7:15; 9:45 - 10:15 or by appointment.

PROPOSED SCHEDULE OF LECTURES AND DISCUSSIONS.

Wed. 13 Jan.   **Orientation.**

Fri. 15 Jan.   **The German Kingdom to 962.**

    N. F. Cantor, Medieval History, pp. 227-240.
    Sources for the History of Medieval Europe from the mid-eighth to the mid-thirteenth century,
        ed. Brian Pullan, pp. 113-117.
    G. Barraclough, The Origins of Modern Germany, pp. 1-53.
    T. Mayer, "The Historical Foundations of the German Constitution," Mediaeval Germany, 911-
        1250, ed. G.Barraclough, II, 1-33.
    B. Schmeidler, "Franconia's Place in the Structure of Mediaeval Germany," ibid., II, 71-93.

Mon. 18 Jan.   **The Ottonian Empire.**

    Barraclough, Origins, pp. 53-71.
    Sources ..., ed. B. Pullan, pp. 117-127.

"Liber de rebus gestis Ottonis," in The Works of Liudprand of Cremona, trans. F. A. Wright, pp. 213-232.
The Rise of the First Reich: Germany in the Tenth Century, ed. B. H. Hill, Jr.

Wed. 20 Jan.   **The Conversion of Hungary and the Coronation of St. Stephen.**

Fri. 22 Jan.   **Secular Influence in Church Reform: Pious Nobles and Rulers.**

Cantor, Medieval History, pp. 240-245.
Barraclough, Origins, pp. 72-98.
The Crisis of Church and State, 1050-1300, ed. B. Tierney, pp. 24-32.
A Source Book of Mediaeval History, ed. F. A. Ogg, pp. 245-249.
Select Historical Documents of the Middle Ages, ed. E. F. Henderson, pp. 267-314; 329-333.
[N.B. These three source books involve some duplication.]
J.-F. Lemarignier, "Political and Monastic Structures in France at the End of the Tenth and the Beginning of the Eleventh Century," Lordship and Community in Medieval Europe: Selected Readings, ed. F. L. Cheyette, pp. 100-127.
U. Stutz, "The Proprietary Church as an Element of Mediaeval Germanic Ecclesiastical Law," Mediaeval Germany, 911-1250, ed. G. Barraclough, II, 35-70.
J. W. Thompson, Feudal Germany, I, 3-124.

Mon. 25 Jan..   **The Reformed Papacy.**

Sources ..., ed. Pullan, pp. 53-56, 58-63, 130-135.
Select Historical Documents ..., ed. Henderson, pp. 336-337; 361-365.

Wed. 27 Jan.   **Eastern and Western Europe Compared.**

Cantor, Medieval History, pp. 247-270.

Fri. 29 Jan.   **The Investiture Contest.**   TERM PAPER TOPICS DUE.

Cantor, Medieval History, pp. 271-304.
Crisis ..., ed. Tierney, pp. 33-95.
Sources ..., ed. Pullan, pp. 135-159.
Source Book ..., ed. Ogg, pp. 261-281.
Select Historical Documents ..., ed. Henderson, pp. 365-409. [Again some duplication!]
Barraclough, Origins, pp. 101-164.
H. Hirsch, "The Constitutional History of the Reformed Monasteries During the Investiture Contest," Mediaeval Germany, ed. G. Barraclough, II, 131-173.
P. Joachimsen, "The Investiture Contest and the German Constitution," ibid., pp. 95-129.

Mon. 1 Feb.   **France: The Capetians to Philip Augustus.**

Wed. 3 Feb.　　**Normandy, the Norman Conquest, and Norman England**.

    Cantor, <u>Medieval History</u>, pp. 305-316.
    <u>Source Book</u> ..., ed. Ogg, pp. 233-244.

Fri. 5 Feb.　　**SLIDES**.

Mon. 8 Feb.　　**The Greater Norman Conquest**.

Wed. 10 Feb.　　**The Background of the Crusading Movement**.

    Cantor, <u>Medieval History</u>, pp. 317-326.

Fri. 12 Feb.　　**The First Crusade**.

    <u>Sources</u> ..., ed. Pullan, pp. 56-58.
    <u>Source Book</u> ..., ed. Ogg, pp. 282-296.

Mon. 15 Feb.　　HOLIDAY: PRESIDENTS' DAY.

Wed. 17 Feb.　　**The Later Crusades**.

    Cantor, <u>Medieval History</u>, pp. 326-331.
    <u>Select Historical Documents</u> ..., ed. Henderson, pp. 333-336; 337-344.
    J. Prawer, "The Nobility and the Feudal Regime in the Latin Kingdom of Jerusalem," <u>Lordship and Community in Medieval Europe: Selected Readings</u>, ed. F. L. Cheyette, pp. 156-179.
    J. Prawer, "Estates, Communities and the Constitution of the Latin Kingdom," <u>ibid.</u>,　　pp. 376-403.

Fri. 19 Feb.　　**Kingship and Law in the Middle Ages**.

    Cantor, <u>Medieval History</u>, pp. 335-349; 421-435.
    K. Bosl, "Ruler and Ruled in the German Empire from the Tenth to the Twelfth Century," <u>Lordship and Community in Medieval Europe: Selected Readings</u>, ed. F. L. Cheyette, pp. 357-375.

Mon. 22 Feb.　　**Church and State in the Twelfth Century**.

    <u>Crisis</u> ..., ed. Tierney, pp. 97-126.
    <u>Sources</u> ..., ed. Pullan, pp. 168-190.
    <u>Select ... Documents</u>, ed. Henderson, pp. 410-430.
    Barraclough, <u>Origins</u>, pp. 167-218.

Wed. 24 Feb.   **The Concept of Empire.**

   G. Barraclough, The Mediaeval Empire: Idea and Reality.

Fri. 26 Feb.   **Feudalism and Its Divergent Tendencies.**

   Cantor, Medieval History, pp. 214-223.
   Sources ..., ed. Pullan, pp. 235-243.
   Source Book ..., ed. Ogg, pp. 203-232.
   Lordship and Community in Medieval Europe: Selected Readings, ed. F. L. Cheyette, pp. 12-61;
       128-136; 198-209; 217-221.
      If you have not already read F.-L. Ganshof, Feudalism, for some other course, I recommend it
      strongly.

Mon. 29 Feb.   **The Hohenstaufen and Feudalism in the Empire.**

   Source Book ..., ed. Thatcher, pp. 202-206.
   Sources ..., ed. Pullan, pp. 160-167.
   O. Freiherr von Dungern, "Constitutional Reorganization and Reform under the Hohenstaufen,"
       Mediaeval Germany, ed. Barraclough, II, 203-233.
   H. Mitteis, "Feudalism and the German Constitution," ibid., II, 235-279.

Wed. 2 Mar.   **SLIDES.**

Fri. 4 Mar.   **HOUR EXAM!**

Mon. 7 Mar.   **Angevin England to Magna Carta.**

   Source Book ..., ed. Ogg, pp. 297-310.
   Select ... Documents, ed. Henderson, pp. 430-431.

Wed. 9 Mar.   **SLIDES!**

Fri. 11 Mar.   **The Renaissance of the Twelfth Century.**

   The Twelfth-Century Renaissance, ed. C. W. Hollister. [Available from Dittos Copies.]
   Cantor, Medieval History, pp. 349-400.

Mon. 14 Mar.   **Trade and Towns in the High Middle Ages.**

   Source Book ..., ed. Ogg, pp. 325-330.
   J. Dhondt, "Medieval Solidarities: Flemish Society in Transition, 1127-1128," Lordship and Com-
       munity in Medieval Europe: Selected Readings, ed. F. L. Cheyette, pp. 268-290.
   [The first chapter of C. Stephenson, Borough and Town, provides a useful survey of the older
       theories on the much-debated subject of medieval town origins.]

Wed. 16 Mar.   **Serfdom, the Markgenossenschaft Theory, and Land**
                Reclamation and Peasant Emancipation.

      C. Stephenson, "The Problem of the Common Man in Early Medieval Europe," <u>American Histori-</u>
<u>cal Review</u>, 51 (1946), 419-439.
      B. Lyon, "Medieval Real Estate Developments and Freedom," <u>Am. Hist. Rev.</u>, 63 (1957), 47-61.
         [Printed without the original full documentation in the Hollister pamphlet assigned for
11 March.]
<u>Source Book</u> ..., ed. Ogg, pp. 330-333.
Thompson, <u>Feudal Germany</u>, II, 545-579.
      T. Mayer, "The State of the Dukes of Zähringen," <u>Mediaeval Germany</u>, ed. Barraclough, II, 175-
202.
      H. Cam, "The Community of the Vill," <u>Lordship and Community</u> ..., ed. Cheyette, pp. 256-267.

Fri. 18 Mar.   **The Wendish Crusade and the Northeastern German**
                          Frontier.   FIRST DRAFT DUE!

      Barraclough, <u>Origins</u>, pp. 249-281.
Thompson, <u>Feudal Germany</u>, II, 387-528.

21 Mar. - 25 Mar. SPRING RECESS. READ BOOKS! WRITE PAPERS! HAVE FUN!

Mon. 28 Mar.   **Land Reclamation and Peasant Emancipation: The Second Phase.**

Wed. 30 Mar.   **SLIDES ON RECLAMATION AND EMANCIPATION.**

Fri. 1 Apr.   HOLIDAY -- GOOD FRIDAY.

Mon. 4 Apr.   **The Stedinger Crusade.**

Wed. 6 Apr.   **New Trends in Monasticism.**

      Cantor, <u>Medieval History</u>, pp. 400-412, 455-459.
<u>Sources</u> ..., ed. Pullan, pp. 77-90.
<u>Source Book</u> ..., ed. Ogg, pp. 250-260; 360-379.
<u>Select ... Documents</u> ..., ed. Henderson, pp. 344-349.

Fri. 8 Apr.   **The Military Orders and the Rise of Prussia.**

Mon. 11 Apr.   **Medieval Heresy and the Inquisition.**

      Cantor, <u>Medieval History</u>, pp. 412-420.
<u>Sources</u> ..., ed. Pullan, pp. 90-98.

Wed. 13 Apr.   The French National Monarchy.

    Cantor, Medieval History, pp. 435-443.
    Sources ..., ed. Pullan, pp. 244-268.

Fri. 15 Apr.   The Papacy and the Secular State in the Thirteenth   Century.

    Cantor, Medieval History, pp. 447-455.
    Crisis ..., ed. Tierney, pp. 127-157.
    Sources ..., ed. Pullan, pp. 191-206.
    Source Book ..., ed. Ogg, pp. 381-388.
    Select ... Documents ..., ed. Henderson, pp. 432-437.

Mon. 18 Apr.   Medieval England after Magna Carta.

Wed. 20 Apr.   SLIDES.

Fri. 22 Apr.   DISCUSSION OF MEDIEVAL TECHNOLOGY, INDUSTRY AND SCIENCE.

    J. Gimpel, The Medieval Machine: The Industrial Revolution of the Middle Ages. (Penguin, 1976)

Mon. 25 Apr.   Medieval Cartography: The Controversial Vinland Map.

Wed. 27 Apr.   Medieval Higher Education.

    Cantor, Medieval History, pp. 461-473.
    Source Book ..., ed. Ogg, pp. 339-359.

Fri. 29 Apr.   New Trends in Politics.

    Cantor, Medieval History, pp. 473-499.
    Sources ..., ed. Pullan, pp. 269-275.
    J. R. Strayer, On the Medieval Origins of the Modern State.
    Select ... Documents, ed. Henderson, pp. 437-439.
    Crisis ..., ed. Tierney, pp. 159-210.
    A. Marongiu, "The Theory of Democracy and Consent in the Fourteenth Century," Lordship and Community ..., ed. Cheyette, pp. 404-421.
    H. Baron, "Cicero and the Roman Civic Spirit in the Middle Ages and the Early Renaissance." ibid., pp. 291-314.
    A. Brackmann, "The Beginnings of the National State in Mediaeval Germany and the Norman Monarchies," Mediaeval Germany, ed. Barraclough, II, 281-299.

Mon. 2 May   **SLIDES.**   DEADLINE FOR TERM PAPERS!

Wed. 4 May   **The Later Middle Ages: "Waning" and Legacy.**

Cantor, <u>Medieval History</u>, pp. 503-547.

FINAL EXAMINATION: Friday, 13 May 1987, 7:30 - 9:30.

INTRODUCTION AND ORIENTATION

F. C. Robinson, "Medieval, the Middle Ages," Speculum, 59 (Oct. 1984), 745-756.

J. van Engen, "The Christian Middle Ages as an Historiographical Problem," American Historical Review, 91 (1986), 519-552.

Medieval Studies: An Introduction, ed. J. M. Powell.

R. W. Southern, The Making of the Middle Ages.

F. Heer, The Medieval World: Europe 1100-1350.

J. H. Mundy, Europe in the High Middle Ages.

Perspectives in Medieval History, ed. K. F. Drew and F. S. Lear.

B. D. Lyon, The Middle Ages in Recent Historical Thought.

R. S. Lopez, "Still Another Renaissance?" American Historical Review, 57 (1951), 1-21.

B. C. Keeney, "A Dead Horse Flogged Again," Speculum, 30 (1955), 606-611.

T. Goldstein, "Medieval Civilization from the World-Historical View," Cahiers d'histoire mondiale, 6 (1960-61), 503-516.

L. White, Jr., "The Legacy of the Middle Ages in the American Wild West," Speculum, 40 (1965), 191-202. See also the objections of O. Ulph, "The Legacy of the American Wild West in Medieval Scholarship," American West, 3 (1966), 50ff.

E. King, England, 1175-1425.

G. Barraclough, The Origins of Modern Germany.

F. H. Bäuml, Medieval Civilization in Germany.

B. H. Hill, Medieval Monarchy in Action: The German Empire from Henry I to Henry IV.

E. S. Duckett, Death and Life in the Tenth Century.

M. Seidlmayer, Currents of Mediaeval Thought With Special Reference to Germany.

G. F. Jones, Honor in German Literature.

H. Daniel-Rops, Cathedral and Crusade.

W. Anderson, Castles of Europe: From Charlemagne to the Renaissance.

F. L. Ganshof, The Middle Ages: A History of International Relations.

J. R. Strayer, Medieval Statecraft and the Perspectives of History: Essays.   With a Foreword by Gaines Post.

J. Le Goff, La Civilisation de l'occident médiéval.

G. Cohen, La grande clarté du moyen age.

H. Focillon, L'an mil.

J. Le Goff, Das Hochmittelalter.

W. von der Steinen, Der Kosmos des Mittelalters.

W. Lammers, Geschichtsdenken und Geschichtsbild im Mittelalter.

H. R. Guggisberg, Das europäische Mittelalter im amerikanischen Geschichtsdenken des 19. und frühen 20. Jahrhunderts.

THE GERMAN KINGDOM TO 962.

K. J. Leyser, Rule and Conflict in an Early Medieval Society: Ottonian Saxony.

K. J. Leyser, "The German Aristocracy from the Ninth to the Early Twelfth Century: A Historical and Cultural Sketch," Past and Present, 41 (1968), 25-53.

K. J Leyser, "Henry I and the Beginnings of the Saxon Empire," English Historical Review, 83 (1968), 1-32.

K. J. Leyser, "The Battle at the Lech, 955: A Study in Tenth-Century Warfare," History, 50 (1965), 1-25.

K. J. Leyser, "Ottonian Government," English Historical Review, 96 (1981), 721-753.

H. L. Adelson, "The Holy Lance and the Hereditary German Monarchy," The Art Bulletin, 48 (1966), 177-192.

T. Reuter, "The 'Imperial Church System' of the Ottonian and Salian Rulers: A Reconsideration," Journal of Ecclesiastical History, 33 (July 1982), 347-74.

C. S. Jaeger, "The Courtier Bishop in Vitae from the Tenth to the Twelfth Century," Speculum, 58 (no. 2, 1983), 291-325.

A. Alföldi, "Hasta - Summa Imperii: The Spear as Embodiment of Sovereignty in Rome," American Journal of Archaeology, 63 (1959), 1-27.

G. Tellenbach, Die Entstehung des deutschen Reiches.

R. Holtzmann, Geschichte der sächsischen Kaiserzeit, pp. 5-174.

M. Lintzel, Ausgewählte Schriften, II, 73-119, 222-275, 583-612.

R. Lüttich, Ungarnzüge in Europa im 10. Jahrhundert.

S. de Vajay, Der Eintritt des ungarischen Stämmebundes in die europäische Geschichte.

H. Büttner, Heinrichs I. Südwest- und Westpolitik.

G. Läwen, Stammesherzog und Stammesherzogtum: Beiträge zur Frage ihrer rechtlichen Bedeutung im 10.-12. Jahrhundert.

Die Entstehung des deutschen Reiches (Deutschland um 900): Ausgewählte Aufsätze aus dem Jahren 1928-1954, mit einem Vorwort von Hellmut Kämpf.

W. von Giesebrecht, Geschichte der deutschen Kaiserzeit, I, 206-447.

Königswahl und Thronfolge in ottonisch-frühdeutscher Zeit, ed. E. Hlawitschka.

F. M. Fischer, Politiker um Otto den Großen.

H.-J. Freytag, Die Herrschaft der Billunger in Sachsen.

G. Waitz, Deutsche Verfassungsgeschichte. 8 vols. [Old but useful!]

W. Kienast, Der Herzogstitel in Frankreich und Deutschland.

H. Zielinski, "Zur Aachener Königserhebung von 936," Deutsches Archiv, 38 (1972), 210-222.

C. Erdmann, "Die Burgenordnung Heinrichs I.," ibid., 6 (1943), 59-101.

C. Erdmann, "Das Grab Heinrichs I.," ibid., 4 (1940-41). 76-97.

THE OTTONIAN EMPIRE.

The Rise of the First Reich: Germany in the Tenth Century, ed. B. H. Hill, Jr.

F. J. Tschan, Bernward of Hildesheim. (3 vols.)

J. B. Morrall, "Otto III: An Imperial Ideal," History Today, 9 (1959), 812-822.

A. Czajkowski, "The Congress of Gniezno in the Year 1000," Speculum, 24 (1949), 339-356.

A. D. Frankforter, "Hroswitha of Gandersheim and the Destiny of Woman," Historian, 41 (Feb. 1979), 295-314.

A. Hauck, Kirchengeschichte Deutschlands, III, 3-338.

E. Hlawitschka, Franken, Alemannen, Bayern und Burgunder in Oberitalien, 774-962.

Festschrift zur Jahrtausendfeier der Kaiserkrönung Ottos des Großen. (3 vols.)

G. A. Bezzola, Das ottonischen Kaisertum in der französischen Geschichtsschreibung des 10. und beginnenden 11. Jahrhunderts.

E. Winter, Rußland und das Papsttum, I, 19-44.

M. Uhlirz, Die Krone des heiligen Stephan, des ersten Königs von Ungarn.
F. Koch, Wurde Kaiser Karl sitzend begraben?
K. und M. Uhlirz, Jahrbücher des deutschen Reiches Unter Otto II. und Otto III, vol. II.
D. Claude, Geschichte des Erzbistums Magdeburg bis in das 12. Jahrhundert, I.
H. Beumann, "Das Kaisertum Ottos des Großen," Hist. Zeit., 195 (1962), 529-573.
H. Keller, "Das Kaisertum Ottos des Großen im Verständnis seiner Zeit., Deutsches Archiv, 20 (1964), 325-388.
D. Jank, "Die Darstellung Ottos des Großen in der spätmittelalterlichen Historiographie," Archiv für Kulturgeschichte, 61 (no. 1, 1979), 69-101.
Z. Wojciechowski, "La 'Renovatio imperii' sous Otton III et la Pologne," Revue historique, 201 (1949) 30-44.
K. Hampe, "Kaiser Otto III. und Rom," Hist. Zeit., 160 (1929), 513-533.
M. Uhlirz, "Kaiser Otto III. und das Papsttum," ibid., 171 (1940), 258-268.
R. Holtzmann, Geschichte der sächsischen Kaiserzeit, pp. 327-382.
Giesebrecht, op. cit., I, 718-743.   [A view now rejected!]
Sylvester II, The Letters of Gerbert, trans. H. P. Lattin.

THE SECULAR ROLE IN CHURCH REFORM: PIOUS NOBLES AND RULERS.

U. Stutz, "The Proprietary Church as an Element of Mediaeval Germanic Ecclesiastical Law," Mediaeval Germany, 911-1250: Essays by German Historians, ed. and trans. G. Barraclough, II, 35-70.
J. W. Thompson, Feudal Germany, I, 3-67.
H. C. Lea, The History of Sacerdotal Celibacy in the Christian Church.
J. Bugge, Virginitas: An Essay in the History of a Medieval Ideal.
G. Constable, Religious Life and Thought (11th.-12th. Centuries).
G. Constable, Monastic Tithes From Their Origins to the Twelfth Century.
F. L. Ganshof, "La dîme monastique, du IXe à la fin du XIIe siècle," Cahiers de civilisation médiévale, 11 (1968), 413-420. [Review article on Constable's book.]
B. H. Rosenwein, Rhinoceros Bound: Cluny in the Tenth Century.   BX2615 .C63 R67 1982
J. Evans, Monastic Life at Cluny, 910-1157.
H. E. J. Cowdrey, The Clunics and the Gregorian Reform.
C. G. Coulton, Five Centuries of Religion. [Use with caution!]
Cambridge Medieval History, III.
K. Hampe, Germany Under the Salian and Hohenstaufen Emperors, pp. 47-59.
K. J. Conant, "Mediaeval Academy Excavations at Cluny, X," Speculum, 45 (1970), 1-39.
K. J. Conant, "Cluny Studies, 1968-1975," ibid., 50 (1975), 383-388, 16 plates.
R. L. Poole, "Benedict IX and Gregory VI," Proceedings of the British Academy, 8 (1917-1918), 199-235.
C. B. Bouchard, "Laymen and Church Reform around the Year 1000: The Case of Otto-William, Count of Burgundy," Journal of Medieval History, 5 (March 1979), 1-10.
E. N. Johnson, "Adalbert of Hamburg-Bremen: A Politician of the Eleventh Century," Speculum, 9 (1934), 147-179.
J. H. Lynch, "Hugh I of Cluny's Sponsorship of Henry IV: Its Context and Consequences," Speculum, 60 (1985), 800-826.

P. Fournier, "Le Décret de Burchard de Worms: Ses caractères, son influence," Rev. d'hist. eccl., 12 (1911), 451-473, 670-701.

T. Schieffer, "Heinrich II. und Konrad II. Die Umprägung des Geschichtsbildes durch die Kirchenreform des 11. Jahrhunderts," Deutsches Archiv, 8 (1950-51), 384-437.

W. Kölmel, "Die kaiserlichen Herrschaft im Gebiet von Ravenna (Exarchat und Pentapolis) vor dem Investiturstreit (10./11. Jahrhundert)," Historisches Jahrbuch, 88 (1968), 257-299.

E. Boshof, "Das Reich in der Kreise: Überlegungen zum Regierungsausgang Heinrichs III.,"Historische Zeitschrift, 228 (1979), 265-287.

B. R. Kemp, "Monastic Possession of Parish Churches in England in the Twelfth Century," Journal of Ecclesiastical History, 31 (Apr. 1980), 133-160.

K. Hallinger, "Zur geistigen Welt der Anfänge Klunys," Deutsches Archiv, 10 (1954), 417-445.

J. Wollasch, "Muri und St. Blasien: Perspektiven schwäbischen Mönchtums in der Reform," ibid., 17 (1961), 420-446.

H. E. Feine, "Klosterreformen im 10. und 11. Jahrhundert und ihr Einfluß auf die Reichenau und St. Gallen," Aus Verfassungs- und Landesgeschichte: Festschrift ... T. Mayer, II, 77-91.

H. E. Feine, "Das Eigenkirchenwesen als Gesamterscheinung," Kirchliche Rechtsgeschichte: Das katholische Kirche. 4. Aufl., pp. 160-182.

E. Sackur, Die Cluniacensur in ihrer kirchlichen und allgemein-geschichtlichen Wirksamkeit bis zur Mitte des elften Jahrhunderts. (2 vols.)

E. E. H. Stengel, Die Immunität in Deutschland bis zum Ende des 11. Jahrhunderts.

A. Schulte, Der Adel und die deutsche Kirche im Mittelalter: Studien zur Sozial-, Rechts- und Kirchengeschichte.

T. Mayer, Fürsten und Staat: Studien zur Verfassungsgeschichte des deutschen Mittelalter.

E. Landers, Die deutschen Klöster vom Ausgang Karls des Grossen bis zum Wormser Konkordat und ihre Verhältnis zu den Reformen.

H. L. Mikoletzky, Kaiser Heinrich II. und die Kirche.

E. Müller, Das Itinerar Kaiser Heinrichs III. (1039 bis 1056) mit besonderer Berücksichtigung seiner Urkunden.

M. Lintzel, Die Beschlusse der deutschen Hoftage von 911 bis 1056.

G. B. Ladner, Theologie und Politik vor dem Investiturstreit: Abendmahlstreit, Kirchenreform, Cluni - und Heinrich III.

Giesebrecht, op. cit., III, 3-230.

Adam of Bremen, History of the Archbishops of Hamburg-Bremen, trans. F. J.   Tschan.

THE REFORMED PAPACY.

W. Ullmann, The Growth of Papal Government in the Middle Ages.

H. Mann, The Lives of the Popes in the Middle Ages, VI.

H. E. J. Cowdrey, The Cluniacs and the Gregorian Reform.

S. Runciman, The Eastern Schism: A Study of the Papacy and the Eastern Churches During the XIth. and XIIth. Centuries.

F. Dvornik, Byzantium and the Roman Primacy.

G. Barraclough, The Medieval Papacy.

P. Partner, The Lands of St. Peter: The Papal State in the Middle Ages and the Early Renaissance.

A. L. Barstow, Married Priests and the Reforming Papacy: The Eleventh-Century Debates.

D. M. Nicol, "Byzantium and the Papacy in the Eleventh Century," Journal of Ecclesiastical History, 13 (1962), 1-20.

P. Charanis, "On the Question of the Hellenization of Sicily and Southern Italy During the Middle Ages," American Historical Review, 52 (1946), 74-86.

J. J. Ryan, "Cardinal Humbert De s. Romana ecclesia: Relics of Roman-Byzantine Relations 1053-1054," Mediaeval Studies, 20 (1958), 206-238.

H. E. J. Cowdrey, "The Peace and the Truce of God in the Eleventh Century," Past and Present, 46 (1970), 42-67.

R. I. Moore, "Family, Community and Cult on the Eve of the Gregorian Reform" Transactions of the Royal Historical Society, 30 (1980), 49-69.

J. Sydow, "Untersuchungen zur kurialen Verwaltungsgeschichte im Zeitalter des Reformpapsttums," Deutsches Archiv, 11 (1954-55), 18-73.

H. Grundmann, "Eine neue Interpretation des Papstwahldekrets von 1059," ibid., 25 (1969), 234-236.

P. Herde, "Das Papsttum und die griechische Kirche in Süditalien vom 11. bis zum 13. Jahrhundert," ibid., 26 (1970), 1-46.

P. E. Schramm, Kaiser, Rom und Renovatio: Studien zur Geschichte des römischen Erneuerungsgedankens vom Ende des karolingischen Reiches bis zum Investiturstreit.

P. E. Schramm, Kaiser, Könige und Päpste: Gesammelte Aufsätze zur Geschichte des Mittelalters. (4 vols.)

H. Pahncke, Geschichte der Bischöfe Italiens deutscher Nation von 951-1264.

F. A. Gregorovius, Geschichte der Stadt Rom im Mittelalter.

A. Hauck, Kirchengeschichte Deutschlands, III, 391-752.

S. Borsari, Il Monachesimo bizantino nella Sicilia e nell' Italia meridionale prenormanne.

EASTERN AND WESTERN EUROPE COMPARED.

F. Oakley, The Medieval Experience: Foundations of Western Cultural Singularity.

F. Heer, The Mediaeval World.

G. Ostrogorsky, History of the Byzantine State.

A. A. Vasiliev, History of the Byzantine Empire, 324-1453.

J. M. Hussey, Church And Learning in the Byzantine Empire, 867-1185.

C. Diehl, Byzantium: Greatness and Decline.

D. M. Nicol, The Last Centuries of Byzantium, 1261-1453. (1972)

D. M. Nicol, Church and Society in the Last Centuries of Byzantium: The Birkbeck Lectures, 1977. (1979)

D. T. Rice, Constantinople from Byzantium to Istanbul.

H. Ahrweiler, Byzance et la mer: La marine de guerre, la politique et les institutions maritimes de Byzance aux VIIe-XVe siècles.

P. K. Hitti, History of the Arabs.

J. J. Saunders, A History of Medieval Islam.

G. E. von Grunebaum, Medieval Islam.

W. M. Watt, The Influence of Islam on Medieval Europe.

R. W. Bulliet, The Camel and the Wheel.

THE INVESTITURE CONTEST.

H. Hirsch, "The Constitutional History of the Reformed Monasteries During the Investiture Contest,"
Mediaeval Germany, 911-1250: Essays by German Historians, ed. and trans. G. Barraclough, II,
131-173.

P. Joachimsen, "The Investiture Contest and the German Constitution," Mediaeval Germany, ed. Barraclough, II, 95-129.

Z. N. Brooke, "Lay Investiture and its Relation to the Conflict of Empire and Papacy," Proceedings of
the British Academy, 25 (1939), 217-247.

S. B. Hicks, "The Investiture Controversy of the Middle Ages, 1075-1122: Agreement and Disagree-
ment Among Historians," Journal of Church and State, 15 (1973), 5-20.

K. F. Morrison, "Canossa: A Revision," Traditio, 18 (1962), 121-148.

R. Nineham, "The So-Called Anonymous of York," Journal of Ecclesiastical History, 14 (1963), 31-45.

G. A. Loud, "Abbot Desiderius of Monte Cassino and the Gregorian Papacy," Journal of Ecclesiastical
History, 30 (1979), 305-322.

R. E. Reynolds, "Liturgical Scholarship at the Time of the Investiture Controversy: Past Research and
Future Opportunities," Harvard Theological Review, 71 (Jan.-Apr. 1978), 109-124.

I. S. Robinson, "Pope Gregory VII, the Princes and the 'Pactum' 1077-1080," English Historical Review,
94 (1979), 721-756.

I. S. Robinson, "Periculosus homo: Pope Gregory VII and Episcopal Authority," Viator, 9 (1978), 103-
131.

W. Ullmann, "Von Canossa nach Pavia: Zum Strukturwandel der Herrschaftsgrundlagen im salischen
und staufischen Zeitalter," Historisches Jahrbuch, 93 (no. 2, 1973), 265-300.

S. N. Vaughn, "St. Anselm and the English Investiture Controversy Reconsidered," Journal of Medieval
History, 6 (Mar. 1980), 484-504.

J. T. Gilchrist, "Canon Law Aspects of the Eleventh Century Gregorian Reform Program," ibid., 13
(1962), 21-38.

S. A. Chodorow, "Magister Gratian and the Problem of 'Regnum' and "Sacerdotium'," Traditio, 26
(1970), 364-381.

S. A. Chodorow, "Ecclesiastical Politics and the Ending of the Investiture Contest: The Papal Election
of 1119 and the Negotiations of Mouzon," Speculum, 46 (1971), 613-640.

G. Tellenbach, Church, State, and Christian Society at the Time of the Investiture Contest.

W. Ullmann, The Growth of Papal Government in the Middle Ages.

Cambridge Medieval History, V, cc. ii, iii.

T. F. Tout, The Empire and the Papacy.

N. Hunt, Cluny Under St. Hugh, 1049-1109.

K. F. Morrison, Tradition and Authority in the Western Church, 300-1140.

T. Schieffer, "Cluny et la querelle des investitures," Rev. hist., 225 (1961), 47-72.

Canossa als Wende: Ausgewählte Aufsätze zur neueren Forschung, ed. H. Kämpf.   [A valuable collection of important German articles on the subject.]

F. Baethgen, "Zur Tribur-Frage," Deutsches Archiv, 4 (1940-41), 394-411.

H. Naumann, "Die Schenkung des Gutes Schleuchsee an St. Blasien: Ein Beitrag zur Geschichte des Investiturstreites," ibid., XXIII (1967), 359-404.
H. Hoffmann, "Ivo von Chartres und die Lösung des Investiturproblems," ibid., 15 (1959), 393-440.
K. Mirbt, Die Publizistik im Zeitalter Gregors VII.
A. Scharnagel, Der Begriff der Investitur im den Quellen und der Literatur des Investiturstreites.
G. Koch, Manegold von Lautenbach und die Lehre von der Volkssouveränitat unter Heinrich IV.
W. Hartmann, "Manegold von Lautenbach und die Anfänge der Frühscholastik," Deutsches Archiv, 17 (1970), 47-149.
H. Mordek, "Proprie auctoritates apostolice sedis: Ein zweiter Dictatus Papae Gregors VII.?" ibid., 28 (1972), 105-132.
R. Kottje, "Zur Bedeutung der Bischofsstädte für Heinrich IV," Historisches Jahrbuch, 97-98 (1978), 131-57.
R. Schieffer, "Gregor VII. - Ein Versuch über die historische Größe," Historisches Jahrbuch, 97-98 (1978), 87-107.
A. Overmann, Gräfin Mathilde von Tuscien.
O. H. Kost, Heinrich V.: Gestalt und Verhängnis des letzten salischen Kaisers.
W. Seegrün, Das Papsttum und Skandinavien, bis zur Vollendung der nordischen Kirchenorganisation (1164).
J. Haller, Das Papsttum: Idee und Wirklichkeit, II.
A. Hauck, Kirchengeschichte Deutschlands, III, 753-923.

Sources on the Investiture Contest.

The Correspondence of Pope Gregory VII: Selected Letters From the Registrum, trans. E. Emerton.
The Epistolae Vagantes of Pope Gregory VII, ed. and trans. by H. E. J. Cowdrey.
A. Murray, "Pope Gregory VII and his Letters," Traditio, 22 (1966), 149-202.
U.-R. Blumenthal, "Canossa and Royal Ideology in 1077: Two Unknown Manuscripts of 'De penitentia regis Salomonis'," Manuscripta, 32 (1978), 91-96.
I. S. Robinson, "The Dissemination of the Letters of Pope Gregory VII During the Investiture Contest," Journal of Ecclesiastical History, 34 (Apr. 1983), 175-193.
Imperial Lives and Letters of the Eleventh Century, trans. T. E. Mommsen and K. F. Morrison.
Die Briefe Kaiser Heinrichs IV., trans. K. Langosch.
Die Texte des normannischen Anonymous, ed. K. Pellens.
The Letters of Peter the Venerable, ed. G. Constable.
Monumenta Germaniae historica: Libelli de Lite Imperatorum et Pontificum saeculis XI et XII conscripti. (3 vols.)
An excellent survey of the period and of the older printed source editions is Jahrbücher des deutschen Reiches Unter Heinrich IV. und Heinrich V., by G. Meyer von Knonau. (7 vols.)

FRANCE: THE CAPETIANS TO PHILIP AUGUSTUS.

R. Fawtier, The Capetian Kings of France.
C. E. Petit-Dutaillis, The Feudal Monarchy in France and England.

M. Bloch, The Royal Touch. Sacred Monarchy. and Scrofula in England and France.
F. Funck-Brentano, The Middle Ages.
J. Evans, Life in Medieval France.
A. R. Lewis, The Development of Southern French and Catalan Society. 718-1050.
T. Evergates, Feudal Society in the Bailliage of Troyes Under the Counts of Champagne. 1142-1284.
S. Painter, The Scourge of the Clergy: Peter of Dreux. Duke of Brittany.
A. W. Lewis, Royal Succession in Capetian France: Studies on Familial Order and the State. (1981).
    JN2375 .L48
C. T. Wood, "Regnum Francie: A Problem in Capetian Administrative Usage," Traditio, 23 (1967),
    117-147.
F. Barlow, "The King's Evil," English Historical Review, 95 (1980), 3-27.
J. F. Benton, "The Revenue of Louis VII," Speculum, 42 (1967), 84-91.
Hallam, Elizabeth M., "The King and the Princes in Eleventh-Century France," Bulletin of the Institute
    of Historical Research, 53 (1980), 143-156.
J. Flach, "La royauté et l'église en France, du IXe au XIe siècle," Revue d'histoire ecclésiastique, 4
    (1903), 432-447.
Ehlers, Joachim, "Elemente mittelalterlicher Nationsbildung in Frankreich (10.-13. Jahrhundert)," His-
    torische Zeitschrift, 231 (1980), 565-587.
W. Kienast, "Der Wirkungsbereich des französischen Königtums von Odo bis Ludwig VI. (888-1137) in
    Südfrankreich," Hist. Zeit., 209 (1969), 529-565.
P. E. Schramm, Der König von Frankreich: Das Wesen der Monarchie vom 9. bis zum 16. Jahrhundert.
    (2. v.)
W. Kienast, Deutschland und Frankreich in der Kaiserzeit.
W. Kienast, Der Herzogstitel in Frankreich und Deutschland.
J.-F. Lemarignier, Le gouvernement royal aux premiers temps Capétiens. (987-1108).
J. Duby, "Le gouvernement royal aux premiers temps capétiens," Le Moyen Age, 72 (1966), 531-544.
Histoire des institutions françaises au moyen âge, ed. F. Lot and R. Fawtier.

NORMANDY, THE NORMAN CONQUEST, AND NORMAN ENGLAND.

R. A. Brown, The Normans and the Norman Conquest.
S. Körner, The Battle of Hastings. England. and Europe. 1035-1066.
D. C. Dougles, William the Conqueror.
F. M. Stenton, The Bayeux Tapestry.   (2nd. ed.)
D. C. Douglas, The Norman Achievement.
D. Bates, Normandy before 1066.
R. A. Brown, Origins of English Feudalism.
R. H. C. Davis, The Normans and Their Myth.
D. F. Renn, Norman Castles in Britain.
C. W. Hollister, The Military Organization of Norman England.
V. H. Galbraith, The Making of Domesday Book.
R. W. Finn, The Domesday Inquest.
G. W. Keeton, The Norman Conquest and the Common Law.

N. F. Cantor, Church, Kingship and Lay Investiture in England, 1089-1135.
H. A. Cronne, The Reign of Stephen, 1135-1154: Anarchy in England.
M. Brett, The English Church Under Henry I.
F. M. Stenton, The First Century of English Feudalism, 1066-1166.
J. W. Alexander, Ranulf of Chester: A Relic of the Conquest.
D. C. Douglas, "The First Century of English Feudalism," Economic History Review, 9 (1939), 128-143.
C. W. Hollister, "1066: The 'Feudal Revolution'," American Historical Review, 73 (1968), 708-723.
C. W. Hollister, "Normandy, France and the Anglo-Norman Regnum," Speculum, 51 (1976), 202-242.
S. B. Hicks, "The Impact of William Clito upon the Continental Policies of Henry I of England," Viator, 10 (1979), 1-21.
R. H. C. Davis, "William of Jumièges, Robert Curthose and the Norman Succession," English Historical Review, 95 (1980), 597-606.
F. Barlow, "William I's Relations with Cluny," Journal of Ecclesistical History, 32 (Apr. 1981), 131-141.
C. Morton, "Pope Alexander II and the Norman Conquest," Latomus, 34 (Apr.-June 1975), 362-382.
J. Gillingham, "Richard I and Berengaria of Navarre," Bulletin of the Institute of Historical Research, 53 (1980), 157-173.
K. Schnith, "Die Wende der englischen Geschichte im 11. Jahrhundert," Historisches Jahrbuch, 86 (1966), 1-53.

THE GREATER NORMAN CONQUEST

J. J. C. Norwich, The Normans in the South, 1016-1130.
J. J. C. Norwich, The Kingdom in the Sun, 1130-1194.
     N. B. Both titles above are good scholarly popularizations.
G. A. Loud, Church and Society in the Norman Principality of Capua, 1058-1197. (1985). BX1546 .C33L68 1985
E. Curtis, Roger of Sicily and the Normans in Lower Italy, 1016-1154.
O. Demus, The Mosaics of Norman Sicily.
A History of the Crusades, ed. K. M. Setton, I & II.
E. Joranson, "The Inception of the Career of the Normans in Italy - Legend and History," Speculum, 23 (1948), 353-396.
A. Brackmann, "The Beginnings of the National State in Mediaeval Germany and the Norman Monarchies," Mediaeval Germany, 911-1250, ed. G. Barraclough,   II, 281-299.
J. H. Pryor, "Transportation of Horses by Sea during the Era of the Crusades: Eighth Century to 1285 A.D.," Mariner's Mirror, 68 (1982), 9-27, 103-125.
M. E. Martin, "An Adriatic Hastings: Normans from Italy Invaded the Byzantine Empire, Robert Guiscard Sought the Imperial Crown," History Today, 27 Apr. 1977), 219-225.
D. Abulafia, "The Reputation of a Norman King in Angevin Naples," Journal of Medieval History, 5 (June 1979), 135-47.
E. Jamison, "The Sicilian Norman Kingdom in the Mind of Anglo-Norman Contemporaries," Proceedings of the British Academy, 24 (1938), 237-85.

A. Marongiu, "A Model State in the Middle Ages: The Norman and Swabian Kingdom of Sicily," Comparative Studies in Society and History, 6 (1963-64), 307-20. See also the "Comment" by J. R. Strayer, ibid., pp. 321-24.

H. Wieruszowski, "Roger II of Sicily, Rex-Tyrannus in Twelfth-Century Political Thought," Speculum, 38 (1963), 46-78.

L.-R. Ménager, "L'institution monarchique dans les Etats normands d'Italie. Contribution à l'étude du pouvoir royal dans les principautés occidentales, aux XIe - XIIe siècles," Cahiers de civilisation médiévale, 2 (1959), 303-31, 445-68.

A. Varvaro, "Les Normands en Sicile aux XIe et XIIe siècles: Présence effective dans l'île des hommes d'origine normande ou gallo romaine," ibid., 23 (1980), 199-213.

H. Enzenberger, "Der 'böse' und der 'gute' Wilhelm: Zur Kirchenpolitik der normannischen Könige von Sizilien nach dem Vertrag von Benevent (1156)," Deutsches Archiv, 36 (1980), 385-432.

A. Brackmann, "Die Wandlung der Staatsanschauungen im Zeitalter Friedrichs I," Historische Zeitschrift, 145 (1932), 1-18.

H. Enzenberger, "Der 'böse' und der 'gute' Wilhelm: Zur Kirchenpolitik der normannischen Könige von Sizilien nach dem Vertrag von Benevent (1156)," Deutsches Archiv, 36 (1980), 385-432.

E. Caspar, Roger II. (1101-1154) und die Gründung der normannisch-sicilischen Monarchie.

THE BACKGROUND OF THE CRUSADING MOVEMENT.

C. Erdmann, The Origin of the Idea of Crusade.

R. W. Southern, Western Views of Islam in the Middle Ages.

B. Z. Kedar, Crusade and Mission: European Approaches towards the Muslims. (1984). BV2625 .K43 1984

D. C. Munro, "The Western Attitude Toward Islam During the Period of the Crusades," Speculum, 6 (1931), 329-343.

W. E. Kaegi, Jr., "The Contribution of Archery to the Turkish Conquest of Anatolia," ibid., 39 (1964), 96-108.

J. Streater, "The Battle of Manzikert," History Today, 17 (1967), 257-263.

E. O. Blake, "The Formation of the 'Crusade Idea'," Journal of Ecclesiastical History, 21 (1970), 11-31.

O. Springer, "Mediaeval Pilgrim Routes from Scandinavia to Rome," Mediaeval Studies, 12 (1950), 92-122.

E. Joranson, "The Problem of the Spurious Letter of Emperor Alexius to the Count of Flanders," American Historical Review, 55 (1949-50), 811-832.

T. A. T. Rice, The Seljuks in Asia Minor.

H. E. Mayer, The Crusades.

A History of the Crusades, ed. K. M. Setton, I.

S. Runciman, A History of the Crusades. (3 vols.)

D. R. Howard, Writers and Pilgrims: Medieval Pilgrimage Narratives and Their Posterity.

V. and H. Hall, The Great Pilgrimage of the Middle Ages: The Road to St. James of Compostella.

C. Courtois, "Grégoire VII et l'Afrique du Nord: Remarques sur les communautés chretiennes d'Afrique au XIe siècle," Rev. hist., 195 (1945), 97-122, 193-226.

G. Constable, "Monachisme et pèlerinage au Moyen Age," ibid., 523 (1977), 3-28.

W. Holtzmann, Beiträge zur Reichs- und Papstgeschichte des hohen Mittelalters, pp. 51-105.
A. Waas, Geschichte des Kreuzzüge. (2 vols.)
U. Schwerin, Die Aufrufe der Päpste zur Befreiung des Heiligen Landes von den Anfängen bis zum Ausgang Innocenz IV.

THE FIRST CRUSADE.

A. C. Krey, "Urban's Crusade - Success or Failure?" American Historical Review, 53 (1948), 235-250.
L. A. M. Sumberg, "The 'Tafurs' and the First Crusade," Mediaeval Studies, 21 (1959), 224-246.
H. E. J. Cowdrey, "Pope Urban's Preaching of the First Crusade," History, 55 (1970), 177-188.
H. Dickerhof, "Über die Staatsgründung des ersten Kreuzzugs," Historisches Jahrbuch, 100 (1980), 95-130.
J. France, "The Election and Title of Godfrey de Bouillon," Canadian Journal of History, 18 (Dec. 1983), 321-29.
B. Stemberger, "Zu den Judenverfolgungen in Deutschland zur Zeit der ersten beiden Kreuzzüge," Kairos, 20 (no. 1 & no 2, 1978), 53-72, 151-157.
R. Crozet, "Le voyage d'Urban II et ses négociations avec le clergé de France," Rev. hist., 179 (1937), 271-310.
J. Riley-Smith, What Were The Crusades?
A. Becker, Papst Urban II (1088-1099).
The First Crusade: The Accounts of Eye-Witnesses and Participants, ed. A. C. Krey.
Fulcher of Chartres, A History of the Expedition to Jerusalem, 1095-1127, trans. F. R. Ryan.
(Setton, Runciman, Mayer and Waas as above.)

THE LATER CRUSADES.

J. Prawer, "The Nobility and the Feudal Regime in the Latin Kingdom of Jerusalem," Lordship and Community in Medieval Europe: Selected Readings, ed. F. L. Cheyette, pp. 156-179.
J. Prawer, "Estates, Communities and the Constitution of the Latin Kingdom," ibid., pp. 376-403.
L. and J. Riley-Smith, The Crusades: Idea and Reality, 1095-1274.
D. C. Munro, The Kingdom of the Crusaders.
A. S. Atiya, Crusade, Commerce and Culture.
B. Z. Kedar, Crusade and Mission: European Approaches towards the Muslims.
M. Purcell, Papal Crusading Policy, 1244-1291: The Chief Instruments of Papal Crusading Policy and Crusade to the Holy Land from the Final Loss of Jerusalem to the Fall of Acre.
E. Joranson, "The Palestine Pilgrimage of Henry the Lion," Medieval and Historiographical Essays in Honor of James Westfall Thompson, ed. J. L.   Cate and E. N. Anderson, pp. 146-225.
G. Constable, "The Second Crusade as Seen by Contemporaries," Traditio, 9 (1953), 213-279.
C. M. Brand, "The Byzantines and Saladin, 1185-1192: Opponents of the Third   Crusade," Speculum, 38 (1962), 167-181.
C. M. Brand, "A Byzantine Plan for the Fourth Crusade," ibid., 43 (1968),   462-475.
R. Chazan, "Emperor Frederick I, the Third Crusade, and the Jews,"   Viator, 8 (1977), 83-93.

P. W. Edbury, "John of Ibelin's Title to the County of Jaffa and Ascalon,"   English Historical Review, 98 (Jan. 1983), 115-133.

A. J. Forey, "Constitutional Conflict and Change in the Hospital of St. John   during the Twelfth and Thirteenth Centuries," Journal of Ecclesiastical History, 33 (Jan. 1982), 15-29.

A. J. Forey, "The Military Orders in the Crusading Proposals of the Late-Thirteenth and Early-Fourteenth Centuries," Traditio, 36 (1980),   317-345.

M. E. Martin, "The Venetian-Seljuk Treaty of 1220," English Historical Review, 95 (1980), 321-330.

D. E. Queller & G. W. Day, "Some Arguments in Defense of of the Venetians on the Fourth Crusade," American Historical Review, 81 (Oct. 1976), 717-737.

D. E. Queller & I. B. Katele, "Attitudes towards the Venetians in the Fourth Crusade: The Western Sources," International History Review, 4 (Feb. 1982), 1-36.

D. E. Queller and S. J. Stratton, "A Century of Controversy on the Fourth Crusade," Studies in Medieval and Renaissance History, 6 (1969), 233-277.

D. E. Queller, T. K. Compton, and D. A. Campbell, "The Fourth Crusade: The Neglected Majority," Speculum, XLIX (1974), 441-465.

R. H. Schmandt, "The Fourth Crusade and the Just War Theory," Catholic Historical Review, 61 (1975), 191-221.

J. Riley-Smith, "The Assise sur la ligece and the Commune of Acre," Traditio, 27 (1971), 179-204.

J. Hill, "From Rome to Jerusalem: An Icelandic Itinerary of the Mid-Twelfth Century," Harvard Theological Review, 76 (Apr. 1983), 175-203.

T. D. Matijasic, "Christian vs. Christian: The Fourth Crusade and the Sack of Zara," Journal of Historical Studies, 5 (no. 2, 1982), 1-19.

H. E. Mayer, "The Origins of the Lordships of Ramla and Lydda in the Latin Kingdom of Jerusalem," Speculum, 60 (1985), 537-552.

J. H. Pryor, "The Naval Architecture of Crusader Transport Ships: A Reconstruction of Some Archetypes for Round-Hulled Sailing Ships," Mariner's Mirror, 70 (1984), 171-219; 275-292, 363-386.

P. Raedts, "The Children's Crusade of 1212," Journal of Medieval History, 3 (1977), 279-323.

E. Meuthen, "Der Fall von Konstantinopel und der lateinische Westen," Historische Zeitschrift, 237 (1983), 1-35.

M. C. Lyons & D. E. P. Jackson,   Saladin: The Politics of the Holy War.

R. C. Smail, Crusading Warfare.

D. Seward, Monks of War: The Military Religious Orders.

A. Ben-Ami, Social Change in a Hostile Environment: The Crusaders' Kingdom of Jerusalem.

J. Prawer, The Crusaders' Kingdom: European Colonization in the Middle Ages.

D. E. Queller, The Fourth Crusade: The Conquest of Constantinople, 1201-1204.

E. D. S. Bradford, The Great Betrayal: Constantinople 1204.

J. Godfrey, 1204: The Unholy Crusade.

J. A. Brundage, Medieval Canon Law and the Crusader.

J. A. Brundage, Richard Lion Heart.

J. Kritzeck, Peter the Venerable and Islam.

J. J. Saunders, Aspects of the Crusades.

R. L. Nicholson, Joscelyn III and the Fall of the Crusader States, 1134-1199.

J. Riley-Smith, The Feudal Nobility and the Kingdom of Jerusalem, 1174-1277.

J. Riley-Smith, The Knights of St. John in Jerusalem and Cyprus, c. 1050-1310.
C. M. Brand, Byzantium Confronts the West, 1180-1204.
A. E. Bakalopoulos, Origins of the Greek Nation: The Byzantine Period, 1204-1461.
B. Lewis, The Assassins: A Radical Sect in Islam.
T. S. R. Boase, Castles and Churches of the Crusading Kingdom.
W. Müller-Wiener, Castles of the Crusaders.
P. W. Edbury, (ed.), Crusade and Settlement: Papers Read at the First Conference of the Society for the Study of the Crusades and the Latin East and Presented to R. C. Smail.
J. Hartmann, Die Persönlichkeit des Sultans Saladin im Urteil der abendländichen Quellen.
H. Vriens, "De kwestie van den vierden kruistocht," Tijdschrift voor geschiedenis, 37 (1922), 50-82.
F. W. Wentzlaff-Eggebert, Kreuzzugsdichtung des Mittelalters.
E. Gerland, Geschichte des lateinischen Kaiserreichs von Konstantinopel.
R. Röricht, Beiträge zur Geschichte der Kreuzzüge.
F. Gabrieli, "Introduction aux historiens arabes des croisades," Cahiers de civilisation médiévale, 13 (1970), 221-228.
H. E. Mayer, "Das Pontificale von Tyrus und die Krönung der lateinischen Könige von Jerusalem: Zugleich ein Beitrag zur Forschung über Herrschaftszeichen und Staatssymbolik," Dumbarton Oaks Papers, 21 (1967), 141-232.
M. L. Bulst, "Zur Geschichte der Ritterorden und des Königreichs Jerusalem im 13. Jahrhundert bis zur Schlacht bei La Forbie am 17. Okt. 1244," Deutsches Archiv, 22 (1966), 197-226.
E. Lavisse, Histoire de France, II, 2, pp. 227-250.
Willliam of Tyre, A History of Deeds Done Beyond the Sea, trans. E. A. Babcock and A. C. Krey.
R. C. Schwinges, "Kreuzzugsideologie und Toleranz im Denken Wilhelms von Tyrus," Saeculum, 25 (1974), 367-385.
Odo of Deuil, De Profectione Ludovici VII in orientem, ed. and trans. by V. G. Berry.
Ambroise, The Crusade of Richard Lion-Heart, trans. M. J. Hubert and J. L. LaMonte.
Arab Historians of the Crusades, ed. and trans. by F. Gabrieli.
Ibn al-Kalanisi, The Damascus Chronicle of the Crusades.
Ceux qui conquirent Constantinople, récits de la quatrieme croisade, ed. N. Coulet.

KINGSHIP AND LAW IN THE MIDDLE AGES.

F. Kern, Kingship and Law in the Middle Ages.
P. E. Schramm, A History of the English Coronation.
H. G. Richardson, "The English Coronation Oath," Speculum, 24 (1949), 44-75.
A. Jones, "The Significance of the Royal Consecration of Edgar in 973," Journal of Ecclesiastical History, 33 (1982), 375-390.
S. J. T. Miller, "The Position of the King in Bracton and Beaumanoir," ibid., 31 (1956), 263-296.
C. W. Hollister and John W. Baldwin, "The Rise of Administrative Kingship: Henry I and Philip Augustus," American Historical Review, 83 (1978), 867-905.
E. Kantorowicz, The King's Two Bodies: A Study in Mediaeval Political Theology.
E. Kantorowicz, Laudes Regiae: A Study in Liturgical Acclamations and Mediaeval Ruler Worship.
E. Peters, The Shadow King: Rex Inutilis in Medieval Law and Literature, 751-1327.

S. Malarkey, "The 'Corones Tweyne': An Interpretation," Speculum, 38 (1963), 473-478.
O. Gierke, Political Theories of the Middle Ages.
H. Mitteis, The State in the Middle Ages: A Comparative Constitutional History of Feudal Europe, trans. H. F. Orton.
A. J. and R. W. Carlyle, A History of Mediaeval Political Theory in the West. (6 vols.)
J. Gardelles, "Les palais dans l'Europe occidentale chrétienne du Xe au XIIe siècle," Cahiers de civilisation médiévale, 19 (Apr.-June 1976), 115-134.
C. Brühl, "Kronen- und Krönungsbrauch im frühen und hohen Mittelalter," Historische Zeitschrift, 234 1982), 1-31.
W. Ullmann, "Der Souveränitätsgedanke in den mittelalterlichen Krönungsordines," Festschrift Percy Ernst Schramm, I, 72-89.
W. Ullmann, "Schranken der Königsgewalt im Mittelalter," Historisches Jahrbuch, 91 (1971), 1-21.
P. E. Schramm, "Die Geschichte des mittelalterlichen Herrschertums im Lichte der Herrschaftszeichen," Hist. Zeit., 178 (1954), 1-24.
H. Beumann, "Die Historiographie des Mittelalters als Quelle für die Ideengeschichte des Königtums," ibid., 180 (1955), 449-488.
R. Buchner, "Der Titel rex Romanorum in deutschen Königsurkunden des 11. Jahrhunderts," Deutsches Archiv, 19 (1963), 327-338.
H. Hoffmann, "Die Unveräußlichkeit der Kronrechte im Mittelalter," ibid., 20 (1964), 389-474.
S. Gagnér, Studien zur Ideengeschichte der Gesetzgebung.
R. Scheyhing, Eide, Amtsgewalt und Bannleihe: Eine Untersuchung zur Bannleihe im hohen und späten Mittelalter.
H. Mitteis, Die deutsche Königswahl: Ihre Rechtsgrundlagen bus zur Goldenen Bulle.
G. Theuerkauf, Lex, Speculum, Compendium Juris: Rechtsaufzeichnungen und Rechtsbewußtsein in Norddeutschland vom 8. bis zum 16. Jahrhundert.
Eike von Repgow, Sachsenspiegel.

CHURCH AND STATE IN THE TWELFTH CENTURY.

J. A. Yunck, "Economic Conservatism, Papal Finance and the Medieval Satires on Rome," Change in Medieval Society: Europe North of the Alps, ed. S. L. Thrupp, pp. 72-85.
M. W. Baldwin, Alexander III and the Twelfth Century.
R. Somerville, "The Council of Pisa, 1135: A Re-examination of the Evidence   for the Canons," Speculum, 45 (1970), 98-114.
N. M. Haring, "Notes on the Council and Consistory of Rheims (1148)," Mediaeval Studies, 28 (1966), 39-59.
J. G. Rowe, "Hadrian IV, the Byzantine Empire, and the Latin Orient," Essays in Medieval History Presented to Bertie Wilkinson, ed. T. A. Sandquist and M. R. Powicke, pp. 3-16.
H. V. White, "Pontius of Cluny, the Curia Romana and the End of Gregorianism in Rome," Church History, 27 (1958), 195-219.
K. Hampe, Germany under the Salian and Hohenstaufen Emperors.
R. Folz, "La chancellerie de Frédéric Ier et la canonisation de Charlemagne," Le Moyen Age, 70 (1964), 13-31.

T. Mayer, "Papsttum und Kaisertum: Werden, Wesen und Auflösung einer   Weltordnung," Hist. Zeit., 187 (1959), 1-53.
A. Brackmann, "Die Ursache der geistigen und politischen Wandlung Europas im   11. und 12. Jahrhundert," ibid., 149 (1934), 229-239.
H.-W. Klewitz, "Das Ende des Reformpapsttums," Deutsches Archiv, 3 (1939),   371-412.
F. J. Schmale, "Papsttum und Kurie zwischen Gregor VII. und Innocenz II.,"   Hist. Zeit., 193 (1961), 265-285.
W. Levison, "Die mittelalterliche Lehre von den beiden Schwerten," Deutsches Archiv, 9 (1951-52), 14-42.
H. Hoffmann, "Die beiden Schwerten im hohen Mittelalter," ibid., 20 (1064),   78-114.
H. Wolter, "Die Verlobung Heinrichs VI. mit Konstanz von Sizilien im Jahre 1184," Historisches Jahrbuch, 105 (1985), 30-51.
G. Baaken, "Die Verhandlungen zwischen Kaiser Heinrich VI. und Papst Coelestin III. in den Jahren 1195-1197," ibid., 27 (1971), 457-513.
J. Goetz, "Kritische Beiträge zur Geschichte der Pataria," Archiv für Kulturgeschichte, 12 (1916), 17-55, 164-194.
M. Pacaut, Alexandre III: Etude sur la conception du pouvoir pontifical dans sa pensée et dans son ouvre .
P. Rassow, Honor Imperii: Die neue Politik Friedrich Barbarossas, 1152-1159.
A. Waas, Heinrich V.: Gestalt und Verhängnis des letzten salischen Kaisers.
F. Böhm, Das Bild Friedrich Barbarossas und seines Kaisertums in den ausländischen Quellen seiner Zeit.
I. Schnack, Richard von Cluny, seine Chronik und sein Kloster in den Anfängen der Kirchenspaltung von 1159.
I. Friedländer, Die päpstlichen Legaten in Deutschland und Italien am Ende des XII. Jahrhundert.
F. Hausmann, Reichskanzlei und Hofkapelle Unter Heinrich V. und Konrad III.
G. Duncken, Die politischen Wirksamkeit der päpstlichen Legaten in der Zeit des Kampfes zwischen Kaisertum und Papsttum in Oberitalien unter Friedrich I.
H. Pahncke, Geschichte der Bischöfe Italiens deutscher Nations von 951-1254.
A. Hauck, Kirchengeschichte Deutschlands, IV, 3-324.
J. Haller, Das Papsttum: Idee und Wirklichkeit, III.
E. Orthbandt, Die Zeit der Staufer.

THE CONCEPT OF EMPIRE.

J. Bryce, The Holy Roman Empire.   [The classic but long out-dated introduction to the subject. Please note that the work was written originally as an undergraduate honors thesis.]
R. Folz, The Concept of Empire in Western Europe From the Fifth to the Fourteenth Century.
G. Barraclough, The Mediaeval Empire: Idea and Reality.
F. Heer, The Holy Roman Empire.
W. Ullmann, "Reflections on the Mediaeval Empire," Transactions of the Royal Historical Society, Fifth Series, 14 (1964), 89-108.
J. A. Brundage, "Widukind of Corvey and the 'Non-Roman' Imperial Idea," Mediaeval Studies, 22 (1960), 15-26.

M. Bloch, "The Empire and the Idea of Empire Under the Hohenstaufen," Land and Work in Mediaeval Europe, pp. 1-43.

R. Buchner, "Der Titel rex Romanorum in deutschen Königsurkunden des 11. Jahrhunderts," Deutsches Archiv, 19 (1963), 327-338.

A. Diehl, "Heiliges römisches Reich deutscher Nation," Hist. Zeit., 156 (1937), 457-484.

R. Holtzmann, "Der Weltherrschaftsgedanke des mittelalterlichen Kaisertums und die Souveränität der europäischen Staaten," ibid., 159 (1939), 251-264.

C. Erdmann, "Das ottonische Reich als imperium Romanum," Deutsches Archiv, 6 (1943), 412-441.

E. E. Stengel, "Kaisertitel und Souveränitätsidee: Studien zur Vorgeschichte des modernen Staatsbegriffs," ibid., 3 (1939), 1-56.

F. Rörig, "Heinrich IV. und der 'Westherrschaftsanspruch' des mittelalterlichen Kaisertums," ibid., 7 (1944), 200-203.

E. E. Stengel, Abhandlungen und Untersuchungen zur Geschichte des Kaisergedankens im Mittelalter.

P. E. Schramm, Kaiser, Rom und Renovatio: Studien zur Geschichte des römischen Erneuerungsgedankens vom Ende des karolingischen Reiches bis zum Investiturstreit.

E. Nellmann, Die Reichsidee in deutschen Dichtung der Salier und frühen Stauferzeit.

W. Smidt, Deutsches Königtum und deutscher Staat des Hochmittelalters während und unter dem Einfluß der italischen Heerfahrten.

U. Allers, The Concept of Empire in German Romanticism and its Influence on the National Assembly at Frankfurt, 1848-1849.

FEUDALISM AND ITS DIVERGENT TENDENCIES.

Lordship and Community in Medieval Europe: Selected Readings, ed. F. L. Cheyette, pp. 12-61, 128-136, 198-209, 217-221.

F. L. Ganshof, Feudalism.

M. Bloch, Feudal Society.

J. Bumke, The Concept of Knighthood in the Middle Ages. Translated by W. T. H. Jackson and Erika Jackson. (1982). CR4513 .B843 1982

S. Painter, Feudalism and Liberty.

H. Mitteis, The State in the Middle Ages: A Comparative Constitutional History of Feudal Europe, trans. by H. F. Orton.

B. D. Lyon, From Fief to Indenture: The Transition from Feudal to Non-Feudal Contract in Western Europe.

J. W. Thompson, Feudal Germany, pp. 232-337.

T. Evergates, Feudal Society in the Bailliage of Troyes Under the Counts of Champagne, 1152-1284.

E. A. R. Brown, "The Tyranny of a Construct: Feudalism and Historians of Medieval Europe," American Historical Review, 79 (1974), 1063-1088.

H. A. Cronne, "The Salisbury Oath," History, 19 (1934-35), 248-252.

K. B. McFarlane, "Bastard Feudalism," Bulletin of the Institute of Historical Research, 20 (1943-1945), 161-180.

B. S. Bachrach, "Enforcement of the Forma Fidelitatis: The Techniques Used by Fulk Nerra, Count of the Angevins (987-1040)," Speculum, 59 (Oct. 1984), 796-819.

B. B. Broughton, Dictionary of Medieval Knighthood and Chivalry: Concepts and Terms.
H. Mitteis, Lehnrecht und Staatsgewalt.
W. Kienast, "Lehnrecht und Staatsgewalt im Mittelalter," Hist. Zeit., CLVIII (1938), 3-51.
R. Boutruche, Seigneurie et féodalité.
E. Perroy, La féodalité en France du Xe au XIIe siècle.
H. Spangenberg, Vom Lehnstaat zum Ständestaat.

THE HOHENSTAUFEN AND FEUDALISM.

O. Freiherr von Dungern, "Constitutional Reorganization and Reform under the Hohenstaufen," Mediaeval Germany, ed. G. Barraclough, II, 203-233.
H. Mitteis, "Feudalism and the German Constitution," ibid, II, 235-279.
P. Munz, Frederick Barbarossa: A Study in Medieval Politics.
P. Munz, "Frederick Barbarossa and Henry the Lion in 1176," Hist. Stud.: Australia and New Zealand, 12 (1965), 1-21.
M. Bloch, "A Problem in Comparative History: The Administrative Classes in France and in Germany," Land and Work in Mediaeval Europe, pp. 82-123.
K. Hampe, "Heinrichs des Löwen Sturz im politisch-historischer Beurteilung," Hist. Zeit., 109 (1912), 49-82.
F. Güterbock, Der Prozeß Heinrichs des Löwen.
E. E. Stengel, "Zum Prozeß Heinrichs des Löwen," Deutsches Archiv, 5 (1942), 493-510.
T. Mayer et al., Kaisertum und Herzogsgewalt im Zeitalter Friedrichs I.
R. Schmidt, "Heinrich der Löwe: Seine Stellung in der inneren und auswärtigen Politik Deutschlands," Hist. Zeit., 154 (1936), 241-284.
H. Meyer, "Bürgerfreiheit und Herrschergewalt unter Heinrich dem Löwen," ibid., 147 (1932), 277-319.
W. Ohnsorge, "Die Byzanzpolitik Friedrich Barbarossas und der 'Landesverrat' Heinrichs des Löwen," Deutsches Archiv, 6 (1943), 118-149.
K. F. Krieger, "Die königliche Lehngerichtsbarkeit im Zeitalter der Staufer," ibid., 26 (1971), 400-433.
J.-L. Kupper, "La politique des ducs de Zähringen entre la Moselle et la mer du Nord dans la seconde moitié du XIIe siècle," Moyen Age, 78 (1972), 427-466.
G. Baaken, "Recht und Macht in der Politik der Staufer," Hist. Zeit., 221 (1975), 553-570.
K. Bosl, Die Reichsministerialität der Salier und Staufer. (2 vols.)
W. Goez, Der Leihezwang.
R. Hildebrand, Der sächsische 'Staat' Heinrichs des Löwen.
E. Gronen, Die Machtpolitik Heinrichs des Löwen und sein Gegensatz gegen das Kaisertum.
D. von Gladiss, Beiträge zur Geschichte der staufischen Reichsministerialität.
H. Büttner, Staufer und Zähringer im politischen Kräftespiel zwischen Bodensee und Genfersee während des 12. Jahrhunderts.
[Thompson and Mitteis as above.]

ANGEVIN ENGLAND TO MAGNA CARTA.

A. L. Poole, From Domesday Book to Magna Carta.
W. L. Warren, Henry II.
A. R. Kelly, Eleanor of Aquitaine and the Four Kings.
J. A. Brundage, Richard Lion Heart: A Biography.
J. T. Appleby, England Without Richard.
E. J. Kealey, Roger of Salisbury: Viceroy of England.
J. W. Alexander, Ranulf of Chester: A Relic of the Conquest.
C. R. Young, Hubert Walter: Lord of Canterbury and Lord of England.
C. R. Cheney, Hubert Walter.
J. T. Appleby, John, King of England.
S. Painter, The Reign of King John.
Z. N. Brooke, The English Church and the Papacy from the Conquest to the Reign of John.
F. M. Powicke, Stephen Langton.
F. Thompson, Magna Carta: Its Role in the Making of the English Constitution, 1300-1629.
S. E. Thorne et al., The Great Charter: Four Essays on Magna Carta and the History of Our Liberty.
W. F. Swindler, Magna Carta: Legend and Legacy.
J. W. Alexander, "The Becket Controversy in Recent Historiography," Journal of British Studies, 9
    (1970), 1-26.
V. H. Galbraith, "Good Kings and Bad Kings in Medieval English History," History, New Series, 30
    (1945), 119-132.
C. W. Hollister, "King John and the Historians," Journal of British Studies, 1 (1961), 1-19.
W. Ullmann, "Arthur's Homage to King John," English Historical Review, 94 (Apr. 1979), 356-64.

THE TWELFTH CENTURY RENAISSANCE.

C. H. Haskins, The Renaissance of the Twelfth Century.
C. Morris, The Discovery of the Individual, 1050-1200.
R. W. Southern, Medieval Humanism and Other Studies.
H. Waddell, The Wandering Scholars: The Life and Art of the Lyric Poets of the Latin Middle Ages.
G. R. Evans, Anselm and a New Generation.
W. Ullmann, Medieval Foundations of Renaissance Humanism.
R. L. Benson, and G. Constable with C. D. Lanham (eds.) Renaissance and Renewal in the Twelfth
    Century. Papers presented at a conference marking the 50th anniversary of the publication of
    Charles Homer Haskins's Renaissance of the Twelfth Century and held in Cambridge, Mass.,
    Nov. 26-29, 1977.
U. T. Holmes, Jr., Daily Living in the Twelfth Century: Based on the Observations of Alexander
    Neckam in London and Paris.
Twelfth-century Europe and the Foundations of Modern Society, ed. M. Clagett, G. Post and R.
    Reynolds.
L. Genicot, "On the Evidence of the Growth of Population in the West from the Eleventh to the Thir-
    teenth Century," Change in Medieval Society, ed. S. Thrupp, pp. 14-29.
H. Gibb, "The Influence of Islamic Culture on Medieval Europe," ibid., pp. 155-167.
J. B. Ross, "A Study of Twelfth-Century Interest in the Antiquities of Rome," Medieval and Histori-
    ographical Essays in Honor of James Westfall Thompson, ed. J. L. Cate and E. N. Anderson, pp.
    302-321.

R. W. Southern, "The Place of England in the Twelfth-Century Renaissance," History, 45 (1960), 201-216.

J. F. Benton, "The Court of Champagne as a Literary Center," Speculum, 36 (1961), 551-591.

J. H. M. McCash, "Marie de Champagne and Eleanor of Aquitaine: A Relationship Reexamined," ibid., 54 (1979), 698-711.

C. W. Bynum, "Did the Twelfth Century Discover the Individual?" Journal of Ecclesiastical History, 31 (Jan. 1980), 1-17.

A. J. Denomy, "Concerning the Accessibility of Arabic Influences to the Earliest Provencal Troubadours," Mediaeval Studies, 15 (1953), 147-158.

A. J. Denomy, "An Inquiry into the Origins of Courtly Love," ibid., 6 (1944), 175-260.

J. C. Moore, "'Courtly Love': A Problem of Terminology," Journal of the History of Ideas, 40 (Oct.-Dec. 1979), 621-32.

T. Stiefel, "The Heresy of Science: A Twelfth-Century Conceptual Revolution," Isis, 68 (Sept. 1977), 347-62.

R. Witt, "Medieval 'Ars Dictaminis' and the Beginnings of Humanism: A New Construction of the Problem," Renaissance Quarterly, 35 (Spring 1982), 1-35.

R. M. Thomson, "England and the Twelfth-Century Renaissance," Past & Present, 101 (Nov. 1983), 3-21.

L. T. Topsfield, Troubadours and Love.

J. Lindsay, The Troubadours and Their World of the Twelfth and Thirteenth Centuries.

J. W. Baldwin, Masters, Princes, and Merchants: The Social Views of Peter the Chanter and His Circle. (2 Vols.)

M. Seidlmayer, Currents of Mediaeval Thought With Special Reference to Germany.

N. F. Partner, Serious Entertainments: The Writing of History in Twelfth- Century England.

B. Stock, The Implications of Literacy: Written Language and Models of Interpretation in the Eleventh and Twelfth Centuries.

C. W. Bynum, Docere Verbo et Exempla: An Aspect of Twelfth-Century Spirituality.

A. V. Murray, Abelard and St. Bernard: A Study in Twelfth-Century Modernism.

Wine, Women and Song: Medieval Latin Student Songs Now First Translated into English Verse, by J. A. Symonds.

A. Fourrier, L'Humanisme médiévale dans les littératures romanes du XIIe au XIVe siècles.

O. Cartellieri, Abt Suger von Saint-Denis, 1081-1151.

J. Flori, "La notion de Chevalerie dans les Chansons de Geste du XIIe siècle: Etude historique du vocabulaire," Moyen Age, 81 (no. 2, 1975), 211-244.

P. Lehmann, "Die Vielgestalt des zwölften Jahrhunderts," Hist. Zeit., 178 (1954), 225-250.

A. Borst, "Abälard und Bernhard,"ibid., 186 (1958), 497-526.

N. M. Häring, "Zur Geschichte der Schulen von Poitiers im 12. Jahrhundert," Archiv für Kulturgeschichte, 47 (1965), 23-47.

F. von Bezold, Das Fortleben der antiken Götter im mittelalterlichen Humanismus.

TRADE AND COMMERCE IN THE MIDDLE AGES.

R.-H. Bautier, The Economic Development of Medieval Europe.

H. L. Adelson, Medieval Commerce.
A. R. Lewis, Naval Power and Trade in the Mediterranean.
A. R. Lewis, The Northern Seas.
P. Dollinger, The German Hansa.
J. A. Gade, The Norwegian Control of Norwegian Commerce During the Late Middle Ages.
M. K. James, Studies in the Medieval Wine Trade.
T. H. Lloyd, The English Wool Trade in the Middle Ages.
S. D. Goitein, A Mediterranean Society: The Jewish Communities of the Arab World as Portrayed in
    the Documents of the Cairo Geniza. (2 vols.)
Essays in Economic History, ed. E. M. Carus-Wilson, Vol. I.
O. Cippola, "Currency Depreciation in Medieval Europe," Change in Medieval Society, ed. S. L.
    Thrupp, pp 227-236.
A. L. Udovich, "At the Origins of Western Commenda: Islam, Israel, Byzantium?" Speculum, 37 (1962),
    198-207.
M. Bloch, "Natural Economy or Money Economy: A Pseudo-Dilemma," Land and Work in Medieval
    Europe, pp. 230-243.
M. Bloch, "The Problem of Gold in the Middle Ages," ibid., pp. 186-229.
J. F. McGovern, "The Rise of New Economic Attitudes - Economic Humanism, Economic Nationalism
    - During the Later Middle Ages and the Renaissance, A.D. 1200-1550," Traditio, 26 (1970),
    217-253.
R. K. Barlow, "The Development of Business Techniques Used at the Fairs of Champagne From the
    End of the Twelfth Century to the Middle of the Thirteenth Century," Studies in Medieval and
    Renaissance History, 8 (1971), 3-52.
A. R. Lewis, "Medieval Social and Economic History as Viewed by North American Medievalists,"
    Journal of Economic History, 35 (Sept. 1975), 630-634.
R. W. Unger, "Warships and Cargo Ships in Medieval Europe," Technology and Culture, 22 (Apr. 1981),
    233-252.
M. Eckoldt, "Navigation on Small Rivers in Central Europe in Roman and Medieval Times," Int. J.
    Nautical Archaeol., 13 (Feb. 1984), 3-10.
W. von Stromer, "Nuremberg in the International Economics of the Middle Ages," Business History
    Review, 44 (1970), 210-225.
G. S. Harrison, "The Hanseatic League in Historical Interpretation," Historian, 33 (1971), 385-397.
U. Dirlmeier, Mittelalterliche Hoheitsträger im wirtschaftlichen Wettbewerb.
Cambridge Economic History of Europe, II, III.
A Source Book for Medieval Economic History, ed. R. C. Cave and H. H. Coulson.
Y. Renouard, "Le grand commerce des vins de Gascogne au moyen áge," Rev. hist., CCXXI (1959),
    261-304.
H. Thomas, "Beiträge zur Geschichte der Champagne-Messen im 14. Jahrhundert," Vierteljahrschrift für
    Sozial- und Wirtschaftsgeschichte, 64 (1977), 433-467.

MUNICIPAL ORIGINS AND URBAN SOCIETY.

C. Stephenson, Borough and Town.   [The first chapter provides a useful survey of the older theories
    on the much-debated subject of medieval town origins.]

J. Tait, The Mediaeval English Borough: Studies on Its Origins and Constitutional History.   [Shows that Stephenson's generalizations are not fully applicable to England.]
H. Pirenne, Medieval Cities.
H. Pirenne, Belgian Democracy: Its Early History.
The Medieval City, ed. H. A. Miskimin, D. Herlihy and A. Udovitch.
F. Rörig, The Medieval Town. [Use with caution.]
P. M. Hohenberg & Lynn Hollen Lees, The Making of Urban Europe, 1000-1950. (1985). HT131 .H58 1985
R. Hodges, Dark Age Economics: The Origins of Towns and Trade A.D. 600-1000.
P. Strait, Cologne in the Twelfth Century.
Herlihy, David, Medieval Households. (Studies in Cultural History.)
C. Platt, The English Medieval Town. (1976). JS3265 .P53 1976
D. M. Nicholas, "Medieval Urban Origins in Northern Continental Europe: State of Research and Some Tentative Conclusions," Studies in Medieval and Renaissance History, 6 (1969), 55-114.
F. Rörig, "Heinrich der Löwe und die Grundung Lübecks: Grundsätzliche Erörterung zur städtischen Ostsiedlung," Deutsches Archiv, 1 (1937), 408-456.
E. Coornaert, "Les ghildes médiévales," Rev. hist., 199 (1948), 22-55, 208-243.
C. Goehrke, "Die Anfänge des mittelalterlichen Städtewesens in eurasischer Perspektive," Saeculum, 31 (1980), 194-220, 221-239.
E. Ennen, "Die Frau im der mittelalterlichen Stadtgesellschaft Mitteleuropas," Hansische Geschichtsblätter, 98 (1980), 1-22.
A. Luchaire, Les communes francaises à l'époque des Capétiens directs.
H. Planitz, Die deutsche Stadt im Mittelalter.
Die Stadt des Mittelalters, ed. C. Haase. (3 vols.)
W. Ebel, Der Bürgereid als Geltungsgrund und Gestaltungsprinzip des deutschen mittelalterlichen Stadtrechts.
J. Bärmann, Die Städtegründungen Heinrichs des Löwen und die Stadtverfassung des 12. Jahrhunderts.
R. Pernoud, Les villes marchandes aux XIVe et XVe siècles.
R. Sprandel, "Die Handwerker in den nordwestdeutschen Städten des Mittelalters," Hansische Geschichtsblätter, 86 (1968), 37-62.

SERFDOM AND THE MARKGENOSSENSCHAFT THEORY.

C. Stephenson, "The Problem of the Common Man in Early Medieval Europe," American Historical Review, 51 (1946), 419-439.
N. D. Fustel de Coulanges, The Origin of Property in Land.
W. J. Bossenbrook, "Justus Möser's Approach to History," Medieval and Historiographical Essays in Honor of James Westfall Thompson, ed. Cate and Anderson, pp. 397-422.
Cambridge Economic History of Europe, I, esp. pp. 224-277.
M. Bloch, French Rural History.
E. Le Roy Ladurie, The Peasants of Languedoc.
W. O. Ault, Open-Field Farming in Medieval England: A Study of Village By-Laws.
C. J. Dahlmann, The Open Field System and Beyond: A Property Rights Analysis of an Economic Institution.

Z. Razi, "The Toronto School's Reconstitution of Medieval Peasant Society: A Critical View," Past and Present, 85 (1979), 141-157.

Z. Razi, "Family, Land, and the Village Community in Later Medieval England," Past & Present, 93 (Nov. 1981), 3-36.

H. Grundmann, "Freiheit als religiöses, politisches und persönliches Postulat im Mittelalter," Hist. Zeit., 233 (1957), 23-53.

G. Grosch, Markgenossenschaft und Grossgrundherrschaft im früheren Mittelalter.

F. Zimmermann, Die Weistümer und der Ausbau der Landeshoheit in der Kurpfalz.

S. Epperlein, Bauernbedrückung und Bauernwiderstand im hohen Mittelalter.

A. Dopsch, Die freien Marken in Deutschland: Beitrag zur Agrar- und Sozialgeschichte des Mittelalters.

A. Dopsch, Herrschaft und Bauer in der deutschen Kaiserzeit.

K. S. Bader, Studien zur Verfassungsgeschichte des mittelalterlichen Dorfes. (3 vols.)

F. Lütge, Studien zur Sozial= und Wirtschaftsgeschichte: Gesammelte Abhandlungen.

G. von Below, Geschichte der deutschen Landwirtschaft des Mittelalters in ihren Grundzügen, ed. by F. Lütge.

LAND RECLAMATION AND PEASANT EMANCIPATION: THE LOW COUNTRIES.

B. Lyon, "Medieval Real Estate Developments and Freedom," American Historical Review, 63 (1957), 47-61.

S. J. Fockema Andreae, "Embanking and Drainage Authorities in the Netherlands During the Middle Ages," Speculum, 27 (1952), 158-167.

B. H. Slicher van Bath, The Agrarian History of Western Europe, 500-1850.

A. M. Lambert, The Making of the Dutch Landscape: A Historical Geography of the Netherlands.

H. Pirenne, Histoire de Belgique, I.

J. F. Niermeyer, "De vroegste berichten omtrent bedijking in Nederland," Tijdschrift voor econmomische en sociale geografie, 49 (1958), 226-231.

G. H. Kurtz, "De oudste dijkbrieven voor de Lekdijkscolleges," Tijdschrift voor geschiedenis, 50 (1935), 276-292.

I. H. Gosses, "De vorming van het graafschap Holland," Verspreide Geschriften, ed. F. Gosses and J. F. Niermeyer, pp. 239-344.

C. A. van Kalveen, "Het polderdistrict Veluwe in de middeleeuwen," Bijdragen en Mededelingen van het Historisch Genootschap, 79 (1965), 219-334.

S. J. Fockema Andreae, Het Hoogheemraadschap van Rijnland: Zijn Recht en zijn Bestuur van den vroegsten Tijd tot 1857.

S. J. Fockema Andreae, Willem I, graaf van Holland, 1203-1222, en de Hollandse hoogheemraadschappen.

S. J. Fockema Andreae, Studiën over Waterschapsgeschiedenis. (7 vols.)

J. F. Niermeyer, Delft en Delftland: Hun Oorsprung en vroegste geschiedenis.

L. A. Warnkönig, Flandrische Staats- und Rechtsgeschichte bis zum Jahre 1305. (3 vols.) [Valuable documentary appendices.]

H. Halbertsma, Terpen tussen Vlie en Eems. (2 vols.)

I. H. Gosses, De rechterlijke organisatie van Zeeland in de middeleeuwen.
I. H. Gosses, Handboek tot de staatkundige geschiedenis der Nederlanden, I: De Middeleeuwen.
Das Rüstringer Recht, ed. W. J. Buma and W. Ebel.

RECLAMATION AND EMANCIPATION: GERMANY IN THE TWELFTH CENTURY.

T. Mayer, "The State of the Dukes of Zähringen,: Mediaeval Germany, 911-1250, ed. G. Barraclough,
    II, 175-202.
J. W. Thompson, Feudal Germany, II, 545-579.
W. Müller-Wille, "Die Hagenhufendörfer in Schaumburg-Lippe," Petermanns Geographische Mit-
    teilungen, 90 (1944), 245-247.
T. Mayer, "Königtum und Gemeinfreiheit im frühen Mittelalter," Deutsches Archiv, 6 (1943), 329-362.
H. K. Schulze, "Rodungsfreiheit und Königsfreiheit: Zu Genese und Kritik neuerer verfassungsges-
    chichtlicher Theorien," Hist. Zeit., 219 (1974), 529-550.
T. Mayer, Mittelalterliche Studien: Gesammelte Aufsätze.

THE WENDISH CRUSADE AND THE NORTHEASTERN GERMAN FRONTIER.

G. Barraclough, The Origins of Modern Germany, pp. 249-281.
J. W. Thompson, Feudal Germany, II, 387-528.
. Dvornik, The Slavs: Their Early History and Civilization, pp. 293-311.
H. Schreiber, Teuton and Slav: The Struggle for Central Europe.
The Cambridge History of Poland from the Origins to Sobieski.
Cambridge Economic History of Europe, I, 361-397.
W. Schlesinger, "Die geschichtliche Stellung der mittelalterlichen deutschen Ostbewegung," Hist. Zeit.,
    183 (1957), 517-542.
H. K. Schulze, "Der Anteil der Slawen an der mittelalterlichen Siedlung nach deutschem Recht im Ost-
    mitteldeutschland," Zeitschrift für Ostforschung, 31 (1982), 321-336.
H. K. Schulze, "Rodungsfreiheit und Königsfreiheit: Zu Genesis und Kritik neuerer verfassungsges-
    chichtlicher Theorien," Historische Zeitschrift, 219 (1974), 529-550.
S. Weinfurter, "Norbert von Xanten - Ordensstifter und 'Eigenkirchherr'," Archiv für Kulturgeschichte,
    59 (1977, ersch. 1979), 66-98.
R. Kötzschke and W. Ebert, Geschichte der ostdeutschen Kolonisation.
H. Conrad, Die mittelalterliche Besiedlung des deutschen Ostens und das deutsche Recht.
W. Schlesinger, Mitteldeutsche Beiträge zur deutschen Verfassungsgeschichte des Mittelalters.
R. Kötzschke, Deutsche und Slawen in mitteldeutschen Osten: Ausgewählte Aufsätze, ed. W.
    Schlesinger.
M. Bünding, Das Imperium Christianum und die deutschen Ostkriege vom zehnten bis zum zwölften
    Jahrhundert.

Heidenmission und Kreuzzugsgedanke im der deutschen Ostpolitik des Mittelalters, ed. H. Beumann.
Die deutsche Ostsiedlung im Mittelalter, ed. K. H. Quirin.
Helmold of Bosau, Chronicle of the Slavs, trans. F. J. Tschan.

NEW TRENDS IN MONASTICISM.

B. K. Lackner, The Eleventh-Century Background of Citeaux.

W. Williams, Saint Bernard of Clairvaux.

Bernard of Clairvaux: Studies presented to Dom Jean Leclercq.

G. R. Evans, The Mind of St. Bernard of Clairvaux.

A. A. King, Citeaux and Her Elder Daughters.

E. R. Elder, (ed.), Goad and Nail: Studies in Medieval Cistercian History, 10. (1985). BX3406.2 .G6
1985.

B. P. McGuire, The Cistercians in Denmark: Their Attitudes, Roles, and Functions in Medieval
Society.

L. J. Lekai, The Cistercians: Ideals and Reality.

P. Fergusson, Architecture of Solitude: Cistercian Abbeys in Twelfth-Century England.

N. F. Cantor, "The Crisis of Western Monasticism, 1050-1130," American Historical Review, 66 (1960),
47-67.

R. Roehl, "Plan and Reality in a Medieval Monastic Economy: The Cistercians," Studies in Medieval
and Renaissance History, 9 (1972), 83-113.

M. W. Bloomfield, "Joachim of Flora," Traditio, 13 (1957), 249-309.

B. McGinn, "The Abbot and the Doctors: Scholastic Reactions to the Radical Eschatology of Joachim
of Fiore," Church History, 40 (1971), 30-47.

R. E. Lerner, "Antichrists and Antichrist in Joachim of Fiore," Speculum, 60 (1985), 553-570.

E. R. Daniel, "The Double Procession of the Holy Spirit in Joachim of Fiore's Understanding of History," Speculum, 55 (1980), 469-483.

C. W. Bynum, "The Cistercian Conception of Community: An Aspect of Twelfth-Century Spirituality,"
Harvard Theological Review, 68 (July-Oct. 1975), 273-86.

D. Burr, "The Correctorium Controversy and the Origins of the Usus Pauper Controversy," Speculum,
60 (1985), 331-342.

M. Reeves, The Influence of Prophecy in the Later Middle Ages: A Study in Joachimism.

D. C. West and S. Zimdars-Swartz, Joachim of Fiore: A Study in Spiritual Perception and History.
BX4705 .J6 W46 1983

B. McGinn, The Calabrian Abbot: Joachim of Fiore in the History of Western Thought.

E. A. Armstrong, Saint Francis, Nature Mystic: The Derivation and Significance of the Nature Stories
in the Franciscan Legend.

M. E. Almedingen, Francis of Assisi.

J. Moorman, A History of the Franciscan Order: From Its Origins to the Year 1517.

E. R. Daniel, The Franciscan Concept of Mission in the High Middle Ages.

M. D. Lambert, Franciscan Poverty: The Doctrine of the Absolute Poverty of Christ and the Apostles
in the Franciscan Order, 1210-1323.

D. Burr, Eucharistic Presence and Conversion in Late Thirteenth-Century Franciscan Thought.

R. M. Bell, Holy Anorexia. Epilogue by William N. Davis.
B. D. Hill, English Cistercian Monasteries and Their Patrons in the Twelfth Century.
W. Braunfels, Monasteries of Western Europe: The Architecture of the Orders.
M. Volke, "Zu einigen Aspekten der Wirtschaftspolitik deutscher Zisterzienserkloster während des 12. und 13. Jahrhunderts," Jahrbuch für Wirtschaftsgeschichte, 1979, II, 169-182.
I. W. Frank, "Die Spannung zwischen Ordensleben und wissenschaftlicher Arbeit im frühen Dominikanerorden," Archiv für Kulturgeschichte, 49 (1967), 164-207.
Chartes et documents concernant l'abbaye de Cîteaux, 1098-1182, ed. J.Marilier.

THE MILITARY ORDERS AND THE RISE OF PRUSSIA.

P. Partner, The Murdered Magicians: The Templars and Their Myth.   CR4743 .P37 1982
F. Carsten, The Origins of Prussia.
E. Christiansen, The Northern Crusades: The Baltic and the Catholic Frontier, 1100-1525.
W. Urban, The Prussian Crusade.
W. Urban, The Baltic Crusade.
J. Fennell, The Crisis of Medieval Russia, 1200-1304.
D. Seward, "The Teutonic Knights," History Today, 20 (1970), 859-866.
A. J. Forey, "The Emergence of the Military Order in the Twelfth Century," Journal of Ecclesiastical History, 36 (1985), 175-195.
A. J. Forey, "Novitiate and Instruction in the Military Orders during the Twelfth and Thirteenth Centuries," Speculum, 61 (1986), 1-17.
K. Slaski, "North-Western Slavs in Baltic Sea Trade from the VIIIth to the XIIIth Century," Journal of European Economic History, 8 (Spring 1979), 83-107.
R. Spence, "Pope Gregory IX and the Crusade in the Baltic," Catholic Historical Review, 69 (Jan. 1983), 1-19.
W. Urban, "The Organization of Defense of the Livonian Frontier in the Thirteenth Century," Speculum, 48 (1973), 525-532.
E. Caspar, Hermann von Salza und die Gründung des Deutschordenstaates in Preussen.
Quellen zur Geschichte des deutschen Ordens, ed. W. Hubatsch.

MEDIEVAL HERESY AND THE INQUISITION.

M. Lambert, Medieval Heresy: Popular Movements from Bogomil to Hus.
H. C. Lea, The Inquisition of the Middle Ages.
A. S. Turberville, Mediaeval Heresy and the Inquisition.
S. Runciman, The Medieval Manichee.
J. Strayer, The Albigensian Crusade.
D. Obolensky, The Bogomils.
W. L. Wakefield, Heresy, Crusade, and Inquisition in Southern France, 1100-1250.
R. E. Lerner, The Heresy of the Free Spirit in the Later Middle Ages.
J. H. Mundy, The Repression of Catharism at Toulouse: The Royal Diploma of 1279. (1985). BX4891.2 .M84 1985

R. I. Moore, "The Origins of Medieval Heresy," History, New Series, 55 (1970),   21-36.
C. N. L. Brooke, "Heresy and Religious Sentiment, 1000-1250," Bulletin of the Institute of Historical Research, 41 (1968), 115-131.
A. P. Evans, "Hunting Subversion in the Middle Ages," Speculum, 33 (1958), 1-22.
D. Walther, "A Survey of Recent Research on the Albigensian Cathari," Church History, 34 (1965), 146-177.
R. Abels & E. Harrison, "The Participation of Women in Languedocian Catharism," Mediaeval Studies, 41 (1979), 215-251.
J. Russell, "Interpretations of the Origins of Medieval Heresy," Mediaeval Studies, 15 (1963), 26-53.
D. Berger, "Christian Heresy and Jewish Polemic in the Twelfth and Thirteenth Centuries," Harvard Theological Review, 68 (July-Oct. 1975), 287-303.
N. J. Housley, "Politics and Heresy in Italy: Anti-Heretical Crusades, Orders and Confraternities, 1200-1500," Journal of Ecclesiastical History, 33 (Apr. 1982), 193-208.
R. E. Lerner, "The Uses of Heterodoxy: The French Monarchy and Unbelief in the Thirteenth Century," French Historical Studies, 4 (1965), 198-202.
D. Radcliff-Umstead, "The Catharists and the Failure of Community," Mediaevalia, 1 (no. 2, 1977), 63-87.
K. Pennington, "'Pro peccatis patrum puniri': A Moral and Legal Problem of the Inqusition," Church History, 47 1978), 137-154.
R. Kay, "The Albigensian Twentieth of 1221-3: An Early Chapter in the History of Papal Taxation," Journal of Medieval History, 6 (1980), 307-315.
G. W. Davis, The Inquisition at Albi.
J. B. Russell, Witchcraft in the Middle Ages.
E. Le Roy Ladurie, Montaillou: The Promised Land of Error.
E. Cameron, The Reformation of the Heretics: The Waldenses of the Alps, 1480-1580.
H. Grundmann, "Ketzerverhöre des Spätmittelalters als quellenkritische Problem," Deutsches Archiv, 21 (1965), 519-575.
L. Christiani, " La tolérance et l'intolérance del'Eglise en matiere doctrinale depuis les premiers siècles jusqu'à nos jours," Cahiers d'histoire mondiale, 5 (1959-60), 71-93.
H. Taviani, "Le mariage dans l'hérésie de l'an mil," Annales, 32 (Nov.-Dec. 1977), 1074-89.
C. Moeller, "Les buchers et les auto-da-fé de l'inquisition depuis le moyen âge," Rev. d'hist. eccl., 14 (1913), 720-751; 15 (1914), 50-69.
J. Musy, "Mouvements populaires et hérésies au XIe siècle en France," Rev. hist., 253 (1975), 33-76.
F. Sanjek, "Le rassemblement hérétique de Saint-Felix-de-Caraman (1167) et les églises cathares au XIIe siècle," ibid., 67 (1972), 767-799.
A. Pales-Gobilliard, "Le Catharisme dans le comté de Foix, des origines au début du XIVe siècle," Revue de l'histoire des religions, 189 (Apr. 1976), 181-200.
A. Borst, "Neue Funde und Forschungen zur Geschichte der Katharer," Hist. Zeit., 174 (1952), 17-30.
P. Braun, "Die Bekämpfung der Ketzerei in Deutschland durch die Päpste bis zum Laterankonzil von 1215," Archiv für Kulturgeschichte, 9 (1911), 475-481.
A. Patschovsky, "Zur Ketzerverfolgung Konrads von Marburg," Deutsches Archiv, 37 (1981), 641-693.
M. Ligniéres, L'hérésie albigeois et la croisade.
J. J. I. Döllinger, Beiträge zur Sektengeschichte des Mittelalters.
L. Förg, Die Ketzerverfolgung in Deutschland unter Gregor IX.

A. Borst, Die Katharer.
Y. Dossat, Les crises de l'Inquisition toulousaine au XIIIe siècle.
Heresies of the High Middle Ages, trans. W. Wakefield and A. P. Evans.
Documents pour servir à l'histoire de l'Inquisition dans le Languedoc, ed. C. Dousais.
The Summa Contra Haereticos Ascribed to Praepositus of Cremona, ed. J. N. Garvin and J. A. Corbett.

THE FRENCH NATIONAL MONARCHY.

R. Fawtier, The Capetian Kings of France.
F. M. Powicke, The Loss of Normandy.
F. C. Pegues, The Lawyers of the Last Capetians.
C. T. Wood, The French Apanages and the Capetian Monarchy, 1224-1328.
T. N. Bisson, Assemblies and Representation in Languedoc in the Thirteenth Century.
M. W. Labarge, Saint Louis: The Life of Louis IX of France.
G. J. Campbell, "The Protest of Saint Louis," Traditio, 15 (1959), 405-418.
G. Post, "Two Notes on Nationalism in the Middle Ages," ibid., 9 (1953), 281-320.
E. A. R. Brown, "Taxation and Morality in the Thirteenth and Fourteenth Centuries: Conscience and
    Political Power and the Kings of France," French Historical Studies, 8 (1973), 1-28.
A. W. Lewis, "The Capetian Apanages and the Nature of the French Kingdom," Journal of Medieval
    History, 2 (June 1976), 119-134.
J. Madaule, The Albigensian Crusade.   [Use with caution!]
M. Bloch, La France sous des deniers Capétiens, 1223-1328.
Y. Renouard, "Essai sur le rôle de l'empire angevin dans la formation de la France et de la civilisation
    française aux XIIe et XIIIe siècles," Rev. hist., 195 (1945), 289-304.
F. Kern, Die Anfänge der französischen Ausdehnungepolitik bis zum Jahre 1308.
Histoire des institutions françaises au moyen áge, ed. F. Lot and R. Fawtier.
J. de Joinville, The Life of Saint Louis.

THE PAPACY AND THE EMPIRE IN THE THIRTEENTH CENTURY.

Innocent III: Vicar of Christ or Lord of the World? ed. J. M. Powell (Heath)   [A useful survey of
    some divergent interpretations.]
K. Pennington, Pope and Bishops: The Papal Monarchy in the Twelfth and Thirteenth Centuries.
    BX1210 .P46 1984
J. A. Watt, The Theory of Papal Monarchy in the Thirteenth Century.
L. E. Elliott-Binns, Innocent III.
J. Clayton, Pope Innocent III and His Times.
W. Ullmann, Medieval Papalism: The Political Theories of the Medieval Canonists.
B. Tierney, Origins of Papal Infallibility, 1150-1350: A Study on the Concepts of Infallibility,
    Sovereignty, and Tradition in the Middle Ages.
P. Andrewes, Frederick II of Hohenstaufen.
T. C. van Cleve, The Emperor Frederick II of Hohenstaufen: Immutator Mundi.

E. Kantorowicz, Frederick the Second, 1194-1250.
D. Abulafia, "Kantorowicz and Frederick II," History, 62 (June 1977), 193-210.
F. Geldner, Konradin, das Opfer eines großen Traumes: Größe, Schuld und Tragik der Hohenstaufen.
J. C. Moore, "Count Baldwin IX of Flanders, Philip Augustus, and the Papal Power," Speculum, 37 (1962), 79-89.
J. W. Baldwin, "The Intellectual Preparations for the Canon of 1215 Against Ordeals," ibid., 36 (1961), 613-636.
J. A. Watt, "The Constitutional Law of the College of Cardinals: Hostiensis to Johannes Andreae," Mediaeval Studies, 33 (1971), 127-157.
D. L. D'Avray, "A Letter of Innocent III and the Idea of Infallibility," Catholic Historical Review, 66 (July 1980), 417-421.
R. Kay, "The Albigensian Twentieth of 1221-3: An Early Chapter in the History of Papal Taxation," Journal of Medieval History, 6 (1980), 307-315.
S. Runciman, The Sicilian Vespers.
Cambridge Medieval History, VI.
H. Tillmann, "Zur Frage des Verhältnisses von Kirche und Staat in Lehre und Praxis Papst Innocenz III.," Deutsches Archiv, 9 (1951-52), 136-181.
A.-D. von den Brincken, "Die Mongolen im Weltbild der Lateiner um die Mitte des 13. Jahrhunderts, unter besondere Berücksichtigung des 'Speculum Historiale' des Vincenz von Beauvais," Archiv für Kulturgeschichte, 57 (1975), 117-140.
H. Marc-Bonnet, "Le Saint Siege et Charles d'Anjou sous Innocent IV et Alexandre IV (1245-1261)," Rev. hist., 200 (1948), 38-65.
F. Kempf, Papsttum und Kaisertum bei Innocenz III.
W. Neumann, Die deutschen Königswahlen und die päpstlichen Machtanspruch während des Inter-regnums.
K. Hampe, Urban IV. und Manfred (1261-1264.
K. Ganzer, Papsttum und Bistumsbesetzung in der Zeit von Gregor IX. bis Bonifaz VIII.: Ein Beitrag zur Geschichte der päpstlichen Reservationen.
J. Haller, Das Papsttum: Idee und Wirklichkeit, IV, V.
A. Hauck, Kirchengeschichte Deutschlands, IV, 684-949; V, 3-582.
Stupor Mundi: Zur Geschichte Friedrichs II. von Hohenstaufen, ed. G. Wolf.
Kaiser Friedrich II. in Briefen und Berichten seiner Zeit, ed. and trans. by
    K. J. Heinisch.

ENGLAND AFTER MAGNA CARTA.

F. M. Powicke, The Thirteenth Century, 1216-1307.
F. M. Powicke, King Henry III and the Lord Edward: The Community of the Realm in the Thirteenth Century. (2 vols.)
R. Wickson, The Community of the Realm in the Thirteenth Century.
J. M. W. Bean, The Decline of English Feudalism, 1215-1540.
R. H. Hilton, A Medieval Society: The West Midlands at the End of the Thirteenth Century.
M. W. Labarge, Gascony, England's First Colony, 1204-1453.

T. W. E. Roche, The King of Almayne.
R. F. Treharne, The Baronial Plan of Reform, 1258-1263.
L. F. Salzman, Edward I.
M. Richter, "The First Century of Anglo-Irish Relations," History, 59(1974), 195-210.

RECLAMATION AND EMANCIPATION IN THIRTEENTH CENTURY GERMANY.

There is no good treatment of this subject in the library. The closest thing is F. D. C. von Cronhelm, "Historisches Bericht von den alten und neueren Rechten und Gerichte in Holstein," Corpus Constitutionum Regio-Holsaticarum, IV, 56-74, which was written in the middle of the eighteenth century. See also E. Finder, Die Vierlande: Beiträge zur Geschichte, Landes- und Volkskunde Niedersachsens, although this should be used with some caution. Some of the readings listed under the headings dealing with reclamation and emancipation in the Low Countries and in North Germany are relevant here also.

MEDIEVAL TECHNOLOGY AND SCIENCE.

L. T. White, Jr., Medieval Technology and Social Change.
J. Gimpel, The Medieval Machine: The Industrial Revolution of the Middle Ages.
Science in the Middle Ages, ed. D. C. Lindberg.
E. Grant, Studies in Medieval Science and Natural Philosophy.
C. H. Haskins, Studies in the History of Mediaeval Science.
A. C. Crombie, Medieval and Early Modern Science.   (2 vols.)
M. Clagett, The Science of Mechanics in the Middle Ages.
R. Mar, Experiments in Gothic Structure.
L. Thorndyke, A History of Magic and Experimental Science.   (6 vols.)
S. C. Easton, Roger Bacon and His Search for a Universal Science.
A. C. Crombie, Robert Grosseteste and the Origins of Experimental Science.
A. Maier, On the Threshhold of Exact Science: Selected Writings of Anneliese Maier on Late Medieval Natural Philosophy. Ed. and trans. Steven D. Sargent.
M. Bloch, "Mediaeval 'Inventions'," Land and Work in Mediaeval Europe, pp. 169-185.
L. T. White, Jr., "Technology and Invention in the Middle Ages," Speculum, 15 (1940), 141-159.
L. T. White, Jr., "Natural Science and Naturalistic Art in the Middle Ages," American Historical Review, 52 (1947), 421-435.
L. T. White, Jr., "Technology Assessment from the Stance of a Medieval Historian," ibid., 79 (1974), 1-13.
L. T. White, Jr., "The Study of Medieval Technology, 1924-1974: Personal Reflections," Technology and Culture, 16 (Oct. 1975), 519-530.
J. A. Weisheipl, "Classification of the Sciences in Mediaeval Thought," Mediaeval Studies, 27 (1965), 54-90.
J. F O'Brien, "Some Medieval Anticipations of Inertia," New Scholasticism, 44 (1970), 345-371.
D. C. Lindberg, "Lines of Influence in Thirteenth-Century Optics: Bacon, Witelo, and Pecham," Speculum, 46 (1971), 66-83.

P. Marshall, "Nicole Oresme on the Nature, Reflection and Speed of Light," Isis, 72 (Sept, 1981), 357-74.
M. R. McVaugh, "Quantified Medical Theory and Practice at Fourteenth-Century Montpellier," Bulletin of the History of Medicine, 43 (1969), 397-413.
E. Rosen, "The Invention of Eyeglasses," Journal of the History of Medicine, 9 (1956), 13-46.
V. Ilardi, "Eyeglasses and Concave Lenses in Fifteenth-Century Florence and Milan: New Documents," Renaissance Quarterly, 29 (1976), 341-360.
K. B. Bales, "Nicole Oresme and Medieval Social Science: The 14th Century Debunker of Astrology Wrote an Early Monetary Treatise," Am. J. Ec. Sociol., 42 (Jan. 1983), 101-12.
E. Grant, "Celestial Matter: A Medieval and Galilean Cosmological Problem," Journal of Medieval and Renaissance Studies, 13 (Fall 1983), 157-86.
J. McEvoy, "The Chronology of Robert Grosseteste's Writings on Nature and Natural Philosophy," Speculum, 58 (no. 3, July 1983), 614-655.
R. C. Dales, "Robert Grosseteste's Place in Medieval Discussions of the Eternity of the World," Speculum, 61 (1986), 544-563.
R. Dales, The Scientific Achievement of the Middle Ages.
M. Clagett, Archimedes in the Middle Ages.
D. Pearsall and E. Salter, Landscapes and Seasons of the Medieval World.
C. Wilson, William Heytesbury: Medieval Logic and the Rise of Mathematical Physics.
V. L. Bullough and B. Bullough, The Care of the Sick: The Emergence of Modern Nursing.
B. Gille, "Les developpements technologiques en Europe de 1100 à 1400," Cahiers d'histoire mondiale, 3 (1956), 63-108.
A. Maier, Die Vorläufer Galileis im 14. Jahrhundert: Studien zur Naturphilosophie der Spätscholastik. 2nd ed. (1966) B734 .M3 1966
A. Maier, Die Vorläufer Galileis im 14. Jahrhundert: Studien zur Naturphilosophie der Spätscholastik. B734 .M3 1966
A. Maier, Zwei Grundproblem der scholastischen Naturphilosophie: Das Problem der intensiven Grosse; die Impetustheorie.
W. Ganzenmüller, Die Alchemie im Mittelalter.
A Source Book in Medieval Science, ed. E. Grant.

MEDIEVAL HIGHER EDUCATION.

H. Rashdall, The Universities of Europe in the Middle Ages. (3 vols.)
A. L. Gabriel, Garlandia: Studies in the History of the Medieval University.
C. H. Haskins, The Rise of Universities.
A. B. Cobban, The Medieval Universities: Their Development and Organization.
J. W. Thompson, The Literacy of the Laity in the Middle Ages.
N. Orme, English Schools in the Middle Ages.
B. Smalley, The Becket Conflict and the Schools: A Study in Intellectuals in Politics.
G. Leff, Paris and Oxford Universities in the Thirteenth and Fourteenth Centuries.
G. R. Evans, Old Arts and New Theology: The Beginnings of Theology as an Academic Discipline.
V. L. Bullough, The Development of Medicine as a Profession: The Contribution of the Medieval University to Modern Medicine.

R. W. Hunt, The Schools and the Cloister: The Life and Writings of Alexander Nequam, 1157-1217.
    Revised by Margaret Gibson. (1984). BX4705 .N395 H86 1984
J. C. Russell, "The Early Schools of Oxford and Cambridge," The Historian, 5 (1943), 61-76.
G. L. Haskins, "The University of Oxford and the 'Jus ubique docendi'," English Historical Review, 56
    (1961), 281-292.
B. Bischoff, "The Study of Foreign Languages in the Middle Ages," Speculum, 36 (1961), 209-224.
J. T. Muckle, "Greek Works Translated Directly Into Latin Before 1350," Mediaeval Studies, 4 (1942),
    33-42; 5 (1943), 102-114.
J. A. Weisheipl, "Curriculum of the Faculty of Arts at Oxford in the Early Fourteenth Century," ibid.,
    26 (1964), 143-185.
L. Thorndyke, "Elementary and Secondary Education in the Middle Ages," Speculum, 15 (1940), 400-
    408.
P. R. McKeon, "The Status of the University of Paris as Parens Scientiarum: An Episode in the Devel-
    opment of Its Autonomy," ibid., 39 (1964), 651-675.
L. DeMaitre, "Theory and Practice in Medical Education at the University of Montpellier in the Thir-
    teenth and Fourteenth Centuries," Journal of the History of Medicine and Allied Sciences, 30
    (Apr. 1975), 103-123.
H. Stehkämper, "Über die geschichtliche Größe Alberts des Großen: Ein Versuch," Historisches
    Jahrbuch, 102 (no. 1, 1982), 72-93.
P. Classen, "Die hohen Schulen und die Gesellschaft im 12. Jahrhundert," Archiv für Kulturgeschichte,
    48 (1966), 155-180.
P. Classen, "Zur Geschichte der 'Akademischen Freiheit', vornehmlich im Mittelalter," Hist. Zeit., 232
    (1981), 529-553.
P. Delhaye, "L'Organisation scholaire aux XIIe siècle." Traditio, 5 (1947), 211-268.
Les Universités du Languedoc au XIIIe siècle.
J. Koch, Artes Liberales von der antiken Bildung zur Wissenschaft des Mittelalters.
University Records and Life in the Middle Ages, ed. L. Thorndyke.
Statuta collegii sapientiae, ed. J. Kerer.

NEW TRENDS IN POLITICS.

A. Brackmann, "The Beginnings of the National State in Mediaeval Germany and the Norman Monar-
    chies," Mediaeval Germany, ed. G. Barraclough, II, 281-299.
J. R. Strayer, On the Medieval Origins of the Modern State.
G. Post, Studies in Medieval Legal Thought: Public Law and the State, 1100-1322.
W. Ullmann, The Individual and Society in the Middle Ages.
J. R. Strayer, The Reign of Philip the Fair.
J. B. Henneman, Royal Taxation in Fourteenth-Century France: The Captivity and Ranson of John II,
    1356-1370.
E. L. Cox, The Eagles of Savoy: The House of Savoy in Thirteenth-Century Europe.
Universities in Politics: Case Studies From the Late Middle Ages and Early Modern Period, ed. J. W.
    Baldwin and R. A. Goldthwaite.
W. E. Brynteson, "Roman Law and Legislation in the Middle Ages," Speculum, 41 (1966), 420-437.

E. Lewis, "King Above Law? 'Quod principi placuit' in Bracton," ibid., 39 (1964), 240-269.
W. Ullmann, "The Development of the Mediaeval Idea of Sovereignty," English Historical Review, 64
    (1949), 1-33.
E. Kantorowicz, "Mysteries of State: An Absolutist Concept and Its Late Medieval Origins," Harvard
    Theological Review, 48 (1955), 65-91.
E. A. R. Brown, "The Ceremonial of Royal Succession in Capetian France: The Funeral of Philip V,"
    Speculum, 55 (1980), 266-293.
B.-A. Procquet de Haut-Jussé, "Une idée politique de Louis IX: La sujéction éclipse la vassalité," Rev.
    hist., 226 (1961), 383-398.
H. Angermeier, Königtum und Landfriede im deutschen Spätmittelalter.
H. Aubin, Die Entstehung der Landeshoheit nach niederrheinischen Quellen.

THE LATER MIDDLE AGES: 'WANING' AND LEGACY.

J. Huizinga, The Waning of the Middle Ages.
The Waning Middle Ages: An Exhibition of French and Netherlandish Art From 1350 to 1500 Com-
    memorating the Fiftieth Anniversary of the Publication of The Waning of the Middle Ages by
    Johan Huizinga.   Catalog by J. L. Schrader.
D. Hay, Europe in the Fourteenth and Fifteenth Centuries.
B. Z. Kadar, Merchants in Crisis: Genoese and Venetian Men of Affairs and the Fourteenth-Century
    Depression.
M. Seidlmayer, Currents of Mediaeval Thought With Special Reference to Germany.
E. B. Bax, German Society at the Close of the Middle Ages.
M. Mollat, The Popular Revolutions of the Late Middle Ages.
F. Oakley, The Western Church in the Later Middle Ages.
S. Ozment, The Age of Reform, 1250-1550: An Intellectual and Religious History of Late Medieval
    and Reformation Europe.
R. S. Gottfried, Epidemic Disease in Fifteenth-Century Europe: The Medical Response and the
    Demographic Consequences.
M. W. Dols, The Black Death in the Middle East.
R. S. Gottfried, The Black Death: Natural and Human Disaster in Medieval Europe.
D. Williman, (ed.) The Black Death: The Impact of the Fourteenth-Century Plague.   RC171 .S8 1977
R. Kieckhefer, European Witch Trials: Their Foundatin in Popular and Learned Culture, 1300-1500.
K. Cohen, Metamorphosis of a Death Symbol: The Transi Tomb in the Late Middle Ages and the
    Renaissance.
B. Tuchman, A Distant Mirror: The Calamitous Fourteenth Century.   [This may be the most wide-
    ly read book ever written on the fourteenth century but, for the reservations of a medievalist,
    see the review by C. T. Wood, Speculum, 54 (1979), 430-435.]
N. J. G. Pounds, "Overpopulation in France and the Low Countries in the Later Middle Ages," Journal
    of Social History, 3 (1970), 225-247.
A. R. Lewis, "The Closing of the Medieval Frontier, 1250-1350," Speculum, 33 (1958), 475-483.
H. S. Lucas, "The Great European Famine of 1315, 1316 and 1317," ibid., 5 (1930), 343-377.
A. R. Bridbury, "Before the Black Death," Economic History Review, 30 (1977), 393-410.

W. J. Courtenay, "The Effect of the Black Death on English Higher Education," Speculum, 55 (1980), 696-714.

R. Gyug, "The Effects and Extent of the Black Death of 1348: New Evidence for Clerical Mortality in Barcelona," Mediaeval Studies, 45 (1983), 385-98.

N. J. Mayhew, "Numismatic Evidence and Falling Prices in the Fourteenth Century," Economic History Review, 27 (1974), 1-15.

P. P. A. Biller, "Birth-Control in the West in the Thirteenth and Early Fourteenth Centuries," Past & Present, 94 (Feb. 1982), 3-26.

E. Pilz, "Die Wirtschaftskrise des Spätmittelalters," Vierteljahrschrift für Sozial- und Wirtschaftsgeschichte, 52 (1965), 347-367.

J. van Klaveren, "Die wirtschaftliche Auswirkung des Schwarzen Todes," ibid., 54 (1967), 187-202.

A. Borst, "Das Erdbeben von 1348: Ein historischer Beitrag zur Katastrophenforschung,", Historische Zeitschrift, 233 (1981), 529-569.

N. Bulst, "Der Schwarze Tod. Demographische, wirtschafts- und kulturgeschichtliche Aspekte der Pestkatastrophe von 1347-1352: Bilanz der neueren Forschung," Saeculum, 30 (no. 1, 1979), 45-67.

H. Rosenfeld, "Der Totentanz als europäischen Phänomen," Archiv für Kulturgeschichte, 48 (1966), 54-83.

La danse macabre de 1485, pref. de P. Vaillant.

Villages désertés et histoire économique, XIe - XVIIIe siècle.

History 238   EUROPE IN THE HIGH MIDDLE AGES

Spring 1988
Charles R. Young
Duke University

** to be purchased for this course
* on reserve, but available also in paperback

I. Feudal Monarchy

*R. Fawtier, The Capetian Kings of France, chs. 1 and 2
Joinville, The Life of St. Louis, Dedication, chs. 1-9, 18-20
   or Joinville in Memoirs of the Crusades pp. 135-223, 304-332
P. Munz, Frederick Barbarossa, 3-43, 315-360
**B. Tierney, The Crisis of Church and State, 91-115
*W. L. Warren, Henry II, 317-361, 399, 447-517
W. L. Warren, The Governance of Norman and Angevin England 1086-1272, 1-63
Leopold Genicot, "Recent Research on the Medieval Nobility," in The Medieval
   Nobility, ed. T. Reuter, 17-29
**Georges Duby, The Chivalrous Society, 81-87, 94-122, 158-177
Maurice Keen, Chivalry, 1-63, 252-253
Benjamin Arnold, German Knighthood, 1-52, 209-224, 248-254

II. Economic Revival (11th and 12th centuries)

Robert Lopez, The Commercial Revolution of the Middle Ages, 85-167
Leonard Cantor, ed., The English Medieval Landscape, 25-53
E. Ennen, The Medieval Town, 1-16, 63-93

III. Cultural Revival (11th and 12th centuries)

**C.Young, The Twelfth Century Renaissance
Michael Willis, ed., The World of John of Salisbury, 1-20
C. Morris, The Discovery of the Individual, 1-19, 48-95, 158-167
**The Letters of Abelard and Heloise (Radice translation)
H. Rashdall, The Universities, I, 271-343
A. B. Cobham, The Medieval Universities, 3-64, 196-217
M. T. Clanchy, From Memory to written record, 1-28, 149-201, 258-265

IV. The Medieval Church at Its Height

J. Powell, Innocent III
**B.Tierney, The Crisis of Church and State, 110-210
Benedicta Ward, Miracles and the Medieval Mind, 1-32, 89-126, 214-218
**The Register of Eudes of Rouen, xv-40
D. Knowles, The Monastic Order in England, 448-471, 679-693
J. Moorman, A History of the Franciscan Order, 3-45, 188-204, 278-294
H. C. Lea, The Inquisition of the Middle Ages, abridged 152-230
W. Wakefield, Heresy, Crusade and Inquisition in Southern France 1100-1251,
   17-80, 237-257
**E. LeRoy Ladurie, Montaillou

V. Medieval Synthesis of Thought and Learning

**D. Knowles, The Evolution of Medieval Thought, 221-288
Columbia Univ., Intro. to Contemporary Civilization in the West
    Vol. I (3rd ed.) 201-255 (Aquinas). (On reserve for History 21-22
T. Van Cleve, The Emperor Frederick II, 283-318, 531-540
Abbot Suger on the Abbey Church of St. Denis
*O. Von Simson, The Gothic Cathedral, 3-39, 50-58, 227-231
*E. Panofsky, Gothic Architecture and Scholasticism, all 88p
P. Frankl, Gothic Architecture, 1-14, 217-242

VI. Representative Institutions

B. Lyon, A Constitutional and Legal History of England, 408-430, 535-561
A. Marongiu, Medieval Parliaments, 9-76, 95-127

VII. End of Middle Ages

*The Fontana Economic History of Europe, I, 25-68
J. Hatcher, Plague, Population, and the English Economy, 1-73
B. Hanawalt, "The Female Felon in Fourteenth Century England," in Women
    in Medieval Society, ed. S. Stuard, 125-138
Barbara Hanawalt, The Ties that Bound, vii-viii, 3-44, 286
**D. Knowles, The Evolution of Medieval Thought, 291-340
*A. Kors and E. Peters, Witchcraft in Europe, 105-189
G. Leff, The Dissolution of the Medieval Outlook, 1-31, 90-102, 118-147

THE BYZANTINE EMPIRE
John Meyendorff
Fordham University

Requirements:
    1. regular participation in class discussions.
    2. two short papers (maximum 5 pages) on topics related to both
class work and readings.
    3. a longer paper on a topic agreed on with the instructor.
    4. a final exam covering the work of the semester.

1. The Empire. The New Capital. The Roman State and the
    Christian Religion.

2. The Christian Church: doctrinal disputes and schisms. Byzantine
    Orthodoxy.
            Reading completed of: Ostrogorsky, 27-68 or
            Vasiliev 1, 43-128; Brand, 5-7.

3. Emperor Justinian and the Reconquest.
            Ostrogorsky, 68-86, or Vasiliev, 129-192.
            Barker, Justinian and the Later Empire

4. Emperor Heraclius and the Persians.
            Ostrogorsky, 92-109; Vasiliev, 193-233.
            Barker, Justinian

5. The Rise of Islam.
            Ostrogorsky, 110-146; Vasiliev, same as above.
            Brand, 135-180.

6. Iconoclasm in Byzantium: a crisis of civilization.
            Ostrogorsky, 147-209; Vasiliev, 234-299.

7. Charlemagne and Byzantium. The cultural and political
    separation between East and West.

8. The Conversion of the Slavs. Patriarch Plotius.
            Ostrogrosky, 210-269; Vasiliev, 301-351.

9. The Macedonian Dynasty: economic reforms and military
    conquests.
            Ostrogorsky, 270-320; Vasiliev, same as above.

10. The Schism between Rome and Byzantium. Crusades begin.
            Ostrogorsky, 320-375; Vasiliev, 351-412.

11. The Commenian Dynasty. The Fourth Crusade.
            Ostrogrosky, 374-417; Vasiliev, 412-505.

12. The Palaeologan Dynasty. Union negociations.
    Ostrogorsky, 418-533; Vasiliev, 506-629.

13. The Council of Florence. The Fall.
    Ostrogorsky, 533-572; Vasiliev, 629-722.

14. Byzantine Civilization. Art, architecture, literature.

REQUIRED READING:

Brand, Ch., Icon and Minaret: Sources of Byzantine and Islamic Civilization
Ostrogorsky, G., History of the Byzantine State, rev. ed., 1969.
Barker, J. W., Justinian and the Later Roman Empire,
Vasiliev, A. A., History of the Byzantine Empire, Vols. I & II.

RECOMMENDED READING:
Jones, A. H. M., The Later Roman Empire, 284-602: A Social, Economic and Administrative Survey, 1964.
Meyendorff, J., Byzantine Theology, 1979.
The Cambridge Medieval History, vol. IV. "The Byzantine Empire" Part 1 & 2. ed. Hussey, 1967.
Nicol, D. M., The Last Centuries of Byzantium, 1972.
Dvornik, F., The Photian Schism: History and Legend, 1948.
Runciman, S., The Eastern Schism: A Study of the Papacy and the Eastern Churches during the XI and XII Centuries, 1955.
Gill, J., The Council of Florence, 1959.
Meyendorff, J., St. Gregory Palamas and Orthodox Spirituality, 1975.

TRANSLATED SOURCES:
Barker, E., Social and Political Thought in Byzantium from Justinian I to the Last Palaeologus, 1957.
Psellus, M., Fourteen Byzantine Rulers: tr. Sewter, 1966.
Procopius, The Secret History
Comena, Anna, The Alexiad, tr. Sewter, 1969.
Porplyrogenitus, Constantine, De Administrando Imperio, tr. Moravczik and Jenkins.

James Alexander
University of Georgia

HISTORY 445F/645F

NORMAN AND EARLY ANGEVIN ENGLAND, 1066-1307

J. W. Alexander
   Office, 542-2053
   Home,   549-3504

required texts for this course are:

Lyon, Constitutional and Legal History of Medieval England
Stephenson, Marcham, Sources of English Constitutional History I

The Normans and England
Lyon, 3-121, 127-138, 200-217

David Douglas, et. al., English Historical Documents, vol. 2
(1042-1189), pp. 107-203, 204-14, 279-89. Undergraduates are
to read enough of the Anglo-Saxon Chronicle to get the flavour
of it; graduate students are to read it in its entirety. This
book is hereafter cited EHD.
Carl Stephenson and Frederic Marcham, Sources of English
   Constitutional History, pp. 33-46, 58-69, 61. This book
   is hereafter cited S-M.

. Henry I and Stephen of Blois, 1100-1154
Lyon, 121-127, 138-200
S-M, 46-58, 59-70

R. W. Southern, "The Place of Henry I in English History," in
   Southern, Medieval Humanism and Other Studies (graduate
   students may wish to own this), or in Proceedings of the
   British Academy, 48 (1962), 127-70.
EHD, 290-313.

I. Crown and Pallium, 1066-1189
Lyon, 200-217, 300-305

EHD, 673-678, 702-776
David Knowles, "Archbishop Thomas Becket," Proceedings of the
   British Academy, 35 (1949), 1-31 (undergraduate only)
David Knowles, The Episcopal Colleagues of Thomas Becket (entire)

. "Perhaps the Greatest English King:" Henry II, 1154-1189
Lyon, 217-234, 279-300

S-M, 71-96
EHD, 322-392
Charles Young, Hubert Walter

'I. Lionheart and Softsword, 1189–1216
    Lyon, 234–279, 305–329
    Sidney Painter, William Marshal

    Harry Rothwell, English Historical Documents, III (hereafter
        EHD), 51–63, 307–332.
    S-M, 96–126

    Asinus coronatus: Henry III, 1216–1272
    Lyon, 329–345, 351–408

    EHD, 63–153, 197–209, 332–350, 351–354, 355–357, 359–60,
        361–367, 370–392, 751–55, 806–23, 899–918.
    S-M, 127–153

    Bertie Wilkinson, Constitutional History of Medieval England,
        1. 110–116, 126–130, 163–186; vol. 3, 170–185, 222–232,
            251–263, 297–305.

    "The English Justinian": Edward I, 1272–1307
    Lyon, 345–350, 408–475
    Haskins, The Growth of English Representative Government (entire)

    EHD, 209–265, 396–410, 414–427, 428–66, 482–87, 496–502
    S-M, 153–189

    Wilkinson, Const. Hist. 1. 211–232; 3. 305–321, 390–98.
    C. H. Lawrence, The English Church and the Papacy, 117–161.

              ADDITIONAL READING FOR HISTORY 645F

    R. W. Southern, "Ranulf Flambard," in his Medieval Humanism or
        in Transactions of the Royal Historical Society, ser. 4, v.
        16 (1933, 95–128.)
    David Douglas, William the Conqueror
    EHD, 232–278; 851–905, 916–919

    H. G. Richardson and G. O. Sayles, The Governance of Medieval
        England 22–135

    R. H. C. Davis, King Stephen (entire)

    EHD, 400–407, 422–428, 434–437, 459–62, 572–75, 928–932

EHD, 609-649

David Knowles, Thomas Becket (entire)

J. W. Alexander, "The Becket Dispute," Journal of British Studies,
    May, 1970, 1-26
Richardson and Sayles, Governance, 285-320

EHD, 407-421, 437-8, 462-82, 906-916, 937-944
Jacques Boussard, Le Gouvernement d'Henri II Plantagenet, 81-158

VI. Charles Duggan, "From the Conquest to the Reign of John," in
        The English Church and the Papacy, ed. C. H. Lawrence, 63-116.
     F. M. Powicke, The Loss of Normandy, 79-169, 280-309
     Sidney Painter, "Norwich's Three Geoffreys" Speculum, 28 (1953),
        808-813

     R. F. Treharne, "The Knights in the Period of Reform and Rebellion,"
        Bulletin of the Institute of Historical Research 21 (1946-8),
        1-12

NORMAN AND EARLY ANGEVIN ENGLAND,
1066-1307

Graduate students should familiarize themselves with the following
documentary and narrative collections, which are the basic source materials
for English medieval history. Undergraduate students should at least be
aware of their existence.

I) Sources

The indispensable set of chronicles is Great Britain, Rerum Brittanicarum
Medii Aevi Scriptores. Commonly known as the Rolls Series, the works
herein vary widely in standards of editing. A detailed list of the contents
of these 99 is in Mullins, Texts and Calendars (below). Nelson's (now
Oxford) Medieval Texts is a relatively new series, still publishing;
it consists of critical Latin texts with facing English translations.
As with the Rolls Series, editors vary, but the series holds to a uniformly
high standard. It includes Glanvill, the histories of Ordericus Vitalis,
the best edition of the Dialogue on the Exchequer, John of Salisbury's
Letters, and other works.

For Church history, valuable material is in both series cited above,
and in the publications of local record societies (again, refer to Mullins
for these). As well, there is William Dugdale's Monasticon Anglicanum,
8 volumes of charter and other evidence relating to the monastic order in
England. Wilkins' Concilia is being superseded by a projected collection
of conciliar and other ecclesiastical documents of the medieval English
Church, of which the first part (actually, vol. II) has appeared: F. M.
Powicke and C. R. Cheney, Councils and Synods, 1205-1313. Papal acta
concerning England can be found in Migne, Patrologia latina, supplemented
by Walther Holtzmann, Papsturkunden in England, and by C. R. and Mary G.
Cheney, the Letters of Pope Innocent III Concerning England and Wales.
Relevant material is also in the superbly-edited series, Corpus christianorum,
series latina (e. g., the works of the Venerable Bede).

The public records are principally found in two great series. The old
Record Commission published records invaluable for the reigns of John
and early Henry III, including the Charter Rolls for John, the letters
patent and close, miscellaneous exchequer documents, Norman Rolls, etc.
Also in this series are Domesday Book (which is translated, county by
county, in the first volume of the Victoria County History of England),
the Hundred Rolls, Placita de quo warranto, the Valor ecclesiasticus,
Statutes of the Realm, etc. The Texts and Calendars of the Public Record
Office picked up the Record Commission's work in the later nineteenth
century, and in some instances (e. g., the Book of Fees) superseded it.
The PRO publications include texts and calendars of exchequer and chancery
enrollments (letters close, patent; charter rolls; ancient correspondence;
diplomatic documents; liberate and fine rolls, etc.), calendars of foreign
archives as they relate to England (from the papacy, Venice, etc.), feudal
inquisitions (the Books of Fees; Feudal Aids), and many miscellaneous
materials (such as the Register of the Black Prince, the Inquisitions post
mortem, etc.). They are listed in Mullins.

The publications of the Selden Society are indispensable for the study
of medieval English law and social history. They include commentaries
(Bracton, Azo, "Fleta," etc.), year books (but those for Edward I, which
are in the Rolls Series), selected cases from the central courts and
from those of justices in eyre, cases and commentaries in forest law and
feudal courts, borough charters, and several important studies (such as
van Caenegem's Royal Writs in England from the Conquest to Glanvill).
All are well-edited, some superbly so, by such scholars as G. O. Sayles,
Plucknett, Lady Stenton, Maitland, and Thorne.

The royal charters and writs of the Norman period are calendared, and
in some cases printed in full, in Regesta regum anglo-normannorum, ed.
H. W. C. Davis (I: 1066-1100), Charles Johnson and H. A. Cronne (II:
1100-1135), and H. A. Cronne and R. H. C. Davis (III and IV: 1135-1154).
Only the charters of Henry II which pertain to continental affairs have
been collected for this reign: Léopold Delisle, Receuil des actes d'Henri
II (4 vols.). Eyton published an inadequate Itinerary of King Henry II,
which calendars some charters. Lionel Landon's Itinerary of Richard I
(Pipe Roll Society) is a model of its type, and calendars or prints most
of Lionheart's charters. The itinerary of King John is not a calendar:
it is printed at the beginning of Sir Thomas Duffus Hardy's edition of the
Patent Rolls of John. There is neither calendar nor itinerary for Henry
III, but H. Gough's Itinerary of Edward I is once again in print; it is
not very good, as may be seen by comparing it with J. B. Trabut-Cussac's
itinerary of Edward in France, 1286-1289 (Bulletin of the Institute of
Historical Research, XXV [1952], 160-203). The lack of calendars for the
charters and writs of the Angevin kings is somewhat compensated for by the
generally excellent indices in the Record Commission and PRO Texts and
Calendars.

The Record Commission published the first extant Pipe Rolls (for 31 Henry I
and 2, 3, and 4 Henry II) and that for 1 Richard I. The others are still
in process of publication by the Pipe Roll Society, commencing with that of
5 Henry II and at present writing extending to 3 Henry III; the pipe and
chancellor's rolls of 14 Henry III are also in the PRS publications, as
are some miscellaneous materials (rolls of the king's court for Henry II
and Richard I, the Rotuli de dominabus of 1185, Feet of Fines for Henry II
and Richard I, the Worcester Cartulary, Interdict Documents, etc.) There
are also pipe roll extracts relating to various counties in the publications
of local record societies (see Mullins).

Many well-edited texts and records are available in the local record and
historical societies of Great Britain. For a comprehensive guide to the
local as well as the national historical society publications, consult
E. L. C. Mullins, Texts and Calendars.

Several continental collections are essential for English medieval history:

> Dom M. Bouquet, et al., Receuil des historiens des Gaules et de la
>   France (24 vols.)
> Publications of the Société de l'histoire de France
> A. Teulet, Layettes de trésor des chartes
> The registers of the French kings often have material pertinent to
>   English medieval history; for a partial guide, v. Robert
>   Fawtier, The Capetian Kings of France, c. i., to whose
>   apparatus add the second through fourth volumes of the Recueil
>   des actes de Phillippe-Auguste

French provincial and municipal historical societies have published
many works indispensable for medieval English history; unfortunately,
no guide comparable to that of Mullins for England exists. The most
important collections for this course are the publications of the
Société des antiquaires de Normandie. For the period beginning in
1154, the publications of societies lying within lands formerly
possessed by the Angevin kings -- Anjou, Brittany, Gascony, etc. --
are relevant as well.

The great German set, the Monumenta Germaniae historica, contains a
great deal of material pertinent to English history in the middle
ages.

II. Research Aids

A. Bibliographies

> Edgar B. Graves, A Bibliography of English History to 1485.
> The volumes of the Oxford History of England for the medieval
> period contain valuable bibliographical essays, and list
> bibliographical guides as well.
>
> > F. M. Stenton, Anglo-Saxon England
> > A. L. Poole, From Domesday Book to Magna Carta
> > F. M. Powicke, The Thirteenth Century
> > May McKisack, The Fourteenth Century
> > E. F. Jacob, The Fifteenth Century

The Conference on British Studies has commenced a bibliographical
series: M. Altschul, Anglo-Norman England, 1066-1154, and Bertie
Wilkinson, The High Middle Ages in England, 1154-1307. See also
English Historical Documents, general ed. David Douglas, vols. 1-3.

For the publications of all national, government, ecclesiastical and
local record and historical societies, a virtually-complete guide is
E. L. C. Mullins, Texts and Calendars.

Since any bibliographical guide is out of date before it sees print, the student should supplement the material in the guides above by book reviews and publication lists in The English Historical Review, the Bulletin of the Institute of Historical Research, the American Historical Review, Speculum, Revue historique, Historische Zeitschrift, the Revue d'histoire ecclésiastique, etc.

Although both incomplete and outdated, Farrar and Evans, English Translations from Medieval Sources is satisfactory for works published before 1945; supplemented by Mary Anne Ferguson, Bibliography of English Translations from Medieval Sources, 1948-1968. The most important translating work now being done in serial publications is in Medieval Texts and in the Columbia University Records of Civilization. Important documents illustrating the development of English constitutional history after 1216 may be found in Bertie Wilkinson, Constitutional History of Medieval England (3 vols.); unlike those in Stubbs' Select Charters, they are printed in translation. Most of the Selden Society volumes also contain translations of the texts which they contain.

B. Handbooks, Manuals, Dictionaries.

V. H. Galbraith, Introduction to the Use of the Public Records

The Royal Historical Society published invaluable research tools; they include:

> Mullins, Texts and Calendars
> F. M. Powicke and E. N. Fryde, Handbook of British Chronology, which includes the regnal years of kings, terms of office of British officers of state, archiepiscopal and episcopal pontifical terms of office, years of incumbancy of the higher nobility, and a great deal of miscellaneous information.
> C. R. Cheney, Handbook of Dates, which is essential for dating documents. The series, "Helps for Students of History"

Charles Trice Martin, The Record Interpreter. Primarily for the research scholar, this little vade mecum is a dictionary of abbreviations (Latin and French), coupled with a glossary of Latin place-names for the British Isles. For the latter, see also Chevin, Dictionnaire des noms latins de lieux and the third (index) volume of the Book of Fees. For help in placing sites in the proper county, see E. Ekwall, Concise Dictionary of English Place-Names. The student in this course will have little need to have a knowledge of paleography or of diplomatics; anyone wishing a bibliography of this field may have the syllabus for my seminar in these disciplines on request.

I. Sanders, English Baronies, is a handbook of origins and descents.
G. E. C. [okayne], Complete Peerage, lists biographical and feudal
information under the names of lordships. The Dictionary of National
Biography gives concise sketches of important medieval English
figures. See also Joseph Strayer (ed.), Dictionary of the Middle Ages.

The Revised Medieval Latin Word-List (ed. Latham) is, despite some
flaws, the best medieval Latin dictionary for English sources. It
should be supplemented with the best one-volume Latin dictionary, which
is that of Lewis and Short (Oxford).

HISTORY 445G/645G:

England in the Later Middle Ages, 1307-1485

312 LeConte Hall
Home phone: 549-3504

James Alexander
University of Georgia

These are the textbooks required for this course; all are in paperback:

Bertie Wilkinson, The Later Middle Ages in England
W.A. Pantin, The English Church in the XIV Century
Jack Lander, Conflict and Stability in Fifteenth-century England
H.S. Bennett, The Pastons and their England
Boris Ford, Medieval Literature

Following is a week-by-week reading list. The additional readings
headed 645G for each week pertain to the graduate students only.

I.   Edward II, 1307-27

   Wilkinson, Later MA, 1-132
   Carl Stephenson and Frederic Marcham, Sources of English
      Constitutional History, 190-205
   Bertie Wilkinson, Constitutional History of Medieval England,
      2.112-76

   645: Margaret Hastings, 'High History or Hack History: England in
      the Later Middle Ages,' Speculum 36 (April, 1961), 225-253

II. Edward III, 1327-77

   Wilkinson, 132-157
   Stephenson/Marcham, 205-232
   Wilkinson. Const. Hist. 2.176-227

   645: Alec Myers, English Historical Documents, IV: 1327-1485,
      35-122, 403, 420-23, 439-49; 482-3, 497-502, 512-15, 533-43.
      W.A. Morris, et al., The English Government at Work, 1327-1337,
      1.394-467, 3.105-41, 467

III. Richard II, 1377-99

   Wilkinson, 157-184
   Stephenson/Marcham, 232-49
   Gervase Mathew, The Court of Richard II
   Wilkinson, Const. Hist. 2.227-329, 3.322-76

   645: Myers, 122-178, 403-14, 449-53, 483-85, 502-3; R.H. Hilton,
      Bond Men Made Free.

IV. England in the Fourteenth Century

   Pantin, English Church in the XIV Century
   Geoffrey Chaucer, Canterbury Tales,

Sir Gawain and the Green Knight (entire)
Langland, Vision of Piers the Ploughman, Prologue and all of part one
Ford, Medieval Literature

645: Myers, 653-65, 785-6, 811-28, 837-50, 878-887, 984-1005,
    1115-17, 1137-43, 1179-94

V. The Regins of Henry IV and Henry V. 1399-1422

Wilkinson, 234-257
Stephenson/Marcham, 249-65, 273-76

645: Myers, 178-213, 414-15, 453-63, 485-87, 543-47
    Bertie Wilkinson, Constitutional History of Enland in the
    Fifteenth Century, Chapter 1

VI. Henry VI, 1422-61

Wilkinson, 237-286
Bennett, The Pastons and Their England
Stephenson/Marcham, 265-71, 276-77

645: Myers, 231-88, 423-36, 463-73, 487-89, 503-7, 515-25, 547-57;
    Wilkinson, Fifteenth Century, chapter 2.

VII. The Yorkist Kings, 1461-85

Wilkinson, 286-305
Lander, Conflict and Stability
Stephenson-Marcham, 272-73, 277-78

Paul Murray Kendall, Richard III, 465-514
Thomas More, History of Richard III
Wilkinson, Fifteenth Century, Chapter 3

645: Myers, 288-351, 514-20, 436-39, 473-82, 489-97, 507-12,
    525-33, 557-60
W.H. Dunham and C.T. Wood, "The Right to Rule England," AHR 81[4]
    (Oct. 1976), pp. 738-761

VIII.England in the Fifteenth Century

Wilkinson, 184-234
W.S. Furnivall, The Babees' Book, pp. 1-9, 31-47, 122-141, 174-5

645: Myers, 655-98, 730-31, 733-35, 828, 837, 850-78, 887-907,
    1005-17, 1117-37, 1143-53, 1194-1208

IX. English Society in the Fifteenth Century

Wilkinson, 305-397
Stephenson/Marcham, 279-96
K.B. MacFarlane, 'Bastard Feudalism,' Bulletin of the Institute of
Historical Research, 20 (1943-45)
F.R.H. duBoulay, An Age of Ambition

History 445G/645G

ENGLAND IN THE LATER MIDDLE AGES, 1307-1485

1) Bibliographical Tools

There is little point in here listing the essential works in this
field; the standard bibliographies for late medieval England are full
guides to both primary and secondary materials. They are included in:

D.J. Guth, Late Medieval England, 1377-1485.
Edgar B. Graves, A Bibliography of English History to 1485.
Margaret Hastings, "High History or Hack History," Speculum, 1961,
    225-53.
E.F. Jacob, The Fifteenth Century.
May McKisack, The Fourteenth Century.
Alec Myers, English Historical Documents, IV.
R.C. Van Caenegem, Guide to the Sources of Medieval History.
Bertie Wilkinson, Constitutional History of Medieval England (3 vols)
_____, Constitutional History of England in the Fifteenth
    Century.

There are both gains and losses in printed sources when later
medieval England is compared with the Norman and early Angevin periods.
We have no pipe rolls in print, the Patrologia latina ends in the early
thirteenth century, and none of the royal acts are calendared as in the
Regesta regum Anglo-Normannorum. The gains are considerable, however:
there are more, and fuller, public records (for an analytical guide, see
Mullins, Texts and Calendars), such as the charter, patent, close, fine,
and liberate rolls. Inquisitions post mortem are fuller than those of
the reign of Henry III. Legal records are more abundant--the Selden
Society publishes many later medieval legal and judicial records. For
military inquests, see Feudal Aids (6 vols.) and The Book of Fees (3
vols.: both PRO).
French history continues to be influential upon that of England in
this period. The more important collections are:

the publications of the Société de l'histoire de France, and of the
various provincial and local record and historical societies.
Documents inédits sur l'histoire de France.
A. Teulet, Layettes de trésor des chartes.
Bibliotheque de l'Ecole des Chartes.
The great Bouquet Recueil does not extend forward in time into our
period.

2) Research Aids

For a splendid bibliographical index to all publications of the
British government, national, ecclesiastical, and local record and
historical societies, see the splendid work Texts and Calendars, by
E.L.C. Mullins. It is to be supplemented, for works published after
1958, by the bibliographical apparatus of the English Historical Review
and of the Billetin of the Institute for Historical Research. For
government publications, see the (periodically revised) Sectional List

#17 (for publications of theRoyal Commission on Historical Manuscripts)
and Sectional List #24 (British National Archives).

Although both incomplete and outdated, Farrar and Evans, English
Translations from Medieval Sources is satisfactory for works published
before 1945. Mary Anne Ferguson, Bibliography of English Translations
From Medieval Sources, 1944-1968. (For works published since 1968, see
the bibliographical information in Speculum). The most important
translating work now being done in serial publications are in the Oxford
Medieval Texts and in the Columbia University Records of Civilization.

A convenient collection of constitutional documents in the original
languages in Chrimes and Brown, Select Documents Of English
Constitutional Histroy, 1307-1485, a successor in time to Stubbs' Select
Charters, which ends in 1307.

Handbooks, Manuals, Dictionaries.

V.H. Galbraith, Introduction to the Use of Publick Records

Guide to the Contents of the Public Record Office, I.

TheRoyal Historical Society published invaluable research tools; they
include:

> Mullins, Texts and Calendars, I (1958), II (1983).
> F.M. Powicke and E.B. Fryde, Handbook of British Chronology, which
> includes the regnal years of kings, terms of office of British
> officers of state, archiepiscopal and episcopal terms of
> office, years of incumbancy of the higher nobility, and a great
> deal of miscellaneous information.

C.R. Cheney, Handbook of Dates, which is essential for dating
documents. The series, "Helps for Students of History."

M Pacaut, Guide de l'étudiant en histoire médievale

Pierre Chaplais, English Royal Documents, 1199-1461

Charles Trice Martin, The Record Interpreter. Primarily for the
research scholar, this little vade mecum is a dictionary of
abbreviations (Latin and French), coupled with a glossary of Latin place
names for the British Isles. For the latter, see also Chevin,
Dictionnaire des noms latins de lieux and the third (index) volume of
the Book of Fees. For help in placing sites in the proper county, see
E. Ekwall, Concise Dictionary of English Place-Names. The studentin
this course will have littel need to have a deep knowledge of
paleography or of deplomatics; anyone wishing a bibliography of this
field may have the syllabus for my seminar in these disciplines on
request.

I. Sanders, English Baronies, is a handbook of origins and descents.
G.E.C. (okayne)., Complete Peerage, lists biographical and feudal
information under the names of lordships. The Dictionary of National
Biography gives concise sketches of important medieval English figures.

The Rivised Medieval Latin Word-List (ed. Latham) is, despite some
flaws, the best medieval Latin dictionary for ENglish sources. It
should be supplemented with the best one-volume Latin dictionary, which
is that of Lewis and Short (Oxford).

3) Supplementary bibliographical recommendations.

     Following are some important books which have appeared since the
publication of the bibliographical aids listed above, or which I wish
particularly to recommend:

S. Armitage-Smith, John of Gaunt
J. M. W. Bean, The Decline of English Feudalism, 1215-1540
S. B. Chrimes, Fifteenth-Century England
_____, Lancastrians, Yorkists, and Henry VII
_____, Introduction to the Administrative History of Medieval
                England
J. Conway Davies, The Baronial Oppositiont to Edward II
M. T. Clanchy, From Memory to Written Record
F. R. H. du Boulay, An Age of Ambition
                , The Lordship of Canterbury
W. H. Dunham, Lord Hastings' Indentured Retainers
John Ferguson, English Diplomacy, 1422-1461
Kenneth Fowler, The King's Lieutenant: Henry de Grosmont
Kenneth Fowler, The Age of Plantagenet and Valois
E. B. Fryde and Edward Miller, Historical Studies of the English
                              Parliament
N. Fryde, The Tyranny and Fall of Richard II
A. Goodman, The Loyal Conspiracy: The Lords Appellant
_____, The Wars of the Roses
Ralph A. Griffiths, The Reign of King Henry VI
A. Hanham, Richard III and His Early Historians, 1483-1535
G. L. Harriss, King Parliament, and Public Finanace in Medieval England
                to 1369
H. J. Hewitt, The Organization of War under Edward III
R. H. Hilton, Bond Men Made Free
             , The Decline of Serfdom in Medieval England
George Holmes, The Good Parliament
Harold Hutchison, King Henry V: A Biography
E. F. Jacob, Henry V and the Invasion of France
R. H. Jones, The Royal Policy of Richard II
C. L. Kingsford, Prejudice and Promise in XV Century England
J. L. Kirby, Henry IV of England
David Knowles, The Religious Orders in England, 2 and 3
Jack Lander, Conflict and Stability in Fifteenth-Century England
_____, Crown and Nobility, 1450-1509
_____, Government and Community in England, 1450-1509
C. H. Lawrence, The English Church and the Papacy in the Middle Ages
Gervase Matthew, The Court of Richard II
K. B. McFarlane, John Wycliffe and English Nonconformity
_____, Lancastrian Kings and Lollard Knights
_____, The Nobility of Later Medieval ENgland
W. A. Morris et al., The English Government at Work, 1327-1336
Colin Morris, Medieval England
G. R. Owst., Literature and Pulpit in Medieval England

W. A. Pantin, The English Church in the XIV Century
J. R. S. Phillips, Aymer de Valence, Early of Pembroke
T. F. T. Plucknett, A Concise History of the Common Law
Michael Powicke, Military Obligation in Medieval England
Michael Prestwich, The Three Edwards
Joel Rosenthal, The Purchase of Paradise
_____, Nobles and the Noble Life, 1295-1500
C. D. Ross, Edward IV: Richard III.
G. O. Sayles, The King's Parliament of England
R. W. Somerville, History of the Duchy of Lancaster
A. L. Storey, The End of the House of Lancaster
T. F.Tout, The Place of Edward II in English History
R. Tuck, Richard II and the English Nobility
J. Vale, Edward III and Chivalry
M. Vale, War and Chivalry

I. General description

Intensive study of selected topics in medieval English history, including the following: the Norman Conquest and its impact on Anglo-Saxon institutions; the development of English feudalism; Magna Carta; the growth of the English church; development of Parliament; the Anglo-Norman, Plantagenet empires; arts, letters and society in medieval England. Attention will be given to the problems of bibliography and source materials. Students will present oral reports on primary and secondary sources, to be written up in brief critical essays. Final examination.

II. Required Books (for general discussion) (LR=Library Reserve)

1) J.J. Bagley & P.B. Rowley, A Documentary History of England, vol. I
(Pelican)

2) G. Barraclough, ed. Social Life in Early England (London 1960)

3) G.W.S. Barrow, Feudal Britain (London 1965)

4) Bede, A History of the English Church and People (Penguin)

5) P.H. Blair, Introduction to Anglo-Saxon England (Cambridge)

6) Z.N. Brooke, The English Church and the Papacy from the Conquest to the
Reign of John (Cambridge UP, repr 1968)

7) D.C. Douglas, William the Conqueror (California)

8) J.C. Holt, Magna Carta (Cambridge 1965)

9) J.E.A. Jolliffe, Angevin Kingship (London 1955)

10) J.E.A. Jolliffe, Constitutional History of Medieval England (Norton)

11) G. Leff, Paris and Oxford Universities in the thirteenth and fourteenth

centuries (Wiley)

12) A.L. Myers, England in the later middle ages (Pelican)

13) W.A. Pantin, English Church in the fourteenth century (Notre Dame)

III. Outline of the Course and Reading Assignments

Jan. 31   Introduction: the sources of medieval English history:
            assignment of reports

Feb. 7   Anglo-Saxon England: the Celtic and Roman background: Anglo-Saxon
            society and institutions

            Reading: Blair, ch. I, II, IV, V

                      Myres, "Roman Britain" (Barraclough, ed. Social Life),
                          pp 1-28

            Reports: L. Alcock, Arthur's Britain (Penguin)
                      Anglo-Saxon Chronicle
                      F. Barlow, Edward the Confessor (U Calif 1970)
                      W.A. Chaney, Cult of Kingship in Anglo-Saxon England
                                  (U Calif 1969)
                      H.R. Loyn, Alfred the Great (OUP 1967)
                      Tacitus, On Britain and Germany (Penguin)

Feb. 14   Anglo-Saxon church: progress of Christianity: letters and arts

            Reading: Bede, Bks. I-V

                      Blair, ch. III, VI

            Reports: F. Barlow, The English Church 1000-1066: a constitutional
                          history (London 1963) (LR)

                      Beowulf (tr. B. Raffel)

                      P.H. Blair, The World of Bede (1971)

                      R.W. Hanning, The Vision of History in Early Britain
                                  (Columbia UP 1965)

                      K. Hughes, Early Christian Ireland (Cornell 1973)

                      Lives of the Saints (Penguin)

Feb. 21   The Norman Conquest

            Reading: Douglas, Parts I-IV

            Reports: Bayeux Tapestry
                      D.C. Douglas, The Norman Fate 1100-1154 (U Calif Pr 1976)
                      E.A. Freeman, History of the Norman Conquest of England
                                  (Oxford 1871-79)
                      C.H. Haskins, The Normans in European History (Norton)
                      C.W. Hollister, The Military Organization of Norman
                          England (Oxford 1965)
                      S. Körner, The Battle of Hastings, England and Europe
                                  1036-66 (1964) (LR)
                      D. Whitelock et al., The Norman Conquest (Scribners)

Feb. 28   Anglo-Norman government and society

             Reading: Bagley & Rowley, no. 2
                       Barrow, Parts I-II
                       Stenton, "Development of Castle" (Barraclough, ed.
                           Social life); pp 96-123

             Reports: F. Barlow, Feudal Kingdom of England 1042-1216 (1955)
                       R.A. Brown, Origins of English Feudalism (N.Y. 1973)
                       H.C. Darby, Domesday England (Cambridge UP 1977)
                       R.H.C. Davis, King Stephen (U. Calif 1967)
                       Eadmer's History of Recent Events in England (tr.
                           Bosanquet, 1964)
                       R.W.Finn, Introduction to the Domesday Book (1963)(L.R.)
                       J.H. Round, Feudal England (4th ed. 1964)
                       F.M. Stenton, First Century of English Feudalism,
                           1066-1166
                       P. Vinogradoff, English Society in the Eleventh Century
                           (Oxford 1908)

Mar. 6   Anglo-Norman church

             Reading: Brooke, ch. I-XII

             Reports: F. Barlow, A History of the Anglo-Norman Church
                           (London 1979)
                       N.F. Cantor, Church, kingship and lay Investiture in
                           England 1089-1135 (Princeton 1958)
                       Eadmer's Life of St. Anselm (ed. Southern, Nelson's
                           Texts 1963)
                       D. Knowles, The Monastic Constitutions of Lanfranc
                       D. Knowles, The Relgious Orders in England, 3 vols.
                       R. W. Southern, St. Anselm and his Biographer
                           (Cambridge 1963) (LR)

Mar. 13   "From Becket to Langton"

             Reading: Brooke, ch. XIII-XIV

             Reports: C.R. Cheney, From Becket to Langton: English Church
                           Government 1170-1213 (1956)
                       C.R. Cheney, Pope Innocent III and England (Stuttgart
                           1976)
                       C.R. Cheney & W.H. Semple, Selected Letters of Pope
                           Innocent III (Nelson Texts)
                       R. Foreville, L'église et la royauté en Angleterre sous
                           Henri II Plantagnet (LR)
                       John of Salisbury, Letters (ed. C.N.L. Brooke)
                       John of Salisbury, Memoirs of the Papal Court
                           (ed. M. Chibnall)
                       D. Knowles, Thomas Becket (London 1970)
                       Materials for the History of Thomas Becket, Archbishop
                           Of Canterbury (ed. Robertson, Rolls Ser., 6 vols.)
                       F.M. Powicke, Stephen Langton (Oxford 1928)

Mar. 20   Angevin Kingship

        Reading: Bagley & Rowley, no. 3-4
                      Barrow, Parts III-IV
                      Jolliffe, Angevin Kingship, Part I

        Reports: J.T. Appleby, England without Richard 1189-1199
                                  (Cornell 1966)
                      John of Salisbury, Stateman's Book (ed. Dickinson)
                      A. Kelly, Eleanor and the Four Kings
                      F.M. Powicke, The Loss of Normandy 1189-1204 (2d ed rev
                                              1961)
                      W.L. Warren, Henry II (U. Calif 1973)

Mar. 27   King John and Magna Carta

        Reading: Bagley & Rowley, no. 6
                      Holt, pp 1-292

        Reports: W.S. McKechnie, Magna Carta (1905)
                      K. Norgate, John Lackland (London 1902)
                      S. Painter, Reign of King John (Baltimore 1949)
                      S. Painter, William Marshall (Baltimore 1933)
                      F. Thompson, Magna Carta: its role in the making of the
                            English Constitution 1300-1629 (Minneapolis 1948)

Apr. 3   Parliament: English Constitutional History and Law

        Reading: Bagley & Rowley, no. 9-10
                      Jolliffe, Constitutional History, esp ch. III-V

        Reports: Bracton, On the laws and customs of England (ed. Thorne
                                          1968)(LR)
                      Glanvill, Treatise on the laws and customs of England
                                  (Nelson Texts 1966)(LR)
                      F.W.Maitland, Constitutional History of England (repr
                                        1961)
                      F. Pollock & F.W. Maitland, History of English Law,
                                          2 vols.
                      F.M. Powicke, HENRY III and the Lord Edward, 2 vols
                                        (1947)
                      H.G. Richardson & G.O. Sayles, Governance of Medieval
                          England, from the Conquest to Magna Carta (1963)
                      W. Stubbs, Constitutional History of England, 3 vols

Apr. 10   English learning: schools and universities

        Reading: Bagley & Rowley, no. 8
                      Leff

        Reports: Bartholomew Anglicus, Medieval Lore (Tr. Steele)
             John of Salisbury, The Metalogicon (Calif)
             H. Rashdall, Universities of Europe in the Middle Ages
                  (edd. Powicke & Emden, 3 vols., 1936)
             P.B. Roberts, Studies in the Sermons of Stephen Langton
                  (Toronto 1968) (LR)
             Roger Bacon, Opus Maius, 2 vols. (tr. Burke, 1928)
             B. Smalley, English Friars and Antiquity (Oxford 1960) (LR)
             B. Smalley, The Becket Conflict and the Schools: a study of
                  Intellectuals in Politics(1973)

Apr. 15-24   No Classes

May   1   Manor, town, and society

              Reading: Bagley & Rowley, no. 5
                        Barraclough, ed. Social Life - essays by Latham pp 29-50;
                           Thompson, pp 139-78; Stenton, pp 179-207; Coulton
                           pp 208-23

              Reports: H.S.Bennett, Life on the English Manor (Cambridge)
                        J.L. Bolton, The Medieval English Economy 1150-1500 (1980)

                        U.T. Holmes, Daily Living in the Twelfth Century (U Wisc)
                        M.W. Labarge, A Baronial Household in the Thirteenth Century (1965)
                        Margery Kempe, Memoirs of a Medieval Woman
                        J.A. Raftis, Tenure and Mobility: Studies in the Social History
                           of the Medieval English Village (Toronto 1964)
                        S.L. Thrupp, Merchant Class of Medieval London (Ann Arbor)
                        G.A. Williams, Medieval London (1963) (LR)

May   8   Aspects and voices of late medieval England, I

              Reading: Bagley & Rowley, no. 11-12
                        Myers

              Reports: J.M.W. Bean. The Decline in English Feudalism, 1215-1540
                                                                        (1968)

                        Froissart, Chronicles
                        A.R. Myers, ed. English Historical Documents IV:
                           1327-1485 (Oxford 1969)
                        J.R. Lander, Conflict and Stability in Fifteenth Century
                           England (1969)
                        E. Perroy, The Hundred Years War

May 15   Aspects and voices of late medieval England, II

              Reading: Pantin

              Reports: Chaucer, Canterbury Tales
                        Cloud of Unknowing (tr. Wolters, Penguin)
                        J. Coleman, Medieval Readers and Writers 1350-1400
                                                          (Columbia UP, 1981)
                        K.B. Macfarlane, John Wycliffe and the Beginnings of
                           English non-conformity (1952)
                        G.R. Owst, Preaching in medieval England, c. 1350-1450
                                                                        (1926)
                        R. Weiss, Humanism in England during the Fifteenth Century
                           (2d ed. 1957)

May 22   FINAL EXAMINATION

Department of History
State University of New York at Stony Brook
Stony Brook, New York 11794-4348
telephone: (516) 246-6500

StonyBrook

History 303: Medieval Society/ Anglo-Saxon England
Spring 1988
Joel Rosenthal

Books (available in the University bookstore)

> G. N. Garmonsway, ed: The Anglo-Saxon Chronicle
> Peter Hunter Blair: Introduction to Anglo-Saxon England
> S Keynes & M Lapidge, eds: Alfred the Great
> Webb & Farmer, eds: The Age of Bede
> Bede: A History of the English Church & People
>
> Class handouts will furnish maps and a translation of
> "The Battle of Maldon"

Part I: Introduction
> For Part I, read Hunter Blair, V.

Week 1: Introduction and basic chronology

Week 2: The sources and how to use them

Part II: The Invasions and the Early Kingdoms of the Heptarchy
> For Part II, read Hunter Blair, I and III, 1-6; The Anglo-
> Saxon Chronicle (mainly the E text) through 797 A.D.:
> Bede's History, Books I & II; Bede's Life of Cuthbert;
> Eddius Stephanus' Life of Wilfrid.

Week 3: Invasions and early settlments (Chronicle to 675 A.D.)

Week 4: Establishment of the Kingdoms (Chronicle to 797 A.D.)

Week 5: Conversion to Christianity (Bede's History, I & II)

Week 6: Heroes & Holy Men (Bede's Life of Cuthbert)

Week 7: Maturity and Stability (Eddius' Life of Wilfrid)

> First (short, in-class) exam

Part III: The Vikings and Alfred the Great
> For Part III, read Hunter Blair, II, 1-5: III, 7: VI,3-6;
> The Anglo-Saxon Chronicle (E text to 948 A.D., plus A text
> for 938 A.D.); Alfred the Great (Asser's Life, 65-110,
> misc. writings, 123-30, 153-60, 163-78).

Week 8: The Viking Invasions (Anglo-Saxon Chronicle to 871 A.D.)

Week 9: Alfred the Great (Anglo-Saxon Chronicle to 900 A.D., Asser's
           Life of Alfred)

Week 10: Alfred: the writings, will, and laws (as indicated in
           Keynes & Lapidge)

Week 11: After Alfred (The Chronicle to 948 A.D., plus the A text for
           937 A.D.)

         Second (short, in-class) exam

Part IV: The Last Days of Anglo-Saxon England
           For part IV, read Hunter Blair, II, 6-8: III, 8-9: IV;
           The Anglo-Saxon Chronicle, to 1067 A.D.

Week 12: Wessex & the Second Viking Invasions (Chronicle, to 1042 A.D.)

Week 13: Edward the Confessor (Chronicle, to 1065 A.D.)

Week 14: The Norman Conquest (The Chronicle, to 1067 A.D.)

The Third short exam will be held after the semester, during the
University's regular exam week

For the course: 3 short exams and a term paper on some topic chosen from a
           close reading of Bede's History of the English Church & People.
           A further sheet will give more information about the paper.
           In addition, both class time and office-hour time will be
           devoted to a selection of topics, advice on bibliography,
           organization, and prose.

           A topic for the term paper is to be submitted by the
           end of Week 6, and the final paper is due by the end
           of Week 12.

Department of History
State University of New York at Stony Brook
Stony Brook, New York 11794-4348
telephone: (516) 246-6500

StonyBrook

History 303: Medieval Society/ Anglo-Saxon England
Spring 1988
Joel Rosenthal

Term paper: Bede: A History of the English Church & People

The largest piece of work for this course is a full-length (15 pages)
term paper, on some aspect of Bede's History. This History is an
extremely rich source of information about Anglo-Saxon England in the
7th century, with particular emphasis upon the conversion to Christianity
and the beginnings of the Church.

There are a great many term-paper topics in Bede, and to get you started
I suggest such obvious ones as the role of women, the nature and power of
kings and kingship, the role of priests, rivalry between paganism and
Christianity, the importance of books and literacy, miracles and miracle
cures, the reasons for conversion, the role of kings in conversion, the
dependence of England upon Rome, the hostility between Anglo-Saxons and
Celts, the role of saints and heroes and holy men and women, etc.

In addition to Bede's History there are a number of scholarly books in the
Melville Library, reserve room. These are on short term reserve and they
have material about Bede and his historical writings. Furthermore,
there are a number of scholarly articles, available in xerox in
the History Department's library (3rd floor, SBS, north side, and open
1-4, Mon-Thursday). You may use the xerox materials in the room; a
history graduate student will sign them out when you ask for them.

A term-paper topic should be chosen by the end of the 6th week of the
semester. You will submit a topic, in writing, along with any bibliography
you have been able to identify, some indication of the parts of Bede's
History that will help you, and any further material (e.g., an outline, if
you have gone that far). These topics will be recorded, approved (with
suggestions and amendments), and returned within a week. Then you are to
write.

Details regarding the form of the papers--footnotes, bibliography, the
rules regarding plagiarism, the need to type or to use a pc, etc--will be
distributed in a few weeks.

One final word: the material we cover in the other books (especially in
Hunter Blair, the Chronicle, and the two saints' lives) will be relevant
and you should use it. Comparisons are worth while, provided you don't
push too far to have a balanced term paper. Remember, Bede is you
basic text, and it is more than rich enough.

FRANCE, from the Stone Age to Joan of Arc.

Jeremy duQuesnay Adams, Southern Methodist University.

       This syllabus consists of a sequence of topics which can be presented on several levels and in several pedagogic directions, depending on which sequence of readings is used to give synchronic dimension to its diachronic narrative continuity.

       At present this course is offered as History 4372, a lecture course with higher expectations than a 3000-level medieval European survey course (for example) and more modest goals than a 5000-level seminar. However, it could easily function as an undergraduate seminar using readings-track A or B, or as a graduate (or advanced honors undergraduate) seminar with track C supplementing track A. Track B is a sequence of readings designed to appeal to students interested in French language or civilization; it should be combined with several of the track A readings for coherence and depth.

       In any of these metamorphoses, the basic course structure suggests a pair of complementary intersecting cones, the vertex of each resting at the center of the other's base (see sketch). Cone D represents the course's commitment to diachronic report, cone S its concern for synchronic analysis.

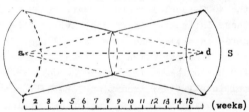

The course's attempt at narrative coverage is widest, both spatially and temporally, in week #1 (Geography and the Paleolithic Era); subsequent sections narrow until in week #15 Jeanne d'Arc becomes the central phenomenon (though far from the sole individual) treated. Conversely, the discrete units of data considered in week #1 can receive only cursory attention; in week #15 Jeanne d'Arc becomes the object of detailed and leisurely analysis. Parity between these two pedagogic principles should be attained as the Franks settle into the region which thereafter comes to bear their name.

       The term _France_, transcendentally significant to Jeanne, is of course blatantly anachronistic when applied to the _Kultur-_

gebiet of Magdalenian and Aurignacian cave-painters. Critique of
the notion of the hexagone géographique, still dear to the contemporary French schoolbook, provides an illuminating point de départ
and orientation point for the semester's discourse. Among the orga-
nizational motifs maintained throughout is a dual regional focus:
on the Paris Basin (broadly defined) and on one other region of
what eventually becomes France. The evolution of the city of Paris,
a persistent motif, is set against the perspective of urban development elsewhere (Marseille, Tours, Reims, Bruges, etc.).

    In its present format, the model week-unit consists of a
Monday lecture, a discursive exposition-cum-slides or other visual
material on Wednesday, and a Friday discussion of one clearly fo-
cussed reading assignment, ideally in a translated primary source
available in paperback edition. Textbook continuity is envisioned
(and required) only for the weeks dedicated to Capetian France, the
course's pedagogic center of gravity.

    The readings assigned as track A are essential to the course
in any of its adaptations, and constitute the required maximum of
the 4000-level lecture format. Track B is designed to appeal to
those interested in French civilization, whether classical or avant-
garde in style, and able to read some French. Track C is designed
to provide selective supplements for advanced students with a taste
for historiographic variety as well as an initiation into continental intellectual traditions. Both tracks offer useful and varied
orientation to the instructor attempting only track A. The Larousse
Histoire de la France under the general direction of Georges Duby
can serve multiple duty; it is a wonderfully convenient réunion of
several current French schools.

    Some salient examples of the supplementary-track approach:
In weeks #3-4 one can track the development of French attitudes toward
the issue of Gallic identity, from the post-Prussian nostalgia of
the early medievalist Lot to Latouche's judicious Common-Market-era
revision to the synthesis attempted twenty years later (1984) by
Harmand, an historian of both Roman and Celtic antiquity; all this
in track C. In the previous week, track B has provided a model
nouvelle-histoire assessment. In weeks #7-9, we encounter the
quintessentially British school of Wallace-Hadrill; in week #13,

attempting assessment of the motives of Philip the Fair, we sample
in brief statements the range of an American school. In the final
week (inspired by Charles T. Wood's Dartmouth seminar on Joan of
Arc), and perhaps also in a term paper, the student following track
C can observe the extraordinary range of significance the Maid has
embodied. For Michelet, she was the precursor of the liberating
tradition of French democracy; for the twentieth-century positivist
Perroy, little more than an annoyingly inflated peripheral episode;
the current feminists Pernoud and Warner go further than Michelet.
Alternatively, the student can explore remorseful revisions across
the Channel just after World War I: Shaw's complex presentation of
Joan as an innocent herald of modern nationalism; Murray's insis-
tence that she was indeed a witch, a category of victim close to
the hearts of Michelet and the feminists). Either option could
fruitfully supplement track B's 60-year sequence of French literary
celebrations of la Pucelle.

History 4372 normally requires one term paper, normally based
the readings assigned. Some typical topics: "Pacification: Caesar according to himself and Louis VI according to Suger"; "Urban sedition in the Gaul of Gregory of Tours and the Flanders of Galbert of
Bruges"; "The communal uprising of Laon, according to Guibert of
Nogent and Suger of Saint-Denis"; "The proper comportment of queens,
according to Gregory of Tours and Jean de Joinville"; "The king's
role in society, as perceived by Jean de Joinville and Jeanne d'Arc".
For other typical topics, see weeks #9 and 15.

J.Adams: Hst.4372

Syllabus of topics and assigned readings, required (Track A) and
recommended in various circumstances (Track B and C)

Week 1 :
Geography and the Paleolithic Era. (The mythic hexagone; presentation of Lower Paleolithic sites at and near Fontainebleau and of
the Upper Paleolithic art - and supposed supporting society - of
the Dordogne.)
Reading: A: André Leroi-Gourhan, "The Evolution of Paleolithic
Art," in C. C. Lamberg-Karlovsky, Hunters, Farmers,
and Civilizations: Old World Archeology (Scientific
American-Freeman, 1979), pp. 36-47.

B: Jacqueline Beaujeu-Carnier, in Histoire de la France, genl. ed.
Georges Duby (Paris: Larousse, 1970), ch. I, "Le pays."

C: P.-R. Giot, intr.; and J.-L. Monnier, pt. I, ch. iv, Préhistoire
de la Bretagne (Rennes: Ouest-France, 1979).

Week 2 :
'Neolithicization' and the Bronze Age. (Cultural definitions; relation (?) of metallurgy and megalith erection; the Seine-Oise-
Marne Culture and the megalithic cult-centers of Brittany, esp.
the Carnac-Locmariaquer-Gavrinnis complex. The modern imagination.)
A: Glyn Daniel, The Megalith-Builders of Western Europe (Penguin
pb, 1958-62), chs. 1, 5, 7.

B: Denise de Sonneville-Bordes, in Duby, Histoire de la France (hereafter,
HF), ch. II, "La préhistoire."

C: Georges Briard, L'age du bronze en Europe barbare: des mégalithes
aux Celtes (Paris: Hespérides, 1976), chs. 4, 5 (pp. 133-47, 165-7),
épilogue.
  - J. L'Helgouach'h, pt. II, ch. i; P.-R. Giot, pt. III, Préhistoire de
la Bretagne.
  - Eleanor Clark, The Oysters of Locmariaquer (Chicago Phoenix pb, 1964,'78

Week 3 :
"Nos Ancêtres les Gaulois": The Iron Age and the Celts. (La Tène hegemony and the first encounter with Greek culture. The Parisii
and Massilia.)
A: G. Bertier de Sauvigny & David Pinkney, History of France,
tr. J. Friguglietti (Forum pb, 1983), intr., ch. 1 (1-10).

B: René Joffroy, in Duby HF, ch. III, "La Gaule avant la conquête romaine."

C: Ferdinand Lot, La Gaule, rev. Paul-Marie Duval (Verviers: Fayard, Marabout, 1967), pt. I, bk. I.

Week 4 :
Caesar. (Division and conquest. The fate of the Haedui; alternatives
  - the Remi (alliance) or the Veneti (genocide)).
A: C. Julius Caesar, The Conquest of Gaul, tr. S.A. Handford
(Penguin pb, 1983).

B: cf. C, infra.

C: Robert Latouche, Gaulois et Francs: de Vercingétorix à Charlemagne
(Paris: Arthaud, 1965), ch. I.

  - F. Lot, La Gaule, pt. I, bk. II.
  - Jacques Harmand, Vercingétorix (Fayard, 1984).

J.Adams: Hst.4372

Syllabus of topics and assigned readings, required (Track A) and recommended in various circumstances (Track B and C)

Week 1 :
Geography and the Paleolithic Era. (The mythic hexagone; presentation of Lower Paleolithic sites at and near Fontainebleau and of the Upper Paleolithic art - and supposed supporting society - of the Dordogne.)
Reading: A: André Leroi-Gourhan, "The Evolution of Paleolithic Art," in C. C. Lamberg-Karlovsky, Hunters, Farmers, and Civilizations: Old World Archeology (Scientific American-Freeman, 1979), pp. 36-47.

B: Jacqueline Beaujeu-Garnier, in Histoire de la France, genl. ed. Georges Duby (Paris: Larousse, 1970), ch. I, "Le pays."

C: P.-R. Giot, intr.; and J.-L. Monnier, pt. I, ch. iv, Préhistoire de la Bretagne (Rennes: Ouest-France, 1979).

Week 2 :
'Neolithicization' and the Bronze Age. (Cultural definitions; relation (?) of metallurgy and megalith erection; the Seine-Oise-Marne Culture and the megalithic cult-centers of Brittany, esp. the Carnac-Locmariaquer-Gavrinnis complex. The modern imagination.)
A: Glyn Daniel, The Megalith-Builders of Western Europe (Penguin pb, 1958-62), chs. 1, 5, 7.

B: Denise de Sonneville-Bordes, in Duby, Histoire de la France (hereafter, HF), ch. II, "La préhistoire."

C: Georges Briard, L'age du bronze en Europe barbare: des mégalithes aux Celtes (Paris: Hespérides, 1976), chs. 4, 5 (pp. 133-47, 165-7), épilogue.
- J. L'Helgouach'h, pt. II, ch. i; P.-R. Giot, pt. III, Préhistoire de la Bretagne.
- Eleanor Clark, The Oysters of Locmariaquer (Chicago Phoenix pb, 1964,'78

Week 3 :
"Nos Ancêtres les Gaulois": The Iron Age and the Celts. (La Tène hegemony and the first encounter with Greek culture. The Parisii and Massilia.)
A: G. Bertier de Sauvigny & David Pinkney, History of France, tr. J. Friugglietti (Forum pb, 1983), intr., ch. 1 (1-10).

B: René Joffroy, in Duby HF, ch. III, "La Gaule avant la conquête romaine."

C: Ferdinand Lot, La Gaule, rev. Paul-Marie Duval (Verviers: Fayard, Marabout, 1967), pt. I, bk. I.

Week 4 :
Caesar. (Division and conquest. The fate of the Haedui; alternatives - the Remi (alliance) or the Veneti (genocide)).
A: C. Julius Caesar, The Conquest of Gaul, tr. S.A. Handford (Penguin pb, 1983).

B: cf. C, infra.

C: Robert Latouche, Gaulois et Francs: de Vercingétorix à Charlemagne (Paris: Arthaud, 1965), ch. I.

- F. Lot, La Gaule, pt. I, bk. II.
- Jacques Harmand, Vercingétorix (Fayard, 1984).

Week 5 :
Gallia Romana. ('Civilization': Lutetia Parisiorum and Durocortorum
Remorum; civitates et viae; the bases of diocesan and departmental
organization.)
A: Bertier de Sauvigny-Pinkney, ch. 1 (pp. 10-13).

B: René Joffroy, in Duby HF, ch. IV, "Les gallo-romains."

C: R. Latouche, Gaulois et Francs, chs. II, III.
- F. Lot, La Gaule,
- Histoire de la France urbaine, genl. ed. Georges Duby: vol. I, La ville
antique, pt. I ("Le réseau urbain"), pt. III ("Les villes de la paix
romaine").
Week 6 :
Gallia Christiana. (The world of Martin of Tours.)
A: Sulpicius Severus, The Life of Martin, Bishop of Tours, tr.
F. R. Hoare in The Western Fathers (Harper Torchbook pb).

- Gregory of Tours, History of the Franks, tr. L. Thorpe (Penguin pb, 1976), bk. I (prol., chs. 1, 28-48).

B: R. Latouche, Gaulois et Francs, ch. IV.

C: Luce Pietri, La ville de Tours, du IVe au VIe siècle: naissance d'une
cité chrétienne (Rome: Ecole Française de Rome, 1983).
- G. Duby, ed. Histoire de la France urbaine, vol. I, pt. IV ("Vetera et
nova"), pp. 423-49, 456-60, 479-93.
- P.-M. Duval, Résumé du Paris antique (Paris: Hermann, 1972).
Week 7 :
The Franks. (The external challenge becomes the new internal ingredi-
ent; 'barbarism' and 'civilization'; the requirements of assimila-
tion -according to whom?; Clovis, the master blender.)
A: Gregory of Tours, History, bk. II (and Thorpe's intr.).

B: Lucien Musset, in Duby HF, ch. V, "Les migrations barbares, IVe-Ve siècle:

C: R. Latouche, Gaulois et Francs, ch. V.
- J. M. Wallace-Hadrill, The Long-Haired Kings and Other Studies in Frank-
ish History (Toronto: MART pb, 1982), chs. I ("Frankish Gaul"), III ("The
Work of Gregory of Tours in the Light of Modern Research"), VII, i & ii
("Reges criniti" and "Pugnator egregius").
Week 8 :
The Merovingians, 451-751. (A dynasty and its domains; the dynamics
of decadence; the place of women.)
A: Gregory of Tours, History: bk. IV, chs. 1, 4, 11, 19, 26-28,
35-6, 49; bk. V; bk. VI, chs. 10, 27, 29, 32, 45-6; bk. VII,
chs. 4-5, 12-13, 15, 19-20, 24, 42, 47; bk. VIII, chs. 15-16
28-29, 33, 40; bk. IX, chs. 2, 9, 18-19, 30, 34, 39-43;
bk. X, chs. 5, 9, 15-17, 20, 27, 30-31. (Students choose
themes to follow: cities, queens and other women, male vil-
lains, model bishops, relations with the Bretons.)

B: Bertier de Sauvigny-Pinkney, ch. 2.
- Pierre Riché, in Duby HF, ch. VI, "Les temps mérovingiens."

C: Latouche, Gaulois et Francs, chs. VI, VII.
- Suzanne Wemple, Women in Frankish Society, 600-900 (Philadelphia: U. Penn-
sylvania Press, 1983).
- J.M. Wallace-Hadrill, Long-Haired Kings, chs. VI ("The Bloodfeud of the
Franks"), VII, iii-v ("Gregory's kings," "Fredegar's kings," "The
rois fainéants").

Week 5 :
Gallia Romana. ('Civilization': Lutetia Parisiorum and Durocortorum
Remorum; civitates et viae; the bases of diocesan and departmental
organization.)
    A: Bertier de Sauvigny-Pinkney, ch. 1 (pp. 10-13).

    B: René Joffroy, in Duby HF, ch. IV, "Les gallo-romains."

    C: R. Latouche, Gaulois et Francs, chs. II, III.
- F. Lot, La Gaule,
- Histoire de la France urbaine, genl. ed. Georges Duby: vol. I, La ville
    antique, pt. I ("Le réseau urbain"), pt. III ("Les villes de la paix
    romaine").
Week 6 :
Gallia Christiana. (The world of Martin of Tours.)
    A: Sulpicius Severus, The Life of Martin, Bishop of Tours, tr.
    F. R. Hoare in The Western Fathers (Harper Torchbook pb).

- Gregory of Tours, History of the Franks, tr. L. Thorpe (Pen-
    guin pb, 1976), bk. I (prol., chs. 1, 28-48).

    B: R. Latouche, Gaulois et Francs, ch. IV.

    C: Luce Pietri, La ville de Tours, du IVe au VIe siècle: naissance d'une
    cité chrétienne (Rome: Ecole Française de Rome, 1983).
- G. Duby, ed. Histoire de la France urbaine, vol. I, pt. IV ("Vetera et
    nova"), pp. 423-49, 456-60, 479-93.
- P.-M. Duval, Résumé du Paris antique (Paris: Hermann, 1972).
Week 7 :
The Franks. (The external challenge becomes the new internal ingredi-
ent; 'barbarism' and 'civilization'; the requirements of assimila-
tion -according to whom?; Clovis, the master blender.)
    A: Gregory of Tours, History, bk. II (and Thorpe's intr.).

    B: Lucien Musset, in Duby HF, ch. V, "Les migrations barbares, IVe-Ve siècles

    C: R. Latouche, Gaulois et Francs, ch. V.
- J. M. Wallace-Hadrill, The Long-Haired Kings and Other Studies in Frank-
    ish History (Toronto: MART pb, 1982), chs. I ("Frankish Gaul"), III ("The
    Work of Gregory of Tours in the Light of Modern Research"), VII, i & ii
    ("Reges criniti" and "Pugnator egregius").
Week 8 :
The Merovingians, 451-751. (A dynasty and its domains; the dynamics
of decadence; the place of women.)
    A: Gregory of Tours, History: bk. IV, chs. 1, 4, 11, 19, 26-28,
    35-6, 49; bk. V; bk. VI, chs. 10, 27, 29, 32, 45-6; bk. VII,
    chs. 4-5, 12-13, 15, 19-20, 24, 42, 47; bk. VIII, chs. 15-16
    28-29, 33, 40; bk. IX, chs. 2, 9, 18-19, 30, 34, 39-43;
    bk. X, chs. 5, 9, 15-17, 20, 27, 30-31. (Students choose
    themes to follow: cities, queens and other women, male vil-
    lains, model bishops, relations with the Bretons.)

    B: Bertier de Sauvigny-Pinkney, ch. 2.
- Pierre Riché, in Duby HF, ch. VI, "Les temps mérovingiens."

    C: Latouche, Gaulois et Francs, chs. VI, VII.
- Suzanne Wemple, Women in Frankish Society, 600-900 (Philadelphia: U. Penn
    sylvania Press, 1983).
- J.M. Wallace-Hadrill, Long-Haired Kings, chs. VI ("The Bloodfeud of the
    Franks"), VII, iii-v ("Gregory's kings," "Fredegar's kings," "The
    rois fainéants").

Week 9 :
Carolingians (687-987). (Less about Charlemagne than about his forbears
and West-Frankish successors - especially Charles the Bald - and the
society which produced that dynasty. Its efforts to reshape that society in turn; grandeur and decline despite the family's commitment
to reform. This week the student experiences a shift in the ratio
of density between lecture and reading. The assigned and suggested
readings are especially heavy in order to provide material for term
papers attempting synthetic research rather than comparative text
analyses.)

A: either Nithard, History of the Sons of Louis the Pious in Bern-
          hard Scholz, Carolingian Chronicles (Ann Arbor pb, 1972)
          (for political-psychological narrative according to the
          Old History),
   or Pierre Riché, Daily Life in the Age of Charlemagne, tr. J. A.
      McNamara (U. Pennsylvania pb, 1978), esp. chs. 1, 3, 7-20,
      23-26 (for the concerns of the New History).

B: Bertier de Sauvigny-Pinkney, ch. 3.
- Adriaan Verhulst, in Duby HF, ch. VII, "La construction carolingienne."
- R. Latouche, Gaulois et Francs, ch. VIII.

C: Einhard and Notker the Stammerer, Two Lives of Charlemagne, tr. L. Thorpe
   (Penguin pb), + the rest of Scholz' Carolingian Chronicles.
- J.M. Wallace-Hadrill, "A Carolingian Renaissance Prince: The Emperor
  Charles the Bald," in Proceedings of the British Academy (London, 1978),
  pp. 155-84.
- Wallace-Hadrill, "History in the Mind of Archbishop Hincmar," in The Writing
  of History, edd. R.H.C. Davis & J.M. Wallace-Hadrill (Oxford U. Press,
  1981), pp. 43-70
- Rosamond McKitterick, "The Carolingians and the See of Reims," in Ideal and
  Reality in Frankish and Anglo-Saxon Society, edd. F. Wormald & R. Collins
  (Oxford U. Press, 1984), pp. 228-49.
Week 10 :
The Capetians, 987-1180. (Another new dynasty, with its variant style
well adapted to its environment. Did it have a 'policy'?)

A: Elizabeth Hallam, Capetian France, 987-1328 (Longman pb, 1980),
   chs. 1-3.
- Suger, Life of Louis the Fat, tr. J. Adams (forthcoming U. Pennsylvania Press pb; now in typescript), sel. chs.

B: Bertier de Sauvigny-Pinkney, ch. 4.
- Georges Duby, in Duby HF, ch. IX, "Les féodaux."

C: Robert Fawtier, The Capetian Kings of France, tr. L. Butler & R.J. Adam
   (New York: St. Martin's pb, 1962), chs. 1-3, 7.
- Georges Duby, The Three Orders: Feudal Society Imagined, tr. A. Goldham-
  mer (Chicago U. Press, 1980): "Revelation;" "Eclipse," ii.
Week 11 :
Capetian France, from Louis the Fat to Philip Augustus. (Cultural atti-
tudes in a time of expanding horizons.)

A: Hallam, Capetian France, ch. 4.
- John Benton, Self and Society in Medieval France: The Memoirs
  of Guibert of Nogent (Toronto: MART pb, 1984).

B: R. Fawtier, Capetian Kings, ch. 12.
- André Joris, in Duby HF, ch. X, "L'essor du XIIe siecle, 1075-1180."

C: Erwin Panofsky, Abbot Suger on the Abbey Church of St.-Denis and Its Art
   Treasures, 2 ed. (Princeton pb, 1977).

Week 9 :
Carolingians (687-987). (Less about Charlemagne than about his forbears
and West-Frankish successors – especially Charles the Bald – and the
society which produced that dynasty. Its efforts to reshape that society in turn; grandeur and decline despite the family's commitment
to reform. This week the student experiences a shift in the ratio
of density between lecture and reading. The assigned and suggested
readings are especially heavy in order to provide material for term
papers attempting synthetic research rather than comparative text
analyses.)

A: either Nithard, History of the Sons of Louis the Pious in Bern-
            hard Scholz, Carolingian Chronicles (Ann Arbor pb, 1972)
            (for political-psychological narrative according to the
            Old History),
   or Pierre Riché, Daily Life in the Age of Charlemagne, tr. J. A.
            McNamara (U. Pennsylvania pb, 1978), esp. chs. 1, 3, 7-20,
            23-26 (for the concerns of the New History).

B: Bertier de Sauvigny-Pinkney, ch. 3.
 - Adriaan Verhulst, in Duby HF, ch. VII, "La construction carolingienne."
 - R. Latouche, Gaulois et Francs, ch. VIII.

C: Einhard and Notker the Stammerer, Two Lives of Charlemagne, tr. L. Thorpe
            (Penguin pb), + the rest of Scholz' Carolingian Chronicles.
 - J.M. Wallace-Hadrill, "A Carolingian Renaissance Prince: The Emperor
            Charles the Bald," in Proceedings of the British Academy (London, 1978),
            pp. 155-84.
 - Wallace-Hadrill, "History in the Mind of Archbishop Hincmar," in The Writing
            of History, edd. R.H.C. Davis & J.M. Wallace-Hadrill (Oxford U. Press,
            1981), pp. 43-70
 - Rosamond McKitterick, "The Carolingians and the See of Reims," in Ideal and
            Reality in Frankish and Anglo-Saxon Society, edd. F. Wormald & R. Collins
            (Oxford U. Press, 1984), pp. 228-49.
Week 10 :
The Capetians, 987-1180. (Another new dynasty, with its variant style
   well adapted to its environment. Did it have a 'policy'?)

A: Elizabeth Hallam, Capetian France, 987-1328 (Longman pb, 1980),
            chs. 1-3.
 - Suger, Life of Louis the Fat, tr. J. Adams (forthcoming U. Penn-
            sylvania Press pb; now in typescript), sel. chs.

B: Bertier de Sauvigny-Pinkney, ch. 4.
 - Georges Duby, in Duby HF, ch. IX, "Les féodaux."

C: Robert Fawtier, The Capetian Kings of France, tr. L. Butler & R.J. Adam
            (New York: St. Martin's pb, 1962), chs. 1-3, 7.
 - Georges Duby, The Three Orders: Feudal Society Imagined, tr. A. Goldham-
            mer (Chicago U. Press, 1980): "Revelation;" "Eclipse," ii.
Week 11 :
Capetian France, from Louis the Fat to Philip Augustus. (Cultural atti-
   tudes in a time of expanding horizons.)

A: Hallam, Capetian France, ch. 4.
 - John Benton, Self and Society in Medieval France: The Memoirs
            of Guibert of Nogent (Toronto: MART pb, 1984).

B: R. Fawtier, Capetian Kings, ch. 12.
 - André Joris, in Duby HF, ch. X, "L'essor du XIIe siecle, 1075-1180."

C: Erwin Panofsky, Abbot Suger on the Abbey Church of St.-Denis and Its Art
            Treasures, 2 ed. (Princeton pb, 1977).

Week 12 :
Capetian France: Urban Explosion and Social Change. (Bruges and Paris.)

A: Galbert of Bruges, The Murder of Charles the Good, Count of
   Flanders, tr. & intr. J.B. Ross (Toronto: ART pb, 1982).

B: Bertier de Sauvigny-Pinkney, ch. 5.
- Jacques Rossiaud, in Duby HF, ch.XI, "La synthèse capétienne."

C: R. Fawtier, Capetian Kings, ch. 11.
- Jacques Le Goff, in Histoire de la France urbaine, vol. II: La ville médiévale, pt. II ("L'apogée de la France urbaine médiévale, 1150-1330").

Week 13 :
The Capetian Ideal and Its Abuse, 1226-1328. (The sainteté of Louis IX
and the hybris of his grandson, Philip the Fair; France - and Paris -
at the center of Europe.)

A: Hallam, Capetian France, chs. 5-6.
- Jean de Joinville, Life of St. Louis, in M.R.B. Shaw (tr.),
  Chronicles of the Crusades (Penguin pb).

B: R. Fawtier, Capetian Kings, chs. 4, 5, 10.
- Elisabeth Carpentier, in Duby HF, ch. XII, "Le grand royaume, 1270-1348."

C: Charles T. Wood, Philip the Fair and Boniface VIII (Holt-Rinehart-Winston
  European Problem Studies: 2 ed., 1971).
- Joseph Strayer, "Philip the Fair - a 'Constitutional' King," in Medieval
  Statecraft and the Perspectives of History (Princeton U. Press, 1971),195-21:
- Elizabeth A.R. Brown, "Philip IV the Fair, of France," Encyclopedia Britan-
  nica, 15th ed. (1983): Macropaedia vol. 14, pp. 223-25.

Week 14 :
The Valois, 1328-1498. (Decline and disaster on all fronts.)

A: Hallam, Capetian France, ch. 7.

B: Bertier de Sauvigny-Pinkney, chs. 6, 7.
- Noël Coulet, in Duby HF, ch. XIII, "Le malheur des temps, 1348-1440."
- Michel Mollat, " " " ch. XIV, "La reconstruction, 1440-1515."

C: Edouard Perroy, The Hundred Years War(1945), tr. W. Wells (New York: Capricorn, 1965), esp. pts. I-IV, VI, VIII(1-3), IX(2, 4).
- Jacques Rossiaud, in Histoire de la France urbaine, vol. II, pt. III ("Crises
  et consolidations, 1330-1530"), pp. 408-553.

Week 15 :
Jeanne d'Arc. (Recovery, real and symbolic; the militant miracle.)

A: The Trial of Joan of Arc, tr. W.F. Scott (Westport, Conn.: Associated Booksellers).

B: Maurice Boutet de Monvel, Joan of Arc (1895), tr. Albert Guérard (Ann Arbor pb
- Paul Claudel, Jeanne d'Arc au Bûcher (w. A. Honegger: 1938).   1957
- Jean Anouilh, L'alouette (1953): The Lark, tr. Christopher Fry (1955).

C: 1) Jules Michelet, Joan of Arc (1843), tr. (Ann Arbor pb, 1957).
      E. Perroy, Hundred Years War, VIII(1).
      Régine Pernoud, Joan of Arc, By Herself and Her Witnesses (New York: Stein
      & Day pb, 1969).
      Marina Warner, Joan of Arc, The Image of Female Heroism (New York: Random
      House pb, 1982).
   2) George Bernard Shaw, Saint Joan (1923).
      Margaret A. Murray, The Witch-Cult in Western Europe (1923; Oxford UP pb,
      1962), appendix IV.

Week 12 :
Capetian France: Urban Explosion and Social Change. (Bruges and Paris.)

A: Galbert of Bruges, <u>The Murder of Charles the Good, Count of</u>
   <u>Flanders</u>, tr. & intr. J.B. Ross (Toronto: HART pb, 1982).

B: Bertier de Sauvigny-Pinkney, ch. 5.
- Jacques Rossiaud, in Duby <u>HF</u>, ch.XI, "La synthèse capétienne."

C: R. Fawtier, <u>Capetian Kings</u>, ch. 11.
- Jacques Le Goff, in <u>Histoire de la France urbaine</u>, vol. II: <u>La ville médi-</u>
   <u>évale</u>, pt. II ("L'apogée de la France urbaine médiévale, 1150-1330").

Week 13 :
The Capetian Ideal and Its Abuse, 1226-1328. (The sainteté of Louis IX
and the <u>hybris</u> of his grandson, Philip the Fair; France - and Paris -
at the center of Europe.)

A: Hallam, <u>Capetian France</u>, chs. 5-6.
- Jean de Joinville, <u>Life of St. Louis</u>, in M.R.B. Shaw (tr.),
   <u>Chronicles of the Crusades</u> (Penguin pb).

B: R. Fawtier, <u>Capetian Kings</u>, chs. 4, 5, 10.
- Elisabeth Carpentier, in Duby <u>HF</u>, ch. XII, "Le grand royaume, 1270-1348."

C: Charles T. Wood, <u>Philip the Fair and Boniface VIII</u> (Holt-Rinehart-Winston
   European Problem Studies: 2 ed., 1971).
- Joseph Strayer, "Philip the Fair - a 'Constitutional' King," in <u>Medieval</u>
   <u>Statecraft and the Perspectives of History</u> (Princeton U. Press, 1971),195-21)
- Elizabeth A.R. Brown, "Philip IV the Fair, of France," <u>Encyclopedia Britan-</u>
   <u>nica</u>, 15th ed. (1983): <u>Macropaedia</u> vol. 14, pp. 223-25.

Week 14 :
The Valois, 1328-1498. (Decline and disaster on all fronts.)

A: Hallam, <u>Capetian France</u>, ch. 7.

B: Bertier de Sauvigny-Pinkney, chs. 6, 7.
- Noël Coulet, in Duby <u>HF</u>, ch. XIII, "Le malheur des temps, 1348-1440."
- Michel Mollat, " "   " ch. XIV, "La reconstruction, 1440-1515."

C: Edouard Perroy, <u>The Hundred Years War</u>(1945), tr. W. Hells (New York: Capricorn, 1965), esp. pts. I-IV, VI, VIII(1-3), IX(2, 4).
- Jacques Rossiaud, in <u>Histoire de la France urbaine</u>, vol. II, pt. III ("Crises
   et consolidations, 1330-1530"), pp. 408-553.

Week 15 :
Jeanne d'Arc. (Recovery, real and symbolic; the militant miracle.)

A: <u>The Trial of Joan of Arc</u>, tr. W.F. Scott (Westport, Conn.: Associated Booksellers).

B: Maurice Boutet de Monvel, <u>Joan of Arc</u> (1895), tr. Albert Guérard (Ann Arbor pb
- Paul Claudel, <u>Jeanne d'Arc au Bûcher</u> (w. A. Honegger: 1938).   1957
- Jean Anouilh, <u>L'alouette</u> (1953): <u>The Lark</u>, tr. Christopher Fry (1955).

C: 1) Jules Michelet, <u>Joan of Arc</u> (1843), tr. (Ann Arbor pb, 1957).
      E. Perroy, <u>Hundred Years War</u>, VIII(1).
      Régine Pernoud, <u>Joan of Arc, By Herself and Her Witnesses</u> (New York: Stein
      & Day pb, 1969).
      Marina Warner, <u>Joan of Arc, The Image of Female Heroism</u> (New York: Random
      House pb, 1982).
   2) George Bernard Shaw, <u>Saint Joan</u> (1923).
      Margaret A. Murray, <u>The Witch-Cult in Western Europe</u> (1923; Oxford UP pb,
      1962), appendix IV.

CAPETIAN AND EARLY VALOIS FRANCE, 987-1498
History 445P/645P

James Alexander
University of Georgia

Required "textbooks," all in paperback:

Robert Fawtier, The Capetian Kings of France
Elizabeth Hallam, Capetian France, 987-1328
J. H. Huizinga, The Waning of the Middle Ages
Emmanuel le Roy Ladurie, Montaillou: The Promised Land of Error
Sidney Painter, French Chivalry
J. R. Strayer, On the Medieval Origins of the Modern State

A spaced line separates readings on reserve from those to be owned by
the student; * indicates a reading selection on reserve which is also
available in paperback, for purchase if you wish to own it. Additional
assignments may be made in class for the graduate students. Assignments
should be read before the week to which they pertain. Cambridge
Medieval History is listed as optional reading.

WEEK   ASSIGNMENT

1   Feudal France in the Eleventh Century: The Early Capetians, 987-1108

         Hallam, 1-108
         Painter, French Chivalry
         Fawtier, Capetian Kings

         Cambridge Medieval History (hereafter cited as CMH), III,
             99-133: Louis Halpehn, "France in the Eleventh Century."
         S. Everett Gleason, An Ecclesiastical Barony of the Middle
             Ages: The Bishopric of Bayeux, 1066-1204 (entire)
         Frederic Cheyette, Lordship and Community in Medieval Europe,
             198-210, 100-128, 137-155

         Graduate students should read as well J. F. Lemarignier, Le
             Gouvernement royal aux premiers temps capetiens, 987-1108,
             first and last chapters, and acquaint themselves with W.
             H. Newman, Le Domaine royal sous les premiers capetiens.

2   Louis VI and Louis VII, 1108-1180

         Hallam, 108-203
         Fawtier, Capetian Kings, 19-24, 137-143, 156-226

         CMH, V, 592-604: Halpehn, "Louis VI and Louis VII"

3   Philip Augustus and Louis VII , 1180-1226

    Fawtier, Capetian Kings, 24-27, 143-151

    Luchaire, Social France in the Age of Philip Augustus
    CMH, VI, 285-330: F. M. Powicke, "The Reigns of Philip Augustus
        and Louis VIII"
    T. Evergates, Feudal Society in the Bailliage of Troyes, 1-15,
        136-154

    Additional reading for first 3 weeks:
        *Odo of Deuill, De profectione Ludovivi VII in orientem
            (entire)
        *Galbert of Bruges, The Murder of Charles the Good
            (entire)

4   St Louis and Philip III, 1226-1285

    Hallam, 204-272
    Fawtier, Capetian Kings, 27-34, 41-109, 151-228

    CMH, VI, 331-361: Ch. Petit-Dutaillis, "St. Louis"
    Sidney Painter, The Scourge of the Clergy
    Jean de Joinville, Life of St Louis (variously titled)
    Eudes Rigaud, The Register of Eudes of Rouen, XV-XXXVI and any
        1 year of the register

5-6 The Last Capetians: Philip "The Fair" through Charles IV, 1285-1328

    Hallam, 273-end
    Fawtier, Capetian Kings, 34-41, 227-230
    le Roy Ladurie, Montaillou

    CMH, VII, 305-339: Hilda Johnstone, "The Last Capetians"
    *Wood, Philip the Fair and Boniface VIII

7   The Hundred Years' War

    Froissart, Chronicles, 1.28-65, 114-151, 174-202; 2.1-31,
        53-104
    CMH, VII, 340-392: A. Couville, "France: The Hundred Years'
        War"
    G. P. Cuttino, "The Causes of the Hundred Years' War," Speculum
        XXXI (1956), 463-472

      Henneman, _French Monarchy_, 123-136
      Huizinga, _The Waning of the Middle Ages_
      Strayer, _On the Medieval Origins of the_ Modern State

      P. S. Lewis, _Later Medieval France_ (and through week 9)
      Geoffrey de la Tour Landry, _The Book of the Knight of the_
          Tower, chapters 6, 14, 15, 16-18, 20-22, 35, 36, 103, 111,
          119, 120, page 29 (lines 36ff.), p. 43 (lines 29ff.), page
          73 (lines 10ff.), pp. 115-119, 122-33, 135-6.

9-10 France at the Close of the Middle Ages

      Henneman, _French Monarchy_, 136-end

      CMH, VII, 232-305:   J. Calmette, "The Reign of Charles VII" and
         "Louis XI"
      P. S. Lewis, _The Recovery of France in the Fifteenth Century_,
         185-216, 242-265, 294-end
      E. Perroy, "Feudalism or Principalities in Fifteenth-Century
         France," _Bulletin of the Institute of Historical Research_,
         XX (1943-45), 181-85
      Philippe de Commynes, _Memoirs_ 1.93-146, 297-368; 2.371-435
      Cheyette, _Lordship and Community_, 240-255
      Shirley, _A Parisian Journal_
      Vaughan, _Valois Burgundy_

    Students should familiarize themselves with the following source
collections, indispendable for the scholarly study of medieval French
history.

    The two great "national" narrative and chronicle series are:

    Dom M. Bouquet, et. al., _Recueil des historiens des Gaules et_
        de la France.

    Société de l'histoire de France: Publications

Government records and collections of charters:

    NB: The _acta_ of many medieval French kings are available, edited
according to reign; some are still incomplete (e.g., the _Recueil des_
actes de Philippe-Auguste has reached only vol. IV). Most are in
the first series below.

    Chartes et deplomes, publiés par les soins de L'Acadmie des
        Inscriptions et Belles-Lettres
    Congregation of St. Maur (eds), _Galla christina_
    Dom de Laurier, et al. (eds), _Ordonnances des rois de France la_
        troisième race
    M. Isambert, et. al. (eds), _Recueil generale des anciennes lois_
        françaises

A. Teulet (ed), <u>Layettes du Trésor des Chartes</u>
<u>Collections des documents inédits sur l'histoire de France</u>
    (which includes, e.g. <u>Les Olim</u>)
The <u>Bibliothéque de l'êcole des Chartes</u> publishes records and
    documents as well as articles. Great Britain's Record
    Commission and Public Record Office have published much
    material pertininet to medieval French history; see E. L.
    C. Mullins, <u>Texts and Calendars</u>, for details of
    publication and contents.

Many excellent editions are among the publications of local French
record and historical societies; they hold to an almost uniformly high
standard of excellence. Unfortunately, there is no French equivalent to
Mullins' <u>Texts and Calendars</u>, an exhaustive analytical index of all
national and local historical society publications in England. A.
Franklin's <u>Les sources de l'histoire de France</u> is a century old, and
Potthast's <u>Bibliotheca hsitorica medii aevi</u>, 70 (a new edition is in
preparation); these are the only comprehensive guides to the French
historical source collections (but see below, A). Frere's <u>Bibliographie</u>
<u>normande</u> pertains to Normandy only.

Among more general series, the following are particularly valuable
lor the history of medieval France:

The Rolls series (Chronicles and Memorials of Great Britain and
    Ireland During the Middle Ages)
J. Mansi, <u>Sacrorum Conciliorum nova et amplissima collectio</u>
Publications in the <u>Monumenta Germaniae historica</u>, especially the
    <u>Scriptores</u> and <u>Leges</u>
J.P. Migne, <u>Patrologiae latinae cursus completus</u>
<u>Recueil des historiens des Croisades</u>
<u>Corpus Christianorum, Series Latina</u>

A. Bibliographies

Since there is no single modern bibliography of medieval French
history, the following must serve as a substitute:

R. C. van Caenegem, <u>Gruide to the Sources of Medieval History</u>
C.V.J. Chevalier, <u>Repertoire des sources historiques de Moyen Age</u>
<u>Collection des inventaires -- sommaires des Archives départmental</u>
    <u>antérieures a 1790</u>
L. H. Cottineau, <u>Répertoire topobibliographique des abbayes et</u>
    <u>prieurés</u>
Fawtier, <u>Capetian Kings,</u> esp C. I.
Franklin and Potthast, <u>supra</u>.
G. Gayet, Sources de l'histoire des intstitutions et de droit
    francais
Louis Halphen, <u>Initiation aux études d'histoire du Moyen Age</u>
L. J. Koenigswarter, <u>Sources et monuments de droit français</u>
    <u>anteérieures au 15e siècle</u>
R. Lasteyrie and A. Vidier, <u>Bibliographie générale des travaux</u>
    <u>historiques et archéologiques publiés par les sociétés</u>
    <u>savants de la France</u> (11 vols., 1898-1950)

J. F. Lemarignier, La France médiévale, pp. 386-402
Gabriel Lepointe and Andre Vandenbossche, Elements de bibliographie
    sur l'histoire des institutions et des faits sociaux, 987-1875
Les Annales (Economies, Sociétés, Civilisations) and continuations
A.L.Molinier, Les sources de l'histoire de France de origines aux
    querres d'Italie
Marcel Pacaut, Guide de l'étudiant en histoire médiévale
L. J. Paetow, A Guide to the Study of Medieval History (Rev. Gray
    C. Boyce)
Ch. Petit-Dutaillis, The Feudal Monarchy in France and England,
    301-409
H. Stein, Bibliographie générale des cartulaires françaises relatifs
    a l'histoire de France
American Historical Society, Guide to Historical Literature

Manuscript collections are frequently described in published French
library catalogues.

For current bibliography, see the reviews and lists in such journals as
    Speculum, English Historical Review, Annals, American Historical
    Review, Revue historique, Historische Zeitschrift, History, Clio:
    Introduction aux Etudes historiques, and other historical
    periodicals. Revue d'histoire ecclésiastique, (thrice
    annually),Bibliographie annuele de l'histoire de France. Theodore
    Besterman, World Bibliography of Bibliographies, Library of
    Congress, Reference Division, Current National Bibliographies

Local history: V. Carriere, Introduction aux êtudes d'histoire
    ecclésiastiqu locale

B. Dictionaries, manuals, etc.

    Chevin, Dictionnaire des noms latins de lieux
    G. Kitson Clark, Guide for Research Students, pp. 40ff, for MS
        collections
    A. de Bourard, Manuel de diplomatique française et pontificale
        (2 volumes of text, three of plates)
    Dom Cottineau, Repertoire topo-bibliographique des abbayes et
        prieures
    A.J.K. Esdaile, A Student's Manual of Bibliography (ed. 3)
    Farrar and Evans, English Translations from Medieval Sources
        although incomplete, remains the only work of its kind,
        supplemented by Mary Anne Ferguson, Bibliography of English
        Translations from Medieval Sources, 1948-1968
    A. Giry, Manuel de diplomatique
    A. Longonon, Atlase historique de la France
    C.T. Martin, The Record Interpreter
    M. Prou, Manuel de Paléographie latine et française du VI au XVII
        siècle
    G. Tessier, Diplomatique royal française
    The Revised Medieval Latin Word-List should be supplemented by the
        best one-volume Latin dictionary, which is that of Lewis and
        Short

c. Fundamental Studies

Most will be found listed in the required readings for this course, or in the bibliographies above. An attempt will be made in the lectures to acquaint students with current historical writing in the field, with the nature of the sources, and with the more interesting and important controversies pertinent to the history of France in the middle ages. The following works are recent enough to have eluded most bibliographies.

John W. Baldwin, Masters, Princes and Merchants
A. Becker, Studien zum Investiturproblem in Frankreich
Thomas Bisson, Assemblies and Representation in Languedoc in the
    Thirteenth Century
Marc Bloch, La France sous les derniers capetiens
Georges Duby, The Chivalrous Society
Georges Duby, La société aux XIe et XIIe siècles dans la région
    mâconnaise
Theodore Evergates, Feudal Society in the Baillage of Troyes
Kenneth Fowler, The Hundred Years War
M. Hallam, Capetian France, 987-1328
John Bell Henneman, Royal taxation in XIV France
Wm. C. Jordan, Louis IX and the Challenge of the Crusade
F. Lavisse (ed.), Histoire de France, vols 2 and 3
J.F. Lemarignier, La France médiévale: Institutions et société
Lemarignier, cited for week 1
E. Lesne, Histoire de la propriété ecclesiastique en France (5
    vols.; much broader than its title would indicate)
Andrew W. Lewis, Royal succession in Capetian France
Archibald Lewis, The Development of Southern France and Catalan
    Society, 718-1750
P.S. Lewis, Later Medieval France
F. Lot and R. Fawtier, Histoire des institutions françaises au moyen
    age
Bryce Lyon and A.E. Verhulst, Medieval Finance
J. Russel Major, Representative Institution in Renaissance France,
    1421-1559
Fliche et Martin, Histoire de l'Eglise
Pacaut, cited for week 2
Frank Pegues, The Lawyers of the Last Capetians
E. Perroy, The Hundred Years Was
Joseph Strayer, Medieval Statecraft and the Perspectives of History
Joseph Strayer, The Administration of Normandy Under St. Louis
J. R. Strayer, The Reign of Philip IV
M.G.A. Vale, Charles VII
M.G.A. Vale, War and Chilvary
Richard Vaughan, Philip the Bold: John the Fearless; Philip the
    Good; Charles the Rash
Charles T. Wood, The French Apanages and the Capetian Monarchy
    1224-1328
Gérardd Sivéry, Saint Louis et son siècle
Jean Richard, St Louis
And see the titles recommended throughout this syllabus for the
    attention of graduate students.

I have not attempted to list the substantial number of exceedingly fine studies of French provinces in the middle ages; many may be found in the apparatus to the Lot and Fawtier set cited above.

Gabrielle M. Spiegel
                                         University of Maryland
                                                College Park
                        Capetian France

General Reference Works:

Achille Luchaire, <u>Histoire des Institutions Monarchiques de la
    France sous les premiers Capétiens</u> (1891) 2 vols.

Achille Luchaire, <u>Manuel des Institutions françaises: Periode
    des capétiens directs</u> (1892).

F.Lot & R. Fawtier, <u>Histoire des Institutions françaises au Moyen
    Age</u> (1952-62) 3 vols.

P. E. Schramm, <u>Der König von Frankreich: Das Wesen der Monarchie
    von 9 zum 16. Jahrhundert</u>.

R. Fawtier, <u>The Capetian Kings of France</u> (1960).

Ch. Petit-Dutaillis, <u>Feudal Monarchy in France & England from the
    Tenth to the Thirteenth Century</u> (1936).

Elizabeth Hallam, <u>Capetian France 987-1328</u> (1980).

Jean Dunbabin, <u>France in the Making 843-1180</u> (1985).

K. F. Werner, <u>Les Origines</u> (before 1000) (1984).

Jean Favier, <u>Le Temps des Principautés 1000-1515</u> (1984).

J. Strayer, <u>On the Medieval Origins of the Modern State</u> (1970).

J.-F. Lemarignier, <u>La France Médiévale Institutions et sociétés</u>
    (1970).

Joseph Declareuil, <u>Histoire Générale du droit français des
    origines à 1789</u> (1925).

                            Topics

1. The Feudal Background

2. The Nature of Monarchy: The Germanic & Carolingian
    Background.

3. The Nature of the Sources: Chronicles

4. The Nature of the Sources: Charters & Legal Records

5. The Capetian Accession: 987 and all that.

6. The Early Capetians (987-1108) - to Philip I

7. Early Feudal Monarchy: Louis VI & Louis VII

8. The Legitimist Debate in the time of Philip Augustus

9. Philip Augustus: The Capetian Revolution

10. Louis VIII and the Appanages

11. Saint Louis: The Golden Age

12. Philip III & the Capetian Bureaucracy

13. The Capetian Apogee: Philip the Fair

Week I: The Feudal Background

F. L. Ganshof, Feudalism

Marc Bloch. Feudal Society (1964) 2 vols.

Joseph Strayer, "The Development of Feudal Institutions," in
    M. Clagett, G. Post & R. Reynolds, eds. Twelfth-Century
    Europe and the Foundations of Modern Society (1961)

Ferdinand Lot, Fidèles ou Vassaux? (1904)

Robert Boutrouche, Seigneurie et Féodalité (1970)

J-P Poly & E. Bournazel La Mutation Féodale Xe-XIIe siècles
    (1980)

Elizabeth A. R. Brown, "The Tyranny of a Construct:
    Feudalism & the Historians of Medieval Europe,"
    American Historical Review, 79 (1974): 1063-88.

Week II: The Nature of Monarchy: The Germanic &
    Carolingian Background

Walter Ullmann, Principles of Government & Politics in the
    Middle Ages (1961)

Walter Ullmann, The Carolingian Renaissance & the Idea of
    Kingship (1969)

F. Kern, Kingship & Law in the Middle Ages

J. M. Wallace-Hadrill, Early Germanic Kingship in England &
    on the Continent (1971)

Marc Bloch, Les Rois Thaumaturges; Eng. Trans.
    Thaumaturgical Kingship/The King's Touch

Week III: The Nature of the Sources: Chronicles

Bernard Guenée, Histoire et Culture Historique dans
    L'Occident médiéval (1980)

Gabrielle Spiegel, The Chronicle Tradition of Saint-Denis:
    A Survey (1978)

Gabrielle Spiegel, "Political Utility in Medieval
    Historiography: A Sketch," History & Theory, 14
    (1975): 314-325.

Bernard Guenée, Politique et Histoire au Moyen Age: Recueil
    d'articles sur l'histoire politique et
    L'historiographie médiévale (1981)

Gabrielle M. Spiegel, "The Cult of Saint-Denis & Capetian
    Kingship," Journal of Medieval History, 1 (1975):
    43-69.

Recueil des Historiens des Gaules et de la France, 24 vols.

Week IV: The Nature of the Sources: Charters & Legal Records

Georges Tessier, Diplomatique royale Française (1962)

M. T. Clanchy, From Memory to Written Record, England 1066-
    1307 (1979)

H.-F. Delaborde, Ch. Petit-Dutaillis, J. Boussard & M.
    Nortier, eds. Recueil des Actes de Philippe-Auguste
    (1916-79) 4 vols.

F. Lot & R. Fawtier, Le Premier Budget de la Monarchie
    française

J. Tardif, Monuments Historiques. Cartons des Rois (1866).

A. Teulet, H.-F. Delaborde, eds. Layettes du Trésor des
    Chartes (1863-1909).

Beugnot, ed. Les Olim ou registres d'arrêt rendus par le roi
    sous les règnes de Louis IX....

Ordonnances des Rois de France de la Troisième Race. (1723)

Philippe de Beaumanoir, Coûtumes de Beauvaisis 3 vols.

Anselme de Sainte-Marie, le Père, Histoire Généalogique et
    Chronologique de la maison royale de France vols.
    I-III. (1726-1728)

Claude Carrozzi, "Le Dernier des Carolingiens: de
    l'histoire au mythe," Moyen Age, 82 (1976): 453-76.

Week V: The Capetian Accession

   Jan Dhondt, "Election et hérédite sous les Carolingiens et
      les premiers Capétiens," Revue Belge de Philologie et
      d'Histoire, 18 (1939): 913-953.

   K. F. Werner, Les Origines, Chap. XVI.

   Andrew Lewis, Royal Succession in Capetian France: Studies
      in Familial Order & the State (1981).

   Joachim Ehler, "Die Historia Francorum Senonensis und der
      Aufstieg des Hauses Capet," Journal of Medieval
      History, 4 (1978): 1-26.

   L. Halphen, "La Place de la Royauté dans le système
      féodale," Revue Historique, 172 (1933): 249-256.

   Julien Havet, "Les Couronnements des rois Hugh & Robert,"
      Revue Historique, 45 (1891): 290-297.

   Ferdinand Lot, Etudes sur le r[gne de Hugh Capet (1903).

   Ch. Pfister, Etudes sur le r[gne de Robert le Pien (996-
      1031) (1885).

Week VI: The Early Capetians to Philip I: 987-1108

   J.-F. Lemarignier, Le Gouvernement royal aux Premiers temps
      Capétiens (1965).

   J. Dhondt, "Une crise du pouvoir Capétien 1032-1034," in
      Miscellanea Medievalia in Memoriam Jan Frederick
      Niemeyer (1967): 137-148.

   Georges Duby, "L'image du prince en France au debut du XIe
      si[cle," Cahiers d'Histoire 17 (1972): 211-216.

   A. Fliche, Le R[gne de Philippe Ier, roi de France 1060-1108
      (1912).

Week VII: Early Feudal Monarchy: Louis VI & Louis VII

   E. Bournazel, Le Gouvernement Capétien au XIIe siecle 1108-
      1180 (1975).

   William Newman, Le Domaine royal sous les premiers Capétiens
      (1937).

   Achille Luchaire, Louis Le Gros: Annales de sa vie et de
      son r[gne. (1890).

   Marcel Pacaut, Louis VII et son royaume

Week VII: cont.:   <u>Louis VI & Louis VII</u>

Marcel Pacaut, <u>Louis VII et les élections episcopales dans</u>
    <u>le royaume de France</u>

John F. Benton, "The Revenue of Louis VII," <u>Speculum</u> (1967):
    84-9.

J.-F. Lemarignier, "Autour de la royaute francaise du IXe au
    XIIIe si[cle." <u>Biblioth[que de L'Ecole des Chartes</u>,
    113 (1955): 5-36.

Achille Luchaire, <u>Etudes sur les Actes de Louis VII</u>

A. Huguenin, <u>Suger et la Monarchie Française au XIIe si[cle</u>
    <u>1108-1152</u>

Gabrielle M. Spiegel, "History as Enlightenment: Suger &
    the Mos Anagogicus," in <u>Abbot Suger and Saint-Denis</u>,
    ed. P. Gerson (1986): 151-58.

Suger, <u>Vie de Louis VI (Vita Ludovici Grossi)</u> ed. Henri
    Wacquet.

Week VIII: <u>The Legitimist Debate in the Time of Philip Augustus</u>

Karl F. Werner, "Die Legitimität der Kapetinger und die
    Entstehung des 'Reditus Regni Francorum ad Stirpem
    Kardoli Magni," <u>Die Welt als Geschichte</u>, 12 (1952):
    203-25.

Gabrielle M. Spiegel, "The Reditus Regni ad Stirpem Karoli
    Magni: A New Look," <u>French Historical Studies</u>, 7
    (1971): 145-174.

Joachim Ehler, "Die Historia Francorum Senonensis und der
    Aufstieg des Hauses Capet," <u>Journal of Medieval History</u>
    4 (1978): 1-26.

Andrew Lewis, "Anticipatory Association of the heir in Early
    Capetian France," <u>American Historical Review</u>, 83
    (1978): 906-927.

Andrew Lewis, "Dynastic Structures & Capetian Throne Right:
    The Views of Giles of Paris," <u>Traditio</u>, 33 (1977):
    225- 52.

Elizabeth Brown, "La Notion de La Legitimité et la Prophétie
    à la cour de Philippe-Auguste," in R.-H. Bautier, ed.
    <u>La France de Philippe-Auguste. Le Temps des Mutations</u>:
    77- 110.

Georgia Wright, "A Royal Tomb Program in the Reign of St.
    Louis," <u>Art Bulletin</u>, 56 (1971): 223-243.

Week IX: Philip Augustus & the Capetian Revolution

John W. Baldwin, The Government of Philip Augustus: Foundations of Royal Power in the Middle Ages (1986).

R.-H. Bautier, ed., La France de Philippe-Auguste Le Temps des Mutations (1982).

Georges Duby, Le Dimanche de Bouvines.

M. Powicke, The Loss of Normandy 1189-1204 Studies in the Angevin Empire (1960).

Week X: Louis VIII & the Appanages

Ch. Petit-Dutaillis, Etude sur la vie et le r[gne de Louis VIII (1894).

Lot & Fawtier, Histoire des Institutions Françaises

Charles T. Wood, The French Appanages & the Capetian Monarchy 1224-1328 (1966).

Andrew Lewis, "The Capetian Appanages & the Nature of the French Kingdom," Journal of Medieval History, 2 (1976): 119-134.

Ch. Wood, "Regnum Francie: A Problem in Capetian Administrative Usage," Traditio, 23 (1967): 117-147.

Week XI: Saint Louis: The Golden Age

William C. Jordan, Louis IX & the Challenge of the Crusade (1979).

Gérard Sivéry, Saint Louis et son Siècle (1983).

Jean Richard, Saint Louis (1982).

G. Sivéry, L'Economie du Royaume de France au siecle de Saint Louis (1986).

Joseph Strayer, The Administration of Normandy under St. Louis (1982).

Septième Centenaire de la Mort de Saint Louis Actes du Colloques de Royaument de Paris (1976).

Gavin, Langmuir, "Judei Nostri:

Week XII: Philip III & the Capetian Bureaucracy

Lot & Fawtier, Histoire des Institutions relevant chap.

Ch. Langlois, Le Règne de Philippe III le Hardi (1887)

6

Week XII cont.: Philip III & the Capetian Bureaucracy

    J. Favier, L'Age des Principautés

    E. Perrot, Les Cas Royaux: Origine et Développement de La
        Théorie aux XIIe et XIVe siècles (1910)

Week XIII: The Capetian Apogee: Philip the Fair

    Joseph Strayer, The Reign of Philip the Fair (19

    Jean Favier, Philippe le Bel

    Joseph Strayer: articles in Medieval Statecraft & the
        Perspectives of History:

        - "Philip the Fair: A Constitutional King,": 195-231.

        - "The Laicization of French & English Society in the
          Thirteenth Century,": 251-265.

        - "Defense of the Realm & Royal Power in France,"
          291-99.

        - "France: The Holy Land, The Chosen People & the Most
          Christian King," 300-328.

    Franklin Pegues, The Lawyers of the Last Capetians

    Joseph Strayer & Charles Taylor, Studies in Early French
        Taxation (1939)

    R.-H. Bautier, "Diplomatique et histoire politique: ce que
        la critique diplomatique nous apprend sur la
        personnalité de Philippe le Bel," Revue Historique, 525
        (1978): 3- 27.

    Gavin Langmuir, "Counsel & Capetian Assemblies," in Etudes
        presentées à la Commission internationale pour
        l'Histoire des Assemblées d'Etats. X Congrès
        International des Sciences historiques (1958): 21-34.

History 343
Fall Semester 1987

W. A. Ernest
University of Hawaii at Manoa

HISTORY OF MEDIEVAL GERMANY TO 1546.

TEXTS: G. Barraclough, The Origins of Modern Germany. (Capricorn)
H. Fuhrmann, Germany in the High Middle Ages, c. 1050-1200. (Cambridge)
The Investiture Controversy: Issues, Ideals, and Results, ed. K. F. Morrison. (Krieger)
The Reformation: Basic Interpretations, ed. L. Spitz. Second edition. (D. C. Heath)

N.B. IN ACCORDANCE WITH UNIVERSITY POLICY, THE TAPING OF LECTURES IS
NOT PERMITTED! Exceptions will be made only for physically handicapped students
having the instructor's written permission.

Barraclough's Origins will serve as the basic text throughout the greater part of the
course, although not during the earlier period. Additional reading is listed in the following
syllabus, but please do not panic! You are not expected to read all of this material or even
the greater part of it. Each item you are asked specifically to read is marked with an
asterisk (*) and, with the exception of the texts listed above, will be found in the Reserve
Room in Sinclair Library. Discussion periods have been scheduled for the Spitz pamphlet
and the Carolingian material, and some other topics may be handled on a discussion or
semi-discussion basis.

You are expected to pursue a research project throughout the greater part of the
semester, dealing with a topic or problem of your choice, which must, however, fall within
the time and subject areas of the course and have the instructor's approval. Submission of
your topic (11 September, on a form which will be furnished) ipso facto will constitute affirmation of the fact that you have checked out the library holdings and that the requisite
primary sources, monographic literature, and periodical material all are available in languages in which you are competent. A first draft of the paper, as nearly as possible in
final form and complete with scholarly apparatus, will be submitted for comment and criticism by 23 October. The final version, impeccable in style, form, and content, and
representing so far as possible a significant original contribution to the sum total of human
knowledge, will be turned in on or before 7 December.

I will gladly furnish advice and a reasonable degree of assistance, both with the paper
and with the course. My office is Sakamaki Hall A-408. See me MWF 7:00 - 7:15; 9:45 -
10:15; W 1:30 - 2:00, or by appointment.

PROPOSED SCHEDULE OF LECTURES AND DISCUSSIONS.

Mon. 24 Aug   **The Geography of Germany and Primitive Germanic Society.**

*A Source Book of Mediaeval History, ed. F. A. Ogg, pp. 19-31.
R. E. Dickinson, The Regions of Germany.
C. T. Smith, An Historical Geography of Western Europe Before 1800.
E. A. Thompson, The Early Germans.
R. E. Oakeshott, The Archaeology of Weapons. (Provocative discussion of the Indo-Europeans.)
M. Todd, Everyday Life of the Barbarians: Goths, Franks and Vandals.
W. Schlesinger, "Lord and Follower in Germanic Institutional History," Lordship and Community
    in Medieval Europe: Selected Readings, ed. F. L. Cheyette (1968), pp. 64-99.
F. S. Lear, "The Idea of Fidelity in Germanic Customary Law," Treason in Roman and Germanic
    Law: Collected Papers (1965), pp. 73-107.

Wed. 26 Aug.   **The Germanic Tribes and the Roman Empire.**

*Source Book ..., ed. Ogg, pp. 32-46.
P. L. MacKendrick, Romans on the Rhine: Archaeology in Germany.
R. MacMullen, Enemies of the Roman Order: Treason, Unrest and Alienation in the Roman Empire.
F. Lot, The End of the Ancient World and the Beginnings of the Middle Ages.
The Transformation of the Roman World: Gibbon's Problem after Two Centuries, ed. L. White, Jr.
M. Rostovtsev, The Social and Economic History of the Roman Empire.
J. B. Bury, The Invasion of Italy by the Barbarians.
T. Hodgkin, Italy and Her Invaders.   (8 vols.)

Fri. 28 Aug.   **The Merovingian Kingdom.**

*Source Book ..., ed. Ogg, pp. 47-67. [A fuller version of the Salic Law appears in Select Historical Documents of the Middle Ages, ed. E. F. Henderson, pp. 176-189.]
J. M. Wallace-Hadrill, The Long-Haired Kings and Other Studies of Frankish History.
S. Dill, Roman Society in Gaul in the Merovingian Age.
B. S. Bachrach, Merovingian Military Organization, 481-751.   [Use with caution!]
B. S. Bachrach, "Procopius, Agathias and the Frankish Military," Speculum, 45 (1970), 435-441.
A. R. Lewis, "The Dukes in the Regnum Francorum, A.D. 550-751," ibid., (1976), 381-410.
R. P. C. Hanson, "The Church in Fifth-Century Gaul: Evidence from Sidonius Apollinaris," Journal of Ecclesiastical History, 21 (1970), 1-10.
Gregory of Tours, History of the Franks.

Mon. 31 Aug.   **The Rise of the Carolingians.**

*Select Historical Documents of the Middle Ages, ed. E. F. Henderson, pp. 319-329.
*Sources for the History of Medieval Europe from the Mid-Eighth to the Mid-Thirteenth Century, ed. Brian Pullan , pp. 3-11.
The Fourth Book of the Chronicle of Fredegar With Its Continuations, trans. J. M. Wallace-Hadrill, pp. 1-121.
W. Goffart, "The Fredegar Problem Reconsidered," Speculum, 38 (1963), 206-241.
A. M. Drabek, Die Verträge der fränkischen und deutschen Herrscher mit dem Papsttum von 754 bis 1020.
A. Angenendt, "Das geistliche Bündnis der Päpste mit den Karolingern (754-796)," Historisches Jahrbuch, 100 (1980), 1-94.

Wed. 2 Sept.   **The Conversion of Germany and the Reform of the Frankish Church.**

W. Levison, England and the Continent in the Eighth Century.
S. J. Crawford, Anglo-Saxon Influence on Western Christendom.
G. W. Greenaway, Saint Boniface: Three Biographical Studies for the Twelfth Centenary Festival.
J. B. Russell, "Saint Boniface and the Eccentrics," Church History, 33 (1964), 235-247.

D. H. Miller, "The Roman Revolution of the Eighth Century: A Study of the Ideological Background of the Papal Separation from Byzantium and Alliance With the Franks," Mediaeval Studies, 36 (1974), 79-133.

R. E. Sullivan, "The Papacy and Missionary Activity in the Early Middle Ages," ibid., 17 (1955), 46-106.

The Letters of Saint Boniface, trans. E. Emerton.

Fri. 4 Sept. **Charlemagne as King and the Conquest of Saxony.**

*Source Book..., ed. Ogg, pp. 108-148.

R. Winston, Charlemagne: From the Hammer to the Cross.

P. Munz, Life in the Age of Charlemagne.

F.-L. Ganshof, "Charlemagne," Speculum, 24 (1949), 520-528.

D. A. Bullough, "Europae Pater: Charlemagne and his Achievement in the Light of Recent Scholarship," English Historical Review, 85 (1970), 59-105. [Review article.]

M. Lintzel, Ausgewählte Schriften, I.

Mon. 7 Sept. HOLIDAY! (Labor Day)

Wed. 9 Sept. **DISCUSSION of the Imperial Coronation of Charlemagne.**

*The Coronation of Charlemagne: What Did It Signify? ed. R. E. Sullivan.

*Sources ..., ed. Pullan, pp. 11-16.

F.-L. Ganshof, The Imperial Coronation of Charlemagne: Theories and Facts. This interpretation should be compared with that of W. Ullmann, The Growth of Papal Government in the Middle Ages, esp. pp. 1-118.

R. Folz, The Concept of Empire in Western Europe From the Fifth to the Fourteenth Century.

P. Munz, The Origin of the Carolingian Empire.

N. Downs, "The Role of the Papacy in the Coronation of Charlemagne," Studies in Medieval Culture, 3 (1970), 7-22.

Zum Kaisertum Karls des Großen: Beiträge und Aufsätze, ed. G. Wolf. [A collection of important articles in German.]

Fri. 11 Sept. **Carolingian Institutions.** [TERM PAPER TOPICS DUE]

*Select Historical Documents ..., ed. Henderson, pp. 189-201, or the same in Source Book ..., ed. Ogg, pp. 134-144.

*Sources ..., ed. Pullan, pp. 18-37.

*W. A. Ernest, "Carolingian and Saxon Institutions."

F.-L. Ganshof, "The Impact of Charlemagne on the Institutions of the Frankish Realm," Speculum, 40 (1965), 47-62.

F. N. Estey, "The Meaning of placitum and mallum in the Capitularies," ibid., 22 (1947), 433-439.

F. N. Estey, "The scabini and the Local Courts," ibid., 26 (1951), 119-129.

J. T. Rosenthal, "The Public Assembly in the Time of Louis the Pious," Traditio, XX (1964), 25-40.

F.-L. Ganshof, "Benefice and Vassalage in the Age of Charlemagne," Cambridge Historical Journal, 6 (1939), 149-175.

P. R. McKeon, "Archbishop Ebbo of Reims (816-835): A Study in the Carolingian Empire and the Church," Church History, 43 (1974), 437-447.
H. Fichtenau, The Carolingian Empire.
F.-L.Ganshof, The Carolingians and the Frankish Monarchy: Studies in Carolingian History.
P. R. McKeon, Hincmar of Laon and Carolingian Politics.
J. W. Thompson, The Dissolution of the Carolingian Fisc in the Ninth Century.

Mon. 14 Sept.   **The Carolingian Renaissance.**

*Source Book ..., ed. Ogg, pp. 144-148.
R. R. Bolgar, The Classical Heritage and Its Beneficiaries.
W. Ullmann, The Carolingian Renaissance and the Idea of Kingship.
K. F. Morrison, The Two Kingdoms: Ecclesiology in Carolingian Political Thought.
E. S. Duckett, Alcuin, Friend of Charlemagne.
F. W. Buckler, Harun al Rashid and Charles the Great.
L. Wollach, Alcuin and Charlemagne: Studies in Carolingian History and Literature.
J. Huber, J. Porcher, W. F. Volbach, The Carolingian Renaissance. [Emphasizes art. Magnificent illustrations; excellent text.]
G. W. Trompf, "The Carolingian Renaissance," Journal of the History of Ideas, 34 (1973). 1-26.
R. J. Gariépy, "Lupus of Ferriéres: Carolingian Scribe and Text Critic," Mediaeval Studies, XXX (1968), 90-105.
J. D. Niles, "The Ideal Depiction of Charlemagne in La Chanson de Roland," Viator, 7 (1976), 123-139.
R. Kottje, "Hrabanus Maurus - 'Praeceptor Germaniae'?" Deutsches Archiv, 31 (1975), 534-545.
"The Letters of Einhard," trans. by H. Preble, Papers of the American Society of Church History, Second Series, I (1913), 107-158.

Wed. 16 Sept.   **SLIDES.**

Fri. 18 Sept.   **The Later Carolingian Empire and the Formation of the German Kingdom.**

*Source Book ..., ed. Ogg, pp. 149-176.
*Select Historical Documents ..., ed. Henderson, pp. 201-207.
*Sources ..., ed. Pullan, pp. 37-42.
*G. Barraclough, The Origins of Modern Germany, pp. 1-23.
*T. Mayer, "The Historical Foundations of the German Constitution," Mediaeval Germany, 911-1250: Essays by German Historians, trans. by Geoffrey Barraclough, II, 1-33.
*B. Schmeidler, "Franconia's Place in the Structure of Mediaeval Germany," ibid., II, 71-93.
K. Bosl, "Ruler and Ruled in the German Empire from the Tenth to the Twelfth Century," Lordship and Community in Medieval Europe: Selected Readings, ed. F. L. Cheyette, pp. 268-290.
K. Leyser, "The German Aristocracy from the Ninth to the Early Twelfth Century: A Historical and Cultural Sketch," Past and Present, 41 (1968), 25-53.
G. Läwen, Stammesherzog und Stammesherzogtum: Beiträge zur Frage ihrer rechtlichen Bedeutung im 10.-12. Jahrhundert.
E. Dümmler, Geschichte des ostfränkischen Reiches. (3 vols.)

Carolingian Chronicles: Royal Frankish Annals and Nithard's Histories, trans. B. W. Scholz and
     B. Rogers.
Son of Charlemagne, trans. A. Cabaniss.

Mon. 21 Sept.   **The Saxon Dynasty: Henry I and Otto I.**

*Barraclough, Origins of Modern Germany, pp. 24-53.
*Sources ..., Pullan, pp. 113-117.
B. H. Hill, Jr., Medieval Monarchy in Action: The German Empire From Henry I to Henry IV,
     pp. 7-42, 111-163.
K. Leyser, Rule and Conflict in an Early Medieval Society: Ottonian Saxony.
K. Leyser, "Henry I and the Beginnings of the Saxon Empire," English Historical Review, 83
     (1968), 1-32.
H. L. Adelson, "The Holy Lance and the Hereditary German Monarchy," The Art Bulletin, 48
     (1966), 177-192.
A. Alföldi, "Hasta - Summa Imperii. The Spear as Embodiment of Sovereignty in Rome,"
     American Journal of Archaeology, 63 (1959), 1-27.
K. Leyser, "The Battle at the Lech, 955: A Study in Tenth-Century Warfare," History, 50
     (1965), 1-25.
W. Schlesinger, "Die Königserhebung Heinrich I., der Beginn der deutschen Geschichte und die
     deutsche Geschichtswissenschaft," Historische Zeitschrift, 221 (Dec. 1975), 529-552.
C. Erdmann, "Das Grab Heinrichs I.," Deutsches Archiv, 4 (1940-41), 76-97.

Wed. 23 Sept.   **The Ottonian Empire.**

*Barraclough, Origins of Modern Germany, pp. 53-71.
*Sources ..., ed. Pullan, pp. 117-120.
B. H. Hill, Jr., The Rise of the First Reich: Germany in the Tenth Century.
J. N. Sunderland, "The Mission to Constantinople in 968 and Liudprand of Cremona," Traditio,
     31 (1975), 55-81.
W. Holtzmann, Geschichte der sächsischen Kaiserzeit, pp 175-249.
A. Hauck, Kirchengeschichte Deutschlands, III, 3-338.
D. Claude, Geschichte des Erzbistums Magdeburg bis in das 12.Jahrhundert, I: Die Geschichte
     der Erzbischöfe bis auf Ruotger (1124).
H. Beumann, "Das Kaisertum Ottos des Großen," Historische Zeitschrift, 195 (1962), 529-573.

Fri. 25 Sept.   **Otto II and Otto III: Renovatio Imperii.**

*Sources ..., ed. Pullan, pp. 120-122.
Hill, Medieval Monarchy in Action, pp. 43-60, 163-183.
J. B. Morrall, "Otto III: An Imperial Ideal," History Today, 9 (1959), 812-822.
A. F. Czajkowski, "The Congress of Gniezno in the Year 1000," Speculum, 24 (1949), 339-356.
F. J. Tschan, Bernward of Hildesheim. (3 vols.)
Z. Wojciechowski, "La 'Renovatio Imperii' sous Otton III et la Pologne," Revue historique, 201
     (1949), 30-44.
K. Hampe, "Kaiser Otto III. und Rom," Hist. Zeit., 160 (1929), 513-533.
M. Uhlirz, "Kaiser Otto III. und das Papsttum," ibid., 171 (1940), 258-268.
K. and M. Uhlirz, Jahrbücher des deutschen Reiches Unter Otto II. und Otto III.   Vol. II.

F. Koch, Wurde Kaiser Karl sitzend begraben?
P. E. Schramm, "Die 'Heilige Lanze,' Reliquie und Herrschaftszeichen des Reiches und ihre Replik in Krakau: Ein Überblick über die Geschichte der Königslanze," Herrschaftszeichen und Staatssymbolik, II, 493-537.
Sylvester II (Pope), The Letters of Gerbert, trans. H. Lattin.

Mon. 28 Sept.　　　　　**Henry II and Conrad II: Domestic and Ecclesiastical Adjustments.**

*Barraclough, Origins of Modern Germany, pp. 72-98.
*H. Fuhrmann, Germany in the High Middle Ages, c. 1050-1200, pp. 1-30.
*Sources ..., ed. Pullan, pp. 122-129.
Hill, Medieval Monarchy in Action, pp. 61-84, 183-208.
K. Hampe, Germany Under the Salian and Hohenstaufen Emperors, trans. R. Bennett (1973), pp. 33-46.
H. J. Lang, "The Fall of the Monarchy of Mieszko II, Lambert," Speculum, 49 (1974), 623-639.
T. Schieffer, "Heinrich II. und Konrad II. Die Umprägung des Geschichtsbildes durch die Kirchenreform des 11. Jahrhunderts," Deutsches Archiv, VIII (1950-51), 384-437.
H. L. Mikoletzky, Kaiser Heinrich II. und die Kirche.

Wed. 30 Sept.　　　　　**The Secular Role in Church Reform: Pious Nobles and Rulers.**

*H. Fuhrmann, Germany in the High Middle Ages, pp. 31-50.
*Sources ..., ed. Pullan, pp. 47-56.
*"The Foundation Charter of Cluny," in Source Book ..., ed. Ogg, pp. 245-249, or in Select Historical Documents ..., ed. Henderson, pp. 329-333.
*Barraclough, Origins of Modern Germany, pp. 72-98. [Assigned above.]
*Thompson, Feudal Germany, I, 68-124.
Hill, Medieval Monarchy in Action, pp. 85-98, 209-214.
Hampe, Germany Under the Salian and Hohenstaufen Emperors, pp. 47-59.
R. L. Poole, "Benedict IX and Gregory VI," Proceedings of the British Academy, 8 (1917-1918), 199-235.
E. N. Johnson, "Adalbert of Hamburg-Bremen: A Politician of the Eleventh Century," Speculum, 9 (1934), 147-179.
H. H. Anton, "Bonifaz von Canossa, Markgraf von Tuszien, und die Italienpolitik der frühen Salier," Historische Zeitschrift, 214 (1972), 529-556.
Adam of Bremen, History of the Archbishops of Hamburg-Bremen, trans. F. J. Tschan.
H. C. Lea, The History of Sacerdotal Celibacy in the Christian Church.
G. Constable, Monastic Tithes From Their Origins to the Twelfth Century.
J. Evans, Monastic Life at Cluny, 910-1157.
K. J. Conant, "Mediaeval Academy Excavations at Cluny, X," Speculum, 45 (1970), 1-39.

Fri. 2 Oct.　　　　　**The Reformed Papacy.**

Mon. 5 Oct.   **Henry IV: Minority and Saxon Wars.**

*Thompson, Feudal Germany, I, 185-216.
*Select Historical Documents ... ed. Henderson, pp. 361-365.
Hill, Medieval Monarchy in Action, pp. 99-106, 214-241.
Hampe, Germany Under the Salian and Hohenstaufen Emperors, pp. 60-79.
J. H. Lynch, "Hugh I of Cluny's Sponsorship of Henry IV: Its Context and Consequences,"
    Speculum, 60 (1985), 800-826.
E. Boshof, "Das Reich in der Kreise: Überlegungen zum Regierungsausgang Heinrichs III.," His-
    torische Zeitschrift, 228 (1979), 265-287.
Meyer von Knonau, Jahrbücher des deutschen Reiches Unter Heinrich IV. und Heinrich V.
    Vols. I-II.

Wed. 7 Oct.   **The Investiture Contest.**

*Barraclough, Origins of Modern Germany, pp. 101-127.
*H. Fuhrmann, Germany in the High Middle Ages, pp. 51-95.
*Sources ..., ed. Pullan, pp. 58-63, 130-159.
*Source Book ..., ed. Ogg, pp. 261-281.
*Select Historical Documents ..., ed. Henderson, pp. 365-409.
    [N.B. These collections will involve quite a bit of duplicaton!]
*P. Joachimsen, "The Investiture Contest and the German Constitution," Mediaeval Germany,
    911-1250, ed. G. Barraclough, II, 95-129.
*J. W. Thompson, Feudal Germany, I, 125-166, 217-265.
Z. N. Brooke, "Lay Investiture and Its Relation to the Conflict of Empire and Papacy," Proceed-
    ings of the British Academy, 25 (1939), 217-247.
D. B. Zema, "The Houses of Tuscany and Pierleone in the Crises of Rome in the Eleventh
    Century," Traditio, 2 (1944), 155-175.
K. F. Morrison, "Canossa: A Revision," Traditio, 18 (1962),121-148.
J. T. Gilchrist, "Canon Law Aspects of the Eleventh Century Gregorian Reform Program," Jour-
    nal of Ecclesiastical History, 13 (1962), 21-38.
S. A. Chodorow, "Magister Gratian and the Problem of 'Regnum' and 'Sacerdotium'," Traditio,
    26 (1970), 364-381.
G. H. Williams, The Norman Anonymous of 1100 A.D.
R. Nineham, "The So-Called Anonymous of York," Journal of Ecclesiastical History, 14 (1963),
    31-45.
G. Tellenbach, Church, State, and Christian Society at the Time of the Investiture Contest.
N. Hunt, Cluny Under Saint Hugh, 1049-1109.
K. F. Morrison, Tradition and Authority in the Western Church, 300-1400.
Hampe, Germany Under the Salian and Hohenstaufen Emperors, pp. 80-107.
P. Segl, "Zum Itinerar Abt Hugos I. von Cluny (1049-1109)," Deutsches Archiv, 29 (1973), 206-
    219.
G. Koch, Manegold von Lautenbach und die Lehre von der Volkssouveränität unter Heinrich IV.
A. Overmann, Gräfin Mathilde von Tuscien.

The Correspondence of Pope Gregory VII: Selected Letters from the Registrum, trans. E.
    Emerton.

The Epistolae Vagantes of Pope Gregory VII, trans. H. E. J. Cowdrey.
A. Murray, "Pope Gregory VII and His Letters," Traditio, 22 (1966), 149-202.
Imperial Lives and Letters of the Eleventh Century, trans. T. E. Mommsen and K. F. Morrison.

Fri. 9 Oct.   **DISCUSSION of the Investiture Contest.**

*The Investiture Controversy: Issues, Ideals, and Results, ed. K. F. Morrison

Mon. 12 Oct.   HOLIDAY (Discoverers' Day)

Wed. 14 Oct.   **Henry V and the End of the Investiture Contest.**
                       [FIRST DRAFT DUE.]
*Barraclough, Origins of Modern Germany, pp. 127-153.
Hampe, Germany Under the Salian and Hohenstaufen Emperors, pp. 108-122.
S. A. Chodorow, "Ecclesistical Politics and the Ending of the Investiture Contest: The Papal
    Election of 1119 and the Negotiations of Mouzon," Speculum, 46 (1971), 613-640.
A. Waas, Heinrich V.
G. Meyer von Knonau, Jahrbücher des deutschen Reiches Unter Heinrich IV. und Heinrich V.
    Vols. VI-VII.

Fri. 16 Oct.   **HOUR EXAMINATION!**

Mon. 19 Oct.   **Cluny, Hirsau, and the German Monarchy.**

*H. Hirsch, "The Constitutional History of the Reformed Monasteries During the Investiture Con-
    test," Mediaeval Germany, 911-1250, ed. G. Barraclough, II, 131-173.
*U. Stutz, "The Proprietary Church as an Element of Mediaeval Germanic Ecclesiastical Law,"
    ibid., II, 35-70.
*J. W. Thompson, Feudal Germany, I, 3-67.
H. E. J. Cowdrey, The Cluniacs and the Gregorian Reform.
T. Mayer, Fürsten und Staat. [An extremely important collection of essays which laid the foun-
    dation for the modern interpretation of the problem.]

Wed. 21 Oct.   **The Summons of 1108 and the Northeastern German Frontier.**

*J. W. Thompson, Feudal Germany, II, 387-528.
M. Bünding, Das Imperium Christianum und die deutschen Ostkriege vom zehnten bis zum
    zwölften Jahrhundert.
Heidenmission und Kreuzzugsgedanke in der deutschen Ostpolitik des Mittelalters, ed. H.
    Beumann.
W. Schlesinger, Mitteldeutsche Beiträge zur deutschen Verfassungsgeschichte des Mittelalters.
Adam of Bremen, History of the Archbishops of Hamburg-Bremen, trans. F. J. Tschan.
Helmold of Bosau, Chronicle of the Slavs, trans. F. J. Tschan.

Fri. 23 Oct.   **Lothar and Conrad III: Decline of the Empire**

   *Barraclough, Origins of Modern Germany, pp. 153-164.
   *Fuhrmann, Germany in the High Middle Ages, pp. 96-134.
   Hampe, Germany Under the Salian and Hohenstaufen Emperors, pp. 123-153.

Mon. 26 Oct.   **An Age of Recovery: Frederick Barbarossa.**

   *Barraclough, Origins of Modern Germany, pp. 167-186.
   *Fuhrmnn, Germany in the High Middle Ages, pp. 135-186.
   *Sources ..., ed. Pullan, pp. 160-189.
   *Source Book ..., ed. Ogg, pp. 398-402.
   *Select Historical Documents ..., ed. Henderson, pp. 410-430.
   Hampe, Germany Under the Salian and Hohenstaufen Emperors, pp. 153-219.
   P. Munz, Frederick Barbarossa: A Study in Medieval Politics.
   M. Pacaut, Frederick Barbarossa.
   M. Baldwin, Alexander III and the Twelfth Century.
   R. Chazan, "Emperor Frederick I, the Third Crusade, and the Jews," Viator, 8 (1977), 83-93.
   J. Fried, "Friedrich Barbarossas Krönung in Arles (1178)," Historisches Jahrbuch, 103 (no. 2,
       1983), 347-71.
   H. Wolter, "Die Verlobung Heinrichs VI. mit Konstanz von Sizilien im Jahre 1184," Historische
       Jahrbuch, 105 (1985), 30-51.

Wed. 28 Oct.   **Social and Economic Developments.**

   B. H. Slicher van Bath, The Agrarian History of Western Europe, A.D. 500-1850.
   G. Duby, Rural Economy and Country Life in the Medieval West.
   L. White, Jr., Medieval Technology and Social Change.
   J. D. Lewis, The Genossenschaft-Theory of Otto von Gierke: A Study in Political Thought.
       (University of Wisconsin Studies in the Political Sciences and History, No. 25.)
   G. Kisch, The Jews in Medieval Germany: A Study of Their Legal and Social Status.
   I. A. Agus, The Heroic Age of Franco-German Jewry: The Jews of Germany and France of the
       Tenth and Eleventh Centuries.
   R. G. Witt, "The Landlord and the Economic Revival of the Middle Ages," American Historical
       Review, 76 (1971), 965-988.
   D. M. Nicholas, "Medieval Urban Origins in Northern Continental Europe: State of Research
       and Some Tentative Conclusions," Studies in Medieval and Renaissance History, 6 (1969),
       55-114.
   L. White, Jr., "The Life of the Silent Majority," Life and Thought in the Early Middle Ages, ed.
       R. S. Hoyt, pp. 85-100.
   The Ruodlieb: The First Medieval Epic of Chivalry from Twelfth-Century Germany, trans. G.
       B. Ford, Jr.

Fri. 30 Oct.   **The Mightiest Vassal: Henry the Lion.**

R. Hildebrand, Der sächsischen 'Staat' Heinrichs des Löwen.
E. Gronen, Die Machtpolitik Heinrichs des Löwen und sein Gegensatz gegen das Kaisertum.
J. Bärmann, Die Städtegründungen Heinrichs des Löwen und die Stadtverfassung des 12.
    Jahrhunderts.

Mon. 2 Nov.   **Germany to the Twelfth Century. SLIDES!**

Wed. 4 Nov.   **The Feudalization of Germany and Barbarossa's Grand Design.**

*Barraclough, Origins of Modern Germany, pp. 186-192.
*Select Historical Documents ..., ed. Henderson, pp. 211-218.
*H. Mitteis, "Feudalism and the German Constitution," Mediaeval Germany, 911-1250, ed. G.
    Barraclough, II, 235-279.
*O. Freiherr von Dungern, "Constitutional Reorganization and Reform Under the Hohenstaufen,"
    ibid., II, 203-233.
*A. Brackmann, "The Beginnings of the National State in Germany and the Norman Monarchies,"
    ibid., II, 281-299.
J. B. Freed, "The Origins of the European Nobility: The Problem of the Ministerials," Viator, 7
    (1976), 211-241.
M. Bloch, "A Problem in Comparative History: The Administrative Classes in France and in
    Germany," Land and Work in Mediaeval Europe (1966), pp. 82-123.
W. Ohnsorge, "Die Byzanzpolitik Friedrich Barbarossas und der 'Landesverrat' Heinrichs des
    Löwen," Deutsches Archiv, 6 (1943), 118-149.
K. Hampe, "Heinrichs des Löwen Sturz in politisch-historischer Beurteilung," Hist. Zeit., 109
    (1912), 49-82.
E. Otto, "Von der Abschliessung des Ritterstandes," ibid., 162 (1940), 19-39.
F. Güterbock, Der Prozeß Heinrichs des Löwen: Kritische Untersuchungen.
W. Goez, Der Leihezwang: Eine Untersuchung zur Geschichte des deutschen Lehnrechts.
H. Mitteis, Lehnrecht und Staatsgewalt: Untersuchungen zur mittel-alterlichen Verfassungsges-
    chichte.
W. Biereye, "Die Kämpfe gegen Heinrich den Löwen in den Jahren 1177 bis 1181," Forschungen
    und Versuche zur Geschichte und der Neuzeit: Festschrift Dietrich Schäfer (1915), pp.
    149-196.
K. Bosl, Die Reichsministerialität der Salier und Staufer. (2 vols.)

Fri. 6 Nov.   **DISCUSSION of Serfdom, the Markgenossenschaft Theory, and**
                     Land Reclamation and Peasant Emancipation: The First Phase.

*C. Stephenson, "The Problem of the Common Man in Early Medieval Europe," American Histor-
    ical Review, 51 (1946), 419-439.
*B. Lyon, "Medieval Real Estate Developments and Freedom," Am. Hist. Rev., 63 (1957), 47-61.
*Source Book ..., ed. Ogg, pp. 330-333.
*Thompson, Feudal Germany, II, 545-579.
T. Mayer, "The State of the Dukes of Zähringen," Mediaeval Germany, ed. Barraclough, II, 175-
    202.
H. Cam, "The Community of the Vill," Lordship and Community ..., ed. Cheyette, pp. 256-267.

A. Dopsch, Die freien Marken in Deutschland: Beitrag zur Agrar- und Sozialgeschichte des
     Mittelalters.
J. F. Niermeier, "De vroegste berichten omtrent bedijking in Nederland," Tijdschrift voor
     economische en sociale geografie, 49 (1958), 226-231.

Mon. 9 Nov.   The Concept of Empire.

*Sources ..., ed. Pullan, pp. 122-127.
J. Bryce, The Holy Roman Empire. [The classic but long outdated introduction to the subject
     which, please note, was written originally as an undergraduate honors thesis!]
G. Barraclough, The Mediaeval Empire: Idea and Reality.
R. Folz, The Concept of Empire in Western Europe From the Fifth to the Fourteenth Century.
F. Heer, The Holy Roman Empire.
W. Ullmann, "Reflections on the Mediaeval Empire," Transactions of the Royal Historical
     Society, Fifth Series, 14 (1964), 89-108.
J. Brundage, "Widukind of Corvey and the 'Non-Roman' Imperial Idea," Mediaeval Studies,
     XXII (1960), 15-26.
M. Bloch, "The Empire and the Idea of Empire Under the Hohenstaufen," Land and Work in
     Mediaeval Europe (1966), pp. 1-43.
A. Diehl, "Heiliges römisches Reich deutscher Nation," Hist. Zeit., 156 (1937), 457-484.
C. Erdmann, "Das ottonische Reich als Imperium Romanum," Deutsches Archiv, 6 (1943), 412-
     441.
P. E. Schramm, Kaiser, Rom und Renovatio: Studien zur Geschichte des römischen
     Erneuerungsgedankens vom Ende des Karolingischen Reiches bis zum Investiturstreit.
E. E. Stengel, Abhandlungen und Untersuchungen zur Geschichte des Kaisergedankens im Mit-
     telalter.
H. Hostenkamp, Die mittelalterlichen Kaiserpolitik in der deutschen Historiographie seit von
     Sybel und Ficker.

Wed. 11 Nov.   HOLIDAY! (Veterans' Day)

Fri. 13 Nov.   The Diversion of Imperial Energies: Henry VI and Frederick II.

*Barraclough, Origins of Modern Germany, pp. 193-246.
*Sources ..., ed. Pullan, pp. 191-231.
*Source Book ..., ed. Ogg, pp. 402-409.
Hampe, Germany Under the Salian and Hohenstaufen Emperors, pp. 220-306.
J. Leuschner, Germany in the Late Middle Ages, pp. 1-64.
T. van Cleve, The Emperor Frederick II of Hohenstaufen: Immutator Mundi.
P. Andrews, Frederick II of Hohenstaufen.
E. Kantorowicz, Frederick the Second, 1194-1250.
W. Seegrün, "Kirche, Papst und Kaiser nach der Anschauungen Kaiser Friedrichs II.", Hist. Zeit.,
     207 (1968), 4-41.
H. Krabbo, Die Besetzung der deutschen Bistümer unter der Regierung Kaiser Friedrichs II.
     (1212-1250).
K. Frey, Die Schicksale des königlichen Gutes in Deutschland unter den letzten Staufern seit
     König Philipp.
The Liber Augustalis or Constitutions of Melfi Promulgated by the Emperor Frederick II for the
     Kingdom of Sicily in 1231, trans. J. M. Powell.

Mon. 16 Nov.   **Land Reclamation and Peasant Emancipation.   The Second Phase.**

[No adequate treatments of this topic have been published.]

Wed. 18 Nov.   **SLIDES ON RECLAMATION AND EMANCIPATION.**

Fri. 20 Nov.   **The Stedinger Crusade.**

H. A. Schumacher, <u>Die Stedinger: Beitrag zur Geschichte der Weser-Marschen</u>.
H. Schmidt, "Zur Geschichte der Stedinger: Studien über Bauernfreiheit, Herrschaft und Religion
    an der Unterweser im 13. Jahrhundert," <u>Bremisches Jahrbuch</u>, 60/61 (1982/1983), 27-94.
R. Kohn, " 'Lieber tot als Sklav': Der Stedingeraufstand in der deutschen Literatur (1836-1975),"
    <u>Oldenburger Jahrbuch</u>, 80 (1980), 1-57; 81 (1981), 83-144; 82 (1982), 99-157.

Mon. 23 Nov.   **Medieval German Expansion into the Baltic Lands.**

*Barraclough, <u>Origins of Modern Germany</u>, pp. 249-281.
*Thompson, <u>Feudal Germany</u>, II, 612-658.
D. Seward, "The Teutonic Knights," <u>History Today</u>, 20 (1970), 859-866.
W. Urban, "The Organization of Defense of the Livonian Frontier in the Thirteenth Century,"
    <u>Speculum</u>, 48 (1973), 525-532.
I. Sterns, "Crime and Punishment Among the Teutonic Knights," <u>ibid.</u>, 57 (1982), 84-111.
R. Spence, "Pope Gregory IX and the Crusade in the Baltic," <u>Catholic Historical Review</u>, 69 (Jan.
    1983), 1-19.
E. Christensen, <u>The Northern Crusades: The Baltic and the Catholic Frontier, 1100-1525</u>.
W. Urban, <u>The Baltic Crusade</u>.
W. Urban, <u>The Prussian Crusade</u>.
F. L. Carsten, <u>The Origins of Prussia</u>.
<u>Cambridge Economic History of Europe</u>, I, 361-397.
F. Benninghoven, <u>Der Orden der Schwertbrüder</u>. [Exemplary monograph!]
K. H. Quirin, <u>Die deutsche Ostsiedlung im Mittelalter</u>.

Wed. 25 Nov.   **The Decline of the Empire to the Mid-Fourteenth Century.**

*Barraclough, <u>Origins of Modern Germany</u>, pp. 282-319.
J. Leuschner, <u>Germany in the Late Middle Ages</u>, pp. 65-147.
N. Denholm-Young, <u>Richard of Cornwall</u>.
T. W. E. Roche, <u>The King of Almayne</u>.
J. R. Strayer, "The Fourth and the Fourteenth Centuries," <u>American Historical Review</u>, 77
    (1972), 1-14.
H. S. Offler, "Empire and Papacy: The Last Struggle," Transactions of the Royal Historical
    Society, Fifth Series, VI (1956), 21-47.
R. Moeller, <u>Ludwig der Bayer und die Kurie im Kampf um das Reich</u>.
H. Wieruszowski, <u>Vom Imperium zum nationalen Königtum</u>.
A. Hauck, <u>Kirchengeschichte Deutschlands</u>, V.

Fri. 27 Nov.   HOLIDAY! [Post-holiday?]

Mon. 30 Nov.   **Emperor Charles IV and the Art of the Possible.**

J. Leuschner, Germany in the Late Middle Ages, pp. 149-178.

P. Moraw, "Kaiser Karl IV. im deutschen Spätmittelalter," Historische Zeitschrift, 229 (1979), 1-24.

R. Schneider, "Karls IV. Auffassung vom Herrscheramt," ibid., 216 (1973), 122-150.

H. Stoob, "Kaiser Karl IV. und der Ostseeraum," Hansische Geschichtsblätter, 88 (1970), 163-214.

N. Bulst, "Der Schwarze Tod. Demographische, wirtschafts- und kulturgeschichtliche Aspekte der Pestkatastrophe von 1347-1352: Bilanz der neueren Forschung," Saeculum, 30 (no. 1, 1979), 45-67.

E. L. Petersen, "Studien zur goldenen Bulle von 1356," Deutsches Archiv, 22 (1966), 226-253.

The Golden Bull of 1356 is translated in Select Historical Documents ..., ed. Henderson, pp. 220-261.

Wed. 2 Dec.   **Late Medieval Germany to the Reformation.**

*Barraclough, Origins of Modern Germany, pp. 320-352.
*Select Historical Documents ..., ed. Henderson, pp. 262-266.

J. W. Stieber, Pope Eugenius IV, the Council of Basel, and the Secular and Ecclesiastical Authorities in the Empire: The Conflict Over Supreme Authority and Power in the Church.

H. J. Cohn, The Government of the Rhine Palatinate in the Fifteenth Century.

P. Dollinger, The German Hansa.

L. W. Spitz, The Religious Renaissance of the German Humanists.

E. Pitz, "Die Wirtschaftskrise des Spätmittelalters," Vierteljahrschrift für Sozial- und Wirtschaftsgeschichte, 52 (1965), 347-367.

J. Aschbach, Geschichte Kaiser Sigmunds.   4 vols.

Fri. 4 Dec.   **SLIDES OF LATE MEDIEVAL GERMANY.**

Mon. 7 Dec.   **The Social and Religious Situation in the Late Medieval German Town: The Example of Würzburg.   [DEADLINE FOR TERM PAPERS!]**

P. Dollinger, The German Hansa.

H. Planitz, Die deutsche Stadt im Mittelalter.

Die Stadt des Mittelalters, ed. C. Haase.   [An extremely valuable three-volume collection of previously published articles.]

K. Trüdinger, Stadt und Kirche im spätmittelalterlichen Würzburg.

Wed. 9 Dec.   **DISCUSSION OF THE REFORMATION IN GERMANYnn.**

*The Reformation: Basic Interpretations, ed. L. W. Spitz. (2nd. ed.)
*Barraclough, Origins of Modern Germany, pp. 355-381.

H. Holborn, A History of Modern Germany: The Reformation.

H. Boehmer, Road to Reformation: Martin Luther to the Year 1521.

R. H. Fife, The Revolt of Martin Luther.
D. C. Steinmetz, Luther and Staupitz: An Essay in the Intellectual Origins of the Protestant
      Reformation.
E. G. Schwiebert, Luther and His Times.
P. Smith, Life and Letters of Martin Luther.
H. Holborn, Ulrich von Hutten and the German Reformation.
C. L. Manschreck, Melanchthon: The Quiet Reformer.
K. Brandi, The Emperor Charles V.
O. von Hapsburg, Charles V.
Luther and the Dawn of the Modern Era, ed. H. A. Obermann.
W. R. Hitchcock, The Background of the Knights' Revolt, 1522-1523.
H. Schilling, "The Reformation in the Hanseatic Cities," Sixteenth Century Journal, 14 (Winter
      1983), 443-56.

FINAL EXAMINATION: Monday, 14 December, 12:00 - 2:00.

THE VIKING AGE

9/5 **Introduction**

9/10–9/12 **Historical Sketch and Introduction to Source Problems**

Jones, *A History of the Vikings*, 1–140
Sawyer, *Kings and Vikings*, 1–38

9/17–9/19 **Mythological Early History**

Saxo Grammaticus, *History of the Danes*, 1–64, 83–101, 113–158.
Snorri Sturlusson, *Heimskringla*, Introduction and *Ynglinga Saga*.

9/24–9/26 **Religion**

Snorri Sturlusson, *Prose Edda*.
Poems of the Vikings, tr. Terry, 3–48, 53–68, 75–92, 166–173,
249–254.

10/1–10/3 **Expansion of Settlement: Iceland and West**

Jones, 269–311
Landnámabók, tr. Palsson and Edwards, 15–80.
Ari Þorgilsson, *Islendingabók*, tr. Hermansson, 59–72.

10/8–10/10 **Vikings in Western Europe, I: Trading and Raiding**

Sawyer, 65–97
Jones, 145–203
Egil's Saga, tr. Palsson and Edwards.

10/15–10/17 **Vikings in Western Europe, II: Settlement**

Sawyer, 98–112
Jones, 204–240, 421–424.
F.M. Stenton, *A Preparatory to Anglo–Saxon England*, ed. D.M.
    Stenton, 136–165, 198–313, 335–345.
R.H.C. Davis, "East Anglia and the Danelaw," *Transactions of the
    Royal Historical Society* 5th ser. 5 (1955), 23–39.
D. Whitelock, "The Conversion of the Eastern Danelaw," *Saga–Book
    of the Viking Society* 12 (1945), 159–176.
P.H. Sawyer, "The Density of the Danish Settlement in England,"
    University of Birmingham Historical Journal 6 (1957–18), 1–17.
G. Fellows Jensen, "The Vikings in England: A Review,"
    Anglo–Saxon England 4 (1975), 181–206.

10/24   **Vikings in the East**

        Sawyer, 113–130
        Jones, 241–268
        Heimskringla: Saga of Harald Hardrada, ch. 1–16.
        N.J. Dejevsky, "The Varangians in Soviet Archaeology Today,"
            Medieval Scandinavia 10 (1977), 7–34.

10/29–10/31   **Kingship and the State**

        Heimskringla: sagas of Harald Fairhair and Olaf Tryggvason
        The Earliest Norwegian Laws, tr. Lawrence Larson: look at *either* the
            Gulathing *or* the Frostathing laws.

11/5–11/7   **Viking Society, I: Legal Sources**

        Sawyer, 39–64
        Lund, "Viking Age Society in Denmark––Evidence and Theories", in
            Skyum–Nielsen and Lund, eds., *Danish Medieval History: New
            Currents*, 22–35.
        Laws of Early Iceland: Gragas

11/12–11/14   **Viking Society, II: Archeological Evidence**

        Randsborg, *The Viking Age in Denmark*
        C.J. Becker et al., "Viking–age Settlements in Western and Central
            Jutland," *Acta Archaeologica* 50 (1979), 89 ff.

11/19–11/21   **Viking Society, III: Literary Sources**

        Njal's Saga, tr. Magnusson and Palsson.
        Rigspula, in *The Poetic Edda*, tr. Hollander.

11/26–12/3   **Conversion and the Integration into Europe**

        Jones, 315–415
        Sawyer, 131–147
        D.M. Wilson, "The Vikings' Relationship with Christianity in Northern
            England," *Journal of the British Archaeological Association*, 3rd
            ser. 30 (1967), 37–46.
        A.E. Christensen, "Denmark between the Viking Age and the Time of
            the Valdemars," *Medieval Scandinavia* 1 (1968), 28–50.

12/5   **In Summary: Uses and Abuses of the Viking Age**

Spain in the Middle Ages
Professor Paul Freedman
Vanderbilt University

1.   Spain in Image and Reality

2.   Geography and Culture of Spanish Regions
     V. S. Pritchett, Spanish Temper (1976), 37-69
     140-152,201-234,245-260.
     Michele Rodde, and Michele Affergan, Spain Observed,tr.
     Stephen Hardman, (N.Y., 1973), (look at pictures).
     Maps

3.   The Course of Medieval Spanish History
     Henry Kamen, Concise History of Spain, (N.Y.,1973), 15-63.

4.   Visigothic and Islamic Spain
     Gabriel Jackson, The Making of Medieval Spain, (1972),
     9-51.

5.   The Reconquista
     El Cid   (complete)

6.   Islamic Civilization
     W. Montgomery Watt, A History of Islamic Spain no. 4,
     Islamic Surveys (Edinburgh, 1965), (complete).

Vacation

7.   Christian Spain
     Jackson, 53-114.

8.   The Jews in Spain
     Y. Baer, The Jews in Christian Spain, introduction, Inner
     Life, Mysticism.
9.   The Late Middle Ages
     Jackson, 117-154.
        FIRST PAPER DUE

10. Everyday Life
     Scholberg, 74-176.
11. Problems in Spanish History
     tba

Subsequent meetings will include presentations of some of your
research. The second paper will be due April 20.

SPAIN IN THE MIDDLE AGES

History 115, Prof. Freedman

Research and Style Handbooks

The Elements of Style. By W. Strunk and E.P. White. (Ref. PE1408.S772 1979)
Historian's Handbook: A Key to the Study and Writing of History. By Wood Gray et. al.
  (Ref. D13.G78 1964)
How to Study History. By Norman Cantor and Richard I. Schreider. (D16.2.C32)
Student's Guide for Writing College Papers. By Kate L. Turabian. (Ref. LB2309.T82 1976)

Atlases, Chronologies, Biographies

The Atlas of Medieval Man. (Ref. CB351.P55 1980)
Cambridge Medieval History. See maps. (Ref. D117.C3)
Chronology of the Medieval World, 800-1491. By R.L. Storey. (Ref. D118.S855 1973b)
The Timetable of History: A Horizontal Linkage of People & Events. By Bernard Grun.
  (Ref. D11.G78)
Who's Who in the Middle Ages. By John Fines. (Ref. D115.F5 1970)

Encyclopedias

Encyclopedia of Islam. (Div. Ref. DS37.E523)
Encyclopedia Judaica. (Div. Ref. DS102.8.E496 v.1-1b)
New Catholic Encyclopedia. Edited by William J. McDonald. (Div. Ref. BX841.N44 1967)

Bibliographies, Indexes and Abstracts, Guides

Bibliographical Essays on Medieval Jewish Studies. (Div. Ref. Z6368.B53)
British Humanities Index. (Ref. AI3.B7 Index Stand 2)
C.R.I.S.: The Combined Retrospective Index Set to Journals in History, 1838-1974.
  (Ref. Z6205.C18 Index Stand 3)
Humanities Index. (Ref. AI3.H85 Index Stand 2)
Index of Articles on Jewish Medieval Studies. (Div. Ref. Z6366.J6)
An Index of Medieval Studies Published in Festschriften, 1865-1946. By Harry F.
  Williams. (Ref. Z6203.W5)
Index to Jewish Periodicals. (Div. Ref. Z6367.I38)
International Bibliography of Historical Sciences. (Ref. Z6205.I61)
  A selected list of historical publications, articles, and books. Section on
  Middle Ages (Historia de la edad media)--sub headings indicated at the beginning of
  the section, e.g. Judios. References are to citation numbers.
International Medieval Bibliography. (Ref. Z6203.I583)

Histories

The Agrarian Life of the Middle Ages. (HC240.C312 v.1)
Cambridge Economic History of Europe. Vols 1-3. (HC240.C3)
The Cambridge History of Islam. (Div. Ref. DS35.6.C3 v.1-2)
The Cambridge Medieval History. (Ref. D117.C3 also Div. Ref. D117.C32 v.1-8)
A History of Medieval Spain. By Joseph F. O'Callaghan. (DP96.025)
A History of the Jews in Christian Spain. By Y. Baer. (Div. Judaica DS135.S7B343)
Jewish Medieval and Renaissance Studies. (Div. Judaica BM180.J59)
The Jews in Spain: Their Social, Political and Cultural Life. (Div. Judaica
  DS135.S7N4 v.1-2)
Spain in the Middle Ages. By Agnus MacKay. (DP99.M23 1977)
The Making of Medieval Spain. By Gabriel Jackson. (DP.J32 1972b)

Some Subject Headings in Card Catalog

Church History--Middle Age 600-1500
Church History--Spain
Inquisition--Spain
Islamic Empire--Civilization
Islamic Empire--History
Jews--History--70-1789
Judaism--History--Medieval and Early Modern Period, 425-1789
Portugal--History--to 1385
Spain--History--Arab Period, 711-1492

Please ask the Reference Librarians for help in finding and using these and other
sources of information in the library.

History 115
Spring, 1981   Some Possible Topics for the First
                             Research Paper

Visigothic institutions   *Thompson, The Goths in Spain

Arab-Christian Cultural Interaction   Anwar Chejne in Islam in
               the Medieval West DS 36.855I76

                      *Watt, Influences of Islam in Medieval
Europe DS 36.85 I8, no. 9
                  Millás Vallicrosa, "Arab and Hebrew
Contributions...," Journal of World History 6 (1961),
732-751 (on microfilm)
               Amerigo Castro, The Structure of Spanish History
               Glick & Sunyer, article in Comparative Studies in
Society & History 11 (1969), 136-154.

Almoravids and Almohads   R. Le Tourneau, The Almohad Movement in
                      North Africa
                      Norris, article in Journal of African
                      History DT 199L4 vol. 12 (1971), 255-268

The Arabs under Christian Rule   John Boswell, The King's Treasure
                  Robert I. Burns, Medieval Colonialism
                  Robert I. Burns, Islam under the Crusaders

Arab Poetry   Nicholson, A Literary History of the Arabs 892.709
                                          N62L1930
          Arberry, Arabic Poetry 892.71008 A66a
          Nykl, Hispano-Arab Poetry 892.710N99h
          Gibb, Arabic Literature 892.709 G43ar1963

The Philosophy of Maimonides, or of Ibn Paqudah

Jewish Poetry: Zinberg, A History of Jewish Literature, vol. 1
                      PJ5008 Z5313
            Ibn Gabirol, Judah Halevi, poems in translation
      *A Jewish Prince in Moslem Spain PJ5050S3A28

Jewish Medicine *Joseph ben Meir Zabara, The Book of Delight

Anti-Semitism Wolff, article in Past & Present 50 (1971), 4-18
               McKay in Past & Present 55 (1972)
               Kamen, The Inquisition (in Divinity Library)

The Origins of Portugal

Military and Social Organization of the Reconquest
           *Lomax, The Reconquest
         (R)McKay, Spain in the Middle Ages

Catalan Expansion   J. Lee Schneidman, Rise of the Aragonese-Catalan
         Empire

Formation of Asturias ↝Lomax, The Reconquest
                O'Callaghan, A History of Medieval Spain

Paul Freedman
History 115
Spring 1981   Second Paper Topic Possibilities

The Jewish <u>Converso</u> and <u>Marrano</u> population and the Spanish
Inquisition.

The Inquisition as a political institution

The expulsion of the Jews (1492)

The seaborne empire of Aragon-Catalonia (conquests of Sardinia,
Sicily, Naples, Athens. . .)

Castilian enterprise before the discovery of America

Arabs under Christian rule (Mudejars)

The powers of the military orders of knights

The conquest and consolidation of Valencia

Romanesque (or Gothic) art and architecture in Spain

The "problem" of Spain (reasons for its differences from
Northern Europe)

The civil wars of the 14th and fifteenth centuries, causes
and results.

Origins of Spanish anti-Semitism and/or anti-Moorish sentiment.

Islamic-Christian Interaction and Exchanges of Technology

                              BIBLIOGRAPHY

Dillard, Heath. "Women in Reconquest Castile: The Fueros of Sepulveda
    and Cuenca." Susan Mosher Stuard. Women in Medieval Society.
    Philadelphia, 1976, 71-94.
Ebbitt, Wilma R. and David R. Ebbitt. Index to English. 7th ed.
    Glenview: Scott Foresman, 1982.
Hillgarth, J.N. "Review of O'Callaghan, History of Medieval Spain,
    Speculum, 52 (July, 1977): 722-26.
Lourie, Elena. "A Society Organized for War: Medieval Spain." Past and
    Present. 35 (December, 1966): 54-76.
O'Callaghan, Joseph F. History of Medieval Spain. Ithaca, 1975.
Powers, James F. "Frontier Municipal Baths and Social Interaction in
    Thirteenth-Century Spain." American Historical Review, 84 (June,   1979):
    649-67.
Shepherd, William R. Historical Atlas. N. Y.: Hammond Co., 1956.
    D12.S5
_____. Westermanns Atlas zur Weltgeschichte. Berlin:
    George Westermann, 1956. G1030.W5

                     SYLLABUS AND READINGS SCHEDULE

1.   Introduction - September 3.

2.   Hispania in Antiquity - September 7, 8, 10.
     O'Callaghan, 11-33. Hillgarth, all.

3.   Barbarian Invasions and Visigothic Hegemony - September 14, 15, 17.
     O'Callaghan, 37-88.

4.   Islamic Invasion & the Rise of the Caliphate - Sept. 21, 22, 24, 28.
     O'Callaghan, 91-162.

5.   Formation of Christian Iberian States, 711-1035 -
     September 29, October 1, 5, 6.
     O'Callaghan, 163-92.

HOUR EXAMINATION 1 -- 8 OCTOBER 1987 -- UNITS 1 - 5

6.   Imperial Hopes and Political Diversity, 1035-1157 -
     October 15, 19, 20, 22.
     O'Callaghan, 193-233.

7.   The Peninsula in the Balance, 1157-1212 - October 26, 27, 29.
     O'Callaghan, 234-330.   Lourie, 54-76.

8.   Reconquest Triumphs and Crises of Consolidation -
     November 2, 3, 5, 9, 10.
     O'Callaghan, 333-406.   Powers, 649-67.   Dillard, 71-94.

9.   14th-Century Reaction, Turbulence & Civil War - Nov. 12, 16, 17.
     O'Callaghan, 407-27.

HOUR EXAMINATION 2 -- 19 NOVEMBER 1987 -- UNITS 6 - 9

---

10. Social, Economic & Religious Institutions - Nov. 23, 24, 30.
     O'Callaghan, 428-520.

11. Emergence of the Trastamaras & the Coming of Peninsular Unity -
     December 1, 3, 7, 8.
     O'Callaghan, 521-676.

FINAL EXAMINATION -- DECEMBER 1987 -- UNITS 1 - 11

Dr. James F. Powers
O'Kane 385
OFFICE HOURS: Monday: 3:15 - 4:45 p. m.
                    Tuesday: 3:15 - 4:45 p. m.
                   Thursday: 3:15 - 4:45 p. m.

If these times are not mutually convenient, we can work out a better time
after class.

The percentage weight of the various elements in the course for determining the final grade are as follows:

Hour Examination 1	17%
Hour Examination 2	17%
Map Quizzes 1 & 2	10%
Term Paper	22%
Final Examination	34%
	100%

ATTENDANCE POLICY

1. Attendance is expected and encouraged at all lectures and discussions in order to achieve an optimum grade and the full benefit of the course.

2. Attendance is demanded by the student for all announced hour examinations and short quizzes. Students who have an unexcused absence from such an examination will not be permitted to take a make-up examination or quiz. Oversleeping will not be considered a valid excuse. Any such excuse must be cleared with your Class Dean.

3. Attendance for the remainder of the lectures and discussions is not demanded, and will not be a factor in the calculation of the final grade as such.

4. Students are, of course, responsible for the content of lectures and discussions given in class on the course examinations. Failure to attend a class presumes that the student has acquired this knowledge through other sources. You are also responsible for being aware of any announcements made by the instructor during a missed class.

LETTER GRADE NUMERICAL SCALE

A	=	100	−	92
A−	=	91.9	−	90
B+	=	89.9	−	87
B	=	86.9	−	83
B−	=	82.9	−	80
C+	=	79.9	−	77
C	=	76.9	−	73
C−	=	72.9	−	70
D+	=	69.9	−	65
D	=	64.9	−	60
F	=	59.9	−	00

Haverford College

Economic and Social History of the High Middle Ages

WF 12:30-2:00   History 219a
Hall 6   Fall, 1987
                                                           Susan Stuard

Books available at the bookstore:
David Herlihy, Medieval Households
Barbara Hanawalt, Women and Work in Pre-industrial Europe
Robert Lopez and Irving Raymond, Medieval Trade in the Mediterranean World
(if it is still in print)
Lynn White, Jr. Medieval Technology and Social Change
(again, if we can get some copies)

    L.S. Stavrianos, a world historian, comparing the late, swift rise of
the West to the earlier rise of other civilizations said, "The root of
[the] fateful difference is to be found in the unique characteristics of
the new civilization - pluralistic, adaptable, and free of the shackles of
tradition."* We shall examine those "unique" characteristics and examine
alternate plausible explanations for their presence in Europe from the 10th
through the 14th centuries. Both the "macro" and the "micro" questions of
development as well as economic and social aspects of the question will be
addressed. Weekly topics will be addressed. Productive debates in the
field will be examined.

    There will be one research paper in the course and two critiques of
assigned articles or chapters. A mid-term quiz may be added if needed.
Please note the reading for October 12 and 14 in the Cambridge Economic
History. These two articles by Postan and Lopez go on for over two hundred
pages. Start this reading by the second week of the course to make sure
you have it ready when that week rolls around.
* L.S. Stavrianos, The World to 1500, 2nd. ed., (Englewood Cliffs, New
Jersey: Prentice Hall, 1975) p. 324.

Weekly Topics and Reading

Wed. Sept. 2 and Fri. Sept. 4 - Posing the question

    Jacques LeGoff, "Confrontation of Clerical and Folk Culture" xerox on

reserve.

    Lynn White, Jr. "Technology Assessment," Medieval Religion and

Technology (Berkeley, 1978) pp. 261-276, on reserve.

    M. Hechter's review of Emmanuel Wallerstein, World Capitalist System

    on reserve.

Jane Schneider, "Was there a Pre-capitalist World System?" Peasant Studies 6 (1977) 20-29, . on reserve.

Wed. Sept. 9 and Fri. Sept. 11 - Economies - Agriculture

Marc Bloch, "The Rise of Dependent Cultivation" and Nellie Neilson, "England" in Cambridge Economic History of Europe, I, ed. M.M. Postan (Cambridge, 1941) pp. 224-277 and 438-466.

Lynn White, Jr. Medieval Technology, chapter 2, pp. 39-78.

Wed. Sept. 16 and Fri. Sept. 18 - Economies - Agriculture

Douglass North and Robert Thomas, "An Economic Theory of the Growth of the Western World" Economic History Review 23 (1970) 1-17, . on reserve.

Ben Thorir, an Icelandic saga, .. on reserve.

Wed. Sept. 23 and Fri. Sept. 25 - Climate

G. Utterstrom, "Climate Fluctuations" Scandanavian Historical Review, . on reserve

J. Anderson and E. Jones, "Natural Disasters and Historical Response" LaTrobe University, Melbourne, Australia, Economics Discussion Papers, on reserve.

Wed. Sept. 30 and Fri. Oct. 2 - Power and Technology

Lynn White, Jr. Medieval Technology, chapter 3, pp. 79-134.

Bert Hansen, "The Complementarity of Science and Magic," American Scientist 74:2 (March-April) 1986, 128-136, . on reserve.

Wed. Oct. 7 and Fri. Oct. 9 - Inventions

Lynn White, Jr. "The Legacy of the Middle Ages in the American Wild West," in Medieval Religion and Technology, pp. 105-147, xerox on reserve

Marc Bloch, "The Watermill" and "Medieval Inventions" in Land and Work in Medieval Europe (New York, 1967) pp. 136-185. On reserve.

Wed. Oct 12 and Fri. Oct. 14 - Trade, South and North

M.M. Postan, "Origins of Trade in the North" and Robert Lopez, "Origins of Trade in the South," in the Cambridge Economic History of Europe II, ed. M.M. Postan, (Cambridge, 1952) pp. 119-354.

Robert Lopez and Irving Raymond, Medieval Trade in the Mediterranean World, Introduction and Part I, pp. 3-50.

Wed. Oct. 21 and Fri. Oct. 23 - Money and Banking

Lopez and Raymond, Medieval Trade, Parts 3 and 5, pp. 157-238 and 341-426.

Carlo Cipolla, Money and Banking in Fourteenth Century Florence (Cambridge, 1982) pp. 1-98, on reserve.

or

Frederic Lane, Venice and History (Baltimore, 1966) "Business and Finance", pp. 36-141. On reserve.

Wed. Oct. 28 and Fri. Oct. 30 - Economic Crisis of the Fourteenth Century

Lopez and Raymond, Medieval Trade, Part 4, --. 239-340.

Robert Lopez, "Hard Times and Investment in Culture," xerox on reserve.

Richard Goldthwaite, "The Renaissance Economy," xerox on reserve.

Wed. Nov. 4 and Fri. Nov. 6 - Societies

David Herlihy, Medieval Households, p. 1-78

Marc Bloch, Feudal Society, (New York, 1963) Volume one, Parts 3 and 4, pp. 123-279. On reserve.

Wed. Nov. 11 and Fri. Nov. 13 - Towns

Lopez and Raymond, Medieval Trade,, Part 2, pp. 51-155.

Barbara Hanawalt, Women and Work in Pre-industrial Europe,, essays by Davis and Howell, pp. 167-222.

Wed. Nov. 18 and Fri. Nov. 20 - Households

David Herlihy, _Medieval Households_, pp. 79-159

Barbara Hanawalt, _Women and Work in Pre-industrial Europe,_, essays by
Bennett, Hanawalt, Otis and Wiesner, pp. 31-114.

Wed. Nov. 25 - Division of Labor

Barbara Hanawalt, _Women and Work in Pre-industrial Europe_, essays by
Stuard and Klapisch-Zuber, pp. 1-30

Wed. Dec. 2 and Fri. Dec. 4 - Conclusion

The fourteenth century in Europe was a time of tremendous crisis, ferment, and change. The bubonic plague cut the population by at least a quarter, and left the survivors to make their way in a different world. Warfare scarred the land and the people, lasting so long that outbreaks could earn the name Hundred Years' War. Such upheavals naturally affected the way men and women viewed their lives and especially their relations with God. The fourteenth century saw great activity in religion and heresy, and in particular saw a larger role played by women in contemplative devotion.

INTRODUCTION--THE FACE OF EUROPE (20 Jan. to 3 Feb.):
During the first weeks of class, we will provide ourselves with basic know-ledge of the political, social, and economic structures across Europe in the fourteenth century--namely, who is ruling when and where, how society is organized, what the economy is like.
Denys Hay, Europe in the Fourteenth and Fifteenth Centuries
Robert E. Lerner, The Age of Adversity
Joseph R. Strayer, "The Promise of the Fourteenth Century," Proceedings of
   the American Philosophical Society 105 (1961), 609-611.
J. R. Hale, et al., eds., Europe in the Late Middle Ages
Daniel Waley, Later Medieval Europe 2nd ed.
Barbara Hanawalt, The Ties that Bound, introduction, ch.3,6,9, epilogue.
Judith Bennett Women in the Medieval English Countryside, ch.7.

DISEASE (10-24 February):
The Black Death brought death, hardship, and terror to most of Europe. We shall be looking at the nature of this disease, the kinds of effects it had on the European population, and how contemporaries expressed their views of it in original sources. We shall also be examining the important changes such mortality inspired in society, the economy, medicine and education. Assign-ments will be made from among the following:
Robert S. Gottfried, The Black Death
The Sources of the Black Death, including readings such as Boccaccio's
   Decameron, Guy de Chauliac's Great Surgery, Henry Knighton's
   Chronicle, and the Strassburg Chronicle. (4 copies on Dinand
   reserve)
John Hatcher, Plague, Population and the English Economy
Graham Twigg, The Black Death: A Biological Reappraisal
Daniel Williman, ed., The Black Death: The Impact of the Fourteenth-
   Century Plague
Zvi Razi, Life, Marriage and Death in a Medieval Parish, ch.2.
William J. Courteney, "The Effect of the Black Death on English Higher
   Education," Speculum 55 (1980), 696-714.
H. S. Lucas, "The Great European Famine of 1315, 1316, 1317,"
   Speculum 5 (1930), 343-77.
Ian Kershaw, "The Great Famine and Agrarian Crisis in England 1315-1322,"
   Past and Present 59 (1973), 3-50.
William McNeill, Plagues and Peoples
Anna Campbell, Black Death and Men of Learning
Glending Olson, Literature as Recreation, ch.5.

Philip Ziegler, The Black Death, ch.9,13.
David Herlihy and Christine Klapisch-Zuber, Tuscans and Their Families
   pages 60-72 (xerox).
"Hunger and History" issue of Journal of Interdisciplinary History,
   volume 14 (autumn 1983), articles by Carmichael, Livi-Bacci, Boserup.
Robert Brenner, "Agrarian Class Structure and Economic Development,"
   Past and Present 70 (1976), 30-75.
T. H. Aston and C. H. E. Philpin, The Brenner Debate

WAR, CRIME, AND VIOLENCE (9-30 March):
The Hundred Years' War, involving (chiefly) England and France, was a major
expression of violence and upheaval in this century. We shall examine how
one writer, Jean Froissart, described his society at war, and study how the
war affected society and economy in general. We will also look at crime and
violence in fourteenth-century society, noting how and why such feelings
were expressed, and how society handled deviant behavior. Some of the
following articles and books will be our guides:
Jean Froissart, The Chronicles
J. J. N. Palmer, Froissart: Historian
Edouard Perroy, The Hundred Years War
George Cuttino, "Historical Revision of the Causes of the Hundred Years'
   War," Speculum 31 (1956), 463-77.
M. M. Postan, "Some Social Consequences of the Hundred Years' War,"
   Economic History Review, series 1, 12 (1942), 1-12.
M. M. Postan, "Costs of the Hundred Years' War," Past and Present
   27 (1964), 34-53.
Cambridge Medieval History vol. 7, pp. 340-92: A. Couville, "France:
   The Hundred Years' War"
Michael Howard, War in European History
John Barnie, War in Medieval English Society
C. T. Allmand, Society at War
John Keegan, The Face of Battle, "Agincourt"
Maurice Keen, Chivalry, ch.1.
Maurice Keen, The Laws of War in the Late Middle Ages
C. D. Crowder, "Peace and Justice Around 1400," Aspects of Late
   Medieval Government and Society ed. J. G. Rowe.
Charles Oman, The History of the Art of War in the Middle Ages
Kenneth Fowler, The Age of Plantagenet and Valois
K. Fowler, "War and Change," The Hundred Years' War
Denys Hay, "The division of the spoils of war in the 14th century
   England," Transactions of the Royal Historical Society, 5th series,
   4 (1954), 91-109.
Philippe Contamine, War in the Middle Ages
Rodney Hilton, Bondmen Made Free
R. H. Hilton, The English Rising of 1381
R. B. Dobson, ed., The Peasants' Revolt of 1381
M. Mollat and P. Wolff, The Popular Revolutions of the Late Middle
   Ages
Guy Fourquin, The Anatomy of Popular Rebellion in the Middle Ages
David Herlihy, "Alienation in Medieval Culture and Society," The
   Social History of Italy and Western Europe, 700-1500
Barbara Hanawalt, Crime and Conflict in English Communities 1300-1348

Barbara Hanawalt, "The Female Felon in 14th-century England," in Susan
    Stuard, ed., Women in Medieval Society
E. L. G. Stones, "The Folvilles of Ashby-Folville, Leicestershire, and
    their Associates in Crime," Transactions of the Royal Historical
    Society, 5th series, 7 (1957), 117-36.
J. G. Bellamy, "The Coterel Gang: An Anatomy of a Band of 14th-century
    Criminals," English Historical Review 74 (1964), 698-717.
Eleanor Searle and R. Burghart, "The Defense of England and the Peasants'
    Revolt," Viator 3 (1972).
Barbara Hanawalt, "Fur Collar Crime: The Pattern of Crime Among the
    Fourteenth-Century English Nobility," Journal of Social History
    8 (1975).

RELIGION, HERESY AND WITCHCRAFT (6-20 April):
By the fourteenth century, the Church was beginning to realize that it was
no longer reaching and inspiring all the Christian population through its
institutions. Many people, especially women, chose to find their own methods
by which to be close to God. Some abandoned Church institutions totally,
frightening the Church with threats of heresy. Accusations of witchcraft
were not unknown. In general, it was the women of the fourteenth century who
found the most imaginative ways to know God. Some of this behavior looks
strange to us, and some writers have compared it to deviant behavior such as
anorexia nervosa. We shall have to judge for ourselves as we read both
primary sources and some controversial modern studies of medieval religion,
to be chosen from the list below:
Julian of Norwich, Revelations of Divine Love
Evelyn Underhill, Mysticism
Elmer O'Brien, Varieties of Mystic Experience: An anthology and inter-
    pretation of the key writing of the major mystics
Ernest W. McDonnell, The Beguines and Beghards in Medieval Culture
Caroline Bynum, "Women Mystics and Eucharistic Devotion in the 13th
    century," Women's Studies 11 (1984), 179-214.
Caroline Bynum, Holy Feast and Holy Fast
Rudolph M. Bell, Holy Anorexia
Richard Kieckhefer, Unquiet Souls: Fourteenth-Century Saints and their
    Religious Milieu
Brenda Bolton, "Mulieres Sanctae," in Susan Stuard, ed., Women in
    Medieval Society
Elizabeth Clark and H. Richardson, ed., Women and Religion: A Feminist
    Sourcebook of Christian Thought
Jeffrey Burton Russell, ed., Religious Dissent in the Middle Ages
Jeffrey B. Russell, "Interpretations of the Origins of Medieval Heresy,"
    Mediaeval Studies 25 (1963), 25-53.
Eleanor McLaughlin, "The Heresy of the Free Spirit and Late Medieval
    Mysticism," Medievalia et Humanistica new series, 4 (1973), 37-54.
Malcolm Lambert, Medieval Heresy
Derek Baker, ed., Schism, Heresy, and Religious Protest, Studies in
    Church History 9, esp. Michael Wilks, "Reformatio regni: Wyclif and
    Hus as leaders of religious protest movements," pp. 109-30.
Walter Wakefield and Austin Evans, Heresies of the High Middle Ages
K. B. McFarlane, John Wycliffe and Beginnings of English Non-Conformity
Gordon Leff, "John Wyclif: The Path to Dissent," Proceedings of
    the British Academy 52 (1966).

Walter L. Wakefield, "Some Unorthodox Popular Ideas of the Thirteenth
  Century," Medievalia and Humanistica new series, 4 (1973),
  25-35.
Margaret Aston, "Lollardy and Sedition 1381-1431," in R. H. Hilton, ed.,
  Peasants, Knights and Heretics
H. G. Richardson, "Heresy and Lay Power under Richard II," English Historical
  Review 51 (1936), 1-28.
K. B. McFarlane, "Education of the Nobility," Nobility of Later
  Medieval England

CONCLUDING WEEK (27 April):
During the final week, we should look at Huizinga's classic statement on the
later Middle Ages, and decide whether this was a time of death and decay, or a
tremendously exciting time of new beginnings.
J. Huizinga, The Waning of the Middle Ages
Joseph R. Strayer, "The Fourth and the Fourteenth Centuries," American
  Historical Review 77 (1972), 1-14.
Barbara Tuchman, A Distant Mirror: The Calamitous 14th Century

CLASS FORMAT:
Discussion and debate of the readings. It is likely that each week, the
entire class will have one book (or part of it) or several articles as common
reading, and that in addition we shall hear individual reports on assigned
chapters or other articles, all of which we will attempt to put into good
order and make sense of.

WRITING ASSIGNMENTS:
There will be one short paper (7-8 pages) due on or before Monday 29 February.
This paper will examine two of the primary sources cited in The Sources of
the Black Death, and show how they illuminate some aspect of the Black Death
as mentioned at greater length in secondary sources such as Gottfried's text
or Ziegler's book. For example, are the secondary sources' conclusions about
persecution of the Jews supported by the documentary evidence found in Source
Number 9?
In addition, a major research of approximately 12-15 pages will be expected
by the end of term. It will be due no later than Wednesday 4 May 1988. By
23 March, I will expect you to submit in writing your choice of a paper
topic and a preliminary bibliography; you should consult with me first before
doing this. Depending on our progress with the syllabus, I would like to
spend one class meeting, probably 13 April, discussing the progress you are
making on your papers and the questions you are or should be raising in them.
This will be a chance to share our research and broaden our inquiries before
final versions are written and graded. This means that you cannot let the
research and planning of your paper slide until the last minute. Presentation
of your topic, the kinds of sources you are using, and the kinds of questions
you are dealing with will become part of the course even though the final
version is not due until classes have ended.

COMPOSITION OF GRADES:
Short paper, 20%. Discussion and class participation, 40%. Research paper,
40%.

James Given
University of California,
Irvine

HISTORY 1176

SOCIAL CONFLICT IN MEDIEVAL EUROPE

Feb. 4: Introduction

Section I: Peasant Unrest

General Reading: *Georges Duby, Rural Economy and Country
Life in the Medieval West, 61-357
*Eric Wolf, Peasants, entire
Recommended for those with no knowledge of medieval history:
R.S. Hoyt and S. Chodorow, Europe in the Middle
Ages (3rd ed.), 181-650

Feb. 11: International Encyclopedia of the Social Sciences
(1968), s.v. Conflict, Vol. 3, pp. 226-241
A.R. Beals and B.J. Siegel, Divisiveness and
Social Conflict, 1-27
*E. Hobsbawm, Primitive Rebels, chs. 1-7
E. Terray, "Class and Class Conflict in the Abron
Kingdom of Gyaman," in Marxist Analyses and
Social Anthropology, ed. by Maurice Bloch,
85-133

Feb. 18: *R.H. Hilton, Bond Men Made Free, entire
R.B. Dobson, The Peasants' Revolt, 1-44

Feb. 25: Mich el Mollat and Philippe Wolff, Popular
Revolutions of the Late Middle Ages, entire

Mar. 4: Guy Fourquin, The Anatomy of Popular Rebellion
in the Middle Ages, entire

Mar. 11: *Norman Cohn, The Pursuit of the Millenium
(rev. ed.), 9-234, 281-286

Mar. 18: *Eric Wolf, Peasant Wars of the Twentieth Century,
Preface, Chs. 1-3, Conclusion

Section II: Heresy

General Reading: Malcolm Lambert, Medieval Heresy, 3-94,
151-216, 335-339
Recommended: R.W. Southern, Western Society and the Church
in the Middle Ages

Apr. 1: *R.I. Moore, The Origins of European Dissent, entire

Section II: Heresy (cont.)

Apr. 8: W. Wakefield, <u>Heresy, Crusade and Inquisition</u>
<u>in Southern France</u>, entire
Lambert, 95-150

Apr. 15: K.B. McFarlane, <u>John Wycliffe and the Beginnings</u>
<u>of English Nonconformity</u>, entire
Lambert, 217-334

Apr. 22: A.P. Evans, "Social Aspects of Medieval Heresy,"
in <u>Persecution and Liberty: Essays in</u>
<u>Honor of George Lincoln Burr</u>, 93-116
J.B. Russell, "Interpretations of the Origins
of Medieval Heresy," <u>Medieval Studies</u>, 25
(1963), 25-53

Reading Period: *Norman Cohn, <u>Europe's Inner Demons</u>, entire

All titles have been placed on reserve in Lamont and Hilles,
except for the <u>International Encyclopedia of the Social Sciences</u>,
which is in the Widener Reference Room. Copies of many of the
assigned works may also be found in the History Department
Library in Robinson Hall. Those works marked with an asterisk (*)
have been ordered for the Coop.

Three papers, each 8-15 pages in length and each worth
one-third of the final grade, are required. There will be
no final examination. The topics for the three essays are as
follows:

Essay #1: Due April 1. Discuss what you believe to be
the principal causes of the major peasant uprisings of the
late middle ages.

Essay #2: Due April 29. Discuss whether or not heresy
can be considered as a form of social protest or resistance
in the middle ages.

Essay #3: Due May 12. Discuss whether or not Europe
in the period of the late twelfth through the early fifteenth
centuries had certain characteristic patterns of social conflict. Is it possible to speak of a specifically medieval
pattern of social conflict?

BARBARA A. HANAWALT, DEPARTMENT OF HISTORY, UNIVERSITY OF MINNESOTA

B350 Knights, Peasants, and Bandits:
A Social History of Medieval England

Spring 1987   B. A. Hanawalt
Sec. no. 2798   Office: BH724
WH 101 TR 2:30-3:45   5-6934 or leave a
                                                                     message at 5-7581
                                                                     Office Hours:
                                                                     W 1:30-3:30 and
                                                                     by appointment

BOOKS AND READINGS

    Joseph and Frances Gies, Life in a Medieval Castle (Harper & Row:
        New York, 1974).
    Barbara Hanawalt, The Ties That Bound: Peasant Families in Medieval
        England (Oxford, 1986). N.B. Royalities from the sale of this book
        for this class will be contributed to the I.U. Foundation to benefit
        the library.
    George Holmes, The Later Middle Ages, 1272-1485.

COURSE DESCRIPTION

    The course emphasizes social history. It explores the ways that ordinary
people and some not so ordinary people coped with the major historical events
that occurred in England from the Norman Conquest to the Tudor dynasty. We
will look at what happened to the Anglo-Saxon population during and after the
Conquest, the life of the serf and free peasants and how this changed over the
centuries, the growth of towns and the bourgeoisie, and the rewards and
problems of being a member of the nobility. In trying to keep up with
historical change, all classes of society resorted to manipulation of the
economy and the law. They also were not slow to use brute force and crime to
achieve their ends. They formed mutual aid societies and relied heavily on
family and neighbors as well. The course is a practical guide on how to
survive the middle ages.

    Some warnings: There is not a comprehensive textbook for this course.
The lecture materials are, for the most part, taken from modern research on the
social history of medieval England. You will have to attend lectures to get
the information that will be on the examinations. You might want to do some
additional reading to keep up with the course. I will be happy to help out
with recommendations.

COURSE REQUIREMENTS

    You must take two midterms and the final examination. In addition an
optional midterm will be offered. The grades on that midterm (if it is higher
than a grade on another midterm) may be substituted for the lower grade. You
may not substitute it for the final examination. You must take the final
examination or receive an incomplete for the course.

The tests are essay examinations. There is a choice between two essays for the first part of the examination. This counts for 2/3 of your grade. The second part of the examination is identifications that count for 1/3 of your grade. You will be able to select three out of six to answer on the identifications.

The major points of the lectures are entered under each topic on the syllabus. In addition you will be given a time line and a brief lecture outline for each class. Experience has shown that you should use these as a guide for studying for the examinations and for taking notes.

COURSE ASSISTANTS

  Katherine Workman
  Shan Harward

SCHEDULE OF LECTURES AND EXAMINATIONS

Jan. 20   Introduction: Discussion of class objectives, requirements, and
          perceptions of the Middle Ages

          I: THE COMPONENT PARTS OF ENGLISH SOCIETY

Jan. 22   ANGLO-SAXON ENGLAND

          Readings: "The Wanderer", "Riddle", "The Wife's Lament"

          Performance Objectives: Note the ties that bound the society
          together. In particular the relationship of the warrior to the lord
          and the wife to the husband.

          Performance Objectives: Lecture
          Understand the social class structure of Anglo-Saxon society. Learn
          the geographical divisions of administration. How did the central
          government function? What role did the people have in government?
          The legal system will be of major importance because we will be
          studying this all semester.

Jan. 27   CONQUESTS OF ENGLAND

          Readings: Florence of Worcester's account of the Conquest, Harald
          Hardrada's Saga, Jumierge's account of the conquest.

          Performance Objectives: Reading
          There were three rivals for the throne in 1066 (Harald of Norway,
          Harold Godwinson, and William the Bastard). You have the description
          of events from three sources that present the three different sides.
          Look for the bias in presentation of events.

          Performance Objectives: Lecture
          What was the basis of the three claims to the throne in 1066? Why
          did William finally win? Why was William still a vassel to the king
          of France even though he became king of England?

Jan. 29   THE ANGLO-SAXON SETTLEMENT

Reading: Gies and Gies, pp. 8-31

Performance Objectives: Reading
What role did castles play in medieval Europe and in the conquest?

Performance Objectives: Lecture
William and his followers were chiefly interested in exploiting
England for their own profit. To do so they had to subdue resistance
and organize efficient government and land use. They tried to keep
as much of the old institutions as they could, but they imposed
feudalism, manorialism, and laws that punished everyone in the
community if a Norman was found dead.

II. KNIGHTS KINGS, SAINTS, SINNERS: 12th AND 13th CENTURIES

Feb. 3   EARLS, BARONS, and FEUDALISM

Reading: Gies and Gies, Life in a Medieval Castle, pp. 32-56

Performance Objective: Reading
What is feudalism and the agreement between the lord and his vassal?
Be able to describe the feudal contract.

Performance Objective: Lecture
This lecture requires concentration because it deals with the feudal
contract between a lord and his vassal. Feudalism forms the basis
for the government, law, and social relations in medieval England so
we will be referring back to this material frequently. You should
understand homage and fealty, fief, subinfeudation, and the terms of
the feudal contract.

Feb. 5   FEUDAL GOVERNMENT AND LAW

Reading: Holmes, ch. 4

Performance Objectives: Reading
You should know about the origins of law and the king's relationship
to it. You should also come to an understanding of how the royal
government worked at both the central administration and the local
level.

Performance Objectives: Lecture
We will be looking at the king's power and the extension of his power
under the Angevine monarchs. Important to get out of the lecture is
the organization of the household government, the use of circuit
justices in the countryside, and the importance of unpaid local
officials in running the country. You should also consider the role
of ordinary people in law enforcement.

Feb. 10   FUNCTIONS OF MEDIEVAL CASTLES

Readings: Gies and Gies, pp. 57-74, 95-108, 186-217

Performance Objectives: Reading
The castles were not simply residences for the nobility. What other
functions did the castle serve? How effective was the castle for
defense?

Performance Objectives: Lecture
Follow the lecture themes through slides. Castles under go profound
changes as the technology of castle building improves. Castles serve
a variety of functions for both the nobility and the monarchy. They
were administrative and legal centers as well as military structures.

Feb. 12   CHIVALRY AND ARISTOCRATIC WOMEN

Readings: Gies, pp. 75-108, 166-185

Performance Objective: Reading
What is the position of the aristocratic woman? What is courtly love
and what does it do for women? What is chivalry?

Performance Objective: Lecture
Note the difference between the romantic, fictional life of
aristocratic women and real life. How much control did women really
have over their lives?

Feb. 17   AMUSEMENTS OF THE NOBILITY

Readings: Gies and Gies, pp. 109-146, 206-217

Performance Objective: Readings
How did the nobility pass time when they were not governing or
fighting?

Performance Objective: Lecture
While we may consider games and play to be light-hearted ventures,
the stakes may be very high. William Marshal, for instance, made his
career on playing war games and conducting himself as a knight.
Politics could also be a game.

Feb. 19   FIRST MIDTERM EXAMINATION

Feb. 24   POLITICS OF KINGS AND BARONS

Reading: Review Holmes, ch. 4

Performance Objective: Lecture
Henry II introduced substantial judicial reforms that led to a
conflict with Archbishop Becket. Why was Henry so determined that
criminous clerks be tried in royal courts? Although Henry II had

imposed a more centrally controlled judicial system on the barons, they came to value it and when John tried to manipulate the system the barons revolted and insisted on a charter (Magna Carta) guaranteeing their rights and making the king subject to the law of the land.

Feb. 26   CRIME AND THE NOBILITY

Performance Objectives: Lecture
Provisions of the Magna Carta and what it accomplished. The judicial role of the nobility and their control of justice. Criminality among the nobility and their ability to elude punishment.

Mar. 3   CLERGY: SECULAR AND REGULAR

Reading: Holmes, ch. 3

Performance Objectives: Reading
What was the difference between the secular and regular clergy? What role did clergy play in politics and in everyday life?

Performance Objectives: Lecture
The lecture will discuss the importance of clergy and religion in everyday life and in the politics of England. The Church was largely an aristocratic institution. Even monasteries in which monks took a vow of poverty recruited from the aristocracy and knights. The Church was organized along hierarchical lines with the archbishop at the top. Archbishops and bishops added to their fame by building fine cathedrals. Those clergy who wanted to escape the world joined monastic orders.

III. PEASANTS AND THE ECONOMY

Mar. 5   MANORIALISM: LAND AND LABOR

Reading: Holmes, ch. 2

Performance Objectives: Reading
What was the physical layout of the manor? How was the land divided? How was the manor made economically profitable for the lord and for the peasant?

Performance Objectives: Lecture
Agriculture formed the basis of the economy of medieval Europe with about 90 percent of the population involved in agricultural production. We are starting a section that will look at the unit of production, the manor, and the agricultural practice and technology. You should be able to distinguish between manorialism and feudalism by this point. There are some technical points to learn in this lecture such as the division of the open fields, the types of work services that the peasant owed his lord, and other charges that the lord could extract from the peasantry.

Mar. 10   VILLAGES AND HOUSING

           Reading: Hanawalt, chs. 1-3

           Performance Objectives: Reading
           Note that there are different status groups within the peasant
           community. There is a primary, well to do group, a secondary group,
           and cottagers. Standards of living depended upon the amount of
           wealth that a person possessed. Note the comforts of life along with
           the discomforts. Also note the interactions with neighbors.

Mar. 12   HOUSEHOLD ECONOMY

           Reading: Hanawalt, chs. 7-10

           Performance Objectives: Reading
           In ch. 7 observe that the peasantry have certain expenditures in
           their budgets as well as certain resources. What supplemental
           activities could the peasantry undertake depending on their
           resources? Again note the different resources of the three status
           groups. Observe the division of labor by age and sex in the peasant
           economy.

Mar. 24   SECOND MIDTERM EXAMINATION

Mar. 26   PEASANT FAMILIES AND DEMOGRAPHIC TRENDS

           Reading: Hanawalt, chs. 4-6

           Performance Objectives: Reading
           There is an assumption in peasant families that all children will get
           some inheritance if it can be managed. Note the various ways that
           parents tried to meet these objectives. What was the family size for
           peasant households? How did they limit size if they did?

           Performance Objectives: Lecture
           The lecture will deal with inheritance, composition of households,
           and the general demographic trends in the population of England.

Mar. 31   STAGES OF LIFE

           Reading: Hanawalt, chs. 11-15

           Performance Objectives: Reading
           How important was age in medieval peasant society? What role did
           love play in choosing a marriage partner or in a marriage? Was
           divorce possible? What arrangements could one make for old age?

           Performance Objectives: Lecture
           Discussion on the stages of life among the peasantry and some of the
           difficulties that they faced.

Apr. 2 COOPERATION AND CONFLICT IN THE VILLAGES

Reading: Hanawalt, chs. 16-17

Performance Objectives: Reading
What institutions outside of the family provided for significant ties among peasants?

Performance Objectives: Lecture
Villages were small communities in which cooperation was necessary but conflict was bound to arise. The lecture will examine the institutions of conflict resolution such as courts and gilds. The lecture will also provide an overview of the patterns of crime in the villages.

Apr. 7 FEASTS, GAMES, AND RELIGION

Performance Objectives: Lecture
The lecture will deal with the various holidays that punctuated the year and also discuss the role of the parish church in the peasants' lives.

Apr. 9 ECONOMIC TRENDS AND URBAN DEVELOPMENT

Reading: Holmes, ch. 7

Performance Objectives: Reading
What conditions permitted the flourishing of towns and trade? How did town life differ from that of the country?

Performance Objectives: Lecture
The lecture will look at the conditions that made urban development possible and the attractions of urban life so popular among the peasantry. We will also discuss town planning, the problems of urban sanitation and policing, and the organization of trades.

Apr. 14 OPTIONAL MIDTERM EXAMINATION

IV. SOCIAL CHANGE OF THE LATER MIDDLE AGES

Apr. 16 THE HUNDRED YEARS' WAR AND THE PEASANT REVOLT

Reading: Holmes, chs. 6, 9, 10

Performance Objectives: Reading
This is a chance to establish the political outline of events in the later middle ages (14th and 15th centuries). Look at the causes of the war, the development of Parliament, and role of the Commons, nobility, and peasantry in government.

Performance Objectives: Lecture
We will discuss the increasing participation of the populace in governemnt including their role in taxation, recruitment of an army, and representative government. We will look at the events of the

Hundred Years' War and the relationship of the Peasant Revolt of 1381 to the war and to the new peasant prosperity of the 14th century.

Apr. 21   SOCIAL CONSEQUENCES OF THE HUNDRED YEARS' WAR

Reading: As for April 16

Performance Objectives: Reading
Look at the changes in government and society that are brought on by the Hundred Years' War.

Performance Objectives: Lecture
The lecture will analyze the effects of the war on the military, government, and society. The role of the nobility in warfare gave way to the importance of the foot soldier and mercenary armies. The autocratic authority of the king became further limited by the development of Parliament. Serfdom demised. The middle classes including gentry and a new professional class became more important in society augmenting the urban middle class as an important force in society.

Apr. 23   EDUCATION AND ITS REWARDS

Reading: Holmes, ch. 9 (review ch. 3)

Performance Objectives: Reading
Look at the way that universities are established and organized. Also look at the causes of heresy. How does the heretical view differ from the orthodox view.

Performance Objectives: Lecture
We will look at the elementary education in England; the establishment of Oxford and Cambridge; the curriculum; and the careers of graduates. We will also look at the intellectual excitement provided by heresies. The lecture will conclude with a discussion of the impact of printing and literacy.

Apr. 24   THE WAR OF THE ROSES AND UNREST IN THE LATE MIDDLE AGES

Reading: Holmes, ch. 11, 12

Performance Objectives: Reading
Do not become bogged down in the geneology of the royal family. Instead look at the causes for the war and the effects of the war on society in the fifteenth century?

Performance Objectives: Lecture
The lecture will cover the causes of the wars, the changes that they brought about, and the general unrest that resulted in the countryside.

Apr. 26   ROBIN HOOD AND OTHER SCOUNDRELS

May   7   7:15-9:15pm FINAL EXAMINATION, WH 101

History 596

Wyclif and the Lollards: A Case Study in the Origins of Dissent

W. R. Jones
Department of History
University of New Hampshire

(Students should use the following bibliographical citations
 as aids both for defining term paper topics and for the compilation of appropriate bibliographies.)

1. Both medieval and modern observers have remarked on the
    relative absence of heresy in pre-Wycliffite England and
    have adduced various explanations for this phenomenon:

    Makower, Felix. The Constitutional History and Constitution
       of the Church of England. London: 1895 (reprint 1960), p.
       183.
    Pollock, Sir Frederick, and Maitland, Frederic William. A
       History of English Law before the Time of Edward I. 2d.
       ed.; 2 vols.; Cambridge: reissue 1968, II, 544.
    Stubbs, William. Report of the Commissioners aapointed to
       inquire into the constitution and working of the ecclesi-
       astical courts .... London; 1883, "Historical Appendix (2),"
       I,52.
    Richardson, H. G. "Heresy and the Lay Power under Richard II,"
       English Historical Review, LI (1936), 1-28.
    Leff, Gordon. Heresy in the Later Middle Ages: the Relation
       of Hereterodoxy to Dissent ca. 1250-1450. 2 vols.; New York:
       1967, II, 33.
    Moore, R. I. The Origins of European Dissent. New York: 1977.
    Lambert, Malcolm. Medieval Heresy: Popular Movements from
       Bogomil to Hus. New York: 1977, p. 269, n. 164.
    Le Goff, Jacques. Hérésies et sociétés dans l'Europe pré-
       industrielle, 11e-18e siècles. Paris: 1968.

    Maitland, Frederic. "The Deacon and the Jewess," Roman Canon
       Law in the Church of England. London: 1898.
    Brooke, C. N. L. "The Missionary at Home: the Church in the
       Towns, 1000-1250," The Mission of the Church and the
       Propagation of the Faith. ed., G. J. Cuming. Studies in
       Church History, 6; Cambridge: 1970, p. 79.
    Brooke, C. N. L. "Heresy and Religious Sentiment: 1000-1250,"
       Medieval Church and Society: Collected Essays. London:
       1971, pp. 139-61.
    Nelson, Janet. "Society, Theodicy and the Origins of Heresy:
       towards a Reassessment of the Medieval Evidence," Schism,
       Heresy and Religious Protest, ed. Derek Baker, Studies in
       Church History, 9. Cambridge: 1972, pp. 66ff.
    Bolton, Brenda. "Tradition and Temerity: Papal Attitudes to
       Deviants, 1159-1216,"Schism, Heresy, etc. ed. Baker, pp.
       79-91.
    Moore, R. I. "Heresy as Disease," The Concept of Heresy in
       the Middle Ages (11th-13th C.). eds. W. Lourdaux and D.
       Verhelst. Leuven and The Hague: 1976, pp. 1-11.
    Wakefield, Walter and Evans, Austin P. Heresies of the High
       Middle Ages. New York and London: 1969. pp. 245-6.
    Russell, Jeffrey B. Dissent and Reform in the Early Middle
       Ages. Berkeley and Los Angeles: 1965, pp. 224-7 and 309-10.

(Some of the questions and issues which should be addressed
are how do the writers account for the religious orthodoxy
of pre-Wycliffite England; what was the role of geography,
political control, social conditions, and the absence or
presence of radical leadership. You might contrast societal
and political conditions in late medieval England, where there
was little heresy before Wyclif, with southern France and
northern Italy, where it abounded.)

2. John Wyclif as Heresiarch

a. General biographies are K. B. McFarlane, John Wycliffe
   and the Beginnings of English Nonconformity. London: 1952;
   and the older work by H. B. Workman, John Wyclif: A Study
   of the English Medieval Church. 2 vols; Oxford: 1926.
   Wyclif's early philosophical career is discussed by J. A.
   Robson, Wyclif and the Oxford Schools, Cambridge: 1966; and
   the general intellectual background in W. A. Pantin, The
   English Church in the Fourteenth Century. Cambridge: 1955,
   pp. 105-85. Consult David Knowles' The Religious Orders in
   England. 3 vols. Cambridge, 1956-9 for the careers and
   writings of some of his more important contemporaries.
   For Wyclif as political activist and religious reformer,
   see Michael Wilks, "Reformatio regni: Wyclif and Hus as Leaders
   of Religious Protest Movements," Schism, Heresy, etc. ed. Baker,
   pp. 109-30; William Farr, John Wyclif as Legal Reformer. Leiden:
   1974; Gordon Leff, "John Wyclif: the Path to Dissent," Proceedings of the British Academy, 52 (1966); Edith Tatnall,
   "John Wyclif and the Ecclesia Anglicana," Journal of Ecclesiastical History, XX (1969), 19-43. A good overview of the
   church's reaction to Wyclif is provided by Joseph H. Dahmus,
   The Prosecution of John Wyclyf, New Haven, 1952.
   (Some questions to be considered are what were the sources
   of Wyclif's theological radicalism; what were his connections
   with the English royal family, especially John of Gaunt and
   the Black Prince's household; what was the rationale of his
   appeal to the crown and lay lords to reform English Christianity;
   what was his role in sparking the Lollard movement.)

3. Wyclif's Early Oxford Critics

   Read the brief biographies of several of the more important
   of Wyclif's academic opponents in Dictionary of National
   Biography, eds. Leslie Stephen and Sidney Lee. 22 vols. London:
   1959-65 (DNB); and Biographical Register of the University
   of Oxford to AD 1500, ed. A. B. Emden. 3 vols; Oxford: 1957-9
   (Emden). For the names of these early academic critics, see
   the brief summaries in Workman, Wyclif, II, 119-48; McFarlane,
   Wycliffe, 148.
      (Kenningham) Robson, Wyclif and Oxford Schools, 162ff;
   DNB, XI, 361-2; Maidstone, DNB, XII, 783-4, Emden, II,
   1204; A. Williams, "Protectorium Pauperis: A Defence of
   the Begging Friars by Richard of Maidstone, O. Carm. (d.
   1396)," Carmelus, V (1958), 132-80; (Patrington) DNB,
   XV, 492-3, Emden, III, 1435-6; (Netter) DNB, XIV, 231-4,
   Emden, II, 1343-4, Robson, Wyclif and Oxford Schools,
   233-40; (Wodeford) DNB, XXI, 867-8, Emden, III, 2081-2;

(Sutherey) Emden, III, 1734; (Wells) Emden, III, 210-11; (Alyngton)
Emden, I, 30-31; (Sharpe) Emden, III, 1680; (Strode) III, 1807-8;
(Binham) DNB, II, 518, Emden, I, 189; (Ashborne) Emden, I, 54;
(Waldby) Emden, III, 1958; and I discuss several of the anti-
Wyclif and anti-Lollard authors in my "Lollards and Images: the
Defense of Religious Art in Later Medieval England," Journal of
the History of Ideas, XXXIV (1973), 39ff. More extended discussions
of the careers and works of individual apologists for orthodoxy
against the Wycliffites may be found in the following: James Crompton,
"Fasciculi Zizaniorum, I, II," Journal of Ecclesiastical History,
XII (1961), 35-45, 155-66; W. A. Pantin, "Two Treatises of Uthred
of Boldon on the Monastic Life," Studies in Medieval History
Presented to Frederick Maurice Powicke, ed. R. W. Hunt, W. A. Pantin
and R. W. Southern (Oxford, 1948), 364-66; Anne Hudson, "The Debate
on Bible Translation, Oxford, 1401," English Historical Review, XC
(1975),9-10; W. A. Pantin, "The Defensorium of Adam Easton," English
Historical Review, LI (1936), 675-80; Michael Hurley, "Sciptura Sola:
Wyclif and His Critics," Traditio, XVI (1960), 275-352; P. Conrad
Walmsley, "Two Long Lost Works of William Wodeford and Robert of
Leicester," Archivum Franciscanum Historicum, XLVI (1953), 458-70;
Andrew G. Little, The Grey Friars in Oxford (Oxford, 1892), 246-9;
Joseph McNulty, "William of Rymington, Prior of Salley Abbey, Chan-
cellor of Oxford, 1372-2," Yorkshire Archaeological Journal, XXX
(1931), 231-47; W. A. Pantin, "A Benedictine Opponent of John Wyclif,"
English Historical Review, XLIII (1928), 73-7; E. F. Jacob, "Reginald
Pecock: Bishop of Chichester," Proceedings of the British Academy,
XXXVII (1952), 121-53; V. H. H. Green, Bishop Reginald Pecock: A
Study in Ecclesiastical History and Thought (Cambridge, 1945); J.
M. Russell-Smith, "Walter Hilton and a Tract in Defence of the
Veneration of Images," Dominican Studies, VII (1954), 180-214;
Eric Doyle, "William Wodeford's 'De dominio civili'clericorum'
against John Wiclif," Archivum Franciscanum Historicum, LXVI (1973),
49-109; Eric Doyle, "William Wodeford, O.F.M., and John Wyclif's
De Religione," Speculum, LII (1977), 329-36; Aubrey Gwynn, The Eng-
lish Austin Friars in the Time of Wyclif (London, 1948); Margaret
Deanley, The Lollard Bible and Other Medieval Biblical Versions.
(Cambridge, 1920);

You should acquaint yourselves (by glancing through the table of
contents and English marginalia) with the unofficial "history"
of Wycliffism in England and Bonhemia compiled by the London
Carmelites and partly published in the Rolls Series, Fasciculi
Zizaniorum Magistri Johannis Wyclif ... Ascribed to Thomas Netter
of Walden, ed. Walter W. Shirley, Rolls Series, 5, London, 1858.
For the authorship and significance of this unique work, see the
article of James Crompton cited above.

(Issues to be considered are: did Wycliffism change intent and
personality in its progress from Oxford classrooms to the English
countryside; what distinguished academic Wycliffism (heterodoxy)
from popular Lollardy (a mass religious movement); what was Wyclif's
connection with the growth of a revolutionary sect; what were the
political objectives (if any) of later Lollardy and how did these
differ from Wyclif's reformist goals; what did the critics of
Wycliffism perceive to be most disturbing or dangerous in his
teaching; how effective was persuasion, as contrasted with the use
of force, in defeating heresy?)

4. The Later Lollards and the Reformation "Connection"

See the general treatments of McFarlane, _Wycliffe_, pp. 107ff; Workman, _Wyclif_, II, 325ff. The definitive work on the subject is John A. F. Thomson, _The Later Lollards: 1414-1520_ (xford, 1965); see also Claire Cross, _Church and People: 1450-1660: the Triumph of the Laity in the English Church_ (Atlantic Highlands, 1976); K. B. McFarlane, _Lancastrian Kings and Lollard Knights_ (Oxford, 1972), on the Lollard gentry; M. E. Aaston, "Lollardy and Sedition, 1381-1431," _Past & Present_, XVII (1960), 1-44, which has been reprinted in _Peasants, Kinights and Heretics: Studies in Medieval English Social History_, ed. R. H. Hilton (Cambridge, 1976), 273-318; A. G. Dickens, _Lollards and Protestants in the Diocese of York: 1509-1558_ (Oxford, 1959); A. G. Dickens, _The English Reformation_ (New York, 1964), pp. 22-37. For the mythical Wyclif, see V. Mudroch, _The Wyclyf Tradition_ (Athans, O., 1979).

For a fascinating glimpse of eccentric forms of religious opinion, see Walter L. Wakefield, "Some Unorthodox Popular Ideas of the Thirteenth Century," _Medievalia et Humanistica_, New Series, IV (1973), 25-35, which discusses manifestations of popular folk belief mentioned by Thomson and Dickens in their treatment of later Lollardy.

There has recently been a revival of interest in Wycliffism, mainly the work of the scholarship of Anne Hudson of Oxford University, whose articles and books show how much more is to be discovered about this tired, old subject. See her "A Lollard Compilation and the Dissemination of Wycliffite Thought," _Journal of Theological Studies_, new series, XXIII (1972), 65-81; "A Lollard Sermon-Cycle and Its Implications," _Medium Aevum_, XL (1971), 142-56; and her edition of Lollard writings, _Selections from English Wycliffite Writings_ (Cambridge, 1978). Dr. Hudson is presently engaged in editing and publishing the Lollard sermons; the first volume of her edition has recently appeared.

(Some matters for thought: what was the connection between later Lollardy and political dissent; what was the social basis (if any) of the Lollard movement (i.e., did the fact that many of the Lollards were enaged in textile manufacturing and sale imply any economic or vocational basis of the sect); what was the relation (if any) of later Lollardy with early Protestantism (did the Wycliffites, in any sense, pave the way for general reform)?)

STATE UNIVERSITY OF NEW YORK
at Stony Brook

DEPARTMENT OF HISTORY

HISTORY 451: Medieval Personalities   Spring 1982
Professor Helen Lemay

COURSE REQUIREMENTS:

1. A research paper, approximately 20 pages long, on a medieval per-
    sonality or group of individuals (e.g. the School of Chartres).
    This paper constitutes the only written requirement for this course,
    and will make up 75% of your final grade. It must include analysis
    of primary source material in translation, and an extensive biblio-
    graphy of secondary sources.

    By Tuesday, March 2 you MUST have chosen your topic. You must come
    into class with TWO copies of a short report giving the following
    information:

        1. Your topic. (e.g., Joan of Arc and Medieval Mystics)
        2. Sources you have consulted that deal with this topic
                Author, Title, Publication Place, date, Stony Brook
                Library call no.
        3. Sources you plan to consult. (same format as above)

    Please TYPE this report and turn it in ON TIME. One copy will be
    given to the reference librarian who will prepare a presentation
    for the class on how to do a good bibliography for this particular
    assignment. Although you will receive hlep from me and from the
    reference librarian, you are responsible for putting in the work
    to develop a good bibliography. Please remember that the quality
    of your bibliography will determine in large measure the quality
    of your paper. If you do your research in general works on medieval
    history, your paper will be general in nature and therefore not very
    good; if you research a specific aspect of your topic, on the other
    hand, you will have a good grasp of it. This means that your biblio-
    graphy will include a good deal of periodical material published in
    scholarly journals.

    The purpose of your research is not merely to collect information;
    you must devote much of your effort to interpreting it. Your research
    is supposed to have direction. You should be investigating the answer
    to a question or testing a hypothesis that you have formulated during
    your preliminary reading. This way your paper will have a THESIS and
    will present, expound and prove the validity of your point of view on
    your chosen subject. For example, you will not simple write a p ,er
    on Joan of Arc that says she had visions which determined the course
    of her military career. Your paper would discuss instead what was
    significant about her hystical experiences: that they occurred to an

unlettered lay woman in a time when femal mystics were educated
members of the monastic orders, that they urged her to take on the
"masculine" military role rather than the "feminine" contemplative
one. You must not only do research, therefore; you must THINK about
what is important about the information you have uncovered.

I would like to see your paper at various stages, if this is
at all possible for you. Since the paper is due on Tuesday, May 4,
do not submit first drafts or partial first drafts on May 3. But
if you get the material to me in March and April (bibliographies,
outlines, a few pages, or an entire draft) I should be able to help
you in its preparation. Please feel free to consult with me often
about your paper. Many students have never conducted a research
project of this magnitude before, and have trouble determining how
to go about it. I consider this project to be one of the most important in your undergraduate career; it trains you in research, analysis
and writing skills that have wide application in your future careers
and in your life in general. If you can do a good job with a problem
pertaining to the middle ages, you have the ability to research topics
relating to business, politics, education, social issues, to name
only a few. This is one of the few truly small classes most of you
will have at Stony Brook, and it is the only really small course that
I teach. The time that I spend in HIS 316 on 200 people I can spend
with you this semester; do not hesitate to take advantage of this
help.

2. Oral reports and participation in class discussion. This will make
up the other 25% of your final grade.

In preparing and presenting oral reports, please keep the following considerations in mind:

First of all, consider yourself as a member of a community of
scholars, not as a student with an assignment to read 30 or 40 pages.
In a seminar, the purpose is to bring to the class what is relevant
to the subject under discussion, and to have the judgement to leave out
what is not. You should try to relate your material to the main topic
at hand (e.g. Peter Abelard and intellectual freedom in the Twelfth
Century) as well as to other topics covered in class (e.g. the role
of women in this scholastic milieu). Please present your material
in such a manner that other students feel free to interrupt you to
clarify or comment on a point you are making, and as a participant
in the seminar please make an effort to take part in class discussion.
This will be a very dull class if it consists of nothing more than
twenty or so "mini-lectures" a month.

If you discover that an article you have read covers almost the
same topic as the ne you are assigned, do not hesitate to present
your material in discussion with the student reporting--your assignment of a class presentation holds only if the material assigned

proves valuable to the class. I have not read all of the works I
have listed; many of them I have merely skimmed, and often the content
appears different after merely skimming them than it does after a
careful reading. Finally, most important of all, try to relate the
secondary material you have been assigned to the primary source reading
which will have been read by all class members. Do not just come to
class and tell us, for example, what Etienne Gilson said about
Abelard and Heloise's love affair. Relate what he said to your own
reading in the Letters and in the Historia Calamitatum and give your
own opinion whenever you have been able to form one.

Please make an effort to inform me in advance if you are unable
to attend class when you are scheduled to report. Telephone the
History Department and leave a message 246-6500 or else telephone
me in my office 246-6511 or at home 928-2312. Please do not telephone
after 8:30 P.M.

Please remember that you are going to have to share the books on
reserve with other members of the seminar. Do not race out of class,
take out the book, and keep it for a week, thereby preventing anyone
else from doing his or her assignment. Stick around for a few minutes
to make arrangements for everyone to have a turn.

James Powell
Syracuse University

HISTORY 344

PLAGUE IN EUROPEAN SOCIETY

Assigned Readings:

William McNeill	Plagues and Peoples
Philip Ziegler	The Black Death
William Bowsky	The Black Death
Carlo Cipolla	Fighting the Plague in Seventeenth Century Italy
John Hatcher	Plague, Population and the English Economy

Requirements: There will be a mid-term and a final examination. Students will write a ten to twelve page essay on a topic of their choice, approved by the instructor.

LECTURES

1. The Nature of Plagues and Epidemics

2. The Plague at Athens

3. Plague in the Roman Empire
    McNeill, 1-131

4. Explanations of the Decline and Fall of the Roman Empire

5. The Demography of the Later Roman Empire

6. The Social and Political Structures of the Later Empire

7. Mohammed and Charlemagne Revisited

8. The Carolingian Renaissance

9. Europe Without Plague: Famine and Disease 850-1347

10. Demographic History, 850-1300

11. The Agrarian Economy, 850-1300

12. Industry, Commerce, and Urbanization, 850-1300

13. Cathedrals and Castles

14. Bureaucrats and Professors

15. Medieval Culture, 1050-1300

16. Prosperity, Poverty, and Dissent

17. Medicine and Public Health, 1150-1350

18. Europe on the Eve of Plague

19. MID-TERM EXAM

20. The Black Death, 1347-1351
    Ziegler, 13-39; Bowsky, 7-64; McNeill, 132-175

21. The Black Death in the Middle East and Italy
    Ziegler, 40-62; Bowsky, 108-113; 122-125

22. The Black Death in France, Germany and England
    Ziegler, 63-223; Bowsky, 65-107

23. Population Decline, 1350 to 1427
    Hatcher, 11-30; Ziegler 224 - 231

24. The Family During the Plague

25. Impact of Plague on the Economy
    Ziegler, 232-258; Hatcher, 31-54

26. Public Health and Medicine

27. The Impact on Religion, Culture, and the Church
    Ziegler, 259-279

28. Plague and Population, 1400-1600
    Hatcher, 55-73

29. The Origins of the Renaissance
    Powell, "Crisis and Culture in Renaissance Europe." On reserve

30. The Formation of the European Elite

31. The European Economy, 1400-1600

32. The Changing Role of the Church

33. The Origins of Modern Slavery

34. Technology and Science

35. The Plague of 1630
    Cipolla, Fighting the Plague

36. Public Health and Medicine

37. The "London" Plague of 1665

38. The Crisis of the Seventeenth Century

39. The End of the Plague in Europe

40. Epidemic Disease, 1700 to Present

41. The Development of Modern Medicine and Public Health
     McNeill, 208-257

42. Population Since the Plague

FINAL EXAMINATION

Rev. 1985/86

History 314   Professor McNamara
Ancient and Medieval Christianity   Room C108N
T 5:40-7:00 Th 5:40-7:05

Textbook: Gonzalez, J, _History of Christianity_
            The New Testament

The textbook is to be read straight through to provide historical
background for the material covered in this course.

Midterm Examination: October 22

Final Examination: December 17

Research Paper (approximately 15-20 pp.)
                December 8

The report will be a historiographical analysis of some problem of
your choice from Christian history up to 1500 AD. Each report
should follow the instructions on the following page. The questions
may be answered in any order but the number of the question being
answered should be placed in the margin for my guidance in grading.

Attribution of material will be footnoted in accordance with the
attached statement regarding plagiarism. Please supply notes for all
statements, even material taken from class lectures and discussion,
in order to familiarize yourselves with the procedures. Proper forms
for footnotes and bibliography must be observed. You are advised to
consult _The MLA Handbook for Writers of Research Papers, Theses and
Dissertations_ for these forms and for all stylistic problems. Copies
are available in the bookstore.

Grades for the reports will be scaled to content and to style
(grammar and spelling included). Errors in the latter will reduce
your grade half a point (i.e., from A to A-).

As a point of departure for your paper, there are general
bibliographies available in any standard text for the entire period
or the appropriate part of the period. For more specific
bibliography use the following journals and periodicals:
    International Medieval Bibliography
    Speculum
    Journal of Ecclesiastical History
    Journal of Medieval Canon Law
    Journal of Medieval History
    Revue d'histoire ecclésiastique
    Constable, G., _Medieval Monasticism: a select bibliography_

Historiography is the study of how history is written—the history of history. It traces the attempts of scholars to use the primary source material at their disposal in a variety of different ways to discover what happened in the past, why it happened and what it means.

1) Choose a problem of limited scope from the subject matter of this course (think small!!)

2) Describe the problem as fully as possible including
    historical context (chronological, geographical, social,
        cultural and economic background where appropriate).
    summary of the particular questions arising from your
        consideration of the problem.

3) Survey the primary sources available including
    all primary sources in existence (including references in
        secondary sources to pictorial, archeological or
literary material in foreign languages or manuscript
        inaccessible to your direct study)
    significant gaps in the information
    a summary of what the primary sources will or will not tell
        you about your problem.
        What facts are established and what contradictions have
            arisen in the sources?

4) Collect a bibliography of secondary sources including
    recent books and articles drawn from specialized
        bibliographies and journals
    foreign language material where pertinent using reviews
        in journals for guidance.

5) Compare and discuss at length the treatment of your problem by as many authors of secondary sources as you can.
    indicate differences in method, interpretation, conclusion

6) Conclude with a summary of the state of modern scholarship
    concerning your problem.

I.   The Primitive Church
      1.   The Roman World at Jesus' Birth
      2.   The evangelican church and the Pauline mission
      3.   Persecution and heresy.
      4.   Church organization: liturgy, sacraments, clergy
      5.   Constantine and Christian imperium
      6.   The church and the fourth century world.

Primary sources consist mainly of the New Testament and Patristic
writings which are available in several collections of translations.
For readers of Latin and Greek, Migne's Patrologia Latina and
Patrologia Graeca are the most complete collections. For readers of
French, Sources Chrétiennes, offers a large collection of
translations for the entire ancient and medieval period. English
translations exist on an individual basis and in the following
series:
The Ante-Nicene Fathers
The Nicene and Post-Nicene Fathers
Ancient Christian Writers
The Fathers of the Church
In addition to the secondary sources listed below, see Classical
World, vol. 76, no. 2 (1982), "A Decade of Patristic Scholarship"
Clark, Elizabeth A., Jerome, Chrysostom and Friends
Hennecke and Schneemelcher, New Testament Apocrypha
Perpetua, The Passion of Perpetua and Felicity
Robinson, The Nag Hammadi Library
Wilkinson, John, Egeria's Travels

Secondary Sources
Barnes, Timothy D., Tertullian
Bell, G L, Monasteries and Monasticism in Central Asia Minor
Bright, William, The Age of the Fathers
Brown, Peter, Religion and Society in the Age of S. Augustine
Cambridge History of the Bible
Dodds, E.R., Pagan and Christian in an Age of Anxiety
Farmer, William R., The Synoptic Problem: A critical analysis
Fiorenza, Elizabeth S, In Memory of Her
Fox, Robin L., Pagans and Christians
Frend, W.H.C., The Rise of Christianity
Guignebert, Charles, The Jewish World at the Time of Jesus
Kelly, J.N.D., Jerome, His LIfe, Writings and Controversies
MacMullen, Ramsay, Christianizing the Roman Empire
McNamara, Jo Ann, A New Song
Meeks, Wayne A., The Moral World of the First Christians
Momigliano, A, Conflict between Paganism and Christianity
Robinson, John A.T., Re-Dating the New Testament
Rousseau, P, Pachomius: The Making of a Community in 4th c. Egypt
Russell, Jeffrey B., The Devil
Wilken, Robert L., The Christians as the Romans Saw Them

II. Latin Christendom in the Early Middle Ages
      7.   The Ascetic MOvement
      8.   The Barbarians and the Roman Church
      9.   The Conversion of the West
      10. The Imperial Church
      11. The Feudal Church
      12. Monastic Reform

Primary Sources
Bede, A History of the English Church and People
Boniface, Letters of Saint Boniface
Caesarius of Arles, The Rule for Nuns
Cassiodorus, Letters
Gregory I, Letters, Pastoral CAre, Dialogues
Gregory of Tours, History of the Franks
Hoare, F.R., The Western Fathers
McNeill, JT, and HM Gamer, Medieval Handbooks of Penance
Peters, E., Monks, Bishops and Pagans
Talbot, C.H., The Anglo-Saxon Missionaries in Germany
Whitelock, D., M. Brett and C.N.L. Brooke, Councils and Synods with
      other documents relating to the English Church, 871-1204,

Secondary Sources:
Amann, E. and A. Dumas, L'église au pouvoir des laïgues
Beck, H&J., The Pastoral Care of Souls in Southeast France
Chadwick, Nora, The Age of Saints in the Early Celtic Church
DeClercq, C, La Législation religieuse franque
Duckett, E., The Wandering Saints of the Early Middle Ages
Dudden, F. Homes, Gregory the GReat
 Eckenstein, Lina, Women under Monasticism, 500-1500
Fisher, J.D.C., Christian Initiation: Baptism in the Medieval West
Geary, Patrick J., Furta Sacra
Hunt, Noreen, Cluniac Monasticism of the Central Middle Ages
McGinn, B. and J, Meyendorff, Christian Spirituality
Morrison, Karl, The Mimetic Tradition of rEform in the West
Nichols, John A. and Lillian T. Shank, Distant Echoes:
Obeldevich, James, ed., Religion and the People 800-1700
 Payer, Pierre J., Sex and the Penitentials
Pelikan, Jaroslav, The Christian Tradition: 4 vols.
Prinz, Friedrich, Frühes Mönchtum im Frankreich
Richards, Jeffrey, Consul of God
Rosenwein, B, Rhinoceros Bound: Cluny in the Tenth Century
 Russell, Jeffrey B., Rebels and Reformers of the Middle Ages
Ryan, John, Irish Monasticism
Sheils, W.J., ed., Monks, Hermits and the Ascetic Tradition
Smith, L.M., Cluny in the Eleventh and Twelfth Centuries
Tavard, Georges, Women in the Christian Tradition
Taylor, H.O., The Emergence of Christian Culture in the West
Tellenbach, Gerd, Church, State adn Christian Society
Ullmann, Walter, Short History of the Papacy in the Middle Ages
Workman, H., The Evolution of the Monastic Ideal

III. The High MIddle AGes
      13. The GRegorian Reform
      14, The Crusades
      15. The Challenge of Capitalism and Urbanism
      16. Law and Orthodoxy
      17. Popular religion and Christian social order
      18. Heresy and Its Control

Primary Sources:
Ancren Riwle
Aquinas, Thomas, Summa Theologica
Armstrong, RJ. and IC. Brady, Francis and Clare
Caesarius of Heisterbach, Dialogue of miracles
Coulton, G.G., ed., From St. Francis to Dante
Emerton, E., The Correspondance of Pope Gregory VII
Eudes de Rouen, Register
Hadewijch, The Complete Works
Hugh Saint Victor, On the Sacraments of the Christian Faith
James, Bruno S., ed., Letters of Saint Bernard of Clairvaux
Lanfranc of Bec, Monastic Constitutions
Mundy, John H., The Repression of Catharism at Toulouse
Peters, Edward, ed. Heresy and Authority in Medieval Europe
Powicke, M. and Cheney, Councils and Synods...English Church
Vitry, Jacques de, Historia Occidentalis
Vitry, Jacques de, The Life of Marie d'Oignies
Wakefield, WL. and Evans, AP., Heresies of the High Middle Ages

Secondary Sources
Boswell, John, Christianity, Social Tolerance and Homosexuality
Brundage, J., Canon Law and the Crusader
Bynum, Caroline, Holy Feast and Holy Fast
Carroll, Michael P., The Cult of the Virgin Mary
Chodorow, S, Christian Political Theory and Church Politics
Duby, Georges, Medieval Marriage
Elliott-Brims, L., Innocent III
Habig, Marion A., St. Francis of Assisi
 Hefele, C.J., and H. Leclercq, Histoire des Conciles
Kirschner, Julius and S. Wemple, eds., Women of the Medieval World
Knowles, D., Archbishop Thomas Becket
Lambert, Malcolm, Franciscan Poverty
Lea, Henry C., History of the Inquisition
LeGoff, Jacques, The Birth of Purgatory
Little, Lester K., Religious Poverty and the Profit Economy
McDonnell, E W., The Beguines and Beghards in Medieval Culture
Moorman, John, A History of the Franciscan Order
Newman, Barbara, Sister of Wisdom: St. Hildegard's Theology
Oldenbourg, Zoe, Massacre at Montségur
Partner, Peter, The Murdered Magicians
Reeves, Marjorie, The Influence of Prophecy in the Later Middle Ages
 Ruether, Rosemary R. and Eleanor McLaughlin, Women of Spirit
Warren, AK., Anchorites and Their Patrons in Medieval England

IV.   The Later Middle Ages
      19.   Innocent III
      20.   The Friars and the People
      21.   The Decline of the Papacy
      22.   The Challenge of Nationalism
      23.   Mysticism and Humanism
      24.   The Waning of the Middle Ages

Primary Sources:
Dante, The Divine Comedy
Dubois, P., On the Recovery of the Holy Land
Loomis, L, The Council of Constance
Langland, The Vision of Piers Plowman
Julian of Norwich, A Book of Showings
The Book of Margery Kempe
The Trial of Joan of Arc
Petrarch, Letters
Pius II, Memoirs

Secondary Sources:
Adam, P. La vie paroissiale en France au XIV siècle
Atkinson, Clarissa W., Mystic and Pilgrim
 Baker, Derek, ed., Sanctity and Secularity
Bossy, John, Christianity in the West, 1400-1700.
Boyd, Catherine E., Tithes and Parishes in Medieval Italy
Bynum, CW., S Harrell and P Richman, eds., Gender and Religion
Clark, J.M., The Great German Mystics
Cohn, N. The Pursuit of the Millenium
Flick, The Decline of the Medieval Church
Gardner, Edmund G., Saint Catherine of Siena
Gaudemet, Jean, La Société écclésiastique dans l'occident
Gougaud, Louis, Devotional and Ascetic Practices in the Middle Ages
Hinnebusch, W. History of the Dominican Order
Jacob, E.F., Essays in the Conciliar Epoch
Kieckhefer, Richard, Unquiet Souls: Fourteenth Century Saints
Lambert, Malcolm, Medieval Heresy
Lerner, Robert E., The Heresy of the Free Spirit
Mollat, Y., The Popes at Avignon
Muldoon, J., Popes, Lawyers and Infidels
Pantin, W. The English Church in the Fourteenth Century
Ruether, Rosemary R. ed., Religion and Sexism
Tierney, B., The Foundations of Conciliar Theory
Ullmann, W., The Origins of the Great Schism
Vauchez, A, La sainteté en occident
Vodola, Elisabeth, Excommunication in the Middle Ages
Warner, Marina, Alone of All Her Sex
Weinstein, D, and Bell, R, Saints and Society
Wilson, Stephen, ed., Saints and Their Cults

Hst U708.1/808.1 Colloquium/Seminar   Spring 1987
Christianity in the Middle Ages   Professor Roberts
Tu 6:30-8:30 P.M.   Ph.D. Program in History
                                              Graduate Center, CUNY

I. General Description

    The emphasis in the course will be on the origins of
Christianity and the subsequent development of the Latin Church
in the Middle Ages. Topics to be included: Hellenistic Palestine;
the New Testament; Graeco-Roman influences on Christianity; the
Patristic period; examples of Christian historiography;
organization and development of the Medieval Church; examples of
biblical criticism and interpretation; the impact of Christianity
on various medieval institutions. Students will be required to
present oral reports on selected readings; two short papers; and
a final examination.

II. Required Books

    G.Barraclough, The Medieval Papacy (Harcourt Brace)
    H.Bettenson, ed. Documents of the Christian Church 2d ed
                        (Oxford)
    E.Bickerman, From Ezra to the last of the Maccabees (Schocken)
    C.N.Cochrane, Christianity and Classical Culture (Galaxy)
    N.Cohn, Pursuit of the Millennium rev ed 1970 (Oxford)
    J.Daniélou, The Bible and the Liturgy (U Notre Dame Pr)
    T.H.Gaster, ed. Dead Sea Scriptures (Anchor)
    King James Bible and Apocrypha
    D.Knowles, Christian Monasticism (World Univ Libr)
    G.Ladner, The Idea of Reform (Harvard)
    J.Pelikan, Emergence of the Catholic Tradition 100-600 (Chicago)
    B.Smalley, Study of the Bible in the Middle Ages (Notre Dame)
    R.W.Southern, Western Society and the Church in the Middle
                Ages (Pelican)

III. Outline of the Course/Reading assignments/Recommended
        Bibliography

Feb. 3 Introduction: bibliography: sources of the history of
            Christianity: assignment of reports
            ANCIENT NEAR EASTERN BACKGROUND

    Recommended: Isaiah 1-12; 40-66/Ezekiel 34/Daniel
                Roland de Vaux, Ancient Israel (1961)
                E.L. Ehrlich, Concise History of Israel (Torchbk)
                H.M. Orlinsky, Ancient Israel (Cornell)

Feb. 10   Hellenistic Palestine

    Reading: E.Bickerman, From Ezra to the last of the Maccabees
                T.H. Gaster, ed. Dead Sea Scriptures (Book of Hymns;
                War of the Sons of Light and Sons of Darkness;
                Commentary on Habakkuk; Manual of Discipline;
                Zadokite Document)
                Book of Job/Proverbs/Ecclesiastes/I & II Macc.(Apoc)

Recommended: M.Black, The Scrolls and Christian Origins (1961)
        F.F.Bruce, New Testament History (Anchor)
        F.M.Cross, The Ancient Library of Qumran (rev 1961)
        M.Grant, The Jews in the Roman World (Scribner 1973)
        C.A.H.Guignebert, The Jewish World in the Time of
                Jesus (N.Y.1965, c.1959)
        Josephus, The Jewish War (Penguin)
        A.Robertson, The Origins of Christianity (rev 1962)
        C.Roth, The Dead Sea Scrolls (N.Y. 1965)
        E.Schürer, Literature of the Jewish People in the
                time of Jesus (Schocken)
        V.Tcherikover, Hellenistic Civilization and the Jews
                (Atheneum)
        G.Vermes, "The Impact of the Dead Sea Scrolls on the
                Study of the NT" J Jewish Stud 27 (no.2 1976)
                107-16

Feb. 17   Historical life and teachings of Jesus: the New
            Testament: its composition: types of literature

  Reading: Synoptic Gospels/Gospel according to John
            Bettenson 26-29; 29-44

  Recommended: D. Bahat, "Does the Holy Sepulchre Church mark
            the Burial of Jesus?" Biblical Archaeol.R. 12 (1986)
        R.Bultmann, Theology of the New Testament, I
                (Scribners 1951)
        E.E. Ellis, "Dating the New Testament" New Test.Stud.
                26 (no. 4, 1980) 487-502
        J.Finegan, Light from the Ancient Past: the
                Archaeological Background of the Hebrew-
                Christian religion (Princeton)
        J.Finegan, The Archeology of the New Testament:
                the life of Jesus and the Beginning of the
                Early Church (1969)
        R.M.Grant, Historical Introduction to the New
                Testament (1972)
        A. von Harnack, Origin of the New Testament (1926)
        H.C.Kee, Jesus in History (1970)
        J.Klausner, Jesus of Nazareth (tr from Hebrew by
                H.Danby, Boston 1964, c. 1925)
        T.W.Manson, The Teaching of Jesus:Studies in its
                Form and Content (CUP 1967)
        J. Pelikan, Jesus through the Centuries: His Place in
                the History of Culture (Yale UP 1985)
        E.Renan, The Life of Jesus (N.Y. 1955)
        A.Schweitzer, Quest of the Historical Jesus (1961)
        A.Schweitzer, The Psychiatric Study of Jesus
                (Boston 1958, c. 1948)
        M.Smith, The Secret Gospel (N.Y. 1973)

Feb. 24   Historical and literary Paul: the definers of doctrine

   Reading: Acts of the Apostles/Romans/I & II Cor./
                  Philippians/Colossians/I & II Thessalonians/
                  Philemon/Hebrews/I & II Peter

                  Bettenson 23-26; 44-62
                  J.Pelikan, The Emergence of the Catholic Tradition
                       100-600, ch. 1-3

   Recommended: Early Christian Writings:the Apostolic
                       Fathers (Penguin)
             I.Edman, The Mind of Paul (1935)
             L.Goppelt, Apostolic and Post-Apostolic Times (Torchbk)
             M. Grant, Saint Paul (Scribner's 1976)
             A.Harnack, History of Dogma, I (Dover)
             A.D.Nock, St Paul (Harper 1963)
             J.C. O'Neill, Paul's Letter to the Romans (Pelican)
             Origen, On First Principles (Torchbook)

Mar.3   Graeco-Roman influences on Christianity: the mysteries

   Reading: Plato, Allegory of the Cave (Republic)
                  Aristotle, Metaphysics XII(Chain of Being)/Ethics VI
                     (Critique of Platonic doctrine of archetypes)
                  Bettenson 1-23
                  C.N. Cochrane, Christianity and Classical Culture

   Recommended: S.Angus, The Religious Quests of the
                       Graeco-Roman World:Historical Background of Early
                       Christianity (N.Y.1967; repr. 1929 ed.)
             J.Campbell, ed. Pagan and Christian Mysteries (Torchbk)
             H.Chadwick, Early Christian Thought and the Classical
                       Tradition (Oxford 1966)
             W.H.C. Frend, Martyrdom and Persecution in the Early
                       Church (1965)
             R.M.Grant, Augustus to Constantine: Thrust of the
                       Christian Movement into the Roman World (1971)
             E.Hatch, Influence of Greek Ideas on Christianity
                       (Torchbook)
             W.Jaeger, Early Christianity and Greek Paideia (Oxford)
             M.L.W. Laistner, Christianity and Pagan Culture in the
                       Later Roman Empire (Cornell)
             R.A.Lanciani, Pagan and Christian Rome (N.Y. 1967)
             H.Mattingly, Christianity in the Roman Empire (1967)
             A.Momigliano, ed. Conflict between Paganism and
                       Christianity in the Fourth Century (1963)
             A.N.Sherwin-White, Roman Society and Roman Law in the
                       New Testament (Oxford 1963)

Mar. 10   Heresy and Orthodoxy in the Early Christian Centuries

Reading: Pelikan, ch. 4-7

Recommended: T.D.Barnes, Tertullian: A Historical and
            Literary Study (Oxford 1971)
    P.Brown, "Pelagius and his Supporters. Aims and
            Environment," J Theolog.Stud. (1968) 93-114
    W.H.C. Frend, The Donatist Church (1952)
    R.M. Grant, Gnosticism and Early Christianity (1959)
    S.L. Greenslade, Schism in the Early Church (1964)
    H. Jonas, The Gnostic Religion (Beacon 1963)
    J.N.D. Kelly, Early Christian Doctrines 2d ed (1960)

Mar. 17   Patristic period: the Latin Fathers

Reading: Ladner, The Idea of Reform

Recommended: Augustine, Confessions (var.editions)
    P.Brown, Augustine of Hippo:A Biography (U Calif.)
    B.Colgrave, ed. The Earliest Life of Gregory the
                Great, by an anonymous monk of Whitby (1968)
    Dialogues of St Gregory the Great (ed. Gardner)
    E.Gilson, The Christian Philosophy of St Augustine (1961)
    J.N.Hritzu, tr. St Jerome, Dogmatic and Polemical Works
                (1965)
    E.Przywara, An Augustine Synthesis (Torchbook)
    Sulpicius Severus et al., The Western Fathers (Torchbook)
    D.S.Wiesen, St Jerome as a Satirist:A Study in Christian
                Latin Thought and Letters (1964)
    H.A.Wolfson, The Philosophy of the Church Fathers (1956)
    F.Van der Meer, Augustine the Bishop (Torchbook)
    H.von Campenhausen, The Fathers of the Latin Church
                (1964)

Mar. 24   Christian Historiography

PRESENTATION OF PAPERS ON CHRISTIAN HISTORIOGRAPHY

Recommended: Augustine, City of God
    Bede, History of the English Church and People
    Eusebius, Ecclesiastical History
    Orosius, The Seven Books of History against the
                Pagans (tr Deferrari 1964)
    Salvian, On the Government of God (repr 1966)

    H.Butterfield, Christianity and History (Scribners)
    G.L. Keyes, Christian Faith and the Interpretation
                of History: a study of St Augustine's
                Philosophy of History (1966)
    R.L.P. Milburn, Early Christian Interpretations of
                History (1954)

Mar. 31   Monasticism in the Western Church: Hagiography: the
           Mendicants

   Reading: D.Knowles, Christian Monasticism
            Bettenson 116-132

   Recommended: N.F. Cantor, "Crisis of Western Monasticism
           1050-1130," AHR 66 (1960)
        L.Z. Daly, Benedictine Monasticism (1965)
        E. Duckett, Wandering Saints of the Early Middle Ages
                (Norton)
        Gregory the Great, St Benedict, Dialogues Bk. II (LLA)
        D. Knowles, The Monastic Order in England 2d ed (1963)
        Lives of the Saints (tr Webb, Penguin)
        J. Moorman, History of the Franciscan Order to the year
                1517 (Oxford 1968)
        J. Van Engen, "The 'Crisis of Cenobitism' Reconsidered:
            Benedictine Monasticism in the Years 1050-1150"
            Speculum (Apr. 1986) 269-304
        H.B.Workman, Evolution of the Monastic Ideal 2d ed
                (1927)
        G. Zarnecki, The Monastic Achievement (1972)

Apr. 7   Latin Christendom on the Offensive: Heretics, Jews,
          Moslems, Byzantine Christians

   Reading: Cohn, Pursuit of the Millennium
            Bettenson 89-97; 132-35

   Recommended: C.N.L.Brooke,"Heresy and Religious Sentiment:
            1000-1250," Bull. Inst. of Hist. Research (1968)
        D.J. Geanakoplos, Byzantine East and Latin West: Two
            Worlds of Christendom in the Middle Ages and
            Renaissance (1966)
        S. Grayzel, The Church and the Jews in the Thirteenth
            Century (1966)
        J.M. Hussey, Church and Learning in the Byzantine
            Empire 867-1185 (1963)
        H.C. Lea, History of the Inquisition of the Middle
            Ages 3 vols, 1888 (1956 repr)
        G.Leff, Heresy in the Later Middle Ages 2 vols (1967)
        E.W. McDonnell, The Beguines and Beghards in Medieval
            Culture (Rutgers UP 1954)
        R.I. Moore, "The Origins of Medieval Heresy"
            History (1970)
        S. Runciman, History of the Crusades 3 vols (1964-67)
        S. Runciman, The Medieval Manichee (Compass)
        J.B. Russell, Dissent and Reform in the Early Middle
            Ages (U Calif Pr 1965)
        A.C. Shannon, Popes and Heresy in the Thirteenth
            Century (1955)
        J. Trachtenberg, The Devil and the Jews (1966)
        W.L. Wakefield & A.P. Evans, edd. Heresies of High
            Middle Ages (Columbia UP 1969, sources)

Apr. 13 - Apr. 19 No classes

Apr. 21   Aspects of Church Organization in the Middle Ages: the
          Papacy: Councils

   Reading: Barraclough, The Medieval Papacy
                Bettenson 79-87; 97-115; 135-36

   Recommended: M.W.Baldwin, The Medieval Papacy in Action (1940)
      S.Baldwin, The Organization of Medieval Christianity (1929)
      R.L.Benson, The Bishop-Elect:A Study in Medieval Ecclesi-
                astical Office (Princeton 1968)
      C.A. Frazeem, "The Origins of Clerical Celibacy in the
                Western Church," Church History (1972) 149-67
      A. Fremantle, The Papal Encyclicals in their Historical
                Context (Mentor)
      E.F. Jacob, Essays in the Conciliar Epoch 3rd ed (1963)
      R.E. McNally, "The History of the Medieval Papacy: A Survey
                of Research 1954-59," Theological Stud. (1960)
      G. Mollat, The Popes at Avignon (1965)
      T.F.X. Noble, The Republic of St. Peter: the Birth of the
                Papal State, 680-825 (U Pennsylvania Pr 1984)
      K.Pennington, Pope and Bishops: the Papal Monarchy in the
                Twelfth and Thirteenth Centuries
                (U Pennsylvania Pr 1984)
      J.T. Shotwell & L.R. Loomis, edd. The See of Peter
                (Columbia Records of Civilization 1965 repr)
      B. Tierney, Foundations of Conciliar Theory (CUP 1955)
      B. Tierney, Origins of Papal Infallibility 1150-1350 (1972)
      W. Ullmann, Growth of Papal Government in the Middle Ages
                2d ed (1962)
      W. Ullmann, Short History of the Papacy in the Middle Ages
                (1972)
      J.A. Watt, Theory of Papal Monarchy in the Thirteenth
                Century (1965)

Apr. 28   The Church and the World: Canon Law, Usury regulation,
          Medieval Political Theory; Just War

   Reading: Southern, Western Society and the Church in the MA

   Recommended: R.H.Bainton, Christian Attitudes toward War
                and Peace (1960)
      S.Chodorow, Christian Political Theory and Church Politics
                in the Mid Twelfth Century (U Calif Pr 1972)
      H.A. Deane, Political and Social Ideas of St Augustine
                (Columbia)
      M. Deanesly, History of the Medieval Church 590-1500 (UP)
      R. de Roover, La pensée économique des scolastiques (1970)
      R. de Roover, Business, Banking and Economic Thought
                (ed. Kirshner 1974)
      J.Gilchrist, The Church and Economic Activity in the MA
                (1969)
      J.T. Joynson, Ideology, Reason and the Limitation of War:
                Religious and Secular Concepts 1200-1740 (1975)

E. Kantorowicz, Laudes Regiae: A Study in Liturgical
    Acclamations and Medieval Ruler Worship (1946)
E. Kantorowicz, The King's Two Bodies (1958)
G. Le Bras et al. Histoire du droit et des institutions de
    l'église en Occident, VII (Paris 1965): Sources et
    théorie du droit
K.F. Morrison, Rome and the City of God: Constitutional
    Relationships of Empire and Church in the Fourth
    Century (Trans. Amer. Philos. Soc. 1964)
R.C. Mortimer, Western Canon Law (U Calif 1953)
J.T. Noonan, Scholastic Analysis of Usury (1957)
F.H. Russell, The Just War in the Middle Ages (CUP 1975)
J.B. Russell, A History of Medieval Christianity: Prophecy
    and Order (Crowell 1968)
M.Spinka, John Hus' Concept of the Church (Princeton 1969)
E. Troeltsch, Social Teaching of the Christian Churches, I
    (Torchbk)
G.Zampaglione, The Idea of Peace in Antiquity (Notre Dame)

May 5   The Liturgy: the Mass: Sermons: Christian literature:
         the Sacraments

    Reading : Daniélou, The Bible and the Liturgy
                 Bettenson 62-79

    Recommended: Augustine, On Christian Doctrine (LLA)
         C.W. Bynum, Jesus as Mother: Studies in the Spirituality
             of the High Middle Ages (U Calif Pr 1984)
         G.Dix, The Shape of the Liturgy (1945)
         J.A.Jungmann, The Early Liturgy to the time of Gregory
             the Great (1961)
         J.A.Jungmann, The Mass of the Roman Rite 2 vols (1951-55)
         H.C. Lea, History of Auricular Confession and Indulgences
             in the Latin Church 3 vols (1896)
         H.C. Lea, History of Sacerdotal Celibacy (1966 repr)
         J.F. McCue, "Doctrine of Transubstantiation from Berengar
             through Trent," Harvard Theol.Rev. (1968)
         R.C. Mortimer, Origins of Private Penance in the Western
             Church (1939)
         G.R. Owst, Literature and Pulpit in Medieval England 2d ed
             (1961)
         G.R. Owst, Preaching in Medieval England (1965 repr)
         F.J.E. Raby, Christian Latin Poetry 2d ed (1953)
         S. Sticca, "Christian Drama and Christian Liturgy,"
             Latomus (1967)
         A.W. Watts, Myth and Ritual in Christianity (Beacon)
         J.L. Weston, From Ritual to Romance [Holy Grail] (Anchor)

May 12   History and Transmission of the Bible: Biblical Criticism
         and Interpretation: Scholastic Theology

   Reading: Book of Revelation/Bettenson 137-50
            Smalley, Study of the Bible in the MA

   Recommended: P.R. Ackroyd, C.F. Evans, edd. Cambridge
        History of the Bible: From the Beginnings to Jerome (1970)
        Cassiodorus, Divine and Human Readings (ed Jones)
        F.C. Copleston, Aquinas (Penguin)
        R.H. Fuller, The New Testament in Current Study (Scribners)
        H. Hailperin, Rashi and the Christian Scholars (1963)
        D. Knowles, Evolution of Medieval Thought (Pelican)
        G.W.H. Lampe, Cambridge History of the Bible: the West from
             the Fathers to the Reformation (1969)
        J.S. Preus, From Shadow to Promise: OT Interpretation from
             Augustine to the Young Luther (Harvard 1969)

May 19 - Thursday schedule

May 26   Final Examination

MOUNT HOLYOKE COLLEGE

History 351: Undergraduate Seminar on Western Monasticism
(one three-hour meeting per week)
Carole E. Straw

A study of Western monasticism, from its origins to the sixteenth century, and its impact on Western culture and institutions, with special emphasis on the individual, the community and their mutual accommodation.

Books Available for Purchase in the College Bookstore

Lawrence, C.H. Medieval Monasticism: Forms of Religious Life in
          Western Europe in the Middle Ages (Longman)
Jean Leclercq, The Love of Learning and the Desire for God (Fordham)
Theodoret of Cyrrhus, A History of the Monks of Syria (Cistercian)
Evagrius Ponticus, Praktikos and Chapters on Prayer (Cistercian)
Dorotheos of Gaza, Discourses and Sayings (Cistercian)
Gregory of Nyssa, The Life of St. Macrina (Peregrina)
Aelred of Rivaulx, Spiritual Friendship (Cistercian)
Teresa of Avila, The Life of Teresa of Jesus: The Autobiography of
          St. Teresa of Avila (Doubleday)
Edward Peters, ed., Monks, Bishops and Pagans: Christian Culture
          in Gaul and Italy, 500-700 (U. of Pennsylvania Press)
Book of Photocopied Texts

Schedule of Class Meetings and Assignments

Week 1   Pre-Christian Monastic Movements and Biblical
                              Justifications for "the Way of Perfection"

                                   The Song of Songs
                                   The Gospel of Saint Matthew
                                   The Gospel of Saint Luke
                                   (And other biblical passages)

Week 2   Flight to the Desert--its Attractions, and
                              Hardships, and Victory. The Cenobitic Life.

                                   Athanasius, Life of Saint Anthony
                                   C.H. Lawrence, Medieval Monasticism, 1-16.

                                   REPORT:
                                   Peter Brown, "The Rise and Function of the

Holy Man in Late Antiquity," Journal of
Roman Studies.

Week 3   Monastic Organization: Authority, Discipleship,
                and Koinonia. The Monastic Life.

Theodoret of Cyrrhus, A History of the Monks of
Syria

REPORT
Philip Rousseau, "The Spiritual Authority of the
'Monk-Bishop': Eastern Elements in Some
Western Hagiography of the Fourth and Fifth
Centuries," Journal of Theological Studies, ser.
2, vol. 22, part 2 (Oct. 1971): 380-419.

Week 4   The Melting Pot of Monastic Spirituality:
                Euanggelion, Stoicism, Hellenistic Philosophies,
                and Far Eastern Traditions

Evagrius Ponticus, Praktikos and Chapters
on Prayer
Dorotheos of Gaza, Discourses and Sayings
Epictetus, The Enchiridion

REPORT:
Herbert Musurillo, "The Problem of Ascetical
Fasting in the Greek Patristic Writers,"
Traditio 12 (1956): 1-64.

Week 5   Forming Ideals of the Life of Perfection

Gregory of Nyssa, On Virginity
                        , The Life of Saint Macrina
Jerome, The Life of Paul the Hermit
        , The Life of Malchus the Captive Monk
Augustine, "Letter of Aurelius Augustine to the
consecrated virgins" (Letter 211)
John Cassian of Marseilles, Conferences
(Selections)

REPORT:
Jo Ann McNamara, "Muffled Voices: The Lives
of Consecrated Women in the Fourth Century,"
in Medieval Religious Women, Vol. 1, pp. 11-
29 (CS 71).

Week 6   The Beginnings of Benedictine Monasticism:
                                Regularity of Life--Work and Prayer

                                     Saint Benedict, The Rule of Saint Benedict
                                     Gregory the Great, The Dialogues (Book II)
                                            , Selections (in Peters)
                                     C.H. Lawrence, Medieval Monasticism, 17-35.
                                     Leclercq, The Love of Learning and the Desire
                                        for God, 1-50.

                                     REPORT:
                                     Adalbert de Vogue, "The Rule of St. Benedict,"
                                        in The Rule of St. Benedict (Collegeville,
                                        Minnesota: The Liturgical Press, 1981),65-112.

Week 7   Peregrinare pro Christo: Missions, Conversions, and
                                     the Movement of Monasticism to the North

                                     Sulpicius Severus, Life of Saint Martin
                                     Jonas, The Life of Columbanus (in Peters)
                                     from The Life of St. Gall, "The Driving Out of
                                        Demons," (in Peters)
                                     Bede, The Ecclesiastical History of the English
                                        People (Selections in Peters)
                                     Life of Leoba [trans. Dorothy
                                        Whitelock, in English Historical
                                     Documents, c. 500-1042, Vol. I.]
                                     C.H. Lawrence, Medieval Monasticism, 36-75.

                                     REPORT:
                                     Jane Tibbets Schulenberg, "Strict Enclosure and
                                        its Effects on the Female Monastic Experience
                                        (500-1100)," in Medieval Religious Women, Vol.
                                        1, pp. 51-86 (CS 71).

Week 8   SEMESTER BREAK

Week 9   Falling Short of the Ideal: Rumors of Dissipation and
                                     Calls for Monastic Reform--From Cluny
                                     to Bury St. Edmund

                                     Jocelin of Brakelond, The Chronicle
                                     Movie: "The Medieval Monastery" (to be shown in
                                        class)
                                     C.H. Lawrence, Medieval Monasticism, 76-144.
                                     Leclercq, The Love of Learning and the Desire
                                        for God, 52-111.

REPORT:
Mary Skinner, "Benedictine Life for Women in
Central France, 850-1100: A Feminist Revival,"
in Medieval Religious Women, Vol. 1, pp. 87
-114 (CS 71).

Week 10   The Flowering of Medieval Monasticism: Affective
                 Spirituality and the Confidence in Reason

                 Saint Bernard (selections)
                 Aelred of Rivaulx, Spiritual Friendship
                 C.H. Lawrence, Medieval Monasticism, 146-175.
                 Leclercq, The Love of Learning and the Desire
                 for God, 112-150.

                 REPORT:
                 Brian Patrick McGuire, "Monastic Friendship and
                 Toleration in Twelfth-Century Cistercian Life,"
                 in Monks, Hermits and the Ascetic Tradition,
                 pp. 147-160.

Week 11   Breaking Monastic Traditions: "The Secular City"
                 Dominic and Francis and the Coming of the Friars:

                 Saint Bonaventure, The Life of Saint Frances
                 Francis of Assisi, The Little Flowers
                     (Selections)
                 Claire of Assisi, The Testament of Saint Claire
                 C.H. Lawrence, Medieval Monasticism, 176-220.
                 Leclercq, The Love of Learning and the Desire
                 for God, 153-190.

                 REPORT:
                 Dennis Devlin, "Feminine Lay Piety in the High
                 Middle Ages: The Beguines," Medieval
                 Religious Women, Vol. 1, pp. 183-196.

Week 12   The Catholic Counter-Reformation and the Medieval
                 Monastic Ideal

                 Teresa of Avila, The Life of Teresa of Jesus
                 Leclercq, The Love of Learning and the Desire
                 for God, 191-235.

                 REPORT:
                 A.D. Wright, "The Religious Life in the Spain of
                 Philip II and Philip III," in Monks, Hermits,
                 and the Ascetic Tradition, pp. 251-274.

Week 13   "Ad Vitam Perfectionis Spectantes": A Monastic
                             Retreat, "Regina Laudis Monastery"

                                   C.H. Lawrence, Medieval Monasticism, 220-233.
                                   Leclercq, The Love of Learning and the
                                         Desire for God, pp. 236-270.

Week 14   Student Presentations

COURSE REQUIREMENTS:

Book/Article Report
Regular Attendance
Active Participation
Monastic Retreat
Final Paper

I.   The Rise of Monasticism

    Workman, Herbert B., <u>The Evolution of the Monastic Ideal</u>
      (Beacon Press, 1962), 1-216

    Knowles, David, <u>Christian Monasticism</u> (McGraw Hill, 1969)
      1-61

    Verdon, Timothy Gregory, <u>Monasticism and the Arts</u>
      (Syracuse, 1984), 1-80

    Leclercq, Jean, <u>The Love of Learning and the Desire for God</u>
      (New American Library 1961), 1-56

II.   The Eleventh and Twelfth Centuries

    Knowles, David, 62-107

    Leclercq, Jean, 57-249

    Gibson, Margaret, <u>Lanfranc of Bec</u> (Oxford, 1978), 1-193

    Johnson, Penelope, <u>Prayer, Patronage, and Power; The Abbey
      of la Trinite, Vendome, 1032-1187</u> (New York University
      Press, 1981), 1-179

    Verdon, Timothy Gregory, <u>Monasticism and the Arts</u>, 81-207

    West, Delno C. and Sandro Zimbards-Schwartz, <u>Joachim of
      Fiore</u> (Indiana, 1983)

    Starnes, Kathleen M., <u>Peter Abelard, His Place in History</u>
      (University Press, 1981), 1-139

    Matthew, Donald, <u>The Norman Monasteries and Their
      Possessions</u> (Greenwood, 1962)

    Hunt, Noreen, <u>Cluny Under Saint Hugh, 1049-1159</u>
      (Notre-Dame, 1967)

III. The Flowering

D'Avray, D.L., <u>The Preaching of the Friars</u> (Oxford, 1985),
1-259

Verdon, pp. 207-269

Erikson, Joan Mowat, <u>Saint Francis et His Four Ladies</u>
(Norton, 1970)

Brooke, Rosalind, <u>The Coming of the Friars</u>,
(London, NY, 1975)

Barbara H. Rosenwein and Lester K. Little, <u>The Social
Meaning of Monks and Friars, The Many Sides of History</u>,
S. Ozment and Frank M. Turner, Vol. 1, 100-120

IV. The Decline

Woodward, G.W.O., <u>The Dissolution of the Monasteries</u>
(NY, Walker, 1966)

Kristeller, P.O., "The Contribution of Religious Orders to
Renaissance Thought and Learning" in <u>Medieval Aspects of
Renaissance Learning</u> (Duke, 1974)

V. Woman in Monasticism

<u>Medieval Women's Visionary Literature</u>, ed. Elisabeth Alvida
Petroff (NY, 1986)

The Three Religions
Jewish-Muslim-Christian Contacts in the Middle Ages

Junior Seminar, Tuesday 1:30-3:320
John Boswell
Yale University

Requirements: readings, attendance at weekly discussions; two
papers. First paper (due at 4th meeting): 3 pages maximum (pages
beyond 3 will be discarded, unread, by instructor) on assigned
topic: criticize one of the three religions from the perspective
of an adherent of another. (Further details in class.)
Second paper (due last day of classes: extensions require at
least one week prior approval): research paper on some aspect of
the interaction of at least two of the three religions or their
adherents. Topic to be chosen by student and approved by
instructor. Minimum 10pp; no maximum, but brevity and high
content>word ratio strongly encouraged. See p.4 for
bibliographical assistance.

Weekly readings:

[a date in parentheses indicates a volume on reserve for this
course in CCL or SML; the name of a press in parentheses
indicates a book (also on reserve) you may wish to purchase for
yourself at the Co-op; both together indicate an expensive book
you could buy but might prefer to consult in the library]

1st week: **Jewish scriptures and lawcodes, Hellenization**
Genesis, Leviticus, Isaiah (use any translation not already
familiar to you or the Masoretic or Septuagint text)
The Mishnah, trans. Herbert Danby (1933).: Moed, Shabbath
(pp.99-120); Nashim, Sotah (pp.293-307); Nezikin, Abodah Zarah
(pp.437-46)
Philo Judaeus, "Selections," ed. H. Lewy, in Three Jewish
Philosophers (1972), pp.27-51, 93-106

2nd week: **Christian scriptures and laws, Hellenization**
Matthew, John, Acts, Galatians (any translation not already
familiar to you, or the Greek text or Vulgate translation)
Canons of the Councils of Elvira, trans. Laeuchli   , and
Nicea, in C. Davis, The Eagle the Crescent and the Cross (1967)
pp.23-28, or in H. Schroeder, Disciplinary Decrees of the
General Councils (1937) pp.18-58 [with commentary]

3d week: Muslim scriptures and law; Hellenization
The Meaning of the Glorious Koran, trans. M.M. Pickthall
(Mentor): Surahs 2, 13, 17
A Manual of Hadith, ed. M.M. Ali (1977), pp.1-30, 41-67, 223-31,
268-81, 293-301, 344-58, 373-408
G. von Grunebaum, Medieval Islam (Univ. of Chicago) pp.142-69,
294-319

4th week: early interaction
J.R. Marcus, The Jew in the Medieval World (Atheneum) pp.3-9,
20-24, 101-15, 349-55
F. Talmage, Disputation and Dialogue: a Reader in the
Jewish-Christian Encounter (KTAV) pp.17-32, 89-99, 134-37
St John Damascene "On the Moslem Heresy," trans. J. Voorhis, The
Moslem World 24 (1934) 392-98 and idem, "The Discussion of a
Christian and a Saracen," ibid. 25 (1935) 266-73
'Abu ʿUthman ʿAmr b. Bahr al-Jahiz, "Risala on the
Christians," trans. Joshua Finkel, Journal of the American
Oriental Society 47 (1927) 322-34
Gregory of Tours and creeds   {NB: less than 100pp.total}

5th week: Islam in Europe (and the Jews in Muslim Spain)
The Poem of the Cid, trans. W.S. Merwin (NAL)
R.W. Southern, Western Views of Islam in the Middle Ages
(Harvard) pp.1-33
N. Stillman, The Jews of Arab Lands (Jewish Publ.Soc.)
pp.152-167
Monroe, J. Hispano-Arabic Poetry (1974) pp.206-212, Stillman,
pp.211-25, and Goldstein, D. The Jewish Poets of Spain (1965)
pp.39-40, 60-71, 119-21, 137-39

6th week: the beginnings of dialogue
Talmage, Disputation, 9-13, 71-81, 117-19, 155-74
Abelard, Dialogue of a Philosopher with a Jew and a Christian,
trans. P.J. Payer (PIMS)
Joseph Kimhi, The Book of the Covenant, trans. F. Talmage (PIMS)
or J. Halevi, Kuzari, ed. I. Heinemann, in Three Jewish
Philosophers, pp.7-130.

**7th week: armed conflict--the Christian view of the
Crusades**
"Spurious Letter of Alexius Comnenus to Count Robert of Flanders
Imploring His Aid against the Turks"--
either The Deeds of the Franks, ed.R. Hill (1962)
or Fulcher of Chartres, A History of the Expedition to
Jerusalem, 1095-1127, trans. F. Ryan (1969) [or in E. Peters,
The First Crusade (1971)]
or Odo of Deuil, De profectione Ludovici VII in orientem (The
Journey of Louis VII to the East), ed. & trans. V. Berry (1948)
or Robert of Clari, The Conquest of Constantinople, trans. E.
McNeal (1964)

or The Song of Roland (any translation you have not read before)

8th week: **armed conflict--other views**
The Jews and the First Crusaders, ed. & trans. S. Eidelberg (U.
of Wisconsin)
one account from F. Gabrielli, Arab Historians of the Crusades
(1969)
or Usamah ibn Murshid Ibn Munquidh, Ibn Munqid, An Arab-Syrian
Gentleman and Warrior in the Period of the Crusades, trans. P.
Hitti (1929)
or Ibn al-Qalanisi, The Damascus Chronicle of the Crusades,
trans. H.A.R. Gibb (1932)

9th week: **philosophical harmony and the appeal to reason**
Averroes [Ibn Rushd], On the Harmony of Religion and Philosophy,
trans. G. Hourani (1976) pp.44-71
Maimonides, The Guide of the Perplexed, in I. Twersky, A
Maimonides Reader (Behrman) pp.234-35, 251,259-65, 274-291,
335-39
Thomas Aquinas, Summa contra Gentiles, trans. the English
Dominican Fathers (1923) or A. Pegis (Doubleday, 1955), Bk 1,
chs.1-8, 11-13; Bk 2, chs. 32-38
creeds

10th week: writing a research paper
class discussion of methods of research, analytical techniques,
varieties of historical approach, organizing and writing papers;
historiographical and technical issues
each student will submit to the class an outline and preliminary
bibliography of his second paper and to one other student a
revision of the first paper

11th week: **sectarian responses: Judaism and Islam**
Maimonides, "Epistle to Yemen," in Maimonides Reader, pp.438-62
The Jewish-Christian Debate in the High Middle Ages: A Critical
edition of the Nizzahon Vetus with an Introduction, Translation
and Commentary, David Berger (Jewish Pub.Soc.) pp.167-230
Samau'al al-Maghribi, "Ifham al-Yahud," ed. & trans. M. Perlmann
in Proceedings of the American Academy for Jewish Research 32
(1964) 31-93

12th week: **darkening clouds: the 13th century**
Marcus, pp.24-28, 34-42, 121-54, 368-69
Ibn Kammuna's Examination of the Three Faiths, trans. M.
Perlmann (1971)
"The Disputation of Rabbi Moses Ben Nachman with Fra Paulo
Christiani on the subject of the Jewish Faith," in O.S. Rankin,
Jewish Religious Polemics (1956), pp.178-210 [or in M. Braude,
Conscience on Trial (1952) pp.69-94]

13th week: **the final storm**
Marcus, pp.43-60
F. Machado, The Mirror of the New Christians (Espelho de
Christãos novos, ed. & trans. M. Vieira (PIMS, 1977)
pp.45-79, 231-83, 311-27

Although part of teaching is helping students to locate sources,
part of writing a paper is learning to locate materials on your
own. Use the notes and bibliographies of assigned texts to
pursue more specialized studies, or consult general
bibliographies for the areas which interest you. Ask the
instructor for bibliographical assistance only after you have
made some effort to familiarize yourself with relevant
bibliographical materials. For Western Europe in the Middle
Ages, e.g., see R.C. van Caenegem and F.L. Ganshof, Guide to the
Sources of Medieval History (1978) or L.J. Paetow, Guide to the
Study of Medieval History (1931), both of which will help you to
find more specialized references by topic. If you read only
English but wish to work with primary sources, it will help you
to consult C.P. Farrar and A. Evans, Bibliography of English
Translations from Medieval Sources (1946), updated by M.
Ferguson, Bibliography of English Translations from Medieval
Sources 1943-67 (1967), to see what is available.
      Materials relating to Jews under Christianity and Islam are
conveniently summarized in the essays and bibliographies in
Bibliographical Essays in Medieval Jewish Studies (The Study of
Judaism, II) (1976). J. Sauvaget, Introduction to the History of
the Muslim East (1965) and the Index Islamicus [ongoing] provide
bibliographical introductions and indices for Islam. For brief
historical background The Cambridge Medieval History and The
Cambridge History of Islam may prove useful, and for specific
topics quick assistance (and small bibliographies) are available
in The Catholic Encyclopedia (the 1908 edition is more detailed,
though also more biassed, than the new one), The Jewish
Encyclopedia and the Encyclopedia Judaica, and The Encyclopaedia
of Islam [2d edition complete only through "K"].

Some suggestions for paper topics, to be taken as food for
thought rather than as constraints:
      Contrast the attitudes toward two religions evinced in the
work of an adherent of a third; e.g., attitudes toward Jews and
Muslims in The Poem of the Cid. Distinguish between personal
relations and attitudes and ideological responses to systems of
belief.
      Using two specific sources from different periods, discuss
the effect on one of the three religions of one or both of the

others (e.g., show that although both Saadia Gaon and Maimonides
were influenced by Islam, the influence of Christianity makes
Maimonides' attitudes substantially different from Saadia's.)
     Analyze the differential impact of some social
issue--assimilation, secularization, intermarriage, church-state
relations, etc.--on two religions. Limit your answer to a
specific and reasonably short time period.
     Contrast the polemical literature of one age or area (but
not both) with that of another.
     Differentiate among the attitudes of proponents of the three
religions at a given time in regard to a social or moral issue
such as divorce, business ethics, warfare, etc.
     Try to account for differences in tolerance of other
religions within one religious tradition over a period of time:
e.g., why does Christian Europe seem so much less tolerant in
the Later Middle Ages than in the early medieval period?
     Compare the developments of one aspect of religious
experience (eschatology, mysticism, orthodoxy, etc.) in two of
the religious traditions during a given period and comment on
the extent to which they can be explained by the particularities
of the tradition itself or appear to be the result of broader
historical trends affecting all religious systems of the time.

<u>THE CRUSADES: A REASSESSMENT</u>
G57.2219

Penny Johnson
spring, 1985

19 Univ. Place
room 410
598-3322/3

This course is designed as a colloquium to explore in great depth the
phenomenon of the medieval crusades, attempting to weigh and balance
the different perspectives of those involved.

Each student is to assume a <u>perspective</u>, for instance, that of a
geographic area: France, Spain, the Germanies, Byzantium;
or of a power: the papacy, the Holy Roman Empire;
or of an ethnic group: the Jews, the Arabs;
or of a problem: the crusade as economic event.
Whatever the perspective adopted, that student is to read
particularly in that area from the general reading list and attempt
to bring an acute sensitivity to the class discussions. I hope that
we can have at a minimum, people to represent the key positions of:
                              western Christendom,
                              Byzantium,
                              the Jews,
                              the Arabs.

The requirements are to do the designated reading and participate in
each class discussion. Students will be expected to attend all
classes with one unexcused absence. There will be no lectures. In
addition, each student will close the course with one of three
options:
                    a paper of between 12 and 20 pages.
                    an oral presentation of 30 minutes.
                    a final exam.
Further reading and research to prepare for this project can come
from the general reading list or from other sources tracked down by
the student.

WEEKLY TOPICS AND ASSIGNMENTS FOR
THE CRUSADES: A REASSESSMENT

Feb. 5   INTRODUCTION

Feb. 12   THE OVERVIEW
+Hans Mayer, The Crusades tr. John Gillingham, Oxford
(1972). Read the whole book, and then reread the
appropriate sections each week.

Feb. 19   EPIC REFLECTIONS OF CRUSADING FERVOR
+The Song of Roland, tr. Sayers, Penguin pb.
+The Cid, tr. W. S. Merwin, NAL pb. (1975).
G. E. von Grunebaum, "The World of Islam: The Face of the
Antagonist," Twelfth Century Europe and the
Foundations of Modern Society, ed. M. Clagett et
al.

Feb. 26   "DEUS VULT." THE LAUNCHING OF THE FIRST CRUSADE
+Fulcher of Chartres, A History of the Expedition to
Jerusalem Norton (1969).
+Anna Comnena, The Alexiad, tr. E. R. Sewter, Penguin (1969)
pp. 333-469.

Mar. 5   JEWS AND ARABS DURING THE FIRST CRUSADE
+F. Gabrieli, Arab Historians of the Crusades U. of Ca.
Press (1978) pp. 3-55.
+The Jews and the Crusaders ed. Shlomo Eidelberg, U.
Wisconsin Press (1977).
+Robert Chazan ed. Church, State, and Jew in the Middle
Ages Behrman pb (1980) pp. 57-63, 113-4.
S. D. Goitein, "Contemporary Letters on the Capture of
Jerusalem," Journal of Jewish Studies 3 (1952).

Mar. 12   ARAB CULTURE
+Usamah Ibn, Memoirs of an Arab-Syrian Gentleman ed. Philip
Hitti AMS Press (1964).
Norman Daniel, "The Developmnent of the Christian
Attitude to Islam," Dublin Review 231 (1957).
W. M. Watt, "Islamic Conceptions of the Holy War," in
The Holy War, ed. Thomas Murphy (1976) pp. 141-156.

Mar. 19   ST. BERNARD AND THE SECOND CRUSADE
+Odo of Deuil, De profectione Ludovici VII in orientem ed.
Virginia Berry, Norton (1948).
Gabrieli, pp. 56-84.
Chazan, pp. 100-8, 114-117.
Constable, "The Second Crusade as Seen by Contemporaries,"
Traditio 9 (1953).

Mar. 26   THE CRUSADE OF THE KINGS
          Gabrieli, pp. 87-252.
          Chazan, pp. 157-165, 309-312.
          Chazan, "Emperor Frederick I, the Third Crusade, and the
              Jews," Viator 8 (1977).
          Gavin Langmuir, "The Jews and the Archives of Angevin
              England: Reflections on Medieval Anti-Semitism,"
              Traditio 19 (1963).
          Amboise, Crusade of Richard Lion-Heart pp. 31-53.

April 9   THE IDEAL ASTRAY: THE FOURTH CRUSADE
          +Villehardouin, in Chronicles of the Crusades, tr. Shaw,
              Penguin (1963).
          +Donald Queller, The Fourth Crusade, U. Pa. Press (1978).

April 16 WOMEN AND CHILDREN
          James Brundage, "The Crusader's Wife," and "The Crusader's
              Wife Revisited," Studia Gratiana 12 & 14 (1967).
          Peter Raedts, "The Children's Crusade of 1212," Journal of
              Medieval History 3 (1977).
          Maureen Purcell, "Women Crusaders: A Temporary Canonical
              Aberration?" In L. O. Frappell Principalities, Powers
              and Estates (1979).
          Hans Mayer, "Queen Melisende of Jerusalem," Dumbarton Oaks
              Papers 26 (1972).

April 23 ST. LOUIS AND THE CRUSADE.
          +Joinville in Chronicles of the Crusades ed. Shaw.
          Gabrieli, pp. 284-304.
          Chazan, pp. 213-220, 283-287.

April 30 THE LAST STAGES
          Gabrieli, pp. 307-350.
          Chazan, pp. 319-322.
          H. A. R. Gibb, "The Influence of Islamic Culture on Medieval
              Europe," Bulletin of the John Rylands Library 38
              (1955).
          A. Luttrell, "The Crusade in the Fourteenth Century," Europe
              in the Late Middle Ages, ed. John R. Hale (1965).

May 7   ORAL PRESENTATIONS

May 14 ORAL PRESENTATIONS

    All books and articles are on reserve in Bobst (books under the
authors' names, and copied articles under P. Johnson).
    All books designated + have been ordered at the Book Center.
    All xeroxed articles are also in my box in the history department
where they can be read in the department lounge, or signed out for a
brief time only to be copied. Please be considerate of each other.

PRIMARY SOURCES:

ISLAM:

Anonymous Syriac Chronicle. "The First and Second Crusades from an
  Anonymous Syriac Chronicle," tr. A. S. Tritton, notes H. A. R.
  Gibb, Journal of the royal Asiatic Society (1933) (1st and 2nd)
Ayyubids, Mamlukes and Crusaders: Selections from the Tarikh al-Duwal
  we'l-Muluk of Ibn al-Furat, tr., U. and M.C. Lyons 2 vols.,
  (1971).
Beha ed-Din ibn Shedad, Life of Saladin, tr. C. W. Wilson, Palestine
  Pilgrim's Texts Society (1897) (3rd).
The Autobiography of Ousâna, 1095-1188, ed. G.R. Potter (1929).
**Gabrieli, Francesco, ed., Arab Historians of the Crusades U. of
  California Press (reprinted 1978) (all crusades).
Ibn-al-Qualanisi, The Damascus Chronicle of the Crusades Extracted
  and tr. by H. A. R. Gibb, "University of London Historical
  Series," no. 5, (1932).
Ibn Battuta,The Travels of Ibn Battuta, a.d. 1325-1354 tr. H. A. R.
  Gibb, 2 vols. ser. 2, nos. 110, 117, (1958 and 1962).
Ibn Jubayr, The Travels of Ibn Jubrayr, tr. R. Broadhurst, (1952)
Medieval Islamic Medicine: Ibn Ridwan's Treatise "On the Prevention
  of Bodily Ills in Egypt, trans. Michael W. Dols ed. Adil S. Gamal
  (Berkeley, 1984).
Nâsir-i-Khusrau, Diary of a Journey through Syria and Palestine in
  1047 tr. G. le Strange, PPTS (1893) (pre-crusades).
Saladin: The Politics of the Holy War, ed. Malcolm Lyons and David
  Jackson (Cambridge, Eng.: 1987).
**Usamah Ibn, Munqidh, Memoirs of an Arab-Syrian Gentleman or An
  Arab Knight in the Crusades ed. Philip K. Hitti, (1964)(2nd)

THE JEWS:

Abu'l Faraj, The Chronography of Gregory Abuy'l Faraj, The Son of
  Aaron, The Hebrew Physician Commonly Known as Bar Hebraeus, tr.
  Ernest A. Wallis Budge, vol. 1, (1932). (1st)
**Chazan, Robert ed., Church, State, and Jew in the Middle Ages
  (1980).
Marcus, Jacob R. ed., The Jew in the Medieval World; A Source Book:
  315-1791 (1975).
**The Jews and the Crusaders: The Hebrew Chronicles of the First and
  Second Crusades ed. Shlomo Eidelberg U. of Wisconsin hb.,
  (1977)(1st & 2nd).

THE CHRISTIANS: edited collections

Bedier, J. P. Aubry, Les chansons de croisade (1909)

Brundage, James ed., <u>The Crusades: A Documentary Survey</u> (1962) (all
   crusades).
Krey, August ed., <u>The First Crusade: The Accounts of Eye-Witnesses</u>
   <u>and Participants</u> (1921) (1st)
Munro, Dana C. ed., <u>Letters of the Crusaders</u> (1894) (all crusades).
Pernoud, Regine ed., <u>The First Crusade</u> (1st)

THE CHRISTIANS:

**Amboise, <u>The Crusade of Richard Lion-Heart</u> tr. M. J. Hubert.(repr.
   1976) (3rd)
**Anna Comnena, <u>The Alexiad</u> Penguin pb., (1969), (1st)
Archer, T. ed., <u>The Crusade of Richard I,</u> (1889), (3rd).
<u>De expugnatione Lyxbonensi,</u> tr., D. W. David, (1936)
Emerton, E. ed., <u>Correspondence of Pope Gregory VII</u> (1st)
**Fulcher of Chartres, <u>A History of the Expedition to Jerusalem,</u>
   <u>1095-1127,</u> tr. F. R. Ryan, ed. Harold Fink Norton pb., (1969).
   (1st)
Helmold, <u>The Chronicle of the Slavs,</u> tr. F. J. Tschan, (1935).
**Joinville and Villehardouin, <u>Chronicles of the Crusades</u> tr. M. R.
   B. Shaw (1963) Penguin pb., (4th, 7th ✛ 8th)
Kohler, Charles ed. "Un sermon comméemoratif de la prise de Jérusalem
   par les croisés, attribué à Foucher de Chartres," <u>Revue de</u>
   <u>l'Orient latin</u> 7 (1901), 158-64. (1st)
**Odo of Deuil, <u>De profectione Ludovici VII in orientem: The Journey</u>
   <u>of Louis VII to the East</u> ed. Virginia Berry, Norton pb., (1948)
   (2nd)
Otto of Freising and his continuator, Rahewin, <u>The Deeds of</u>
   <u>Frederick Barbarossa</u> Norton pb. (1956) (3rd).
"Pèlerinage en Palestine de l'Abbesse Euphrosyne, Princesse de
   Polotsk" tr. de Khitrowo <u>Revue de l'Orient Latin</u> 3 (1896).
Raymond of Aguilers, <u>Raymond of Aguilers, Historia Francorum qui</u>
   <u>ceperunt Jerusalem,</u> tr. J.; H. and L. L. Hill (1968).
Richard of Devizes, <u>Chronicle of Richard of Devizes of the Time of</u>
   <u>King Richard the First,</u> tr. J. T. Appleby (1963) (3rd).
**<u>The Poem of the Cid,</u> tr. W. S. Merwin, (1975) NAL pb.
   (reconquista).
Tudebode, Peter, <u>Peter Tudebode, Historia Hierosolymitano itinere,</u>
   tr. J. H. and L. L. Hill (1974).
William of Tyre, <u>William of Tyre: A History of the Deeds done beyond</u>
   <u>the Sea,</u> tr. E. Babcock and A. C. Krey, 2 vols. (repr. 1971)
   (1st).

**Designates a work which is required to be read for this course and
is on reserve in Bobst.
*Designates a work which is optional, but is on reserve in Bobst.

SECONDARY SOURCES:

Alphandery, P., and A. Dupront, La chrétienté et l'idée de croisade 2 vols, (1954-59).

Atiya, A. S., Crusade, Commerce, and Culture (1962).

Barber, Malcolm, "Lepers, Jews and Moslems: The Plot to Overthrow Christendom in 1321," History 66 (1980).

_____, The Trial of the Templars (1978).

Beebe, B., "The English Baronage and the Crusade of 1270," Bulletin of the Institute of Historical Research 48 (1975).

Blake, E. O., "The Formation of the 'Crusade Idea'", Journal of Ecclesiastical History 21 (1970).

Brundage, James, "'Cruce Signari': The Rite for Taking the Cross in England," Tradition 22 (1966).

_____, Canon Law and the Crusader.

**_____, "The Crusader's Wife," and "The Crusader's Wife Revisited," Studia Gratiana 12 (1967) and 14 (1967).

_____, "The Army of the First Crusade and the Crusade Vow: Some Reflections on a Recent Book," Medieval Studies 33 (1971).

Bulliet, Richard W., Conversion to Islam in the Medieval Period: An Essay in Quantitative History (1979).

Burns, Robert I., Islam under the Crusaders. Colonial Survival in the Thirteenth-Century Kingdom of Valencia (1973).

_____, Muslims, Christians, and Jews in the Crusader Kingdom of Valencia (1984).

Cahen, Claude, "Une lettre d'un prisonnier musulman des Francs de Syrie," in Melanges Edmond-René Labande (1974).

Christiansen, E., The Northern Crusades (1980).

**Constable, Giles, "The Second Crusade as Seen by Contemporaries," Traditio 9 (1953).

Cowdrey, H. E. J., "Pope Urban II's Preaching of the First Crusade," History 55 (1970).

Crocker, Richard L., "Early Crusade Songs," in T. P. Murphy, ed., The Holy War (1976).

Daniel, Norman, Islam and the West: The Making of an Image (1962).

**_____, "The Development of the Christian Attitude to Islam," Dublin Review 231 (1957).

Delaville le Roulx, J., La France en Orient au XIVe siècle: Expéditions du maréchal Boucicaut 2 vols. (1885-6).

Duncalf, F. "The Peasants' Crusade," AHR 26 (1920-1).

Erdmann, Carl, The Origin of the Idea of Crusade, tr. of 1935 ed. notes by Baldwin and Goffart (1977).

Favreau, M.-L., Studien zur Fruhgeschichte des Deutschen Ordens (1974).

**Gibb, H. A. R., "The Influence of Islamic Culture on Medieval Europe," Bulletin of the John Rylands Library 38 (1955).

Hehl, E.-D., Kirche und Kreig im 12. Jahrhundert (1980).

Housley, Norman, The Italian Crusades: The Papal-Angevin Alliance and the Crusades Against Christian Lay Powers 1254-1343 (1982).

Jacoby, D. "Crusader Acre in the Thirteenth Century: Urban Layout and Topography," Studi Medievali 3rd ser., 20 (1979).

Jordan, William, Louis IX and the Challenge of the Crusade (1979).

Kedar, Benjamin Z., "The Passenger List of a Crusade Ship, 1250: Towards the History of the Popular Element on the Seventh Crusade," Studi Medievali, 3rd ser. 13 (1972).
_____, Crusade and Mission: European Approaches toward the Muslims (1984).
Lomax, D. M., The Reconquest of Spain (1978).
_____, La Ørden de Santiago, 1170-1275 (1965).
**Luttrell, A., "The Crusade in the Fourteenth Century," Europe in the Late Middle Ages, ed. J. A. Hale et al. (1965).
Martin, M. E., "The Venetian-Seljuk Treaty of 1220," EHR 95 (1980).
Moorhead, J., "The Earliest Christian Theological Response to Islam," Religion 2 (1981).
**Mayer, Hans, The Crusades, tr. John Gillingham (1965).
Munro, D. C. , "The Children's Crusade," AHR 19 (1914).
_____ "A Crusader" Speculum 7 (1932).
*_____ The Kingdom of the Crusaders .
Murphy, Thomas, ed., The Holy War (1976).
Nesbitt, J. W., "The Rate of March of Crusading Armies in Europe: a Study and Computation," Traditio 19 (1963).
Ø'Callaghan, J. F., The Spanish Military Ørder of Calatrava and its Affiliates (1975).
Pennington, Kenneth, "The Rite for taking the Cross in the Twelfth Century," Traditio 30 (1974).
**Purcell, Maureen, "Women Crusaders: A Temporary Canonical Aberration?" in Frappell, L. Ø. ed., Principalities, Powers and Estates,
Pflaum, H., "A Strange Crusaders' Song," Speculum 10 (1935).
Pissard, H., La guerre sainte en pays chrétien (1912).
Prawer, Joshua, The Crusaders' Kingdom (1972).
_____, The Latin Kingdom of Jerusalem 1099-1291 (1947).
Prutz, H., Die geistlichen Ritterorden (1908).
Purcell, M., Papal Crusading Policy 1244-1291 (1975).
Porges, Walter, "The Clergy, the Poor, and the Non-Combatants on the First Crusade," Speculum 21 (1946).
Powell, James, Anatomy of a Crusade, 1213-1221 (1986).
Queller, Donald E. and Susan Stratton, "A Century of Controversy on the Fourth Crusade," Studies in Medieval and Renaissance History 6 (1969).
**Queller, Donald E., The Fourth Crusade (1978).
**Raedts, Peter, "The Children's Crusade of 1212," Journal of Medieval History 3 (1977).
Richard, Jean, "An Account of the Battle of Hattin, Referring to the Frankish Mercenaries in Øriental Moslem States," Speculum 27 (1952).
Riley-Smith, Jonathan, "Peace Never Established: The Case of the Kingdom of Jerusalem,"Trans. Roy. Hist. Soc., 5th ser., 28 (1978).
_____, "Crusading as an Act of Love," History 65 (1980).
_____, "An Approach to Crusading Ethics," Reading Medieval Studies 6 (1980).
_____, The First Crusade and the Idea of Crusading (1986).
_____, The Knights of St. John in Jerusalem and Cyrprus, c. 1050-1310 (1967).

Riley-Smith, Louise and Jonathan, <u>The Crusades: Idea and Reality</u>
<u>1095-1274</u> (1981).
Robinson, I. S. "Gregory VII and the Soldiers of Christ," <u>History</u> 58
(1973).
Roscher, H., <u>Papst Innocenz III und die Kreuzzuge</u> (1969).
Rouche, Michel, "Cannibalisme sacré chez les croises populaire," in
Yves-Marie Hilaire, ed., <u>La religion popularie</u> (1981).
Roussett, P. "La notion de Chrétienté aux XIe et XIIe siècles," <u>Moyen</u>
<u>âge</u> 69 (1963).
*Runciman, Steven, <u>A History of the Crusades</u> 3 vols. (1951-54).
Schmandt, R. H., "The Fourth Crusade and the Just-War Theory,"
<u>Catholic Historical Review</u> 61 (1975).
Setton, Kenneth Meyer, <u>A History of the Crusades</u> 6 vols., (1955-).
_____, <u>The Papacy and the Levant 1204-1571</u> 2 vols. (1976-8).
Sivan, E., <u>L'Islam et la croisade</u> (1968).
Smail, R. C., <u>Crusading Warfare (1097-1193)</u> (1956).
Somerville, Robert, "The Council of Clermont and the First Crusade,"
<u>Studia gratiana</u> 20 (1976).
Southern, R. W., <u>Western Views of Islam in the Middle Ages</u> (1980).
Spence, Richard, "Pope Gregory IX and the Crusade in the Baltic," <u>EHR</u>
69 (1983), 1-19.
Sumberg, L. A. M., "The <u>Tafurs</u> and the First Crusade," <u>Medieval</u>
<u>Studies</u> 21 (1959).
Synan, <u>The Popes and the Jews in the Middle Ages.</u>
Throop, Palmer A., <u>Criticism of the Crusade: A Study of Public</u>
<u>Opinion and Crusade Propaganda</u> (1940).
Villey, M. <u>La croisade: Essai sur la formation d'une théorie</u>
<u>juridique</u> (1942).
_____, "L'idée de croisade chez les juristes du moyen âge,"
<u>Relazioni del X congresso internazionale di scienze storiche:</u>
<u>III, Storia del medio evo (1955).</u>
**Watt, W. M., "Islamic Conceptions of the Holy War," in Murphy, <u>Holy</u>
<u>War.</u>
_____, <u>Islam and the Integration of Society</u> (1961).
_____, <u>The Influence of Islam on Medieval Europe</u> (1972).

THE JEWS:

Abrahams, Israel, <u>Jewish Life in the Middle Ages</u> (1969).
Baron, Salo, <u>A Social and Religious History of the Jews</u> 2nd ed. Vols
3-8 (1957).
_____, <u>Ancient and Medieval Jewish History</u> (1972).
**Chazan, Robert, "Emperor Frederick I, the Third Crusade, and the
Jews," <u>Viator</u> 8 (1977).
Dunlop, D. M. <u>The History of the Jewish Khazaqrs</u> (1954).
Goitein, S. D., <u>A Mediterranean Society: The Jewish Communities of</u>
<u>the World as Portrayed in the Documents of the Cairo Geniza</u> vol
1, <u>Economic Foundations</u> (1968); vol. 2, <u>The Community</u> (1971).
**_____, "Contemporary Letters on the Capture of Jerusalem,"
<u>Journal of Jewish Studies</u> 3 (1952).
Grant, Michael, <u>The Jews in the Roman World</u> (1973).

**Langmuir, Gavin, "The Jews and the Archives of Angevin England: Reflections on Medieval Anti-Semitism," Traditio 19 (1963), 183-244.

_____, "From Ambrose of Milan to Emicho of Leiningen: The Transformation of Hostility against Jews in Northern Christendom," Settimane di studio del Centro italiano di studi sull' alto medievo (Mar.-Apr., 1978) 26 (1980).

Roth, Cecil and I. H. Levine eds. The Dark Age: Jews in Christian Europe 711-1096, vol. 2 of Cecil Roth gen. ed., The World History of the Jewish People, Second Series; The Medieval Period (1966).

Starr, Joshua, The Jews in the Byzantine Empire, 641-1204 (1970).

Trachtenberg, Joshua, The Devil and the Jews: The Medieval Conception of the Jew and its Relation to Modern Antisemitism (1943).

**von Grunebaum, G. E., "The World of Islam: The Face of the Antagonist," in Twelfth Century Europe and the Foundations of Modern Society ed. M. Clagett, G. Post, R. Reynolds (1966).

ISLAM:

Andrae, Tor, Mohammed: The Man and his Faith (1960).

Bell, R. Introduction to the Qu'ran (1970).

Daniel, Norman The Arabs and Medieval Europe (1974).

Dunlop, D. M. Arab Civilization to 1500 (1971).

Gabrieli, Francesco, Muhammad and the Conquests of Islam (1968).

Jourani, A. H. and S. M. Stern, eds., The Islamic City (1970).

Ketton, K. M., ed. A History of the Crusades vols. 1 + 2 (1969).

Lewis, Bernard, The Arabs in History (1960).

Lane, E. W. Arabian Society in the Middle Ages (1971).

Lombard, Maurice, The Golden Age of Islam (1975).

Rosenthal, F.I. J., Political Thought in Medieval Islam (1962).

Richards, D. S. ed. Islam and the Trade of Asia (1971).

von Grunebaum, G. E., Medieval Islam (1961).

BYZANTIUM:

Baynes, Norman and H. St. L. B. Moss, eds., Byzantium: An Introduction to East Roman Civilization (1961).

Geanakoplos, D. J., Interaction of the Sibling Byzantine and Western Cultures in the Middle Ages and Italian Renaissance (300-1600) (1976).

Haussig, H. W., A History of Byzantine Civilization (1971).

Hussey, Joan M., The Byzantine World (1961).

_____, ed., The Byzantine Empire in The Cambridge Medieval History vol. 4, (1966).

Kempt, Friedrich, ed al., eds., The Church in the Age of Feudalism chaps. by Hans-Georg Beck on religion (1969).

Øbolensky, Dimitri, The Byzantine Commonwealth (1971).

Østrogorsky, George, A History of the Byzantine State, 2nd ed., (1968).

Runciman, Steven, The Byzantine Theocracy (1977).

BIBLIØGRAPHY:
Atiya, Azia, The Crusade: Historiography and Bibliography (1976).

NB: Bobst has an excellent collection on the crusades. Look in the D150-D182, and DS90-135 stacks. You may be able to take out library books for some of the required reading.

MEDIEVAL CHRISTIAN MYSTICISM
E. Ann Matter
University of Pennsylvania

This course covers a selection of writings from some of the great mystical and spiritual Christian writers of the 5th-16th centuries. The main focus will be on the primary sources. These have, however, been grouped according to Christian mystical themes; each section will be opened by a secondary reading, which will be available in xerox from the instructor. These secondary readings are meant to help us ask important questions of the texts: what distinguishes "mysticism" from "spirituality?", what are the sources of Christian mystical language?, what do the mystics say about personal experience, as distinguished from cosmology or theology?

Each student has a choice of writing:

1) Two 7-10 page papers (critical, exegetical work) on one of the primary texts, or a selection from one of the primary texts; or

2) One paper as described above, and one short research paper (10-15 pp.) on a mystical treatise by an author not covered by the course. A list of possible topics for this paper will be distributed the first week of classes.

COURSE OUTLINE

I. BIBLICAL THEMES: ALLEGORY / THE SONG OF SONGS
    P.P. Parente, "The Canticle of Canticles in Mystical Theology," Catholic Biblical Quarterly 6 (1944) 142-158

1) Introduction, The Song of Songs, Parente

2) Origen of Alexandria and Hugh of Saint Victor on the Song of Songs

3) Bernard of Clairvaux, On the Song of Songs v.1

4) Hildegard of Bingen, Ordo Virtutum (a liturgical morality play)
   Alain of Lille, On the Six Wings of the Cherubim

II. THE DARK WAY
    D. Knowles, "The Influence of Pseudo-Dionysius on Western Mysticism" Christian Spirituality, ed. P. Brooks (London, 1975) 80-94
    and E. Underhill, "The Dark Night of the Soul," Mysticism, chapter 9.

5) Dionysius the Areopagite (Pseudo-Dionysius), Introduction and The Mystical Theology, Knowles, Underhill

6) Pseudo-Dionysius, The Divine Names

7) The Cloud of Unknowing

III.   THE TRINITY E.   Underhill,   "Mysticism   and   Theology,"
       Mysticism, chapt. 5
       or J. Leclerq, "Monastic Theology," The Love of Learning
       and the Desire for God, chapter 9.

8) Augustine, Confessions, books 1-9, Underhill, Leclerq

9) Augustine, Confessions, books 10-13, Bonaventure, The Mind's Road
       to God

IV.   INCARNATION AND CRUCIFIXION C.   Talbot, "Christina of Markyate:
      A Monastic Narrative of   the Twelfth Century," Essays and
      Studies 1962, pp. 13-26
      and E. McLaughlin, "'Christ My Mother':   Feminine Naming
      and Metaphor in Medieval Spirituality," Nashotah Review 15
      (1975, no. 3) 230-248

10) Julian of Norwich, A Revelation of God's Love

11) Teresa of Avila, The Interior Castle

V.   THE TREMBLER BEFORE THE COSMOS / THE PILGRIM D.   T.   Suzuki,
     "Meister Eckhart and Buddhism," Mysticism Christian and
     Buddhist, chapter 1

12) Meister Eckhart, The Book of Divine Comfort, About Disinterest,
       Selected Sermons, Suzuki

13) The Way of a Pilgrim

EASTERN CHRISTIANITY IN THE MIDDLE AGES
John Meyendorff
Fordham University

<u>Requirements</u>: Three short papers (no more than five pages) on
subjects announced at least one week in advance, and related to the
required readings. The final examination covering the whole
content of the course.

<u>Required readings</u>:
    <u>The New Testament</u>, esp. Mark 1-6; John 1-2, 18-21; Acts 1-5,
8-9; 1 Cor. and Gal.
    Henry Chadwick, <u>The Early Church</u>, Penguin Books, 1967.
    Colin McEvedy, <u>The Penguin Atlas of Medieval History</u>, 1969
    Alexander Schmemann, <u>The Historical Road of Eastern Orthodoxy</u>
1978.
    John Meyendorff, <u>Byzantine Theology</u> (particularly part I:
Historical Trends), Fordham Press, 2nd ed., 1978.
    Francis Dvornik, <u>Byzantium and the Roman Primacy</u> Fordham Press,
1966.

1. Basic Acquaintance with Christian Origins
        New Testament. Chadwick, 9-73.

2. The Early Church: intellectual life, persecutions.
        Chadwick, 74-124; Schmemann, 3-61.

3. Emperor Constantine. The transfer of the imperial capital
    to Constantinople.
        Chadwick, 125-132; Schmemann, 62-80

4. From Constantine to Theodosius: The establishment of
    Christianity. Paganism surviving. Monasticism. Arianism.
        Chadwick, 133-191; Schmemann, 80-112.

5. The Controversy on the Identity of Jesus Christ: different
    trends in Alexandria and Antioch.
        Chadwick, 192-200.

6. Church and State in Byzantium. The ecumenical councils.
        Schmemann, 113-134.

7. The Council of Chalcedon and the Schism of the Monophysites.
        Chadwick, 200-205; Schmemann, 134-142.

8. Emperor Justinian (527-565): The Roman dream of universality.
        Schmemann, 142-168; Chadwick, 205-210.

9. The Rise of Islam and its Consequences for Eastern
   Christianity.   Iconoclasm.
       Schmemann, 168-214.

10. Byzantium and Rome: The gradual estrangement and the schism.
       Schmemann, 214-251; Dvornik, 27-153.

11. Further Discussion of Materials related to the Schism.
       Meyendorff, 91-102.

12. The Missionary Expansion of the Byzantine Orthodox Church.
       Schmemann, 255-270, 292-313.

13. The Doctrinal Positions of Byzantine Orthodoxy.
       Meyendorff, particularly chapters 8, 9, 15, 16, & 17.

14. The Crusades, their Impact on Christian Disunity. Attempts at
    reunion; Lyons, Florence.
       Dvornik, 154-167; Schmemann, 251-254.

CHURCH AND STATE IN THE MIDDLE AGES   Brian Tierney
Cornell University

HISTORY 367

READING LIST   Fall 1981

Paperbacks

   B. Tierney, THE CRISIS OF CHURCH AND STATE, 1050-1300.
   W. Ullmann, HISTORY OF POLITICAL THOUGHT (=MEDIAEVAL POLITICAL THOUGHT)
   J. A. Watt, JOHN OF PARIS
   G. Barraclough, THE MEDIEVAL PAPACY.
   J. R. Strayer, ON THE MEDIEVAL ORIGINS OF THE MODERN STATE

Other Assigned Readings

   M. V. Clarke, MEDIEVAL REPRESENTATON AND CONSENT, Ch. 12, 13.
   P. Hughes, HISTORY OF THE CHURCH, II, pp. 209-238.
   E. Kantorwicz, THE KING'S TWO BODIES, pp. 143-164.
   F. Kempf, "Die papstliche Gewalt in der mittelalterlichen Welt,"
      MISCELLANEA HISTORIAE PONTIFICIAE (1959). (English summary).
   F. Kern, KINGSHIP AND LAW, pp. 149-205.
   G. Post, STUDIES IN MEDIEVAL LEGAL THOUGHT, pp. 241-269, 301-309.
   J. R. Powell, INNOCENT III
   J. R. Strayer, "Laicization of Society in the Thirteenth Century,"
      reprinted in S. Thrupp, CHANGE IN MEDIEVAL SOCIETY.
   G. Tellenbach, CHURCH, STATE, AND CHRISTIAN SOCIETY, Introduction
   B. Tierney, "Some Recent Works on...the Medieval Canonists,"
      TRADITIO, 10 (1954).
   B. Tierney, "Medieval Canon Law and Western Constitutionalism,"
      CATHOLIC HISTORICAL REVIEW, 62 (1966).
   W. Ullmann, GROWTH OF PAPAL GOVERNMENT, pp. 1-31, 262-309, 340-343.

For Reference

   R. W. and A. J. Carlyle, HISTORY OF POLITICAL THEORY (6 vols.)

All works listed above are on Reserve in Uris Library. The source materials
and other books mentioned on the following sheet of Term Paper Topics are
also on the Reserve shelf.

The paperbacks may be purchased at the Campus Bookstore.

1. The Early Centuries (to 800 A.D.)

        Introduction - Problems of Church and State
        Foundations - Scripture and the Early Church
        Rome and the Barbarians - St. Augustine
        The Papacy to Gelasius I
        Rome, Byzantium, and Gaul, 500-750
        Charlemagne - The Medieval Empire

        Readings: CRISIS OF CHURCH AND STATE, pp. 1-32; Ullmann, GROWTH OF
                  PAPAL GOVERNMENT, pp. 1-31; Ullmann, POLITICAL THOUGHT,
                  pp. 7-99; Kempf, Review of Ullmann (translated summary);
                  Barraclough, MEDIEVAL PAPACY, pp. 7-61.

2. Empire and Papacy (800-1150)

        Disintegration - Feudal Kingship
        Recovery - Theocratic Kingship
        The Papal Reform Movement
        Papacy versus Empire - Gregory VII and Henry IV
        End of the Conflict - Effects on Church and State

        Readings: CRISIS, pp. 33-95; Hughes, HISTORY OF THE CHURCH, II, pp.
                  209-238; Ullmann, GROWTH, pp. 262-309; Tellenbach, CHURCH,
                  STATE AND CHRISTIAN SOCIETY, INTRODUCTION; Barraclough,
                  MEDIEVAL PAPACY, pp. 63-101.

3. The Revival of Law (1150-1200)
        Law and Administration - the Church
        Law and Administration - England, France, Germany
        Empire versus Papacy - Frederick I and Alexander III
        Canonistic Theories of Church and State
        Canonistic Theories of Empire and Kingdoms

        Readings: CRISIS, pp. 97-126; Kern, KINGSHIP AND LAW, pp. 149-205;
                  Post, STUDIES, pp. 241-269, 301-309; Ullmann, GROWTH,
                  pp. 340-343; Tierney, "Some Recent Works on ... the
                  Medieval Canonists"; Strayer, MEDIEVAL ORIGINS, pp. 3-56.

4. Papal Theocracy? (1200-1250)

        Innocent III: Personality and Problems
        Innocent III: Political Theory
        Papal Sovereignty and its Limitations
        Royal Sovereignty and its Limitations
        Empire versus Papacy - Frederick II and Innocent IV

        Readings: CRISIS, pp. 127-157; Powell, INNOCENT III; Tierney, POPE
                  AND COUNCIL; SOME NEW DECRETIST TEXTS; W. Ullmann,
                  POLITICAL THOUGHT, pp. 100-158; Barraclough, pp. 101-140;
                  Kantorowicz, KING'S TWO BODIES, pp. 143-164.

5. <u>Aristotelianism, Nationalism, and the Constitutional State</u> (1250-1300)

       Thomas Aquinas
       Factors in Medieval Constitutionalism
       The Rise of Representative Government
       Church versus State - Boniface VIII and Philip IV
       Political Theory - Giles of Rome and John of Paris

       Readings: CRISIS, pp. 159-210; Ullmann, POLITICAL THOUGHT, pp. 159-
                 232; M. V. Clarke, REPRESENTATION AND CONSENT, Ch. 12, 13;
                 Tierney, "Western Constitutionalism and Medieval Canon
                 Law;" Strayer, "Laicization of Society;" J. A. Watt, JOHN
                 OF PARIS.

History 595

Medieval Crime

W. R. Jones   University of New Hampshire
Department of History   Semester I, 1982-3

The following bibliographical citations should be used both for
the definition of term paper topics and for the assembling of pertinent bibligraphical materials for them.

I. The Social and Economic Contexts of Medieval Crime

For a recent, but classic statement of the economic determinants
of crime in medieval and early modern England, see J. M. Beattie,
"The Pattern of Crime in England, 1600-1800," Past & Present,
62 (1974), 47-95. Compare with Michael Weisser's attempt to
fashion general societal models for explaining criminality in
Crime and Punishment in Early Modern Europe (Atlantic Highlands,
1979). Compare both with the older work of L. O. Pike, A History
of Crime in England, 2 vols.; London, 1893 and the popular treatment of the subject by Andrew McCall, The Medieval Underworld
(London, 1979). Note that different methodologies and models
produce quite different results. What are the weaknesses and
strengths of the methodologies and models employed by individual
authors?

II. Felony in Medieval England

A recent attempt to write legal and social history using the
records of criminal justice is Barbara Hanawalt's Crime and
Conflict in English Communities, 1300-1348 (Cambridge, MA and
London, 1979). Look up the critical reviews of this book in
the scholarly journals (Journal of Interdisciplinary History,
American Journal of Legal History, etc.) Compare Hanawlt's
description of homicide in medieval England with the similar
work of James Given, Society and Homicide in Thirteenth Century
England (Palo Alta, CA, 1977). Did they find any significant
differences between the thirteenth and fourteenth centuries?

III. Politics, Justice and Crime

Did the existence of an efficient criminal justice system
and of strong royal authority inhibit the incidence of criminal
disorder? Read John Bellamy, Crime and Public Order in England
in the Later Middle Ages (London and Toronto, 1973); W. R. Jones,
Rex et ministri: English Local Government and the Crisis of 1341,"
Journal of British Studies, 13 (1973), 1-20; idem, "Keeping the
Peace: English Society, Local Government, and the Commissions
of 1341-44," American Journal of Legal History, 18 (1974), 307-
20; John Langbein, Torture and the Law of Proof (Chicago, 1977);
Alfred Soman, "Deviance and Criminal Justice in Western Europe,
1300-1800: An Essay in Structure," Criminal Justice History,
I (1980), 1-28· John Langbein, Prosecuting Crime in the
Renaissance (Cambridge 1974).

IV. Organized Crime in the Middle Ages

See the articles of E. L. G. Stones, "The Folvilles of Ashby-Folville, Leicestershire, and Their Associates in Crime, 1326-1341," Transactions of the Royal Historical Society, 5th series, 7 (1957), 117-36, and J. G. Bellamy, "The Coterel Gang: An Anatomy of a Band of Fourteenth Century Criminals," English Historical Review, 74 (1964), 698-717; and the recent monograph of J. C. Holt, Robin Hood (London, 1982).

Can one speak of "professional criminals" in premodern Europe? Does Robin Hood conform to the "social bandit" described by Eric J. Hobsbawm in his classic work, Bandits?

V. The Criminal in Literature

In addition to Holt's Robin Hood, see M. H. Keen, The Outlaws of Medieval England (London, 1977).

VI. Cultural Determinants of Crime

W. R. Jones, "Violence, Criminality and Culture Disjunction on the Anglo-Irish Frontier: the Example of Armagh, 1350-1550," Criminal Justice History, 1 (1980), 29-47; Timothy Curtis, "Explaining Crime in Early Modern England," ibid., 117-37; I. A. Thompson, "A Map of Crime in Sixteenth Century Spain," Economic Hist. Review, 21 (1968) 244-67

VII. Changing Paterns of Crime

Joel Samaha, Law and Order in Historical Perspective: the Case of Elizabethan Essex (New York, 1974); E. P. Thompson, Albion's Fatal Tree (London, 1975); J. C. Cockburn, Crime in England: 1500-1800 (London, 1977); E. P. Thompson, Whigs and Hunters (London, 1975) V. A. C. Gatrell, B. Lenman, and G. Parker, Crime and the Law since 1500 (London, 1979); J. J. Tobias, Crime and Industrial Society in the Nineteenth Century (London, 1967); idem, Urban Crime in Victorian England (New York, 1972).

VIII. Imprisonment

Contrast the approaches of R. B. Pugh, Imprisonment in Medieval England (Cambridge, 1968) and Michel Foucault, Discipline and Punish, the Birth of the Prison (New York, 1977). What are the implications of Foucault's thesis?

Geoffrey Koziol
Harvard University

History 1124
The Pursuit of Justice in the Early Middle Ages

Books to be purchased (should also be on reserve):

Fritz Kern, Kingship and Law in the Middle Ages
F-L Ganshof, Frankish Institutions under Charlemagne
Njal's Saga
Casebook (at Kinko's)

Schedule of Classes and Readings

R = on reserve at Lamont and Hilles
RH = on reserve in history department library

2/9   Introduction

2/16   The traditional view of early medieval law: Kern, Kingship
       and Law, 3-180

2/23   The revised version: Patrick Wormald, "'Lex Scripta' and
       'Verbum Regis': Legislation and Germanic Kingship," in
       P.H. Sawyer and Ian Wood, Early Medieval Kingship (Leeds,
       1979) [R, RH]; Selections from Anglo-Saxon laws, in
       English Historical Documents, vol. 1, ed. Dorothy
       Whitelock, 2 ed. (London, 1979), 357-69 (skim), 391-94,
       399-430 [R,   RH]

3/1   Carolingian justice: Ganshof, Frankish Institutions, 3-34,
       45-55, 71-97; The Reign of Charlemagne, ed. H.R. Loyn and
       John Percival (New York, 1976), 46-98 [R, RH]

3/8   Carolingian justice: Rosamund McKitterick, "Some Carolingian
       Law Books and their Function," Studies on Medieval Law and
       Government presented to Walter Ullmann, ed. Brian Tierney
       and Peter Linehan (London, 1980), 13-28 [R, RH]; Janet
       Nelson, "Dispute settlement in Carolingian West Francia,"
       Patrick Wormald, "Charters, law, and the settlement of
       disputes in Anglo-Saxon England," and Chris Wickham, "Land
       disputes and their social framework in Lombard-Carolingian
       Italy," all in The Settlement of Disputes in Early
       Medieval Europe, ed. Wendy Davies and Paul Fouracre (London,
       1986) [R,   RH]

3/15   "Feudal anarchy": Georges Duby, "The Evolution of Judicial
       Institutions: Burgundy in the 10th and 11th Centuries,"
       in idem, The Chivalrous Society (Berkeley, 1980), chapter
       2 [R,   RH]; Stephen Weinberger, "Cours judiciaires,
       justice et responsabilité sociale dans la Provence médiévale,"
       Revue historique 542 (1982), 273-88 [English translation,

. . ., RH]; <u>Casebook</u>, nos. 1-38

3/22   "Feudal anarchy" part 2: Stephen White, "<u>Pactum legem</u> <u>vincit</u> <u>et</u> <u>amor</u> <u>judicium</u>:" The Settlement of Disputes by Compromise in 11th-century Anjou," <u>Am</u>. <u>Journ</u>. <u>of</u> <u>Legal</u> <u>Hist</u>. 22 (1978), 281-308 [R, xerox RH]; <u>Casebook</u>, nos. 1-38; Patrick Geary, "Vivre en conflit dans une France sans État: typologie des mécanismes de règlement des conflits (1050-1200)," <u>Annales</u>, <u>E</u>.<u>S</u>.<u>C</u>. 41 (1986), 1107-33 [English translation,   RH]

4/5   Feuds & and the question of legal formalism: <u>Njal's</u> <u>Saga</u>

4/12   Feuds: William Ian Miller, "Avoiding Legal Judgment: The Submission of Disputes to Arbitration in Medieval Iceland," <u>Am</u>. <u>Journ</u>. <u>of</u> <u>Legal</u> <u>Hist</u>. 28 (1984), 95-134; <u>idem</u>, "Justifying Skarphedinn: Of Pretext and Politics in the Icelandic Bloodfeud," <u>Scandinavian</u> <u>Studies</u> 55 (1983), 316-44; <u>idem</u>, "Gift, Sale, Payment, Raid," <u>Speculum</u> 61 (1986), 89-50 [all R,   RH]

4/19   Ordeals: Robert Bartlett, <u>Trial</u> <u>by</u> <u>Fire</u> <u>and</u> <u>Water</u> (Oxford, 1987), 1-42, 42-7 (skim), 49-53, 103-13, 113-26 (skim) [book & . . . . RH]; Peter Brown, "Society and the Supernatural," <u>Society</u> <u>and</u> <u>the</u> <u>Holy</u> <u>in</u> <u>Late</u> <u>Antiquity</u> (Berkeley, 1982), 302-332 [R, RH]; Rebecca Colman, "Reason and Unreason in Early Medieval Law," <u>Journal</u> <u>of</u> <u>Inter-</u> <u>disciplinary</u> <u>Hist</u>. 4 (1974), 571-91 [R, xerox RH]; Sources on ordeals [RH]

4/26   Law and religion: Steven Sargent, "Religious Responses to Violence," <u>Historical</u> <u>Reflections</u> 12 (1985), 219-40 [R, xerox RH]; Geoffrey Koziol, "Monks, Feuds, and the Making of Peace," <u>ibid</u>. 14 (1987), 532-49 [offprint RH]; Patrick Geary, "Humiliation of Saints," <u>Saints</u> <u>and</u> <u>Their</u> <u>Cults</u>, ed. Stephen·Wilson (Cambridge, 1983) [R,   RH]; <u>Casebook</u>, nos. 39-42

5/3   Susan Reynolds, <u>Kingdoms</u> <u>and</u> <u>Communities</u> (Oxford, 1984), chapter 1 [R]; Sally Falk Moore, "Law and Social Change" and "Law and Anthropology," in <u>Law</u> <u>as</u> <u>Process</u> (London, 1978) [.   RH]

Comment: I owe the English versions of the articles by Weinberger
and Geary to the authors. The Casebook provides my translations
of some forty-three disputes, ordeals and battles, prayers, and
curses from tenth- and eleventh-century France. Sources on
ordeals includes the ordeals and battles from Guibert of Nogent
and Galbert of Bruges and the blessings printed in Tierney, The
Middle Ages, vol. 1, Sources.

I also recommend the following recent works:

H.H. Anton, "Zum politischen Konzept karolingischer Synoden und
    zur karolingischen Brüdergemeinschaft," Hist. Jahrbuch 99
    (1979): 55-132
Pierre Bonnassie, "Les conventions féodales dans la Catalogne du
    XIe siècle," Annales du Midi, vol. 80
John Bossy, ed., Disputes and Settlements. Law and Human
    Relations in the West (Cambridge, 1983)
James Campbell, "Observations on English Government from the
    Tenth to the Twelfth Century," TRHS, 5th series 25 (1975):
    39-54
F. Chiovaro, "Discretio pastoralis et scientia canonica au XIe
    siècle," Studia moralia 15 (1977): 445-68
Heinrich Fichtenau, Lebensordnungen des 10. Jahrhunderts: Studien
    über Denkart und Existenz im einstigen Karolingerreich
    (Stuttgart, 1984)
Hans-Werner Goetz, "Kirchenschutz, Rechtswahrung und Reform. Zu
    den Zielen und zum Wesen der frühen Gottesfriedensbewegung in
    Frankreich," Francia 11 (1983): 193-223
                "Herrschaft und Recht in der frühmittel-
    alterlichen Grundherrschaft," Historisches Jahrbuch 104 (1984):
    392-410
Aron Gurevic, "Représentations et attitudes à l'égard de la
    propriété pendant le haut moyen âge," Annales 27 (1972):
    523-47
Jurgen Hännig, Consensus fidelium: Frühfeudale Interpretationen
    des Verhältnisses von Königtum und Adel am Beispiel des
    Frankenreiches (Stuttgart, 1982)
Reinhold Kaiser, "Selbtshilfe und Gewaltmonopol. Königliche
    Friedenswahrung in Deutschland und Frankreich im Mittelalter,"
    Frühmittelalterliche Studien 17 (1983): 55-72
Simon Keynes, The Diplomas of King Aethelred the Unready
    (Cambridge, 1980)
Geoffrey Koziol, "Lord's Law and Natural Law," The Medieval
    Tradition of Natural Law, ed. H. Johnson (Kalamazoo, 1987)
K. Kroeschell, "Konigtum und Rechtsordnung in der Zeit der
    sächischer und salier Herrscher," ZSSRG, Germ. Abt. 82 (1965):
    1-98
K.J. Leyser, Rule and Conflict in an Early Medieval Society
    (Bloomington, 1980)
H.R. Loyn, The Governance of Anglo-Saxon England (Stanford, 1984)

Colin Morris, "Judicium Dei: the social and political
    significance of the ordeal in the eleventh century," _Studies in
    Church History_ 12 (1975): 95-111
Janet Nelson, "Kingship, law and liturgy in the political thought
    of Hincmar of Reims," _EHR_ 92 (1977): 241-79
Paul Ourliac and J. de Malafosse, _Histoire du droit privé_, 3
    vols. (Paris, 1968-71)
Henri Platelle, "La violence et ses remèdes en Flandre au XIe
    s.," _Sacris erudiri_ (1971): 101-73
Susan Reynolds, "Law and Communities in Western Christendom, c.
    900-1140," _Am. J. Legal Hist._ 25 (1981): 205-24
T.J. Rivers, _The Laws of the Alamans and Bavarians_
            The Laws of the Salian and Ripuarian Franks
Clausdieter Schott, "Der Stand der Leges-Forschung," _Frühmittel-
    alterliche Studien_ 13 (1979): 29-55
K.F. Werner, "Missus--marchio--comes: Entre l'administration
    centrale et l'administration locale de l'Empire carolingien,"
    Histoire comparée de l'administration (IVe-XVIIIe siècles).
    Actes du XIVe colloque historique franco-allemand, Tours, 1977
    (Munich/Zurich, 1980), 191-239
Patrick Wormald, "Ethelred the Lawmaker," _Ethelred the Unready:
    Papers from the Millenary Conference_, ed. D. Hill, British
    Archaeological Reports 59 (Oxford, 1978)

Janet Loengard
NYU Law School

ENGLISH LEGAL HISTORY
(LO6.3011)

Spring Term, 1988   Professor Loengard

Tuesday, January 26. (1) Introduction to the common law. (2) Before the
common law: Anglo-Saxon England.
For 2/2: Harding 13-29, 35-41; The Law Courts of Medieval England, docs.
2,3,5,6,9,11,18 (reserve).

Tuesday, February 2. Of courts and jurisdiction.
For 2/9: Harding 59-87; The Law Courts of Medieval England, docs. 10, 12
(crown pleas only); Britton, vol. I, 104-106 (reserve); Lowe v. Paramour, Dyer
301 (mimeographed).

Tuesday, February 9. The King's peace, the King's justice: pleas of the
crown.
For 2/16 and 2/23: Harding 41-47, 88-96; Baker & Milsom 11-36, 48-64, 177-182,
199-208.

Tuesday, February 16 and Tuesday, February 23. "Under all is the land":
tenures and their consequences, estates in land, and the development of the
real actions.
For 3/1: Harding 96-106; Baker & Milsom 264-277, 209-215, 300-301, 320-337,
340-351, 358-362, 370-377, 383-384, 391-395, 398-402, 420-441, 584-610.

Tuesday, March 1.   The personal actions. The origins of debt, detinue,
account, covenant, replevin. A first look at trespass and its offspring: case,
trover, and assumpsit.
A classroom colloquium: One (not terribly significant) action and how it grew:
an exercise in tracing the evolution of law.
For 3/8: Harding 194-215, 167-193, 123-143; Register of Writs (MS Rawlinson C
292 ff. 9a-104a [Bodleian Library, Oxford]), secs. 57-66 and 257-329 in Early
Registers of Writs, 122-123 and 171-183 (reserve).

Tuesday, March 8.   An excursus on writs, sources of law, and the rise of
the legal profession.
For 3/22: Baker & Milsom 37-64; Helmholz 74-100 (reserve); Walker, "Widow
and Ward: the Feudal Law of Child Custody in Medieval England" (reserve);
Loengard, "'Of the Gift of her Husband': English Dower and its Consequences in
the Year 1200" (reserve); S.F.C. Milsom, "Inheritance by Women in the Twelfth
and Early Thirteenth Centuries" (reserve).

Tuesday, March 15   NO CLASS. SPRING BREAK.

Tuesday, March 22.   Married, divorced, widowed, or orphaned: domestic
circumstances and their legal consequences.
For 3/29: Harding, 110-113, 143-149; Baker & Milsom 94-114; The Law Courts of
Medieval England, docs. 21, 22, 23, 25, 30; Kiralfy 70-72 (reserve).

Tuesday, March 29.   (1) Administration of law in theory and fact before 1485. (2) A rival for the common law courts: the Chancellor and Equity. For 4/5: Harding 149-166; The Law Courts of Medieval England docs. 27, 28; Bennett, The Pastons and their England, ch. XII (reserve).

Tuesday, April 5.   The other non-common-law courts and why and how they grew: Star Chamber, the Court of Requests, and others, significant and otherwise (what is a Court of the Verge?) For 4/12: Harding 216-239; The Law Courts of Medieval England, doc. 29; Blatcher, "Touching the Writ of Latitat: An Act 'of no great moment'" (reserve); Wurzel, "The Origin and Development of Quo Minus" (reserve); Baker and Milsom 420-441; Nicholas Fuller's Case, 12 Co. Rep. 41, 77 Eng. Rep. 1322 (Ex. Chamb. 1607); Courtney v. Glanvil, Cro. Jac. 343, 79 Eng. Rep. 294 (K.B. 1615); Woodley v. Manneringe, H. 18 Jac. (unprinted: C.P. 1621) (mimeographed).

Tuesday, April 12.   The response of the common law courts: form-stretching and legal fictions, and their substantive effects. For 4/19: Harding 307-329; Blackstone, bk. III ch. 9 (reserve).

Tuesday, April 19.   The development of tort and contract in the early modern period: the rise of commercial law. For 4/26: Harding 265-277.

Tuesday, April 26.   The development of criminal law in the early modern period. For 5/3: Harding 242-262; The Case of Prohibitions, 13 Co. Rep. 30, 77 Eng. Rep. 1440 (1609); The Five Knights' Case, Howell, State Trials III, 51 (1627) (excerpt mimeographed); The King v. John Hampden, Howell, State Trials III, 1089 (1637) (excerpt mimeographed).

Tuesday, May 3.   Who shall control the law? The 17th century dilemma and its solution: the background to modern understandings.

TEXTS

Alan Harding, A Social History of English Law. (Peter Smith: Gloucester, Mass., 1973).
J.H. Baker and S.F.C. Milsom, Sources of English Legal History: Private Law to 1750. (Butterworths: London, 1986).

RESERVE TEXTS AND ARTICLES

Bennett, Helen, The Pastons and their England (1st paperback ed. Cambridge, 1968).
Blackstone, William, Commentaries on the Laws of England (any edition).
Blatcher, Marjorie, "Touching the Writ of Latitat: An Act 'of no great moment'" in Elizabethan Government and Society, ed. Bindoff, Hurstfield and Williams (London, 1961).
Britton, ed. and tr. F.M. Nichols. 2 vols. (Oxford, 1865; repr. Holmes Beach, Fla., 1983).

Early Registers of Writs, ed. Elsa de Haas and G.D.G. Hall (Selden Society
    vol. 87; London, 1970).
Harding, Alan, The Law Courts of Medieval England (London, 1973)
Helmholz, R.H., Marriage Litigation in Medieval England (Cambridge, 1974).
Kiralfy, A.K.R., A Source Book of English Law (London, 1957)
Loengard, Janet, "'Of the Gift of her Husband': English Dower and its
    Consequences in the Year 1200" in Women of the Medieval World, ed.
    Kirshner and Wemple (New York and London, 1985).
Milsom, S.F.C., "Inheritance by Women in the Twelfth and Early Thirteenth
    Centuries" in On the Laws and Customs of England, ed. Arnold, Green,
    Scully and White (Chapel Hill, 1981).
Walker, Sue Sheridan, "Widow and Ward: The Feudal Law of Child Custody in
    Medieval England" in Women in Medieval Society, ed. Stuard (Philadelphia,
    1976).
Wurzel, Karl G., "The Origin and Development of Quo Minus", 49 Yale Law
    Journal 39 (1939)

All readings are in English. Various other mimeographed materials - primarily
statutes and case reports - will be handed out in class during the semester.

NOTE

In the event that you feel the need for background material of a general
nature, I have put the following books on reserve in the library. I have not
assigned any material in them, but if you have never had a course in English
history you might find it useful to look at one of them.

Keir, Sir David Lindsay, The Constitutional History of Modern Britain since
    1485 (9th ed. New York, 1969).
Lyon, Bryce, A Constitutional and Legal History of Medieval England (2nd ed.
    New York, 1980).

MAGNA CARTA THROUGH THE AGES

Description: Approximately the first half of the term will be spent on Magna Carta in its early thirteenth-century setting: its causes, its contents, its meaning in its own day. The second half of the term will trace the role which Magna Carta has played in English and American constitutional and legal development from the thirteenth century to the present and the interpretations and mis-interpretations to which it has been subjected in the process.

Class mode: discussion seminar.

Grades will be based on:

participation in class discussion (30%)

two written book reviews, one also to be delivered orally (20% each). The instructions for these reviews are on a separate sheet.

a final examination (30%). This examination will be given at the scheduled time, Thursday, June 6, 5:45-7:45; but the questions will be handed out in advance, probably in the last class. I invite any of you who might like to do so to submit possible questions for inclusion on the exam. I retain abso-lute discretion as to whether to include a question, but I shall be happy to explain why a question was rejected should I choose not to use one which you submit.

Office hours: Tuesdays and Thursdays, 1:15-2:45, and by appoint-ment in 306A Morrill Hall (telephone: 353-9039). You may leave messages in 301 Morrill Hall (telephone: 355-7500).

* * * * *

Background: Students who do not have some background in medieval and early modern English history should read S. B. Chrimes, English Constitutional History (any edition). You may also wish to consult Alan Harding, A Social History of English Law. A copy of each book is on 2-hour reserve for this course.

Reading assignments: The following pages contain the reading as-signments for each class. They are followed by an alphabetical listing of all the works assigned for the course, giving full cita-tions for each and indicating where they are available. The order in which required readings are listed in the class-by-class assign-ments is the order in which you should, if it is at all possible, read them.

Because this is a discussion seminar, the reading must be com-pleted before the class for which it is assigned.

All sources assigned are contained in the sourcebook which I have compiled for the course. Most of the articles and excerpts from books assigned are contained in the coursebook which I have compiled for the course. Both the sourcebook and the coursebook are on 2-hour reserve. Each is also available for purchase in photocopy at Kinko's on Division Street.

Class # 1 (March 28): Introduction

    no reading assignment

PART I: MAGNA CARTA IN ITS OWN DAY

Classes # 2-5 (April 2, 4, 9, 11): Reading the charter

  Required reading:

    Sources: Magna Carta
             Coronation charters of Henry I, Stephen and Henry II
             "Unknown" Charter
             Articles of the Barons

    Secondary: Thorne, "What Magna Carta Was"
              Painter, "Magna Carta"
              Cam, Magna Carta—Event or Document?

    Recommended reading: Davis, Magna Carta
                        Dickinson, The Great Charter
                        Galbraith, "Magna Carta"
                        Goodhart, "Law of the Land"
                        Howard, Magna Carta
                        Jennings, Magna Carta

  Note: there are extended clause-by-clause commentaries on Magna
    Carta in:

    McKechnie, Magna Carta, pp. 191-480
    Swindler, Magna Carta, pp. 244-351

Class # 6 (April 16): The reign of John

  Required reading: Jones, King John and Magna Carta

  Recommended reading: Hollister, "King John and the Historians"

  Books for review: Warren, King John
                  Painter, The Reign of King John
                  Powicke, The Loss of Normandy
                  Norgate, John Lackland

Class # 7 (April 18): Concepts behind Magna Carta

  Required reading: Holt, "The Barons and the Great Charter"
                  Holt, "Rights and Liberties in Magna Carta"
                  Jolliffe, selections from Angevin Kingship

  Books for review: Holt, Magna Carta
                  Young, The Royal Forests of Medieval England
                  Richardson, English Jewry under Angevin Kings

Class # 8 (April 23): The motives of the barons

  Required reading: Stubbs, <u>Constitutional History</u>, section 155
                    Jenks, "The Myth of Magna Carta"
                    Petit-Dutaillis, "The Great Charter"
                    Holt, <u>Magna Carta</u>, Chapter VII

  Books for review: Jolliffe, <u>Angevin Kingship</u>
                    Holt, <u>The Northerners</u>
                    Painter, <u>William Marshal</u>
                    Powicke, <u>Stephen Langton</u>

Class # 9 (April 25): Magna Carta, clause 34

  Required reading: McKechnie, <u>Magna Carta</u>, commentary on c. 34
                    Hurnard, "Magna Carta, Clause 34"
                    Clanchy, "Magna Carta, Clause Thirty-Four"

Class # 10 (April 30): Magna Carta, clause 39

  Required reading: McKechnie, <u>Magna Carta</u>, commentary on c. 39
                    McIlwain, "Due Process of Law in Magna Carta"
                    Powicke, "Per iudicium parium vel per legem
                      terrae"
                    Keeney, <u>Judgment by Peers</u>, Chapter III
                    Holt, <u>Magna Carta</u>, pp. 226-29

  Book for review: Keeney, <u>Judgment by Peers</u>

              PART II: MAGNA CARTA IN ENGLAND AFTER 1215

Class # 11 (May 2): The Middle Ages

  Required reading:

    Secondary: Cam, <u>Magna Carta</u>, pp. 11-20 (review)
               Dunham, "Magna Carta and British Constitutionalism,"
                 pp. 26-36
               Stenton, <u>After Runnymede</u>

    Sources: Charter of the Forest
             Confirmation of the Charters
             Articles on the Charters
             The Six Statutes

  Books for review: Thompson, <u>The First Century of Magna Carta</u>
                    Turner, <u>The King and his Courts</u>

Class # 12 (May 7): The Tudors

  Required reading: Butterfield, <u>The Englishman and his History</u>,
                      pp. 1-30
                    Radin, "The Myth of Magna Carta"
                    Butterfield, "Magna Carta in the Historiography
                      of the Sixteenth and Seventeenth Centuries,"
                      pp. 3-14

  Books for review: Thompson, <u>Magna Carta: Its Role</u> . . .
                    Shakespeare, <u>King John</u>
                    Bale, <u>King Johan</u>
                    Anonymous, <u>The Troublesome Raigne of King John</u>

Class # 13 (May 9): The early Stuarts

  Required reading:

    Secondary: Cam, <u>Magna Carta</u>, pp. 20-24 (review)
              Dunham, "Magna Carta . . . ," pp. 36-42
              Butterfield, <u>The Englishman and his History</u>, pp. 31-72
              Ashley, <u>Magna Carta in the Seventeenth Century</u>,
                  pp. 3-33
              Butterfield, "Magna Carta . . . ," pp. 15-25

    Sources: Debates in Commons, 26 April 1628, on the Lords' Propo-
            sitions of 25 April
          The Petition of Right
          Penn, <u>The Excellent Priviledge of Liberty and Property</u>

  Books for review: Pocock, <u>The Ancient Constitution and the Feudal
                    Law</u>
                 Relf, <u>The Petition of Right</u>
                 White, <u>Sir Edward Coke</u> . . .

Class # 14 (May 14): Two seventeenth-century revolutions

  Required reading:

    Secondary: Dunham, "Magna Carta . . . ," pp. 42-46
              Butterfield, <u>The Englishman and his History</u>, pp. 72-78
               Ashley, <u>Magna Carta</u> . . . , pp. 33-62
               Pallister, <u>Magna Carta</u>, pp. 1-42

    Sources: Walwyn, <u>Englands Lamentable Slaverie</u>
          Lilburne, <u>Englands Freedome, Souldiers Rights</u>
          Brady, <u>A Complete History of England</u>, prefatory material
          The Declaration of Rights

  Books for review: Gough, <u>Fundamental Law</u> . . .
                 Schwoerer, <u>The Declaration of Rights</u>

Class # 15 (May 16): Modern England

  Required reading: Blackstone, <u>Commentaries</u>, IV, pp. 416-18
                  Pallister, <u>Magna Carta</u>, pp. 43-107

  Book for review: Blackstone, <u>The Great Charter</u>, pp. i-lxxvi

PART III: MAGNA CARTA IN AMERICA

Class # 16 (May 21): General

  Required reading: Cam, <u>Magna Carta</u>, pp. 24-26 (review)
                  Hazeltine, "The Influence of Magna Carta"
                  Kurland, "Magna Carta and Constitutionalism . . . "

  Books for review: Howard, <u>The Road from Runnymede</u>
                 Pound, <u>The Development of Constitutional Guaran-
                   tees of Liberty</u>

Class # 17 (May 23): The colonial period

  Required reading:

    Secondary: Swindler, Magna Carta, Chapter VII
                Colbourn, The Lamp of Experience, pp. 25-39
                Howard, The Road from Runnymede, pp. 35-48, 133-38,
                  156-64, 188-202

    Sources: Penn, The Excellent Priviledge (review)
              The Massachusetts "Parallels" of 1646
              Instructions of the Town of Braintree (1765)

    Books for review: Colbourn, The Lamp of Experience
                       Mullett, Fundamental Law . . .
                       Schwartz, The Great Rights of Mankind

Class # 18 (May 28): Habeas Corpus and Magna Carta

  Required reading:

    Secondary: Meador, Habeas Corpus and Magna Carta

    Source: Habeas Corpus Act of 1679

    Book for review: Duker, A Constitutional History of Habeas Corpus

Class # 19 (May 30): Summary and review

    no reading assignment

BIBLIOGRAPHY

Except as noted, all the works listed are on 2-hour or 7-day reserve
at Assigned Reading. Two asterisks indicate that a work should be
available for purchase in the bookstores. One asterisk indicates
that the work—or the part of it assigned—is in the coursebook.
Some of the books assigned for report are in print (some are even
paperbound) and may therefore be purchased, though they have not
been ordered for the course.

**Ashley, Maurice, Magna Carta in the Seventeenth Century (1965)
  Bale, John, King Johan (Huntington Library edition, 1969)
  Blackstone, William, The Great Charter and the Charter of the
    Forest (1759). Available only in Special Collections.
 *Butterfield, Herbert, The Englishman and his History (1944)
 *_____, "Magna Carta in the Historiography of the Sixteenth and
    Seventeenth Centuries," The Stenton Lecture, University of
    Reading, 1968
**Cam, Helen Maud, Magna Carta—Event or Document? (1965)
  Chrimes, S. B., English Constitutional History, 4th ed. (1967)
 *Clanchy, M. T., "Magna Carta, Clause Thirty-Four," English Histo-
    rical Review, LXXIX (1964), 542-48
 *Colbourn, H. Trevor, The Lamp of Experience: Whig History and
    the Intellectual Origins of the American Revolution (1965)
  Davis, G. R. C., Magna Carta (1971)
  Dickinson, J. C., The Great Charter (1955)
  Duker, W. F., A Constitutional History of Habeas Corpus (1980)

*Dunham, William Huse, Jr., "Magna Carta and British Constitu-
    tionalism," in Thorne et al., The Great Charter, pp. 26-50
 Galbraith, V. H., "Magna Carta," in his Studies in the Public
    Records (1948), pp. 122-50
 Goodhart, Arthur L, "Law of the Land" (1966)
 Gough, J. W., Fundamental Law in English Constitutional History
    (1955)
 Harding, Alan, A Social History of English Law (1966)
*Hazeltine, H. D., "The Influence of Magna Carta on American Con-
    stitutional Development," in Malden, MCCE, pp. 180-225
 Hollister, C. Warren, "King John and the Historians," The Journal
    of British Studies, I (1961), 1-19
*Holt, James C., "The Barons and the Great Charter," English Histo-
    rical Review, LXX (1955), 1-24
*_____, Magna Carta (1965)
 _____, The Northerners (1961)
*_____, "Rights and Liberties in Magna Carta," Album Helen Maud Cam,
    I (1960), 57-69
 Howard, A. E. Dick, Magna Carta: Text and Commentary (1964)
*_____, The Road from Runnymede: Magna Carta and Constitutionalism
    in America (1968)
*Hurnard, Naomi D., "Magna Carta, Clause 34," in Studies in Medie-
    val History presented to Frederick Maurice Powicke (1948), pp.
    157-79
*Jenks, Edward, "The Myth of Magna Carta," Independent Review, IV
    (1904-5), 260-73
 Jennings, Ivor, Magna Carta and its Influence in the World Today
    (1965)
 Jolliffe, J. E. A., Angevin Kingship, 2nd ed. (1963)
*_____, excerpts from Angevin Kingship, in Norman F. Cantor and
    Michael S. Werthman (edd.), The English Tradition, I (1967),
    pp. 45-52
**Jones, J. A. P., King John and Magna Carta (1971)
*Keeney, Barnaby C., Judgment by Peers (1949)
*Kurland, Philip B., "Magna Carta and Constitutionalism in the
    United States: 'The Noble Lie,'" in Thorne et al., The Great
    Charter, pp. 51-75
*McIlwain, Charles H., "Due Process of Law in Magna Carta" (1914),
    reprinted in Constitutionalism and the Changing World, pp. 86-126
*McKechnie, William S., Magna Carta, 2nd ed. (1914)
 Malden, H. E. (ed.), Magna Carta Commemoration Essays (1917)
 Meador, Daniel John, Habeas Corpus and Magna Carta (1966)
 Mullett, Charles F., Fundamental Law and the American Revolution,
    1760-1776 (1933)
 Norgate, Kate, John Lackland (1902)
*Painter, Sidney, "Magna Carta," American Historical Review, LIII
    (1947), 42-49
 _____, The Reign of King John (1949)
 _____, William Marshal: Knight-Errant, Baron and Regent of Eng-
    land (1933)
 Pallister, Ann, Magna Carta: The Heritage of Liberty (1971)

*Petit-Dutaillis, Charles, "The Great Charter," in <u>Studies and Notes Supplementary to Stubbs' Constitutional History</u> (1908), pp. 127-45

Pocock, J. G. A., <u>The Ancient Constitution and the Feudal Law</u> (1957)

Pound, Roscoe, <u>The Development of Constitutional Guarantees of Liberty</u> (1957)

Powicke, Frederick Maurice, <u>The Loss of Normandy, 1189-1204: Studies in the History of the Angevin Empire</u> (1913, 1961)

* ____ , "Per iudicium parium vel per legem terrae," in Malden, <u>MCCE</u>, pp. 96-121

____ , <u>Stephen Langton</u> (1928)

*Radin, Max, "The Myth of Magna Carta," <u>Harvard Law Review</u>, LX (1947), 1060-91

Relf, Frances Helen, <u>The Petition of Right</u> (1917)

Richardson, H. G., <u>English Jewry under Angevin Kings</u> (1960)

Schwartz, Bernard, <u>The Great Rights of Mankind: A History of the American Bill of Rights</u> (1977)

Schwoerer, Lois G., <u>The Declaration of Rights, 1689</u> (1981)

Shakespeare, William, <u>King John</u> (any edition)

Stenton, Doris Mary, <u>After Runnymede: Magna Carta in the Middle Ages</u> (1965)

*Stubbs, William, <u>Constitutional History of England</u>, I (first edition, 1873)

*Swindler, William F., <u>Magna Carta: Legend and Legacy</u> (1965)

Tabuteau, Emily Z. (comp.), Sourcebook on Magna Carta

Thompson, Faith, <u>The First Century of Magna Carta</u> (1925)

____ , <u>Magna Carta: Its Role in the Making of the English Constitution</u> (1948)

*Thorne, Samuel E., "What Magna Carta Was," in Thorne et al., <u>The Great Charter</u>, pp. 11-25

____ et al., <u>The Great Charter</u> (1965)

<u>The Troublesome Raigne of King John</u>, ed. J. W. Sider (1979)

Turner, Ralph V., <u>The King and his Courts: The Role of John and Henry III in the Administration of Justice, 1199-1240</u> (1968)

Warren, W. L., <u>King John</u> (1961)

White, Stephen D., <u>Sir Edward Coke and "The Grievances of the Commonwealth"</u> (1979)

Young, Charles R., <u>The Royal Forests of Medieval England</u> (1979)

BOOKS:

1. Warren, King John. For class # 6.

2. Holt, Magna Carta. For class # 7.

3. Thompson, The First Century of Magna Carta. For class # 11.

4. Thompson, Magna Carta: Its Role in the Making of the English Constitution. For class # 12.

5. Pocock, The Ancient Constitution and the Feudal Law. For class # 13.

6. Howard, The Road from Runnymede: Magna Carta and Constitutionalism in America. For class # 16.

7. Colbourn, The Lamp of Experience: Whig History and the Intellectual Origins of the American Revolution. For class # 17.

8. Mullett, Fundamental Law and the American Revolution. For class # 17.

9. Gough, Fundamental Law in English Constitutional History. For class # 14.

10. Schwoerer, The Declaration of Rights, 1689. For class # 14.

11. Jolliffe, Angevin Kingship. For class # 8.

12. Keeney, Judgment by Peers. For class # 10.

13. Turner, The King and his Courts: The Role of John and Henry III in the Administration of Justice, 1199-1240. For class # 11.

14. Relf, The Petition of Right. For class # 13.

15. Blackstone, The Great Charter and the Charter of the Forest. For class # 15.

16. Painter, The Reign of King John. For class # 6.

17. Young, The Royal Forests of Medieval England. For class # 7.

18. Richardson, English Jewry under Angevin Kings. For class # 7.

19. Holt, The Northerners. For class # 8.

20. Painter, William Marshal. For class # 8.

21. White, Sir Edward Coke and "The Grievances of the Commonwealth". For class # 13.

22. Pound, The Development of Constitutional Guarantees of Liberty. For class # 16.

23. Schwartz, The Great Rights of Mankind: A History of the American Bill of Rights. For class # 17.

24. Powicke, The Loss of Normandy, 1189-1204: Studies in the History of the Angevin Empire. For class # 6.

25. Powicke, Stephen Langton. For class # 8.

26. Shakespeare, King John. For class # 12.

27. Duker, A Constitutional History of Habeas Corpus. For class # 18.

28. Norgate, John Lackland. For class # 6.

29. Bale, King Johan. For class # 12.

30. The Troublesome Raigne of King John. For class # 12.

INSTRUCTIONS:

1. One book review is to be delivered orally in the class to which the book is most directly relevant.

    a. The correlation between books and classes is indicated both on the list above and on the syllabus.

    b. Each student must review a different book. Assignments of books to individual students will be made early in the term, probably on April 9. Before then, students should have familiarized themselves with the books sufficiently to be able to make an informed choice. All these books are on 7-day reserve at the Assigned Reading desk of the Library. Until the assignments have been made, however, please do not take one of these books out more than overnight, as the books must be available to all students in the class.

    c. An oral review should take about fifteen minutes and do three things:

        1. describe to the class the author's subject, approach and conclusions;

        2. explain the relevance of the book to the subject of the course and the particular class;

        3. evaluate the book (as explained below).

    The reviewer should be prepared, also, to add insights derived from the book in the course of general class discussion and/or to entertain questions after presenting the review.

    d. The written version of this review should be submitted within a week after the oral review is delivered. During the interim, the reviewer should have a conference with me about the review.

2. The other review, to be submitted in writing only, may be done on any of the books listed above. This review may be submitted at any time during the term. I advise you not to submit it before attending the class to which the book is relevant but also to submit it fairly soon thereafter. NO REVIEW WILL BE ACCEPTED LATER THAN THE LAST MEETING OF THE COURSE, that is, May 30.

3. You may rewrite either or both of your reviews and resubmit the revised version(s) for reconsideration of grades. Pressure of time means that this opportunity will be available only for reviews initially submitted no later than May 16. Revised versions must be submitted no later than the last meeting of the course, that is, May 30.

4. Each written review should aim to do two things:

   a. discuss the contents of the book in the context of this course. In other words: what is the subject of the book? what does it say about its subject? what are its theses? what light does it cast on the subject of this course in general and of the particular class for which the book is assigned? does it support or refute any other works which you have read for the course or any theses which we have developed in class?

   b. evaluate the book as a piece of historical investigation. In other words: what sources does the author use (the evidence)? how are the sources used (the methodology)? how well does the evidence support the author's thesis or theses? are there flaws in the methodology or the reasoning? does the author miss anything? do other conclusions (complementary or antithetical) emerge from the evidence? if the book differs in one or more conclusions from other works which you have read for the course or from a thesis developed in class discussion, which conclusion(s) seem to you more nearly correct, and why? In short, it the book, good, bad or indifferent? (Here, in effect, I am asking you to grade the book.)

   For more guidance on how to approach these assignments, see the accompanying handout "How to Analyze a Book."

5. Written reviews should be as long as you find necessary to say what you have to say. Between five and seven typed pages should be sufficient. Papers <u>must</u> be typed. For toher matters of form, see the attached sheet "Remarks concerning the Form of Papers."

6. Note: I have read most but not all of the books available for review. Before writing your reviews, you should ascertain whether I have read the books on which you are writing, as you will have to describe what the books say at greater length if I have not than if I have. With regard to oral reviews, remember that most, if not all, of your audience will not have read the book.

7. Please feel free to consult me, either in office hours or by appointment, at any stage in the production of these reviews.

Bennett
Medieval Synthesis, 1050-1250
Department of History
Fall, 1987

Texts: A Scholastic Miscellany, Anselm to Ockham, ed. Eugene Fairweather
The Letters of Abelard and Heloise, ed. and trans. Betty Radice
Brian Tierney, The Crisis of Church and State, 1050-1300
Lester K. Little, Religious Poverty and the Profit Economy in Medieval
    Europe
M.-D. Chenu, Nature, Man and Society in the Twelfth Century, trans.
    Little and Taylor
Renaissance and Renewal in the Twelfth Century, ed. Robert Benson and
    Giles Constable
David Knowles, The Evolution of Medieval Thought
xeroxed collection of additional primary source readings

Also on order, but recommended only:
        C.W. Previté-Orton, The Shorter Cambridge Medieval History
        Georges Duby, The Early Growth of the European Economy

Requirements: One long paper (approx. 15 pp.) and take-home final; the odd
        report

Readings (an (S) indicates that only selections from the work will be read):

I. Beginnings of the New Learning

        David Knowles, The Evolution of Medieval Thought, Ch. 8 (93-106)
        Anselm, Proslogion (Fairweather, Scholastic Miscellany, 69-96)
        ------ Letter on the Incarnation of the Word (Fairweather 97-99)

II. New Learning and New Institutions: Schools, Teachers, and Curricula in the
        First Half of the Twelfth Century

        Hugh of St. Victor, Didascalicon (S)
        Abelard, Historia calamitatum (in The Letters of Abelard and Heloise)
        Knowles, Evolution, Chs. 9-12 (107-141)
        Southern, "The Schools of Paris and the School of Chartres," Renais-
            sance and Renewal in the Twelfth Century, ed. Benson and
            Constable (hereafter R. and R.)   (113-137)

III. Other Aspirations: The Reform of the Church and Religious Life

Tierney, Crisis of Church and State, 1.3, 2.1-3 (24-73)
Constable, "Renewal and Reform in Religious Life," R. and R. (37-67)
Little, Religious Poverty and the Profit Economy in Medieval Europe,
      Chs. 2, 4-7 (19-41, 61-112)
Chenu, Nature, Man, and Society (hereafter NMS), Ch. 6, "Monks, Canons,
      and Laymen in Search of the Apostolic Life" (202-238)

IV. Theology of the Reformers

Bernard of Clairvaux, Sermons on the Song of Songs (S)
Hugh of St. Victor, On the Sacraments (S)
Richard of St. Victor, On the Trinity (S) (Fairweather 324-331)

V. The Clash of Cultures: Reform Theology Versus the New Learning

Abelard, Ethics (Scito te ipsum) (S)
------- Exposition of the Epistle to the Romans (S) (Fairweather 276-
      87)
School of Anselm of Laon, Question on Original Sin (Fairweather 263-6)
Hugh of St. Victor, On the Sacraments (Fairweather 302-9)
Bernard of Clairvaux, Letters against Abelard
Otto of Freising, account of Abelard (from Gesta Friderici
      Imperatoris)
Leclercq, "The Renewal of Theology," R. and R. (68-109)

VI. The Sense of History: Apocalypse Soon

Hugh of St. Victor, On the Sacraments (S) (Fairweather 300-318)
Otto of Freising, Chronica, Prologue
Joachim of Fiore, Selections from works
Classen, "Res gestae, Universal History, Apocalypse," R. and R. (387-
      417)
Chenu, NMS, Ch. 5, "Theology and the New Awareness of History" (162-
      201)

VII. Unexpected Consequences: Women and "Reform"

Abelard and Heloise, Letters (S)
Additional reading to be assigned

VIII. A Change in World-View: From Symbolism to Science

Chenu, NMS, Ch. 1, "Nature and Man..." (1-48)

244

Chenu, _NMS,_ Ch. 3, "The Symbolist Mentality" (99-145)
d'Alverny, "Translations and Translators," _R. and R._ (421-462)
Bernard Sylvestris, _Cosmographia_ (S)
Robert Grosseteste, _On Light_

IX. The Institutionalization of the New Learning: The Universities

Chenu, _NMS,_ Ch. 8, "The Masters of the Theological 'Science'" (270-309)
Baldwin, "Masters at Paris from 1179 to 1215," _R. and R._ (138-172)
Knowles, _Evolution_, Chs. 13-15, 18-19, 21 (153-192, 221-248, 255-268)
Documents relating to the University of Paris
Aquinas, _Summa Theologica_ (S)
Matthew of Aquasparta, _Disputed Questions on Faith_ (S)(Fairweather
    402-427)

X. The Spiritualization of Society: St. Francis et al.

Francis of Assisi, _Writings_ (S)
Celano, _First Life of St. Francis_
Little, _Religious Poverty_, Chs. 8-9 (113-169)
Chenu, _NMS,_ Ch. 7, "The Evangelical Awakening" (239-269)

XI. The Secularization of Culture: Views of Law and Government

Kantorowicz, "Kingship under the Impact of Scientific Jurisprudence,"
    in _Twelfth-Century Europe and the Foundations of Modern_
    Society, ed. Clagett et al. (89-111)
Tierney, _Crisis,_ 2.4-3.1, 3.3-6, 4.1-2 (74-109,116-157,159-171)
Kuttner, "The Revival of Jurisprudence," _R. and R._ (299-323)
Nörr, "Institutional Foundations of the New Jurisprudence," _R. and R._
    (324-338)

XII. A Second Reading

Stock, _The Implications of Literacy,_ Chs. 1, 4-5, and Conclusion (12-87,
    326-531)

MEDIEVAL DISCUSSIONS OF THE ETERNITY OF THE WORLD
Dr. Richard Dales
University of Southern California, Los Angeles

I.   The sources: Loci classici of the Problem.
        Timaeus; Clacidius; Augustine, Confessions and City of
        God; Boethius, Consolation of Philosophy; Genesis I.

II. Eriugena and his Followers
        Eriugena, Division of Nature; Anonymous Commentator on the
        Consolation;   Bernard of Chartres;   Hugh of St. Victor;
        Didascalicon and Homilies on Ecclesiastes.

III. The Early Twelfth Century
        William of Conches; Anonymous On the Elements; Hermes, On
        the Six Principles of Things; Richard of St. Victor, On
        the Trinity; Bernard Silvestris, Cosmographia.

IV. The Re-assertion of the Traditional View
        Peter Lombard, Sentences.

V.   A Different Presentation of the Question
        Aristotle, Decaelo, Metaphysics, Physics; Algazel,
        Metaphysics;   Avicenna, Metaphysics;   Maimonides, Dux
        dubitantium.

VI. The Initial Latin Response
        Gundissalinus, De processione mundi; Alexander of Hales,
        Summa tneologiae and Questio utrum mundus sit eternus.

VII. The Alarm Sounded
        Robert Grosseteste, Hexameron and De finitate motus et
        temporis.

VIII. The Development of the Franciscan Position
        Thomas of York, Sapientiale; John Pecham, Utrum mundus sit
        eternus;   William of Baglione, Utrum mundus sit eternus;
        Bonaventure, Commentary on the Sentences, II, I; Matthew of
        Aquasparta, Could the World Have Been Created from Eternity.

IX. The Position of the Philosophers
        Boethius of Dacia, The Eternity of the World; Ps.-Siger of
        Brabant, Questions on the Physics; Tnomas of Aquino, The
        Eternity of the World; Siger of Brabant, The Eternity of
        the World.

X.   The Condemnations of 1277

XI. The Aftermath of the Condemnations
     Anonymous, <u>Could the World Have Been Created from Eternity</u>;
     Arlotto of Prato, <u>Utrum mundus sit eternus</u>;   Henry of
     Harclay, <u>Could the World Have Been Created from Eternity</u>;
     William of Alnwick, <u>Determinations</u>.

  **Prof. Dales has translated all the above texts which are generally
    only available in Latin.

RELIGIOUS STUDIES 236
CHRISTIAN THOUGHT TO THE REFORMATION
E. Ann Matter
University of Pennsylvania

This course will trace the development of normative
Christianity from the early church to the beginning of the age
of reform (200-1350). The focus will be on the interrelation
of institutional expressions ("The Church") with popular piety
("the people"). Topics considered will include
heresy/orthodoxy, the development of the clerical hierarchy,
and the place of women in the Christian tradition. Readings
will include primary sources, and both traditional and
"unorthodox" secondary interpretations.

Tuesday classes will be, for the most part, presentation
and explanation of the weekly theme by the instructor.
Thursdays will be given over to discussion of the readings,
especially the primary materials, assigned for the week.
Particiaption in the Thursday discussions is an important
requirement of the course.

Each student will write two 3-5 page "thought papers" on
one or more of the primary sources. The nature of these papers
will be discussed in class; their due-dates are given in the
class outline. There will also be a take-home midterm, given
out on October 20, due October 29, and a final exam during exam
week.

1. INTRODUCTION: THE VARIED BACKGROUND OF CHRISTIANITY
        Chadwick, The Early Church, 1-3.

2. HELLENISM AND CHRISITANITY
        Dodds, Pagan and Christian in an Age of Anxiety
        Apuleius, The Golden Ass, selections

3. CHRISTIAN PLATONISM
        Chadwick, 4-6;
        Knowles, The Evolution of Medieval Thought, I
        Justin Martyr and Origen of Alexandria, selections

4. THE QUESTION OF PERSECUTION AND THE IDEAL OF MARTYRDOM
        Chadwick, 7, 10
        Gibbon, Decline and Fall of the Roman Empire XVI
        The Martyrdom of Saint Polycarp
        The Passion of Perpetua and Felicitas

5. THE DIALECTIC OR ORTHODOXY/THE COUNCILS
        Chadwick, 8, 9, 11, 14
        Macmullen, Constantine, IV

        PAPER DUE

6. THE GREEK FATHERS, SPIRITUAL AND ASCETIC TRADITIONS
        Chadwick, 12, 13
        Basil the Great and John Chrysostom, selected homilies
        Gregory of Nyssa, The Life of Saint Macrina

7. THE LATIN FATHERS, DOGMA AND DISCIPLINE
        Chadwick, 15-16
        Augustine of Hippo, Enchiridion
        A. Yarborough, "Christianization in the Fourth Century"

        MIDTERM GIVEN OUT

8. MONKS AND MISSIONARIES

        Chadwick, 17-18
        Gibbon, XXXVII
        Gregory the Great, The Life of Saint Benedict
        Benedict of Nursia, A Rule for Monks
        The Venerable Bede, Ecclesiastical History of the
        English Church II, 1

        MIDTERM DUE

9. THE FRANKS AND THE BYZANTINES
        Knowles, VI-VII
        Pelikan, The Spirit of Eastern Christendom, 3-4
        Einhart and Notker, Two Lives of Charlemagne

10. SPECULATIVE THEOLOGY EAST AND WEST
        Knowles, VIII-XII
        Pelikan, 5
        Hroswitha, Paphnutius, Sapientia
        Anselm of Canterbury, Cur Deus Homs, selections

11. RELIGION AND HUMANISM IN THE TWELFTH CENTURY
        Knowles, III
        Peter Abelard, Historia calamitatum, letters to and
        from Heloise.
        Bernard of Clairvaux, De diligendo Deo

12. THE CRUSADES
        Peters, ed. Christian Society and the Crusades
        Marcus, The Jew in the Medieval World, selections
        Abrahams, Jewish Life in the Middle Ages, IV
        Cohn, The Pursuit of the Millennium, 3,2 (pp. 61-71)

13. THE SCHOLASTIC SYNTHESIS
Knowles IV-V
Pelikan, 6
Thomas Aquinas, <u>Summa Theologica,</u> selections

PAPER DUE

14. SPIRITUAL MOVEMENTS OF THE HIGH MIDDLE AGES
<u>The Little Flowers of Saint Francis</u>
Bolton, "Mulieres Sanctae"

Books to purchase:

Augustine of Hippo, <u>The Enchiridion on Faith, Hope, and Love</u>
(Gateway)
R. Brown, tr., <u>The Little Flowers of Saint Francis</u>(Image)
Henry Chadwick, <u>The Early Church</u> (Penguin)
E. R. Dodds, <u>Pagan and Christian in an Age of Anxiety</u>(Norton)
Gregory of Nyssa, <u>Life of Saint Macrina</u>(Eastern Orthodox Bks)
Gregory the Great, <u>Dialogues Book II: Saint Benedict,</u> tr.
Uhlfelder.(Bobbs-Merrill)
David Knowles, <u>The Evolution of Medieval Thought</u>(Vintage)
A. C. Meisel and M. L. del Mastro, eds., <u>The Rule of Saint</u>
<u>Benedict</u>(Image)
Jaroslav Pelikan, <u>The Christian Tradition 2: The Spirit of</u>
<u>Eastern Christendom</u>(Chicago)
Edward Peters, ed., <u>Christian Society and the Crusades</u>
<u>1198-1229</u>(Penn Press)
Betty Radice, ed., <u>The Letters of Abelard and Heloise</u>(Penguin)
Lewis Thorpe, tr., <u>Einhard and Notker the Stammerer, Two Lives</u>
<u>of Charlemagne</u>(Penguin)

History 223   Katharine Park
Spring 1987   Wellesley College

FROM CLOSED WORLD TO INFINITE UNIVERSE

The following books have been ordered from the Bookstore:
  *C.S. Lewis, The Discarded Image
  *Richard C. Dales, The Scientific Achievement of the Middle Ages
  *Francis Bacon, The Great Instauration and the New Atlantis
  *René Descartes, Discourse on Method
  *Isaac Newton, Newton's Philosophy of Nature
  Edward Grant, Physical Science in the Middle Ages
  Allen Debus, Man and Nature in the Renaissance
  Alexandre Koyré, From the Closed World to the Infinite Universe
  Arthur Koestler, The Watershed
  Richard Westfall, The Construction of Modern Science
*Required purchase (all others recommended).

Course requirements: 1. Two 5-7 page papers
                       2. Midterm examination
                       3. Final examination
                       4. Class attendance and participation

General reference works:
     Dictionary of Scientific Biography (Reference room: qQ 141 D5)
       This work contains compact essays on the life and work of important
       scientists, with helpful bibliographies.
     Isis Cumulative Bibliography, 1913-1965 (Reference: qZ 7405 H612)
     Isis, annual bibliography issue (Reference: Z 7405 H618)
       Both of these provide bibliography in the history of science arranged
       by subject matter and period.
     Dictionary of the History of Ideas (Reference: qCB 5 D52)
     Encyclopedia of Philosophy (Reference: qB 41 E5)

Syllabus:

1. Introduction

Part I: SCIENCE IN THE MIDDLE AGES

2. The Medieval Cosmos

    Lewis, The Discarded Image, chs. 1, 2, 5, and pp. 139-52 (chs. 3 and
    4 optional).

3. The Renaissance of the 12th Century: Nature and the Elements

    Dales, The Scientific Achievement of the Middle Ages, pp. 1-38.
    Adelard of Bath, from the Natural Questions, in Dales, pp. 38-51.
    Lewis, pp. 165-74.
    Recommended: M.-D. Chenu, Nature, Man and Society in the Twelfth
    Century, ch. 1.

4. From School to University: Aristotle and Scholasticism

   Grant, A Source Book in Medieval Science, pp. 42-4, selections 9-11.
   Grant, Physical Science in the Middle Ages, pp. 20-8.
   Recommended: New Catholic Encyclopedia, articles on "Scholasticism",
      "Scholastic Method".

5. Grosseteste on the Physical World

   Dales, chs. 3-4.
   Recommended: Crombie, "Robert Grosseteste," Dictionary of Scientific
      Biography.

6. Science and Religion: Nature and Miracles

   Thomas Aquinas, Summa contra gentiles, III, chs. 99-103.
   Condemnations of 1277, in Grant, Source Book, pp. 45-50.
   Grant, "Science and Theology in the Middle Ages," in Lindberg and
      Numbers, eds., God and Nature, ch. 2.

7. Criticizing Aristotle: Physics

   Dales, ch. 6.
   Recommended: Grant, Physical Science, ch. 4.

8. Criticizing Aristotle: Cosmology

   Dales, ch. 7.
   Grant, Physical Science, ch. 5.
   Alexandre Koyré, From the Closed World to the Infinite Universe,
      ch. 1.

Part II: THE SCIENTIFIC RENAISSANCE

9. From Middle Ages to Renaissance: Science and Magic

   Debus, Man and Nature in the Renaissance, ch. 1.
   Dales, ch. 8.
   Recommended: Bert Hansen, "Science and Magic," in Lindberg, ed.,
      Science in the Middle Ages, ch. 15.

10. From Middle Ages to Renaissance: Science and the Arts

   Leonardo da Vinci, from the Notebooks, in Gundersheimer, ed., The
      Italian Renaissance, pp. 163-81.
   Debus, ch. 3.
   Recommended: Rossi, Philosophy, Technology and the Arts, pp. 1-41.

11. The New Medicine: Paracelsus

   Paracelsus, from On the Miners' Sickness, in Paracelsus, Four
      Treatises, pp. 56-80.
   Debus, ch. 2.
   Recommended: Koyré, "Paracelsus," in Ozment, ed., The Reformation in
      Medieval Perspective, pp. 185-218.

12. The New Anatomy: Vesalius

   Vesalius, Preface to On the Fabric of the Human Body, in O'Malley,
      Andreas Vesalius of Brussels, pp. 317-26.
   Vesalius, from the Epitome, in Saunders and O'Malley, The
      Illustrations from the Works of Andreas Vesalius of Brussels, pp.
      203-27.
      Construct either the male or the female figure, using the sheets of
      organs handed out in class.
   Debus, pp. 54-63.

13. The New Astronomy: Copernicus

   Kuhn, The Copernican Revolution, ch. 5.
   Gingerich, "Crisis vs. Aesthetic in the Copernican Revolution," Vistas
      in Astronomy 17 (1975): 85-97.
   Debus, pp. 74-84.

14. Midterm

15. Breaking the Spheres: Brahe and Kepler

   Koestler, The Watershed.
   The World according to Norman Bloom (class handout).

16. Thinking the Unthinkable: Bruno

   Koyré, From the Closed World, ch. 2.

17. Renaissance Magic and Modern Science: The Great Debate

   Yates, "The Hermetic Tradition in Renaissance Science," in Singleton,
      ed., Art, Science and History in the Renaissance, pp. 255-75.
   and one of the following:
   Vickers, "Introduction," in his Scientific and Occult Mentalities
      in the Renaissance.
   Rosen, "Was Copernicus a Hermetist?" Minnesota Studies in the
      Philosophy of Science, vol. 5, pp. 163-71.
   Hesse, "Hermeticism and Historiography: An Apology for the Internal
      History of Science," ibid., pp. 134-60.
   Westman, "Magical Reform and Astronomical Reform: The Yates Thesis
      Reconsidered," in Westman and McGuire, Hermeticism and the
      Scientific Revolution.

18. Seeing the Invisible: Galileo I

   Galileo, The Starry Messenger and from The Assayer, in
      Discoveries and Opinions of Galileo, pp. 23-58, 274-79.
   Kuhn, pp. 219-37.
   Koyré, From the Closed World, ch. 4.

Part III: THE SCIENTIFIC REVOLUTION

19. Motion and Mathematics: Galileo II

   Galileo, from Dialogue concerning the Two Chief World Systems, in
      Marie Boas Hall, Nature and Nature's Laws, pp. 78-96.
   Westfall, The Construction of Modern Science, pp. 13-24.
   Debus, pp. 109-15.

20. Academies and Experiments: Bacon

   Bacon, The Great Instauration and the New Atlantis.
   Boas, The Scientific Renaissance, ch. 8.
   Westfall, ch. 6.

21. The Circulation of the Blood: Harvey

   Harvey, from On the Motion of the Heart and Blood, in Hall, pp. 136-59.
   Debus, pp. 66-73.
   Westfall, ch. 5.

22. Mechanism and Method: Descartes

   Descartes, Discourse on Method, Parts I, II, IV, V, VI.
   Westfall, ch. 2.
   Debus, pp. 105-9.

23. The Mechanical Philosophy

   Boyle, from The Excellency and Grounds of the Mechanical Hypothesis,
      in Hall, pp. 311-23.
   Merchant, The Death of Nature, ch. 7 (chs. 1-4 recommended).

24. Newton I: Science and Personality

   Newton, A New Theory of Light and Color, in Thayer, Newton's
      Philosophy of Nature, pp. 68-81.
   Westfall, ch. 8.
   Manuel, A Portrait of Isaac Newton, chs. 1-4.

25. Newton II: Metaphysics and Theology

   Koyré, From the Closed World, chs. 9-12.
   Lewis, The Discarded Image, Epilogue.

History 235   Katharine Park
Fall 1987   Wellesley College

               THE FORMATION OF EUROPEAN CULTURE:
               MIDDLE AGES AND RENAISSANCE

The following books have been ordered from the Bookstore:
    R.W. Southern, The Making of the Middle Ages
    Peter Abelard, The Story of Abelard's Adversities
    Andreas Capellanus, The Art of Courtly Love
    Bonaventure, The Mind's Road to God
    Etienne Gilson, Reason and Revelation in the Middle Ages
    Ernst Cassirer, ed., The Renaissance Philosophy of Man
    Christine de Pizan, The Book of the City of Ladies
    Thomas More, Utopia
    Niccolo Machiavelli, The Prince
    Michel de Montaigne, Selections from the Essays
    Francis Bacon, The Great Instauration and the New Atlantis
    J. Weinberg, A Short History of Medieval Philosophy (optional).

Course requirements: 1. Two 5-7 page papers
                       2. Midterm examination (take-home)
                       3. Final examination
                       4. Class attendance and participation.

General reference works:
    Dictionary of the History of Ideas (Reference: qCB 5 D52)
    Encyclopedia of Philosophy (Reference: qB 41 E5)
    New Catholic Encyclopedia (Reference:qBX 841 N44).

Syllabus:

I. THE RENAISSANCE OF THE TWELFTH CENTURY

Week 1: Anselm and Monastic Culture

    Southern, The Making of the Middle Ages, pp. 154-93.
    Note: By the end of the third week of class you should have read
    also pp. 15-153 of Southern.
    Anselm, Proslogion, in Fairweather, Scholastic Miscellany, pp.
    69-93.
    Recommended: Weinberg, A Short History of Medieval Philosophy, ch. 4.
                 or Copleston, A History of Medieval Philosophy, ch. 6.

Week 2: Abelard, Heloise, and the Schools

    Southern, pp. 193-218.
    Abelard, The Story of Abelard's Adversities. (See also next page.)

Heloise, from her first letter to Abelard, and Radice, "The French
Scholar-Lover: Heloise," in Katharina M. Wilson, _Medieval Women
Writers_, pp. 90-108.
Recommended: Weinberg, ch. 5
                 or Copleston, chs. 6 (second half)-7.

Week 3: Andreas Capellanus and Courtly Culture

Southern, ch. 5.
Andreas Capellanus, _The Art of Courtly Love_.
C.S. Lewis, _The Allegory of Love_, ch. 1.

II. SCHOLASTIC CULTURE AND ITS CRITICS

Week 4: Mystical Theology and the New Orders: Bernard of Clairvaux and
         Bonaventure

Wimsatt, "St. Bernard, The Canticle of Canticles, and Mystical Piety,"
   in Paul Szarmach, ed., _An Introduction to the Mystics of Medieval
   Europe_, chs. 4.
Bernard of Clairvaux, letter against Abelard and from _The Love of
   God_, in Petry, ed., _Late Medieval Mysticism_, pp. 54-65.
Bonaventure, _The Mind's Road to God_.
Recommended: Weinberg, ch. 8
                 or *Copleston, chs. 10-11.

Week 5: Philosophy in the University: Aquinas, Siger and Boethius of Dacia

Gilson, _Reason and Revelation in the Middle Ages_.
Aquinas, _Summa theologiae_, I, Q. 46, arts. 1-2.
Boethius of Dacia, _Question on the Eternity of the World_.
Recommended: Copleston, chs. 12-13.

Week 6: Petrarch and the Birth of Humanism

Kristeller, _Eight Philosophers of the Italian Renaissance_, ch. 1.
Petrarch, from his letters and _On His Own Ignorance and That of Many
   Others_, in Cassirer, ed., _The Renaissance Philosophy of Man_, pp.
   47-143.
Recommended: Hay, _The Italian Renaissance in its Historical
   Background_, chs. 1-4.

Week 7: Christine de Pizan and the Defense of Women

Christine de Pizan, _The Book of the City of Ladies_, including
   introduction by Earl Jeffrey Warner.
Christine de Pizan, from _Lavision Christine_, in Petroff, ed.,
   Medieval Women's Visionary Literature, pp. 335-39.

III. RENAISSANCE AND REFORMATION

Week 8: Civic Humanism: Barbaro and Bracciolini

> Lauro Martines, Power and Imaginationn, ch. 11.
> Francesco Barbaro, On Wifely Duties, in Kohl and Witt, eds., The
>   Earthly Republic, pp. 179-227.
> Poggio Bracciolini, On Nobility, in Watkins, ed., Humanism and
>   Liberty, pp. 118-48.
> Recommended: Hay, ch. 5
>   or Garin, Italian Humanism, ch. 2.

Week 9: Pico and the Jewish Tradition

> Kristeller, ch. 4.
> Pico, Oration [On the Dignity of Man], in Cassirer, pp. 223-54,
>   and from the Heptaplus, in Pico, On the Dignity of Man and Other
>   Works, pp. 65-84, 170-74.
> Recommended: Roth, A History of the Jews of Italy, ch. 5 (also 4).

Week 10: More on the Best Society

> Hexter, More's Utopia: The Biography of an Idea, parts I (skim)
>   and II (read).
> More, Utopia.
> Recommended: Hay, ch. 7.

Week 11: Machiavelli on the Real World

> Berlin, "The Originality of Machiavelli," in his Against the
>   Current, pp. 25-79.
> Machiavelli, The Prince.
> Recommended: Gilbert, "The Humanist Concept of the Prince and The
>   Prince of Machiavelli," Journal of Modern History 11 (1939):
>   449-83 (in stacks).

Week 12: Montaigne and the Problem of Certainty

> Popkin, A History of Skepticism, chs. 1-3.
> Montaigne, Selections from the Essays.

Week 13: Francis Bacon: Knowledge and Power

> Carolyn Merchant, The Death of Nature, ch. 7
> or Paolo Rossi, Francis Bacon: From Magic to Science, ch. 1.
> Bacon, The Great Instauration and the New Atlantis.

MEDIEVAL CULTURE:
THE AGE OF SPIRITUALITY

INDS 293, ENGL 279, FNAR 159, HIST 255
Drs. Brauner, Masi, Rosenwein

Required books:
William Cook and R. Herzman, The Medieval World View: an Introduction
    (Oxford University Press)
Geoffrey of Monmouth, History of the Kings of Britain (Penguin)
Anon., Quest of the Holy Grail (Penguin)
Chrétien de Troyes, Arthurian Romances (Xerox at Kinko's)
St. Benedict, Rule of St. Benedict (Liturgical Press)
Peter Abelard, The Letters of Abelard and Heloise (Penguin)
Selected readings, marked below with an ×; Xerox copies will be available.

Recommended Books:
W.T.H. Jackson, Medieval Literature, A History and a Guide (Collier) [out of
    print; see copy on reserve]
Bernard of Clairvaux, On the Song of Songs, I (Cistercian Fathers series,
    no.4)
E. Holt, A Documentary History of Art, vol.1 (Doubleday)
A. Seay, Music in the Medieval World (Prentice-Hall)
    [All books ordered at Loyola Bookstore and Beck's. Copies of recommended
    texts are on reserve]

Syllabus and Assignments

Jan.19 Introduction to the course

Jan.21 Pagan and spiritual love (Song of Songs, Ovid)
    ×Bible, **The Song of Songs**
    ×Ovid

Jan.26- Cook and Herzman (2 classes)
  28   [Jan.26, chs.1-3; Jan.28, chs.8-9]

TOPIC 1: THE COURT MILIEU

Feb.2-   Princes, kings, lords, and vassals
  4   ×Suger, **Life of Louis the Fat**
        Begin reading Geoffrey of Monmouth, History of the Kings , pp.166-
          261, and Chrétien de Troyes, Lancelot

Feb.9- Geoffrey of Monmouth: historical context and sources for Arthurian
  11   literature
        Geoffrey of Monmouth, History, pp.166-261

Feb.16– Troubadours: lyric poetry and medieval song
18   *Troubadour poems

Feb.23– Chrètien de Troyes: the court at Troyes; Arthurian literature between
25   Geoffrey and Chrètien; Chrètien's other poetry
       Chrètien de Troyes, Lancelot

Mar.1   MID-TERM EXAM

ΕΟΡΙC ΙΙ: ΕΗΕ ΜΟΝΑΣΕΙC ΜΙLΙΕU

Mar.3   Monasticism: video tape: Life in a Medieval Monastery

Mar.8– SPRING VACATION
10

Mar.15   FIRST REPORT DUE
         Monastic architecture

Mar.17   **The Rule of St. Benedict**

Mar.22– Gregorian chant: The Liturgy of monastic life.
24   Begin reading The Quest of the Holy Grail

Mar.29– St. Bernard and Suger
31   **Bible, The Song of Songs**
       St. Bernard, Sermons 1, 7, 20 (on reserve)
       **St. Bernard, "Apologia to William of St. Thierry," and Suger, "The
         Book of Suger," in Holt, Documentary History of Art, pp.18-48 (on
         reserve**

Apr.5– **Anon., The Quest of the Holy Grail**
7

ΕΟΡΙC ΙΙΙ: ΕΗΕ URBAN ΜΙLΙΕU

Apr.12   RESEARCH PAPER DUE
         The rise of cities

Apr.14 Realism/Nominalism; Peter Abelard's life
        Abelard, Story of My Misfortunes

Apr.19 *Abelard, Sic et Non

Apr.21 Gothic architecture and the mysticism of light: Suger and St. Denis

Apr.26– Chartres
28

Apr.28 SECOND REPORT DUE

Ground Rules

You are expected to do the readings assigned for each class and to participate in class discussions. One-third of your grade is based on class participation.

Examinations will combine short answer and essay questions. The final exam will be comprehensive. Cheating will result in a grade of F on that examination. There will be no make-up exams unless the student calls an instructor <u>on the day</u> of the exam with his or her excuse and <u>arranges for the make-up at that time</u>. Otherwise, a missed exam will result in a grade of F. Exams count one-third of your grade.

There are three papers. Two are to be reports on off-campus excursions relevant to the topics in the course, such as visits to churches built in medieval style, to concerts of early music, to museums, lectures, plays, to libraries housing medieval manuscripts, and so on. The topics should be chosen in consultation with a professor. The reports, 2 pages long, should relate your excursion to what you are learning in class. You may not do two of the same type of excursion, but the topics may be the same, i.e., you may not write about two concerts, but you may write about a concert and a lecture on early music. These reports will be graded Pass/Fail. Late papers will be marked F.

The third paper is a research paper. You will be given a list of suggested topics to start you thinking; you may wish to relate the topic of your research paper to that of your excursions. Your final choice should be approved by a professor. Papers should be 5-7 pages long, not counting footnotes and bibliography (both to be attached to the back of the paper). Late papers will be downgraded 1/2 grade for every day late (e.g. A- one day late will be B+).

Reports and papers should be typewritten or computer-printed, double-spaced, with one inch margins, **proofread**. Plagiarism will result in a grade of F on the paper; there will be no chance to rewrite it. Plagiarism means not only simply quoting another person's work without acknowledgment but also paraphrasing without acknowledgment. It also means stringing together <u>acknowledged</u> quotes or paraphrases. Consult a professor if you have questions. Papers count one-third of the grade; the two reports together are worth one-half as much as the research paper.

Grades for papers, exams, and the course are given by the three instructors in consultation.

Nota bene: a complete performance of a medieval Mass with chant, polyphony, and traditional ceremony will be presented by the Harwood Early Music Ensemble on Saturday, February 20, at 8:00 p.m. in the First Baptist Church, Chicago and Lake Streets, Evanston, and on Sunday, February 21, at 3:00 p.m. in the Church of the Ascension, 1133 North LaSalle Street, Chicago.

MEDIEVAL INSTITUTIONS
Donald Queller
University of Illinois, Urbana

THE GERMANS AND THE GERMANIC KINGDOMS

Topics:

The Anglo-Saxons
Sources for the Early Germans*
Peaceful Germanization of the Roman Empire
Visigoths
Vandals
Huns
Ostrogoths*
Lombards
Salian Franks
Social and Political Structure

Bibliography:

Bury, J.B., THE INVASION OF EUROPE BY THE BARBARIANS. 940.1-B975i
Lot, F., THE END OF THE ANCIENT WORLD AND THE BEGINNING OF THE MIDDLE AGES.
 841.09-L882e
Tacitus, GERMANIA. 870 - T118- tG.E7
Gregory of Tours, HISTORY OF THE FRANKS (Dalton translation) 944.01 - G821h-
 1927
Hodgkin, T., ITALY AND HER INVADERS. 945 - H689i
Moss. H. St. L. B., THE BIRTH OF THE MIDDLE AGES
Dill, S., ROMAN SOCIETY IN GAUL IN THE MEROVINGIAN AGE. 914.401 - D598r
Drew, Katherine Fisher, comp., THE BARBARIAN INVASIONS
THE BURGUNDIAN CODE, D. Fischer translation
Cassiodorus, LETTERS, Hodgkin translation. 879 - C345 - d.E4
Hodgkin, T., THEODORIC THE GOTH. 92 - T388h
Villari, P., THE BARBARIAN INVASIONS OF ITALY
Arragon, R.F., THE TRANSITION FROM THE ANCIENT TO THE MEDIEVAL WORLD.
 937.09 - A.773t
Wallace-Hadrill, J.M., THE BARBARIAN WEST, 400-1000. 940.1 - W1956 - 1961
Pirenne, Henri, MOHAMMED AND CHARLEMAGNE. 940.1 - P666mo - paper
Bark, Wm., ORIGINS OF THE MEDIEVAL WORLD. 330 - S785p - V.14 - paper
Thompson, E.A., THE EARLY GERMANS
Sullivan, Richard E., HEIRS TO THE ROMAN EMPIRE
Latouche, Robert, CAESAR TO CHARLEMAGNE
Thompson, E.A., THE GOTHS IN SPAIN
Duckett, E.S., GATEWAY TO THE MIDDLE AGES
Thompson, E.A., THE VISIGOTHS IN THE TIME OF ULFILAS
_____, A HISTORY OF ATTILA AND THE HUNS
Wallace-Hadrill, J.M., THE LONG-HAIRED KINGS AND OTHER STUDIES IN FRANKISH
 HISTORY
_____, EARLY GERMANIC KINGSHIP IN ENGLAND AND ON THE CONTINENT
Maenchen-Helfen, J. Otto, THE WORLD OF THE HUNS
Paul the Deacon, HISTORY OF THE LOMBARDS
Musset, Lucien, THE GERMANIC INVASIONS
Bachrach, Bernard, FRANKISH MILITARY HISTORY

Mr. Queller
THE CAROLINGIANS

Bibliography:

    THE CORONATION OF CHARLEMAGNE (Problems in European Civilization)
    Einhard, LIFE OF CHARLEMAGNE
    Davis, H.W.C., CHARLEMAGNE
    Duckett, Eleanor S., ALCUIN, FRIEND OF CHARLEMAGNE
    Fichtenau, Heinrich, THE CAROLINGIAN EMPIRE
    Cabaniss, Allen, SON OF CHARLEMAGNE; A CONTEMPORARY LIFE OF LOUIS THE PIOUS
    Easton, Stewart, THE ERA OF CHARLEMAGNE
    Boussard, Jacques, THE CIVILIZATION OF CHARLEMAGNE
    Seelinger, G., Chaps. on Carolingian Empire in CAMBRIDGE MEDIEVAL HISTORY, II, 19
        and 21
    Thompson, James Westfall, THE DISSOLUTION OF THE CAROLINGIAN FISC
    Ganshof, Francois Louis, FRANKISH INSTITUTIONS UNDER CHARLEMAGNE
    Thorpe, Lewis G.M., TWO LIVES OF CHARLEMAGNE
    CAROLINGIAN CHRONICLES, trans. by Bernhard Walter Scholz
    Munz, Peter, LIFE IN THE AGE OF CHARLEMAGNE
    Duckett, E.S., CAROLINGIAN PORTRAITS
    Ganshof, Francois Louis, THE CAROLINGIANS AND THE FRANKISH MONARCHY
    Cabaniss, James A., CHARLEMAGNE
    Folz, Robert, THE CORONATION OF CHARLEMAGNE, 25 DECEMBER 800
    Barruclough, Geoffrey, THE CRUCIBLE OF EUROPE
    Folz, Robert, THE CONSTITUTION OF CHARLEMAGNE
    Loyn, H.R., and John Percival, THE REIGN OF CHARLEMAGNE: DOCUMENTS ON
        CAROLINGIAN ADMINISTRATION

FEUDALISM

<u>Topics</u>:

Origins
The Combination of the Elements of Feudalism under the Carolingians
The Feudal Contract
Homage and Fealty
Subinfeudation and the Demesne
The Feudal Nobility
Military Training and Equipment
The Castle and Castle Life
Chivalry

<u>Bibliography</u>:

RAOUL DE CAMBRAI, trans. by Jessie Crosland
THE SONG OF ROLAND
University of Pennsylvania Translations and Reprints, Vol. IV, No. 3 (Documents
 Illustrative of FEUDALISM)
Stephenson, Carl, MEDIEVAL FEUDALISM
————, AMERICAN HISTORICAL REVIEW, Vol. XLVI (1941), pp. 788-812
Bloch, Marc, FEUDAL SOCIETY
Stenton, Sir Frank, THE FIRST CENTURY OF ENGLISH FEUDALISM, 1066-1166
Seignobos, Charles, THE FEUDAL REGIME
Painter, Sidney, STUDIES IN THE HISTORY OF THE ENGLISH FEUDAL BARONY
Ganshof, Francois L., FEUDALISM, trans. by Philip Grierson
Vinogradoff, Sir Paul, "Feudalism," CMH, III, Ch. 18
White, Lynn, MEDIEVAL TECHNOLOGY AND SOCIAL CHANGE
Coulborn, Rushton, FEUDALISM IN HISTORY
Painter, S., FRENCH CHIVALRY
Strayer, Joseph R., FEUDALISM
Herlihy, David, ed., THE HISTORY OF FEUDALISM
Lewis, Archibald R., KNIGHTS AND SAMURAI: KNIGHTS IN NORTHERN RANCE AND
 JAPAN
Brown, R. Allen, ORIGINS OF ENGLISH FEUDALISM
Brown, Elizabeth A.R., "The Tyranny of a Construct: Feudalism and Historians of
 Medieval Europe," AHR, LXXIX (1974), 1063-1800"
Round, J.H., FEUDAL ENGLAND
Critchley, J.S., FEUDALISM

Mr. Queller

EARLY MEDIEVAL MONARCHY

Topics:

Sources
Theory of Feudal Monarchy
East Frankland
    Sources of royal strength
    The Stem Ducies
    The Ottonians
West Frankland
    Early Capetians
    Deterioration of the Demesne
    Capetian Government
    The Great Baronies
Anglo-Saxon England
    Before the Danes
    The Danes and the Rise of Wessex
    Anglo-Saxon Monarchy
    Local Government

Bibliography:

THE WORKS OF LUIDPRAND OF CREMONA, trans. by F.A. Wright
Barraclough, Geoffrey, MEDIEVAL GERMANY, 2 vols.
_____, THE ORIGINS OF MODERN GERMANY
_____, THE MEDIEVAL EMPIRE
Johnson, Edgar N., SECULAR ACTIVITIES OF THE GERMAN EPISCOPATE
Thompson, James Westfall, FEUDAL GERMANY
Hill, Boyd, ed., RISE OF THE FIRST REICH
Heer, Friedrich, THE HOLY ROMAN EMPIRE
Fawtier, Robert, THE CAPETIANS
Haskins, Charles Homer, THE NORMANS IN EUROPEAN HISTORY
Petit-Dutaillis, Charles, FEUDAL MONARCHY IN FRANCE AND ENGLAND
ENGLISH HISTORICAL DOCUMENTS, ed. by David Douglas, vol. I, ed. by Dorothy
    Whitelock
Blair, Peter Hunter, ANGLO-SAXON ENGLAND
Kirby, D.P., THE MAKING OF EARLY ENGLAND
Larson, L.M., CANUTE THE GREAT
Oman, Charles, ENGLAND BEFORE THE NORMAN CONQUEST
Stenton, Sir Frank M., ANGLO-SAXON ENGLAND
Whitelock, Dorothy, THE BEGINNINGS OF ENGLISH SOCIETY
Duckett, Eleanor Shipley, ALFRED THE GREAT
Deanesly, Margaret, THE PRE-CONQUEST CHURCH IN ENGLAND
Hollister, C.W., ANGLO-SAXON MILITARY INSTITUTIONS
Plummer, Christopher, LIFE & TIMES OF ALFRED THE GREAT
Cheney, C.R., THE CULT OF ANGLO-SAXON KINGSHIP

Mr. Queller

MANORIALISM

Bibliography:

Bennett, H.S., LIFE ON THE ENGLISH MANOR
Boissonade, P., LIFE AND WORK IN MEDIEVAL EUROPE
CAMBRIDGE ECONOMIC HISTORY, Vol. I
Kosminsky, E.A., STUDIES IN THE AGRARIAN HISTORY OF ENGLAND
Nielson, Nellie, MEDIEVAL AGRARIAN ECONOMY
Power, Eileen, "Peasant Life and Rural Conditions," CAMBRIDGE MEDIEVAL HISTORY,
    Vol. VII, Chap. XXIV
Ernle, R.E. Prothero, ENGLISH FARMING, PAST AND PRESENT
Orwin, C.S. & C.S., THE OPEN FIELDS
Lennard, Reginald, RURAL ENGLAND, 1086-1135
Bloch, Marc, FRENCH RURAL HISTORY
Raftis, James, TENURE AND MOBILITY
Ault, Warren, OPEN-FIELD HUSBANDRY AND THE VILLAGE COMMUNITY
Duby, Georges, RURAL AND COUNTRY LIFE IN THE MEDIEVAL WEST
Hilton, R.H., THE DECLINE OF SERFDOM IN MEDIEVAL ENGLAND
LeRoy Ladurie, E., THE PEASANTS OF LANGUEDOC
Bloch, Marc, SLAVERY AND SERFDOM IN THE MIDDLE AGES
Vinogradoff, Paul, VILLEINAGE IN ENGLAND
Ault, Warren, OPEN-FIELD FARMING IN MEDIEVAL ENGLAND
Homans, George, ENGLISH VILLAGERS IN THE THIRTEENTH CENTURY
Vinogradoff, Paul, GROWTH OF THE MANOR
_____, ENGLISH SOCIETY IN THE ELEVENTH CENTURY
Duby, Georges, THE EARLY GROWTH OF THE EUROPEAN ECONOMY
White, Lynn, MEDIEVAL TECHNOLOGY AND SOCIAL CHANGE

MEDIEVAL TOWNS

Topics:

Origins
The Middle Class
Town Charter & Urban Government
Social and Political Unrest in Medieval Towns
The Rise of Despots
Any Particular Town

Bibliography:

Pirenne, Henri, MEDIEVAL CITIES
_____, ECONOMIC AND SOCIAL HISTORY OF MEDIEVAL EUROPE
Stephenson, Carl, BOROUGH AND TOWN
Boissonade, P., LIFE AND WORK IN MEDIEVAL EUROPE
Lipson, E., INTRODUCTION TO THE ECONOMIC HISTORY OF ENGLAND
Pirenne, Henri, EARLY DEMOCRACIES IN THE LOW COUNTRIES
CAMBRIDGE ECONOMIC HISTORY, vol. II
Schevill, Ferdinand, HISTORY OF FLORENCE
Butler, W.F., THE LOMBARD COMMUNES
Hill, J.W., MEDIEVAL LINCOLN, 942.53-H646W
Thompson, James Westfall, ECONOMIC AND SOCIAL HISTORY OF THE MIDDLE AGES
_____, ECONOMIC AND SOCIAL HISTORY OF EUROPE IN THE LATTER MIDDLE AGES
    1300-1530
Power, Eileen, MEDIEVAL PEOPLE
Benson, E., LIFE IN A MEDIEVAL CITY
Evans, J., LIFE IN MEDIEVAL FRANCE
Salzman, L.F., ENGLISH LIFE IN THE MIDDLE AGES
Bland, A.E., P.A. Brown & R.H. Tawney, ENGLISH ECONOMIC HISTORY: SELECT
    DOCUMENTS (part I)
Mundy & Riesenberg, THE MEDIEVAL TOWN
Thrupp, Sylvia, THE MERCHANT CLASS OF MEDIEVAL LONDON
Herlihy, David, PISA IN THE EARLY RENAISSANCE
Waley, Daniel P., MEDIEVAL ORVIETO
Espinas, George, LA VIE URBAINE DE DONAI AU MOYEN AGE
Herlihy, David, MEDIEVAL & RENAISSANCE PISTOIA
Waley, Daniel, THE ITALIAN CITY-REPUBLICS
Baker, Timothy, MEDIEVAL LONDON
Williams, Gwyn A., MEDIEVAL LONDON: FROM COMMUNE TO CAPITAL
Schevill, Ferdinand, SIENA
Brucker, Gene, RENAISSANCE FLORENCE
Brooke, Christopher N.L. & Gillian Kerr, LONDON, 800-1216
Lane, Frederic C., VENICE
Platt, Colin, THE MEDIEVAL ENGLISH TOWN
Reynolds, Susan, AN INTRODUCTION TO THE HISTORY OF ENGLISH MEDIEVAL TOWNS
Beresford, Maurice, NEW TOWNS IN THE MIDDLE AGES
Holmes, Urban T., DAILY LIFE IN THE TWELFTH CENTURY

COMMERCE AND INDUSTRY

<u>Topics</u>:

Medieval Banking
Medieval Money
Partnerships, Regulated Companies and Joint Stock
Fairs of Champagne
Textile Industry
The Guild System

<u>Bibliography</u>:

Lopez, Robert S., THE COMMERCIAL REVOLUTION OF THE MIDDLE AGES, 950-1350
CAMBRIDGE ECONOMIC HISTORY, vol. II-III
Pirenne, Henri, ECONOMIC AND SOCIAL HISTORY OF MEDIEVAL EUROPE
Power, E., MEDIEVAL PEOPLE
Thompson, J.W., ECONOMIC AND SOCIAL HISTORY OF EUROPE IN THE LATER MIDDLE
    AGES
Boissonade, P., LIFE AND WORK IN MEDIEVAL EUROPE
Thompson, J.W., ECONOMIC AND SOCIAL HISTORY OF THE MIDDLE AGES
Byrne, E.H., GENOESE SHIPPING IN THE XII-XIII CENTURIES
Lane, F.C., VENETIAN SHIPS AND SHIPBUILDERS
De Roover, Raymond, THE RISE AND DECLINE OF THE MEDICI BANK
Reynolds, Robert L., EUROPE EMERGES
Cipolla, Carlo, MONEY, PRICES & CIVILIZATION IN THE MEDIEVAL WORLD
Salzman, L.F., ENGLISH TRADE IN THE MIDDLE AGES
_____, ENGLISH INDUSTRIES IN THE MIDDLE AGES
Renard, Georges Francis, GUILDS IN THE MIDDLE AGES
Dollinger, Philippe, THE GERMAN HANSA
Miskimin, Harry A., THE ECONOMY OF EARLY RENAISSANCE EUROPE, 1300-1460
Postan, M.M., MEDIEVAL TRADE AND FINANCE
De Roover, Raymond A., BUSINESS, BANKING AND ECONOMIC THOUGHT IN LATE
    MEDIEVAL AND EARLY MODERN EUROPE
Lane, Frederic C., ANDREA BARBARIGO
Sapori, Armando, ITALIAN MERCHANT IN THE MIDDLE AGES
Power, Eileen, THE WOOL TRADE IN ENGLISH MEDIEVAL HISTORY
Lloyd, Terence, THE ENGLISH WOOL TRADE IN THE MIDDLE AGES
De Roover, Raymond, THE MEDICI BANK
_____, MONEY AND BANKING IN MEDIEVAL BRUGES
Usher, Abbot Payson, THE EARLY HISTORY OF DEPOSIT BANKING
Lopez, R.S. & I.W. Raymond, MEDIEVAL TRADE IN THE MEDITERRANEAN WORLD

Mr. Queller

THE CRUSADES

<u>Topics</u>:

The Reconquista   Relations of Latins with the Byzantine Empire
First Crusade
Second Crusade   Latin States in the East
Third Crusade
Fourth Crusade   Later Crusades

<u>Bibliography</u>:

Strayer, Joseph R., THE ALBIGENSIAN CRUSADES
Anna Comnena, THE ALEXIAD
Fulcher of Chartres, CHRONICLE OF THE FIRST CRUSADE
Krey, A.C., THE FIRST CRUSADE
William of Tyre, HISTORY OF THE CRUSADES
LaMonte, J.L., FEUDAL MONARCHY IN THE LATIN KINGDOM OF JERUSALEM
Munro, D.C., THE KINGDOM OF THE CRUSADERS
Newhall, R.S., THE CRUSADES
Paetow, L.J., ed., THE CRUSADES AND OTHER ESSAYS PRESENTED TO D.C. MUNRO
Stevenson, W., THE CRUSADERS IN THE EAST
Robert of Clari, CONQUEST OF CONSTANTINOPLE
Runciman, S., A HISTORY OF THE CRUSADES
Hitti, P.K., AN ARAB-SYRIAN GENTLEMAN AND WARRIOR IN THE PERIOD OF THE
    CRUSADES
Archer, T.A., THE CRUSADE OF RICHARD I
Duncalf, F., and Krey, A.D., PARALLEL SOURCE PROBLEMS IN MEDIEVAL HISTORY,
    pp. 95-133
Joinville, Jean de, LIFE OF ST. LOUIS
Villehardouin, THE CONQUEST OF CONSTANTINOPLE
Setton, Kenneth, et al., HISTORY OF THE CRUSADES
Andressohn, J.C., ANCESTRY AND LIFE OF GODFREY OF BOUILLON
Yewdale, R.B., BOHEMOND I OF ANTIOCH
Nicholson, R., TANCRED
Southern, Richard W., WESTERN VIEWS OF ISLAM IN THE MIDDLE AGES
Brand, Charles, BYZANTIUM CONFRONTS THE WEST, 1180-1204
Riley-Smith, Jonathan, THE KNIGHTS OF ST. JOHN IN JERUSALEM AND CYPRUS
Brundage, James, CANON LAW AND THE CRUSADES
Prawer, Joshua, THE CRUSADERS' KINGDOM: MEDIEVAL COLONIALISM IN THE MIDDLE
    AGES
Mayer, Hans Eberhard, THE CRUSADES
Riley-Smith, Jonathan, THE FEUDAL NOBILITY AND THE KINGDOM OF JERUSALEM,
    1174-1277
Nicolson, R.L., JOSCELIN III AND THE FALL OF THE CRUSADER STATES, 1134-1199
Smail, R.C., CRUSADING WARFARE
_____, THE CRUSADERS IN SYRIA AND THE HOLY LAND
Brundage, James A., RICHARD LION-HEART
Urban, William L., THE BALTIC CRUSADE
Queller, D.E., THE FOURTH CRUSADE
Erdmann, Carl, THE ORIGINS OF THE IDEA OF CRUSADE
Grousset, René, THE EPIC OF THE CRUSADES

THE ANGEVIN EMPIRE

<u>Topics</u>:

      Formation of the Angevin Empire
      Eleanor of Aquitaine
      Judicial and Administrative Reforms of Henry II
      Magna Carta

<u>Bibliographical suggestions</u>:

      Morris, W.A., THE MEDIEVAL ENGLISH SHERIFF TO 1300
      Pollock, F., and F.W. Maitland, THE HISTORY OF ENGLISH LAW BEFORE THE TIME OF
          EDWARD I
      McKechnie, W.S., MAGNA CARTA
      Poole, R.L., THE EXCHEQUER IN THE TWELFTH CENTURY
      Powicke, F.M., STEPHEN LANGTON
      _____, THE LOSS OF NORMANDY
      Barlow, F., THE FEUDAL KINGDOM OF ENGLAND, 1042-1216
      Stubbs, W., CONSTITUTIONAL HISTORY OF ENGLAND
      Petit-Dutaillis, C., FEUDAL MONARCHY IN FRANCE AND ENGLAND
      ENGLISH HISTORICAL DOCUMENTS, ed. by D.C. Douglas and G.W. Greenway, Vol. 2
      Norgate, Kate, ENGLAND UNDER THE ANGEVIN KINGS
      _____, RICHARD THE LION HEART
      _____, JOHN LACKLAND
      Painter, S., THE REIGN OF KING JOHN
      Salzman, L.F., HENRY II
      Ramsay, J.J., THE ANGEVIN EMPIRE, 1154-1216
      Maitland. F.W.. CONSTITUTIONAL HISTORY AND ENGLAND
      MAGNA CARTA COMMEMORATION ESSAYS
      Warren, W.L., KING JOHN
      Kelly, Amy, ELEANOR AND THE FOUR KINGS
      Lyon, Bryce, CONSTITUTIONAL HISTORY
      Davis, R.H.C., KING STEPHEN
      Holt, J.C., MAGNA CARTA
      Jolliffe, John E.A., ANGEVIN KINGSHIP
      Knowles, David, THOMAS BECKETT
      Cronne, H.A., THE REIGN OF KING STEPHEN
      Caeneghem, R.C. Van, THE BIRTH OF THE ENGLISH COMMON LAW
      Sutherland, Donald W., THE ASSIZE OF NOVEL DISSEISIN
      _____, QUO WARRAUTO
      Warren, W.L., HENRY II
      Lloyd, Alan, KING JOHN
      Bennetts, Pamela, THE BARONS OF RUNNYMEDE
      Thompson, Faith, FIRST CENTURY OF MAGNA CARTA

Mr. Queller

MEDIEVAL HISTORY

France in the Thirteenth Century

Topics:

The Extension of Royal Power	National Assemblies
under Philip Augustus	Brothers of St. Louis
Blanche of Castile	Philip III
The Character of St. Louis	Philip IV
Royal Authority under St. Louis	

Bibliography:

Jordan, W.C., LOUIS IX AND THE CHALLENGE OF THE CRUSADE

Luchaire, Achille, SOCIAL FRANCE IN THE AGE OF PHILIP AUGUSTUS

Petit-Dutaillis, C., FEUDAL MONARCHY IN FRANCE AND ENGLAND FROM THE 10th TO THE 13th CENTURY

Strayer, J., ADMINISTRATION OF NORMANDY UNDER ST. LOUIS

Hutton, W.H., PHILIP AUGUSTUS

Perry, F., ST. LOUIS

Walker, Williston, ON THE INCREASE OF ROYAL POWER IN FRANCE UNDER PHILIP AUGUSTUS

Joinville, Jean de, LIFE OF ST. LOUIS

Strayer, Joseph R., "The Crusade Against Aragon," SPECULUM, Jan., 1953

Strayer, J.R., "Philip the Fair - A Constitutional King," AMERICAN HISTORICAL REVIEW, Oct., 1956

Fawtier, Robert, THE CAPETIAN KINGS OF FRANCE

Pegues, Frank, LAWYERS OF PHILIP IV

Labarge, Margaret Wade, ST. LOUIS

Strayer, Joseph R., THE MEDIEVAL ORIGINS OF THE MODERN STATE

Wood, Charles T., THE FRENCH APPANAGES & THE CAPETIAN MONARCHY, 1224-1328

Powicke, F.M., THE LOSS OF NORMANDY, 1189-1204

Hollister, C.Warren & John Baldwin, "The Rise of Administrative Kingship: Henry I & Philip Augustus," AHR, LXXXIII (1978), 867-905

THE DISINTEGRATION OF THE EMPIRE

Topics:

Frederick II
The Fall of the Hohenstaufens
The Interregnum
The German Constitution in the Later Middle Ages
Reasons for the Failure of the Holy Roman Empire

Bibliography:

Barraclough, Geoffrey, MEDIEVAL GERMANY
————, ORIGINS OF MODERN GERMANY
Thompson, J.W., FEUDAL GERMANY
Kantorowicz, Ernst, FREDERICK II
Bayley, C.C., THE FORMATION OF THE GERMAN COLLEGE OF ELECTORS
Bryce, James, THE HOLY ROMAN EMPIRE
Henderson, E.F., A HISTORY OF GERMANY IN THE MIDDLE AGES
Stubbs, William, GERMANY IN THE EARLY MIDDLE AGES
————, GERMANY IN THE LATER MIDDLE AGES
Einstein, D., EMPEROR FREDERICK II
Dollinger, Philippe, THE GERMAN HANSA
Heer, Friedrich, THE HOLY ROMAN EMPIRE
Van Cleve, Thomas, FREDERICK II
Hampe, K., GERMANY UNDER THE SALIAN & HOHENSTAUFEN EMPERORS

ITALY IN THE LATE MIDDLE AGES

Topics:

The Communes	Venice
Naples and Sicily	The Lesser States
The Papal States	Machiavelli's Prince
Florence	The Triumph of Despotism
Milan	

Bibliography:

Armstrong, E., LORENZO DE' MEDICI

Baron, H., THE CRISIS OF THE EARLY ITALIAN RENAISSANCE

_____, HUMANISTIC AND POLITICAL LITERATURE IN FLORENCE AND VENICE AT THE
   BEGINNING OF THE QUATTROCENTO

Brown, H., VENICE, AN HISTORICAL SKETCH

Burckhardt, J., THE CIVILIZATION OF THE RENAISSANCE IN ITALY

De Roover, Raymond, THE MEDICI BANK

Emerton, E., HUMANISM AND TYRANNY

Herlihy, David, PISA IN THE EARLY RENAISSANCE

Hodgson, F.C., VENICE IN THE FOURTEENTH AND FIFTEENTH CENTURIES

Mattingly, Garrett, RENAISSANCE DIPLOMACY

Molmenti, Pompeo, VENICE

Scheville, F., A HISTORY OF FLORENCE

_____, THE MEDICI

_____, SIENA

Symonds, J.A., THE RENAISSANCE IN ITALY

Young, George F., THE MEDICI

Waley, Daniel, THE PAPAL STATE IN THE THIRTEENTH CENTURY

Martin, Alfred von, SOCIOLOGY OF THE RENAISSANCE

Gilbert, Felix, MACHIAVELLI & GUICCIARDINI

Rubinstein, Nicolai, THE GOVERNMENT OF FLORENCE UNDER THE MEDICI,
   1434-1494

Herlihy, David, MEDIEVAL AND RENAISSANCE PISTOIA

Martines, Lauro, LAWYERS AND STATECRAFT IN RENAISSANCE FLORENCE

Becker, Marvin B., FLORENCE IN TRANSITION

Goldthwaite, Richard, PRIVATE WEALTH IN RENAISSANCE FLORENCE

FLORENTINE STUDIES, ed. by Nicolai Rubinstein

Smith, Denis Mack, MEDIEVAL SICILY

Brucker, Gene, RENAISSANCE FLORENCE

Molho, Anthony, SOCIAL AND ECONOMIC FOUNDATIONS OF THE ITALIAN RENAISSANCE

Butler, William F.T., THE LOMBARD COMMUNES

Bowsky, William, FINANCE OF THE COMMUNE OF SIENA

Chambers, D.S., THE IMPERIAL AGE OF VENICE, 1380-1580

Garin, Eugenio, PORTRAITS FROM THE QUATTROCENTO

Hale, John R., ed., RENAISSANCE VENICE

Lane, Frederic C., VENICE

Pullan, Brian S., A HISTORY OF EARLY RENAISSANCE ITALY

Ferguson, Wallace, THE RENAISSANCE IN HISTORICAL THOUGHT

Jones, P.J., THE MALATESTA OF RIMINI AND THE PAPAL STATE

Partner, Peter, THE LANDS OF ST. PETER

Hyde, John Kenneth, SOCIETY & POLITICS IN MEDIEVAL ITALY; THE EVOLUTION OF
   THE CIVIL LIFE, 1000-1350

Brentano, Robert, ROME BEFORE ANIGNON

Kedar, Benjamin Z., MERCHANTS IN CRISIS: GENOVESE AND VENETIAN MEN OF
   AFFAIRS & THE 14th C. DEPRESSION

PARLIAMENTARY INSTITUTIONS

Topics:

Origins
English House of Commons
Estates General
Cortes

Roman and Canon Law and Parliamentary
   Institutions
Principle of Consent

Bibliography:

SPECULUM, April, 1954, part 2- Given over to essays on Medieval Representation in
   Theory and Practice
Madden, M.R., POLITICAL THEORY AND LAW IN MEDIEVAL SPAIN
Adams, G.B., COUNCILS AND COURTS IN ANGLO-NORMAN ENGLAND
Baldwin, J.F., THE KINGS' COUNCIL IN ENGLAND DURING THE MIDDLE AGES
Wilkinson, B., STUDIES IN CONSTITUTIONAL HISTORY OF THE XIII AND XIV CENTURIES
Haskins, G.L., THE GROWTH OF ENGLISH REPRESENTATIVE GOVERNMENT
McIlwain, C.H., THE HIGH COURT OF PARLIAMENT
Pollard, A.F., THE EVOLUTION OF PARLIAMENT
Gray, N.L., THE INFLUENCE OF THE COMMONS ON EARLY LEGISLATION
Pasquet, D., AN ESSAY ON ORIGINS OF OF THE HOUSE OF COMMONS
Clarke, M..W., MEDIEVAL REPRESENTATION AND CONSENT
Weske, D.B., CONVOCATION OF THE CLERGY
McIlwain, THE GROWTH OF POLITICAL THOUGHT IN THE WEST
Lyon, Bruce, A CONSTITUTIONAL & LEGAL HISTORY OF MEDIEVAL ENGLAND
Wilkinson, Bertie, THE CONSTITUTIONAL HISTORY OF ENGLAND, 1216-1399, 3 v.
Jolliffe, J.E.A., CONSTITUTIONAL HISTORY OF MEDIEVAL ENGLAND
Tierney, Brian, FOUNDATIONS OF THE CONCILIAR THEORY
Wilkinson, Bertie, CONSTITUTIONAL HISTORY OF ENGLAND IN THE FIFTEENTH
   CENTURY
Post, Gaines, MEDIEVAL LAW AND POLITICAL THOUGHT
O'Callaghan, Joseph, "The Beginnings of the Cortes of Leon-Castile," in AMERICAN
   HISTORICAL REVIEW, LXXIV (1969), pp. 1503-1537
Marongiu, Antonio, MEDIEVAL PARLIAMENTS
McKisack, May, THE PARLIAMENTARY REPRESENTATION OF THE ENGLISH BOROUGHS
   DURING THE MIDDLE AGES
Bisson, Thomas W., ASSEMBLIES AND REPRESENTATION IN LANGUEDOC
Powicke, Michael R., THE COMMUNITY OF THE REALM, 1154-1485   942.03
   P8753c
Sayles, G.O., THE KING'S PARLIAMENT IN ENGLAND
Fryde, E.B., and Edward Miller, eds., HISTORICAL STUDIES OF THE ENGLISH
   PARLIAMENT
Harris, G.L., KING, PARLIAMENT AND PUBLIC FINANCE
Stubbs, William, CONSTITUTIONAL HISTORY OF ENGLAND
Petit-Dutaillis, Charles, STUDIES SUPPLEMENTARY TO STUBBS CONSTITUTIONAL
   HISTORY

MEDIEVAL ADMINISTRATION

Topics:

Household Administration
Chancellor
Curia regis (or ducis or comitis)
Financial administration
Sheriffs
Baillis and Clerks

Bibliography:

Petit-Dutaillis, Charles, FEUDAL MONARCHY IN FRANCE AND ENGLAND
Luchaire, A., HISTOIRE DES INSTITUTIONS MONARCHIQUES DE LA FRANCE
Strayer, J., ADMINISTRATION OF NORMANDY UNDER ST. LOUIS
Taylor, C.H., and J.R. Strayer, STUDIES IN EARLY FRENCH TAXATION
Adams, G.B., COUNCIL AND COURTS IN ANGLO-NORMAN ENGLAND
Baldwin, J. F., THE KINGS' COUNCIL IN ENGLAND DURING THE MIDDLE AGES
Round, J.H., KINGS' SERJEANTS
Tout, T.F., CHAPTERS IN THE ADMINISTRATIVE HISTORY OF MEDIEVAL ENGLAND
Cuttino, C.P., ENGLISH DIPLOMATIC ADMINISTRATION, 1259-1339
Willard, J.F., and W.A. Morris, ENGLISH GOVERNMENT AT WORK, 1327-1336
Ramsey, J.H., THE REVENUES OF THE KINGS
Ballard, A., THE DOMESDAY INQUEST
Morris, W.A., THE MEDIEVAL SHERIFF TO 1300
Poole, R.L., THE EXCHEQUER IN THE TWELFTH CENTURY
Haskins, C.H., NORMAN INSTITUTIONS
Lunt, W., PAPAL REVENUES IN THE MIDDLE AGES
Chrimes, S.B., AN INTRODUCTION TO THE ADMINISTRATIVE HISTORY OF MEDIEVAL
    ENGLAND thru Chap. IV
Luchaire, Archille, MANUEL DES INSTITUTIONS FRANCAISES
    PERIOD DES CAPETIENS DIRECTES
Monier, Raymond, LES INSTITUTIONS FINANCIERES DU COMPTE DE FLANDRE DU XI
    SIECLE A 1384
Nowe, Henri, LES BAILLIS COMTAUX DE FLANDRE
Monier, Raymond, LES INSTITUTIONS CENTRALES DU COMPTE DE FLANDRE DE LA FIN
    DU IXE S. A 1384
Morris, W.A. THE EARLY ENGLISH COUNTY COURT
Lyon, Bryce, CONSTITUTIONAL AND LEGAL HISTORY OF MEDIEVAL ENGLAND
Wilkinson, Bertie, CONSTITUTIONAL HISTORY OF ENGLAND, 1216-1399
_____, STUDIES IN THE CONSTITUTIONAL HISTORY OF THE 13TH & 14TH CENTURIES
Lyon, Bryce, and Adriaan Verhulst, MEDIEVAL FINANCE
Strayer, Joseph R., ON THE MEDIEVAL ORIGIN OF THE MODERN STATE
BRITISH GOVERNMENT AND ADMINISTRATION: STUDIES PRESENTED TO S.B.CHRIMES,
    ed. by H.Mearder & H.R. Loyn

Janet Loengard
Moravian College

HISTORY 370

Seminar: A Thousand Years of Women, c.500 - 1500

Mrs. Loengard

Spring, 1988

February 3   The preliminaries: A note on purposes and methods.
"Housekeeping": some comments about required texts, reserve
readings, suggested sources for term papers, attendance
policy, and that kind of thing. Choice of topics for term
papers/presentations.
Introduction: At the beginning of a thousand years: Women and
late antiquity. To be read for today's meeting and discussion: The Life of Melania the Elder from Palladius, The
Lausiac History, tr. R.T. Meyer, 123–125, 134–137, 141–144;
St. Jerome, Letter to Eustochium, in Charles Christopher
Mierow, tr., The Letters of St. Jerome, Letter 22; Egeria,
excerpt from the Itinerarium, in Marcelle Thiebaux, tr., The
Writings of Medieval Women (hereafter Thiebaux, tr.) 1–13;
St. Augustine, Letter to Ecdicia, in Sister Wilfred Parsons,
tr., Saint Augustine: Letters, Volume V, 261–269. (We are
cheating here: these women and their correspondents date from
the fourth and fifth centuries. But they are a good
introduction.)
For next time: Susan Groag Bell, ed., Women: From the Greeks
to the French Revolution (hereafter Bell, ed.) 55–63, 84–89;
Angela M. Lucas, Women in the Middle Ages (hereafter Lucas)
19–29, 61–82; Jo Ann McNamara and Suzanne F. Wemple,
"Marriage and Divorce in the Frankish Kingdom" in Susan
Mosher Stuard, ed., Women in Medieval Society (hereafter
Stuard, ed.) 95–124; Letters of Amalasuntha in Thiebaux, tr.,
15–23; Gregory of Tours, History of the Franks, ed. Ernest
Brehaut, 89–90, 99–100, 106, 145–146, 211–216 (all about
Brunhilda).

February 10   Colloquium. Women, civilized East and barbarian West.
For next time: Shulamith Shahar, The Fourth Estate: A History
of Women in the Middle Ages (hereafter Shahar) 22–52; Bell,
ed. 102–117; Lucas 30–58; Eileen Power, Medieval Women
(hereafter Power) 89–99; Jo Ann McNamara, "The Ordeal of
Community: Hagiography as a disciplinary tool in Merovingian
convents" (mimeographed unpublished text used by permission);
Hroswitha of Gandersheim, Dulcitius and Abraham.

February 17   First Paper. Women and Religion: The Alternative Career.
For next time: Susan Millinger, "Humility and Power: Anglo-
Saxon Nuns in Anglo-Norman Hagiography" in John A. Nichols
and Lillian Thomas Shank, eds., Distant Echoes 115–129;
Michael Goodich, "Ancilla Dei: The Servant as Saint in the

Late Middle Ages" in Julius Kirshner and Suzanne F. Wemple, eds., _Women of the Medieval World_ (hereafter Kirshner and Wemple, eds.) 119-136; Rosalind B. Brooke and Christopher N.L. Brooke, "St. Clare" in Derek Baker, ed., _Medieval Women_ (hereafter Baker, ed.) 275-287; Baudonivia of Poitiers, _The Life of St. Radegund_ in Thiebaux, tr. 43-56; _The Little Flowers of St. Clare_ (The _Testament_ of St. Clare), tr. Fr. Edmund O'Gorman, chs. 4, 10.

February 24   Second Paper. Women and Religion: The Female Saint. For next time: Shahar 65-90; Lucas 83-104; Power 35-52; Georges Duby, _The Knight, The Lady and the Priest_ 57-74, 87-106; R.H. Helmholz, _Marriage Litigation in Medieval England_ 74-100; Letters I and II of Abelard and Heloise in _The Letters of Abelard and Heloise_, tr. Betty Radice.

March 2   Third Paper. Women and Marriage: Maiden and Wife. For next time: Shahar 93-98; Christiane Klapsich-Zuber, "The 'Cruel Mother': Maternity, Widowhood, and Dowry in Florence in the Fourteenth and Fifteenth Centuries" in _Women, Family, and Ritual in Renaissance Italy_ (hereafter Klapisch-Zuber) 117-131; Sue Sheridan Walker, "Feudal Constraint and Free Consent in the Making of Marriages in Medieval England: Widows in the King's Gift" in _Historical Papers, 1979_ 97-109; Janet Loengard, "Of the Gift of her Husband: English Dower and its Consequences in the Year 1200" in Kirshner and Wemple eds. 215-255; _The Goodman of Paris_, tr. Eileen Power, 41-43, 110-1152, 205-220, 223-229.

March 9   Fourth Paper. Women and Marriage: Wife and Widow. For next time: Klapisch-Zuber, "Childhood in Tuscany at the Beginning of the Fifteenth Century" and "Blood Parents and Milk Parents: Wet Nursing in Florence 1300-1530" 94-116, 132-164; Shahar 98-106; Sue Sheridan Walker, "Widow and Ward: the Feudal Law of Child Custody in Medieval England" in Stuard, ed., 159-172; David Herlihy, _Medieval Households_ 120-130; "How the Good Wife Taught her Daughter" and "How the Wise Man Taught his Son", in Edith Rickert, ed. _The Babees' Book_, 31-47.

March 16   Fifth Paper. Women and Marriage: Mother and Child. For next time: Penny Schine Gold, "The Lady and the Virgin" 116-144; Kay E. Lacey, "Women and Work in Fourteenth and Fifteenth Century London" in Lindsey Charles and Lorna Duffin, eds., _Women and Work in Pre-Industrial England_ (hereafter Charles and Duffin eds.) 24-82; Ruth Kittel, "Women under the Law in Medieval England 1066-1485" in Barbara Kanner, ed., _The Women of England from Anglo-Saxon Times to the Present_ 124-137; Susan Mosher Stuard, "Women in Charter and Statute Law: Medieval Ragusa/Dubrovnik" in Stuard, ed., 199-208.

March 23   Sixth Paper. Women and Law.
            For next time: Barbara Hanawalt, "The Female Felon in
            Fourteenth Century England" in Stuard, ed. 125-140; Barbara
            A. Kellum, "Infanticide in England in the Later Middle Ages"
            in History of Childhood Quarterly i (1974) 367-388; John M.
            Carter, "Rape in Medieval English Society: The Evidence of
            Yorkshire, Wiltshire, and London 1218-1276" in Comitatus
            xiii (1982) 33-63; Elisabeth Kimball, ed., Some Sessions of
            the Peace in Lincolnshire, 1381-1396, selected cases which I
            have translated for you (on reserve).

March 30   SPRING BREAK

April 6   Seventh paper. Women as Criminals and Victims.
            For next time: Shahar 251-280; Gwendolyn Bryant, "The French
            Heretic Beguine: Marguerite Porete" in Katharina M. Wilson,
            ed., Medieval Women Writers (hereafter Wilson, ed.) 204-215;
            William Monter, "The Pedestal and the Stake" in Renate Brid-
            enthal and Claudia Koontz, eds., Becoming Visible (hereafter
            Bridenthal and Koontz, eds.) 119-136; W. Butler-Bowden, ed.,
            The Book of Margery Kempe, 94-124.

April 13   Eighth paper. Women as Heretics.
            For next time: Bell, ed. 89-95, 190-195; Christine de Pisan,
            selections from The City of Ladies and The Book of Three
            Virtues in Wilson, ed., 333-363; Meg Bogin, The Women
            Troubadours 37-76, 89, 109-113; Lucas 137-169; Joan M.
            Ferrante, "The Education of Women in the Middle Ages in
            Theory, Fact, and Fantasy" in Patricia Labalme, ed., Beyond
            Their Sex: Learned Women of the European Past (hereafter
            Labalme, ed.) 9-42; Marie de France, two fables from Isopet
            in Thiebaux, tr. 203-205. (Also Heloise's first letter to
            Abelard, as above.)

April 20   Ninth paper. Women, the Pen and the Brush.
            For next time: Kathryn L. Reyerson, "Women in Business in
            Medieval Montpellier" in Barbara Hanawalt ed., Women and Work
            in Preindustrial Europe 117-144; Judith M. Bennett, "The
            Village Ale-Wife: Women and Brewing in Fourteenth-Century
            England", ibid. 20-36; Diane Hutton, "Women in Fourteenth
            Century Shrewsbury" in Charles and Duffin, eds. 83-99;
            Merry E. Wiesner, Working Women in Renaissance Germany 11-35;
            Bell 151-158; Mary Bateson, ed., Borough Customs I, 185-186,
            227, 229-230, 309; II, 172-183.

April 27   Tenth paper. Women at Work.
            For next time: Janet L. Nelson, "Queens as Jezebels: the
            careers of Brunhild and Balthild in Merovingian history" in
            Baker, ed. 31-78; Bernard Hamilton, "Women in the crusader
            states: the queens of Jerusalem 1100-90", ibid. 143-174;
            Frances and Joseph Gies, "A Reigning Queen: Blanche of
            Castile" in Women in the Middle Ages 97-119; Marion Facinger,
            "A Study of Medieval Queenship" in Studies in Medieval and
            Renaissance History 5 (1968) 1-47; Patricia-Ann Lee, "Reflec-

tions of Power: Margaret of Anjou and the Dark Side of
Queenship" in <u>Renaissance Quarterly</u> 39 (1986) 183-217;
Joseph M. Levine, ed., <u>Great Lives Observed</u>: <u>Elizabeth I</u>,
13-14, 17-20, 221-23, 41, 66-67, 139-145.

May 4   Eleventh Paper. Women Rulers and Perceptions of them.
For next time: Joan Kelly-Gadol, "Did Women Have a Ren-
aissance?" in Bridenthal and Koontz, eds. 137-164; Margaret
L. King, "Book-Lined Cells: Women and Humanism in the Early
Italian Renaissance" in Labalme, ed., 66-90; Bell, ed.
200-214.

May 11   Colloquium. The other end of a thousand years: Women in
the Renaissance.

Textbooks

You should buy the following texts, available in the bookstore:

Bell, Susan Groag, ed., <u>Women from the Greeks to the French Revolution</u>.
    Stanford, 1973, 1980.
Shahar, Shulamith, <u>The Fourth Estate</u>: <u>A History of Women in the Middle
    Ages</u>. London, 1983.
Stuard, Susan Mosher, ed., <u>Women in Medieval Society</u>. Philadelphia, 1976,
    1982.

Reserve Readings

At least one copy of all readings assigned above will be on reserve in Reeves
Library for your use there. These volumes may not be removed from the
Library, so it should be possible for everyone to obtain them in time to do
the readings before the class for which they are due.

Baker, Derek, ed., <u>Medieval Women</u>. (Oxford, 1978)
Bateson, Mary, ed., <u>Borough Customs</u>, Vols. I and II. (Selden Society vols.
      18, 21: London, 1904, 1906).
Bridenthal, Renate, and Claudia Koontz, <u>Becoming Visible</u>: <u>Women in European
      History</u>. (Boston, 1977).
Bogin, Meg, <u>The Women Troubadours</u>. (New York, 1980)
Butler-Bowden, W., ed., <u>The Book of Margery Kempe</u> (London, 1936).
Charles, Lindsey and Lorna Duffin, eds., <u>Women and Work in Pre-Industrial
      England</u>. (London, 1985)
Duby, Georges, <u>The Knight, the Lady and the Priest</u>: <u>The Making of Modern
      Marriage in Medieval France</u>. (New York, 1983)
Facinger, Marion, "A Study of Medieval Queenship" in <u>Studies in Medieval and
      Renaissance History</u> 5 (1968).
Gies, Frances and Joseph Gies, <u>Women in the Middle Ages</u>. (New York, 1978)
Gold, Penny Schine, <u>The Lady and the Virgin</u>: <u>Image, Attitude and Experience
      in Twelfth-Century France</u>. (Chicago, 1985)
Gregory of Tours, <u>History of the Franks</u>, ed. Ernest Brehaut (New York, 1969).
Hanawalt, Barbara, <u>Women and Work in Preindustrial Europe</u>. (Bloomington,
      Ind., 1986)
Helmholz, R.H., <u>Marriage Litigation in Medieval England</u> (Cambridge, 1974).

Herlihy, David, Medieval Households. (Cambridge, Mass., 1985).

Hroswitha of Gandersheim, Plays, tr. Larissa Bonfante with collaboration of
    Alexandra Bonfante-Warren (New York, 1979).

Kanner, Barbara, The Women of England from Anglo-Saxon Times to the Present.
    (Hamden, Conn., 1979)

Kimball, Elisabeth, ed., Some Sessions of the Peace in Lincolnshire,
    1381-1396 (Lincoln Record Society vol. 49: Lincoln, 1955).

Kirshner, Julius, and Suzanne F. Wemple, eds., Women of the Medieval World.
    (London and New York, 1985).

Klapisch-Zuber, Christiane, Women, Family, and Ritual in Renaissance Italy,
    tr. Lydia G. Cochrane. (Chicago, 1985)

Labalme, Patricia H., ed., Beyond Their Sex: Learned Women of the European
    Past. (New York, 1984).

Lee, Patricia-Ann, "Reflections of Power: Margaret of Anjou and the Dark Side
    of Queenship", Renaissance Quarterly 30 (1986).

Lucas, Angela M., Women in the Middle Ages: Religion, Marriage and Letters.
    (New York, 1983)

McNamara, Jo Ann, "The Ordeal of Community: Hagiography as a disciplinary
    tool in Merovingian convents" (mimeographed unpublished text of a
    paper read at Columbia University, November, 1981; used by per-
    mission). NOTE: Professor McNamara has been kind enough to allow us
    to use her text; since it is not yet published, please do not make
    copies of it.

Mierow, Charles Christopher, tr., The Letters of St. Jerome, Vol. I.
    [Ancient Christian Writers: The Works of the Fathers in Translation,
    No. 33]. Intro. and notes by Thomas Comerford Lawler. (Westminster,
    Md., and London, 1963).

Nichols, John A. and Lillian Thomas Shank, eds., Distant Echoes. (Kalamazoo,
    Mich., 1984).

O'Gorman, Fr. Edmund O.F.M. Conv., tr., The Little Flowers of Saint Clare
    (Padua, 1972).

Palladius, The Lausiac History, tr. & annot. R.T. Meyer [Ancient Christian
    Writers, Vol. 34]. (New York, 1964).

Parsons, Sister Wilfrid S.N.D., tr., St. Augustine: Letters, Vol. V.
    [The Fathers of the Church, Vol. 32]. (New York, 1956).

Power, Eileen, Medieval Women. (Cambridge, 1975)

Power, Eileen, tr., The Goodman of Paris. (Le Menagier de Paris). (New York,
    1928).

Radice, Betty, tr. and ed., The Letters of Abelard and Heloise. (London,
    1974; paperback repr. 1986).

Rickert, Edith, ed., The Babees' Book. From texts of Dr. F.J. Furnivall.
    (New York, 1966).

Thiebaux, Marcelle, trans. and ed., The Writings of Medieval Women. (New
    York, 1987)

Walker, Sue Sheridan, "Feudal Constraint and Free Consent in the Making of
    Marriages in Medieval England: Widows in the King's Gift", Historical
    Papers, A Selection from the Papers Presented at the Annual Meeting
    [of the Canadian Historical Association] Held at Saskatoon, 1979.

Wiesner, Merry E., Working Women in Renaissance Germany. (New Brunswick,
    N.J., 1986)

Wilson, Katharina M., ed., Medieval Women Writers. (Athens, Ga., 1984)

Presentations and Term Papers

At the time of your presentation, you should be prepared to hand in any translations you have done or any extended text(s) you are using, together with an outline of your presentation and at least a preliminary bibliography. You should have enough copies so that each member of the seminar can receive one. If your presentation was given at a class meeting before April 6, you should hand in your term paper at that meeting. If your presentation was on April 6 or thereafter, you should hand in your term paper at the class meeting following your presentation. The typed paper should run between 10 and 15 pages and should, of course, be properly footnoted; you should append your final bibliography. We will talk at the first class meeting about footnote style and usage, the form of your bibliography, and so on, but let it be said now that plagiarism will result in a student's failing the course. If you are unclear about what constitutes plagiarism in a given instance, please consult with me.

Since this is a seminar, participation is essential for the success of the course. And since this is true, participation will count for 40% of the final grade; the oral presentation will count for 30% and the written paper 30%. Obviously, this makes attendance at each session very important. If you must miss a class meeting, please let me know in advance if possible; I will attempt to help you in catching up on anything you missed.

ASMR 5000:   Concepts of Eve and Mary in the Middle Ages and Renaissance

SYLLABUS

Texts: Marina Warner Alone of All Her Sex   Abreviations AS
       Andreas Capellanus The Art of Courtly Love   CAL
       R. Bridenthal and C. Koonz Becoming Visible   BV
       E. Clark and H. Richardson Women and Religion   WR

Time: 6:30-9:00   Place: Brewster 303C

Professors: N. Mayberry, Brewster 438A; John Carter, Brewster 341A; C. Peters,
           Jenkins 1332

Assignment Schedule

Jan.   14 Overview of course, discussion of materials, methods, speakers,
         texts, goals. Choosing semester projects. The time frame of the
         Middle Ages and Renaissance.
         Lecture topic: "Theological Concepts of Eve and Mary" Read WR
              26-52, BV Intro., AS 3-74.
         In library read Chapter I in A. Lucas, Women in the Middle Ages and
         pp. 19-27 in S. Wemple, Women in Frankish Society.

     21 Lecture topic: John Carter, "Boethius, Fortuna and the Classical
                   Heritage of the Middle Ages."
         Assignment: BV 60-89, WR 15-25, AS 333-339.
         In library consult: J. Peradotto & J. Sullivan Women in the Ancient
                        World and
                          A. Cameron & A. Kuhrt Images of Women in
                          Antiquity
         Discussion of Assignment

     28 Lecture topic: John Carter "Eve and Mary on Trial: Judges
                        Decision Regarding Women in Medieval
                        England"
         Assignment: Eileen Powers, Medieval Women Chapter I

         SEMESTER TOPICS DUE Discussion of assignment and semester topics

Feb.   4 Lecture topic, "Images of Eve and Mary in Medieval Art."
         Assignment: Read, Taylor, Learning to Look
         Discussion: Henry Kraus "Eve and Mary, Conflicting Images of
                    Medieval Woman" in The Living Theatre
                    of Medieval Art, pp. 41-62.

     11 Lecture topic: Ruth Moskop "Hildegard von Bingen"
         Assignment: Read Chapter I of Medieval Writers
                pp. 63-96 of Women in the Middle Ages
                pp. 78-115 in WR
         Discussion

         BIBLIOGRAPHIES DUE

     18 Lecture topic: N. Mayberry, "The Cult of Mary and the Rise of
                    Courtly Love"
         Assignment: AS 68-117, 236-269, BV 119-136
               Consult: In Pursuit of Perfection: Courtly Love in
                      Medieval Literature
         Discussion

Feb.   25 Lecture topic "Peter Lombard's Portrait of Eve"
           Assignment: Read all of CL and Chapter X of WR
                           pp. 18-22 of Book II of <u>The Sentences of Peter Lombard</u>
           Discussion

           OUTLINES DUE

March   4 Guest Visiting Lecturer

       18 Lecture topic: M. Bassman, "The Romance of the Rose"
           Assignment: Dahlburg: <u>The Romance of the Rose</u>

           FIRST DRAFT OF PROJECT DUE - PEER EDITING IN CLASS

       25 Lecture topic: M. Malby "Dante's Beatrice"
                           C. Peters "Images of Eve and Mary in the Art of
                                      Giotto'
           Assignment: AS 160-174
           Read: pp. 69-100 of J. Stubblebine, <u>Giotto</u>: <u>The Arena Chapel
                                     Frencoes</u>

April   1 Lecture topic: Paul Dowell "The Wife of Bath"
                           Bodo Nischan "Women of the Renaissance"
           Assignment: WR Chapter 11, BV Chapters 6 & 7
           Consult: La Clavière, <u>The Women of the Renaissance</u>
                      <u>Sixteenth Century Journal</u> 15 (1984) 401-418
                      <u>Sixteenth Century Journal</u> 12 (1981) 3-13
           Discussion of projects, peer editing.

        8 Lecture topic: F. Daughtery "Images of Eve and Mary in Northern
                                        Renaissance Art"
           Assignment
           Discussion
       15 Lecture topic: M. South, "The Virgin and the Unicorn"
           Assignment:

           FINAL DRAFT DUE

       22 Lecture topic: M. Schwarz "Montaigne's Essays on the Education of
                                      Women"
           Assignment: Read Montaigne's Essay "On Education" in Vol. I of
                        Montaigne's Essays

       29 Overview of course subject, review and assignment of open book,
           take home exam to be turned in by May 2.

COLLOQUIUM ON WOMEN IN THE MIDDLE AGES
G57.2109

Penny Johnson
Monday 6:10
fall, 1986

Office hrs: M 3-5
Rm: 513 19 Univ. Pl.
598-3322/3

This course examines women's experience in and contributions to medieval Europe as well as the context and factors which shaped women's lives. The colloquium can be taken on either of two tracks.

Track A: This is for the new-comer to the history of women in pre-modern European history. The student will read and prepare to discuss all of the assigned reading for each meeting. (Weekly reading is quite short: 186 pp. average, but often the primary sources are demanding.) In addition, the student will hand in a weekly journal of responses to that reading. Class participation will be an important component of the student's input, and the grade will reflect the quality of both the journal and class participation.

Track B: This is for the student already familiar with the literature of the history of women in pre-modern European history. This student will be expected to be conversant with all the reading and to be prepared to discuss it each week in class. Early in the term the student will define (in consultation with the instructor) either a reading or a research paper topic. A summary of the findings will be presented informally in class in a brief oral report at one of the final two class meetings, and a paper of between 12-20 pages will be due at the end of exam period. The grade for Track B will be based primarily on the paper.

N.B.: To choose which of these tracks is appropriate for your level, look at the assigned reading; if you have already read better than half of it, you belong on Track B.

CLASS MEETINGS

Mon. Sept. 22   Introduction

Sept. 29 The Shaping of Attitudes (88pp.)
     The Bible Genesis 1-3
               Leviticus 12, 15:19-32; 20:10-21.
               1 Corinthians 5-7; 11:1-15; 14:34-6.
               Galatians 3:26-29.
               1 Timothy 2:9-15; 5:3-16.
     *Aristotle, Politics, Bk. 1, Ch. 12-13.
     *Jerome, Letter 22 to Eustochium. Select Letters of St. Jerome, tr.
          F. A. Wright, (Cambridge, Eng.:1933).
     *Rosemary Ruether, "Misogynism and Virginal Feminism in the Fathers of
          the Church," Religion and Sexism ed. R. Ruether (1974), 150-183.
     *Vern Bullough,"Medieval Medical and Scientific Views of Women,"
          Viator 4 (1973), 484-501.

Oct. 6 The Early Middle Ages (235 pp.)
    Medieval Women Visionary Literature, ed. Elizabeth Petroff
        (Oxford:1986) Perpetua, "The Passion of Ss. Perpetua and
        Felicitas." pp. 70-77.
    Elaine Pagels, The Gnostic Gospels (N.Y.:1981) intro., ch. 1-3.
    Rosemary Rader, Breaking Boundaries: Male/Female Friendship in Early
        Christian Communities (N.Y.:1983).

Oct. 13 Yom Kippur no class

Oct. 20 The Barbarian Period (205 pp.)
    St. Leoba, "The Life of St. Leoba." pp. 106-114 in Petroff.
    Suzanne Wemple, Women in Frankish Society (Philadelphia:1981).

Oct. 27 Life, Death, and Influence (99 pp.)
    *David Herlihy, "Life Expectancies for Women in Medieval
        Society," in The Role of Woman in the Middle Ages
        ed. Rosmarie Morewedge (Albany:1975), 1-22.
    *_____, "Land, Family, and Women," Traditio
        18 (1962), 89-120 and in Women in Medieval Society, ed. Susan
        Stuard (Philadelphia:1976), 13-45.
    *Vern Bullough, "Female Longevity and Diet," Speculum
        55 (1980).
    Emily Coleman, "Infanticide in the Early Middle Ages", in
        Stuard 47-70.
    *Jo Ann McNamara and Suzanne Wemple, "The Power of Women
        through the Family in Medieval Europe: 500-1000,"
        Feminist Studies 1 (1973), 126-141 and in Clio's Consciousness
        Raised, ed. Mary Hartmann and Lois Banner (N.Y.:1976), 103-118.

Nov. 3 Women and the Family (187 pp.)
    Christina of Markyate pp. 144-150 in Petroff.
    David Herlihy, Medieval Households (Cambridge:1985).
    *Robert Hajdu, "Family and Feudal Ties in Poitou, 110-1300,"
        J.I.H. 8 (1977), 117-139.
    Barbara Hanawalt, "Childrearing Among the Lower Classes of Late
        Medieval England," JIH 8 (1977), 1-22.

Nov. 10 Marriage (383 pp.)
    *The Marriage Ceremony from the Old Sarum Missal, (my translation)
    Georges Duby, The Knight, The Lady and The Priest tr. Barabara
        Bray (N.Y.:1983).
    *Emily Coleman, "Medieval Marriage Characteristics: A Neglected Factor
        in the History of Medieval Serfdom,"J.I.H. 2 (1971), 205-219.
    *John Noonan, "Power to Choose," Viator 4 (1973), 419-434.
    *Michael Sheehan, "The Influence of Canon Law on the Property Rights
        of Married Women in England," Medieval Studies 25 (1963),
        109-124.
    *_____, "The Formation and Stability of Marriage in
        Fourteenth Century England: Evidence of an Ely Register,"
        Medieval Studies 33 (1971), 228-263.
    Judith Bennett, "The Tie that Binds: Peasant Marriages and Families in
        Late Medieval England," JIH 15 (1984), 111-129.

Nov. 17 The Cloister: The Alternate for Women (162 pp.)
Medieval Women Writers, ed. Katharina Wilson (Athens, Ga.:1984),
Heloise in pp. 90-108.
Hrotsvit of Gandersheim pp. 114-135, Hildegard of Bingen and
Elisabeth of Schonau, pp. 151-170, Clare of Assisi, pp. 242-5 in
Petroff.
Brenda Bolton, "Mulieres Sanctae" in Stuard, 141-158.
*Penelope D. Johnson, "The Stereotype of the Naughty Nun: Sexual
Scandal in Thirteenth-century Norman Monastic Communities."

Nov. 24 Courtly Love and Social Reality (96 pp.)
Marie de France, pp. 64-89 in Katharina Wilson.
Castelloza, pp. 131-152 in Katharina Wilson.
Christine de Pizan, pp. 340-346 in Petroff.
*John Benton, "Clio and Venus," in The Meaning of Courtly Love,
ed. Francis Newman (Albany:1968), 19-42.
*Herbert Moller, "The Social Causation of the Courtly Love Complex,"
Comparative Studies in Society and History, 1 (1959), 137-63.

Dec. 1 The Mystical Route (261 pp.)
Catherine of Siena, pp. 263-275 and Julian of Norwich, pp. 308-314 in
Petroff.
*Caroline Bynum, "Fast, Feast, and Flesh: The Religious Significance
of Food to Medieval Women," Representations 11 (1985), 1-25.
*Mary Mason, "The Other Voice: Autobiography of Women Writers," Auto-
biography: Essays Theoretical and Critical ed. James Olney
(Princeton:1980), 207-235.
Rudolf Bell, Holy Anorexia (Chicago:1985).

Dec. 8 Women Active in Society (262 pp.)
Christine de Pizan, The Book of the City of Ladies tr. Jeffrey
Richards (N.Y.:1982).
*"The Case of a Woman Doctor in Paris," The Portable Medieval Reader
ed. James B. Ross and Mary McLaughlin (Harmondsworth:1977),
635-40.

Dec. 15 The Constriction of the Late Middle Ages (76 pp.)
Marie d"Oignies, Christina Mirabilis, Hadewijch pp. 179-200 and Na
Prous Boneta pp. 284-290 and Marguerite Porete, pp. 294-8 in
Petroff.
*Diane Owen Hughes, "Earrings for Circumcision: Distinction and
Purification in the Italian Renaissance City," Persons in Groups
ed. Richard C. Trexler (Binghamton:1985), 155-177.
*Leah Otis, "Prostitution and Repentance in Late Medieval
Perpignan," Women of the Medieval World, ed. J. Kirshner & S.
Wemple (1985), 137-160.

Winter vacation

Jan. 5   oral reports by Track B students

Jan. 12 oral reports by Track B students

SUPPLEMENTARY READING FOR THE COLLOQUIUM

I have added a supplemental reading list that is extremely idiosyncratic.
It can be added to infinitely by looking through the bibliographies
mentioned here as well as by using the bibliographies and footnotes from
the works we are reading. The purpose of appending this list is to bring
readily to your hand either very recent titles which may not yet appear in
other lists or what are to my mind the best of the older studies which are
truly deserving of note.

Important bibliographic tools:

*Dietrich, Sheila C., "An Introduction to Women in Anglo-Saxon Society
    (c. 600-1066)", in The Women of England, Interpretive Bibliographical
    Essays ed. Barbara Kanner (Hamden, Ct:1979), 32-56.
*Erickson, Carolly and Kathleen Casey. "Women in the Middle Ages: a
    Working Bibliography." Medieval Studies 37 (1975).
Frey, Linda, Marsha Frey, and Joanne Schneider. Women in Western Europe
    and History: A Select Chronological, Geographical, and Topical
    Bibliography from Antiquity to the French Revolution. Westport, CT:
    1982.
*Kelly, Joan, et. at. Bibliography in the History of European Women. 5th
    ed. A Sarah Lawrence College Women's Studies Publication: 1982.
*Krueger, Roberta L., and E. Jane Burns. A Selective Bibliography
    of Criticism: Women in Medieval French Literature. Romance Notes 26
    (1985), 375-390.

Bibliographic and Historiographic Essays:

Davis, Natalie. "Women's History in Transition: The European Case."
    Feminist Studies 3 (1976), 83-103.
Hartman, Mary and Lois Banner, ed. Clio's Consciousness Raised: New
    Perspectives on the History of Women. N.Y.: 1974.
Kelly, Joan. Women, History and Theory: The Essays of Joan Kelly.
    Chicago: 1984.

NOTE:

*All citations marked with an asterix are available in xerox both on
reserve in Bobst and in the department. You may check out the
departmental copies for a few hours only   Please
be considerate of your fellow class members.
    All of the books on the reading list have been requested for reserve
so that, for instance, you can get Jerome by looking under my name for a
xerox of the letter, or by requesting the Select Letters in which the
letter appears and which is also on reserve. Library books on reserve are
usually under the author's or editor's name (but occasionally under the
title). Be creative and persistent; the reading should be there
somewhere.

General Bibliography:

Atkingon, Clarissa. Mystic and Pilgrim: The Book and the World of
    Margery Kempe. Ithaca: 1983.
Barstow, Anne. Married Priests and the Reforming Papacy: The
    Eleventh-century Debates. N.Y.: 1982.
Boyd, Catherine. A Cistercian Nunnery in Mediaeval Italy: The
    Story of Rifreddo in Saluzzo, 1220-1300. Cambridge: 1943.
Brooke, Christopher. "Marriage and Society in the Central Middle
    Ages" Marriage and Society: Studies in the Social History of
    Marriage. Ed. R. B. Outhwaite. London: 1981.
Bynum, Caroline. Jesus as Mother: Studies in the Spirituality of
    the High Middle Ages. Berkeley: 1982.
_____. Holy Feast and Holy Fast: The Religious
    Significance of Food to Medieval Women (Berkeley: 1987).
Dronke, Peter. Women Writers of the Middle Ages: A Critical Study
    of texts from Perpetua (+203) to Marguerite Porete (+1310).
    Cambridge, Eng.: 1984.
*Eckenstein, Lina. Women under Monasticism. Cambridge, Eng.:
    1896, reissued 1963.
Farmer, Sharon. "Persuasive Voices: Clerical Images of Medieval
    Wives," Speculum 61 (1986), 517-543.
Fell, Christine. Women in Anglo-Saxon England. Bloomington, Ind.:
    1984.
Flandrin, Jean-Louis. "Contraception, Marriage, and Sexual
    Relations in the Christian West." Biology of Man in History,
    ed. Robert Forster and Orest Ranum.
Glasser, Marc. "Marriage in Medieval Hagiography," Studies in
    Medieval and Renaissance History 4 (1981), 3-34.
Gazeau, R. "La clôture des moniales au XIIe siècle en France."
    Revue Mabillon 58 (1974).
Gold, Penny. The Lady and the Virgin: Image and Attitude, and
    Experience in 12th-Century France. Chicago: 1985.
Goodrich, Michael. "The Contours of Female Piety in Later Medieval
    Hagiography." Church History 50 (1981), 20-32.
Hanawalt, Barbara A. The Ties that Bound: Peasant Families in
    Medieval England. Oxford: 1986.
_____. ed. Women and Work in Preindustrial Europe
    (Bloomington: 1986).
Herlihy, David. Women in Medieval Society. Houston, TX: 1971.
_____. Medieval Households. Cambridge, MA.: 1985.
Howell, Martha C. Women, Production, and Patriarchy in Late
    Medieval Cities. Chicago: 1986.
Hughes, Diane. "Urban Growth and Family Structure in Medieval
    Genoa." Past and Present 66 (1975).
Hughes, Muriel. Women Healers in Medieval Life and Literature.
    Reissued Freeport, N.Y.: 1968.
Jordan, William. "Jews on Top: Women and the Availability of
    Consumption Loans in Northern France in the Mid-Thirteenth
    Century." Journal of Jewish Studies 29-30 (1978-9).
Klinck, Anne. "Anglo-Saxon Women and the Law." Journal of
    Medieval History 8 (1982).
Kraus, Henry. "Eve and Mary: Conflicting Images of Medieval
    Women." in The Living Theatre of Medieval Art. Bloomington:
    1967.

Labalme, Patricia A. Ed. Beyond Their Sex: Learned Women of the
    European Past (N.Y.: 1980).
Leclercq, Jean. "Medieval Feminine Monasticism: Reality versus
    Romantic Images." Benedictus: Studies in Honor of St. Benedict
    of Nursia. Ed. Rozanne Elder (1981).
Lucas, Angela. Women in the Middle Ages: Religion, Marriage and
    Letters. N.Y.: 1983.
McDonnell, Ernest. The Beguines and Beghards in Medieval Culture.
    New Brunswick, NJ: 1954.
McNamara, Jo Ann. A New Song: Celibate Women in the First Three
    Christian Centuries. N.Y.: 1983.
Macfarlane, Alan. Marriage and Love in England: Modes of
    Reproduction 1300-1840. London:
Milsom, S. F. C. "Inheritance by Women in the Twelfth and Early
    Thirteenth Centuries." On the Laws and Customs of England:
    Essays in Honor of Samuel E. Thorne. Chapel Hill: 1981.
Mitterauer, Michael & Reinhard Sieder. The European Family:
    Pataricarchy to Partnership from the Middle Ages to the
    Present. Chicago: 1977.
Moller, Herbert. "The Meaning of Courtly Love," Journal of
    American Folklore 73 (1960), 39-52.
Moore, John "'Courtly Love': A Problem of Terminology," Journal of
    the History of Ideas 40 (1979), 621-632.
Newman, Barbara. Sister of Wisdom: St. Hildegard's Theology of
    the Feminine (Berkeley: 1987).
Nicholas, David. The Domestic Life of a Medieval City: Women,
    Children, and the Family in Fourteenth-Century Ghent. Lincoln,
    NE.: 1985.
Nichols, John and Lillian Shank, eds. Distant Echoes: Medieval
    Religious Women. Kalamazoo, MI: 1984.
Otis, Leah. Prostitution in Medieval Society: History of an Urban
    Institution in Languedoc. Chicago: 1985.
Parisse, Michel. Les nonnes au Moyen âge. LePuy: 1983.
_____ ed. Les religieuses en France au XIIIe siècle.
    Nancy: 1985.
Pernoud, Regine. Blanche of Castile. N.Y.: 1972.
_____. La femme au temps des cathédrales. Paris: 1980.
Petroff, Elizabeth. Consolation of the Blessed. N.Y.: 1979.
Plummer, John F. ed. Vox Feminae: Studies in Medieval Woman's Songs
    Kalamazoo, MI: 1981.
Power, Eileen. "The Position of Women." The Legacy of the Middle
    Ages. Ed. C. G. Crump and E. F. Jacob. Oxford: 1926.
_____. Medieval English Nunneries 1275-1535. Cambridge, Eng.:
    1922.
Reilly, Bernard. The Kingdom of Leon-Castilla under Queen Urraca,
    1109-1126. Princeton: 1982.
Rose, Mary Beth ed. Women in the Middle Ages and the Renaissance:
    Literary and Historical Perspectives. Syracuse: 1986.
Searle, Eleanor. "Seigneurial Control of Women's Marriage: The
    Antecedents and Function of Merchet in England." Past and
    Present 82 (1979).
Shahar, Shulamith. The Fourth Estate: A History of Women in the
    Middle Ages. Tr. Chaya Galai. London: 1983.
Walker, Sue Sheridan. "Free Consent and Marriage of Feudal Wards
    in Medieval England." Journal of Medieval History 8 (1982).

Ward, Benedicta. "The Image of the Prostitute in the Middle Ages," _Monastic Studies_ 16 (1985).

Warner, Marina. _Joan of Arc: The Image of Female Heroism_. N.Y.: 1982.

_____. _Alone of all her Sex: The Myth and Cult of the Virgin Mary_. N.Y.: 1976.

Warren, Ann K. _Anchorites and their Patrons in Medieval England_. Berkeley: 1985.

Wilson-Kastner, Patricia et. al. eds. _A Lost Tradition: Women Writers of the Early Church_. Washington, D.C.: 1981.

Wood, Charles T. "Queens, Queans, and Kingship: An Inquiry into Theories of Royal Legitimacy in Late Medieval England and France." _Order and Innovation in the Middle Ages_. Ed. William C. Jordan, Bruce McNab, Teofilo F. Ruiz. Princeton: 1976.

RELIGIOUS STUDIES   232

THE MOTHERS OF THE CHURCH: WOMEN IN THE CHRISTIAN TRADITION

E. Ann Matter
University of Pennslyvania
243-8614

        This course is intended to fill in the gaps left by traditional histories
of Christianity by looking at the roles women played in the development of the
Christian tradition. We will examine accounts by and about women in a chronological
period ranging from the early church to the Reformation. The organization will
be roughly topical within the mold of historical development.

        Tuesday classes will feature lectures on the background of the readings,
intended to raise the major questions for discussion on Thursdays. Regular
attendance and class participation are essential for the success of the course.
In addition, each student will write two 4/5 page papers: the first on units I and
II, due one week after the completion of unit II, the second on units VI and VII,
due one week after the completion of unit VII. There will also be a final
examination, for which students may substitute a research paper on any topic
relating to the course and cleared with the instructor.

BOOKS ORDERED FROM THE UNIVERSITY BOOK STORE:

E. Clark and H. Richardson, eds., WOMEN AND RELIGION: A FEMINIST SOURCEBOOK OF
        CHRISTIAN THOUGHT (New York 1977) [abbreviated as WR]
J. Engelsman, THE FEMININE DIMENSION OF THE DIVINE. (Philadelphia 1979)
Heloise, LETTERS, in B. Radice, trans., THE LETTERS OF ABELARD AND HELOISE (Penguin 197
R. Pernoud, ed., JOAN OF ARC: BY HERSELF AND HER WITNESSES (New York 1969)
R. Ruether, NEW WOMAN, NEW EARTH (New York 1975) [abbreviated NW]
_____, ed., RELIGION AND SEXISM: IMAGES OF WOMEN IN THE JEWISH AND CHRISTIAN
        TRADITIONS (New York 1974)   [abbreviated RS]
K. Stendahl, THE BIBLE AND THE ROLE OF WOMEN (Philadelphia 1966)
Teresa of Avila, AUTOBIOGRAPHY (Doubleday edition, trans. A. Peers)
S. Undset, KRISTEN LAVRANSDATTER III: THE CROSS (Bantam edition)

OPTIONAL (also on reserve):

R. Bainton, WOMEN OF THE REFORMATION IN GERMANY AND ITALY
Gregory the Great, DIALOGUES
E. Power, MEDIEVAL WOMEN, ed. M. Postan
S. Stuard, WOMEN IN MEDIEVAL SOCIETY

All other assigned readings will be on reserve. [abbreviated as R]

COURSE OUTLINE:

I. INHERITED IMAGES OF WOMEN
    A) The Biblical Perspectives:
JAN. 15 LECTURE
Readings: Bible passages suggested in WR (3/4)
               P. Bird, "Images of Women in the OLd Testament" (RS)
               P. Trible, "Depatriarchalizing in Biblical Interpretation," JAAR 41
                 (1973) 30-48 (R)
               C. Parvey, "The Theology and Leadership of Women in the New Testament" (RS)
               K. Stendahl, THE BIBLE AND THE ROLE OF WOMEN

    B) The Theological Question:
JAN. 22 LECTURE
Readings: J. Engelsman, THE FEMININE DIMENSION OF THE DIVINE

II. THE IDEAL WOMAN: THE BLESSED VIRGIN MARY
JAN. 29 LECTURE
Readings: R. Ruether, "Mistress of Heaven " (NW)
               _____, "Misogynism and Virginal Feminism" (RS)
               Selections from Infancy and Marian Pseudepigrapha (R)

III. THE IDEAL WOMAN: VIRGINITY, SERVICE, AND MARTYRDOM
FEB. 5 LECTURE
Readings: Clement of Alexandria, Augustine, Jerome (WR 5/7)
               Tertullian(?), THE PASSION OF SAINTS PERPETUA AND FELICITY (R)
               Gregory of Nyssa, THE LIFE OF SAINT MACRINA (R)
               A. Yarbrough, "Christianization in the Fourth Century: The Example
                 of Roman Women," CH 45 (1976) 1-17 (R)

IV. SERVING AND RULING: WOMEN IN CHRISTIAN LEADERSHIP
    A) The Church
FEB. 12 LECTURE
Readings: R. Ruether, "Guarding the Sanctuary" (NW)
               E. McLaughlin, "Equality of Souls, Inequality of Sexes: Women in
                 Medieval Theology" (RS)
               Thomas Aquinas selections in WR (8)
               F. Cardman, "The Medieval Question of Women and Orders," The Thomist
                 42(1978) 582-99 (R)

    B) The State
FEB. 19 LECTURE
Readings: E.A.R. Brown, "Eleanor of Aquitaine: Parent, Queen and Duchess," in
                 ELEANOR OF AQUITAINE ed. W.W. Kibler (R)
               R. Pernoud, ed. JOAN OF ARC (1-6)
               V. Scudder, ed. SAINT CATHERINE OF SIENA AS SEEN IN HER LETTERS, sel. (R)

V. THE TRIUMPHANT INSTITUTION: MONASTICISM
    A) Origin and Development
FEB. 26 LECTURE
Readings: Caesarius, RULE FOR NUNS, selections (R)
               E. Power, "Nunneries," in MEDIEVAL WOMEN
               B. Bolton, "Mulieres Sanctae," in WOMEN IN MEDIEVAL SOCIETY

B) Individual Self-Expression

MARCH 4 LECTURE

Readings: Gregory the Great, DIALOGUES, selections
             P.A. Crusack, "ST. Scholastica: Myth or Real Person?" DOWNSIDE REVIEW
                92(1974) 145-59 (R)
             J.H. Wansbrough, "St. Gregory's Intention in the Stories of St.
                Scholastica and Sy. Benedict," REVUE BÉNÉDICTINE 75 (1965) 145-51 (R)
             Hroswitha of Gandersheim, SAPIENTIA, PAPHNUTIUS, DULCITIUS (R)
             Heloise, LETTERS

VI. THE TRIUMPHANT TRADITION: MYSTICISM
   A) Traditional Feminine Spirituality

MARCH 18 LECTURE

Readings: E. Underhill, MYSTICISM, selections (R)
             C.H. Talbot, THE LIFE OF CHRISTINA OF MARKYATE (R)
             Butler, LIVES OF THE SAINTS, lives of Gertrude the Great, Elisabeth of
                Schönau, Mechtilde of Hackeborn, Teresa of Avila, Catherine of
                Genoa, Brigid of Sweden, Lydwine of Schiedam

   B) The Mystical and the Saintly

MARCH 25 LECTURE

Readings: Julian of Norwich, Margery Kempe in WR (9)
             Mechtilde of Magdeburg, THE FLOWING LIGHT OF THE GODHEAD, tr. L. Menzies,
                selections (R)

VII THE QUESTION OF WITCHCRAFT

APRIL 1 LECTURE

Readings: MALLEUS MALEFICARUM, selections in WR (10)
             R. Ruether, "Witches and Jews: the Demonic Alien in Christian Culture" (NW)
             R. Pernoud, JOAN OF ARC (7-9)

VIII. THE DAWN OF THE MODERN ERA

APRIL 8 LECTURE

Readings: Luther and Milton, selections in WR (11/12)
             J. Irwin, "Anna Maria von Schurman: From Feminism to Pietism" CH (1977) (R)
             Teresa of Avila, AUTOBIOGRAPHY, selections
             R. Bainton, WOMEN OF THE REFORMATION IN GERMANY AND ITALY, selections
             J.D. Douglas, "Women and the Continental Reformation" (RS)

IX. AN ORDINARY LIFE

APRIL 15 LECTURE

Reading: S. Undset, KRISTIN LAVRANSDATTER III: THE CROSS

APRIL 22   SUMMARY AND OVERVIEW

Medieval Women Writers

September

Thurs. 10: Introduction. Basic texts: Petroff, Medieval Women's Visionary Literature; Wilson, Medieval Women Writers, Dronke, Women Writers of the Middle Ages. Read "Introduction" in Petroff, pp. 3-59.

Tues. 15: "Women in the Early Church" in Petroff, pp. 60-69, "The Passion of St. Perpetua" and "The Life of St. Macrina," pp. 70-77 and 77-82.

Thurs. 17: "St. Perpetua" and "St. Macrina"

Tues. 22: Hrotsvit (Hroswitha) of Gandersheim: "Basilius" and "Dulcitius" in Wilson, pp.30-63; "Pelagius" and "Abraham" in Petroff, pp. 114-135; "Hrotsvitha" in Dronke, pp.55-83.

Thurs. 24: continue with Hrotsvit.

Tues. 29: "Heloise" in Wilson, pp. 90-108; "Heloise" in Dronke, pp. 107-143.

October

Thurs. 1: continue Heloise.

Tues. 6: Marie de France: Lais. "Guigemar," "Le Fresne," "Bisclavret." Trans. Joan Ferrante and Robert Hanning.

Thurs. 8: Marie de France: "Lanval," "Yonec," "Eliduc."

Tues. 13: Women Troubadours, in Meg Bogin, The Women Troubadours. "Personal Poetry by Women," in Dronke, pp. 84-106, and his article on Castelloza in Wilson, pp. 131-152.

Thurs. 15: continue women troubadours.

Tues. 20: Hildegard, the "Seer of the Rhine." Dronke, "Hildegard of Bingen," pp. 144-201; "The German Visionary: Hildegard of Bingen," in Wilson, pp. 109-130; "Visionaries of the early twelfth century" and "Hildegard" in Petroff, pp. 136-143, 151-158.

Thurs. 22: continue Hildegard. xeroxed handouts from Scivias and essay by Joan Ferrante.

Tues. 27: The Beguine movement in northern Europe. "New Styles of Feminine Spirituality" in Petroff, pp. 171-178; "Marie d'Oignies," "Christina of St. Trond," "Hadewijch of Brabant," "Beatrijs of Nazareth," pp. 179-206.

Thurs. 29: "Mechthild of Magdeburg" and "Hadewijch" in Wilson, pp. 153-203.

November

Tues. 3: A Women's Movement in southern Europe. "Women and Spirituality in Medieval Italy," in Petroff, pp. 231-241; "Testament of St. Clare," "St. Umilta," "Angela da Foligno," pp. 242-263.

Thurs. 5: "Women, Heresy, and Holiness," in Petroff, pp.276-283; "Na Prous Boneta," "Marguerite Porete," pp. 284-290, 294-298. "Marguerite Porete" in Wilson, pp. 204-226; "From Hildegard to Marguerite Porete" in Dronke, pp. 202-228.

Tues. 10: St. Catherine of Siena: "Letters" in Petroff, pp. 263-275; "Catherine of Siena" in Wilson, pp. 252-268.

Thurs. 12: Interpretations of Catherine: selections from Bell, Holy Anorexia, and Bynum, Holy Feast and Holy Fast.

Tues. 17: "Women Writers of the Late Fourteenth Century" in Petroff, pp. 299-307; texts of Julian of Norwich, Margery Kempe, Dona Leonor Lopez de Cordoba, pp. 308-334.

Thurs. 19: "Julian of Norwich," "Margery Kempe," in Wilson, pp. 269-296, 297-319.

Tues. 24: Interpretations of Margery Kempe and Julian of Norwich. Selections from Atkinson, Mystic and Pilgrim.

Thurs. 26: THANKSGIVING

December

Tues. 1: "Christine de Pizan," in Wilson, pp. 333-363. Selections from City of Ladies.

Thurs. 3: continue Christine de Pizan.

Tues. 8: Joan of Arc; selections from her trial.

Thurs. 10: selections from A Lesbian Nun in Renaissance Italy.

Paper Topics: CL 391/WOST 393   E. Petroff

Paper 1 (due Nov.10)
     A creative response to the works of one of the writers we have read. I
am interested in seeing a connection between you and the medieval woman whose
writings you choose; you might write an imaginary interview with her, a
dialogue between yourself and her, a letter to her, a story about her. One of
you is writing a letter to Dhuoda; the persona writing is another woman who is
taking care of Dhuoda's little son and telling Dhuoda how he is doing. (Dhuoda
is the Frankish woman who wrote a book on how to be a good man for the son who
was taken away from her in infancy.) Another person is writing a tenzone in
the stgyle of the women troubadours. I imagine these papers will be three to
five pages long, about 1,000 words, typed.

Paper 2 (due Nov.24)
     A report on library work so far. This may take the form of a book
report, a journal entry of 3-5 pages responding to a specific issue you have
encountered in your reading, a analysis or critique of something you feel is
particularly insightful or wrong-headed about medieval women. You may want to
write on something about the Crusades, or prostitution, or women and religion,
or address an article or book on one of the women writers we've read. I'm not
expecting a lengthy report here, but I do want to see some real critical
thinking on women's issues. Try to stay under five pages.

The FINAL EXAM will be a take-home final that you'll have about two weeks to
work on. It will be both creative and scholarly, and we'll write it together.

THE JEWS IN THE MIDDLE AGES
Professor Judith Baskin
University of Massachusetts/Amherst

This course surveys Jewish history and civilization under Islam and in the Christian world from the fourth to the fifteenth century. Emphasis is placed both on Judaism's internal development, and on Jewish responses to the medieval civilizations of Islam and Christianity. The first half of the course considers the Islamic milieu, the second the Christian.

Course requirements are a midterm, a final, an oral report, and an 8-10 page paper based on that report. Possible report topics are suggested at the end of the syllabus. Students should consult with the Professor for bibliography and for approval of alternative topics. A helpful collection of bibliographical essays, on reserve in the library, is **Bibliographical Essays in Medieval Jewish Studies. The Study of Judaism** Vol.2 (published by KTAV for the Anti-Defamation League of B'nai B'rith, New York, 1976). The **Encyclopedia Judaica**, and the older **Jewish Encyclopedia**, in the reference section of the library, are also basic tools for beginning research, as are the bibliographical sections in our assigned texts.

Required Texts:

Robert Seltzer   **Jewish People. Jewish Thought**   JPJT

Norman Stillman   **The Jews of Arab Lands**   JAL

Jacob Marcus   **The Jew in the Medieval World**   JMW
             (a sourcebook)

Jacob Neusner   **Understanding Rabbinic Judaism**   URJ
   (a collection of essays by major scholars on important medieval
         Jewish ideas, trends and personalities)

Leon Poliakov   **The History of Antisemitism** vol. 1   HA

Strongly Recommended:

Israel Abrahams   **Jewish Life in the Middle Ages**   JLMA

Jacob Katz   **Exclusiveness and Tolerance**
             Tradition and Crisis

Louis Jacobs   **Jewish Ethics. Philosophy and Mysticism**   JEPM
             (a sourcebook)

S. D. Goitein   **Jews and Arabs**.

Jan. 13: Rabbinic Backgrounds of Medieval Judaism. URJ 39-70.

Jan. 18: Judaism and Islam. JPJT 323-334; JAL 3-21, 113-151.

Jan. 20: Baghdad and the Achievements of the Geonim. JPJT 334-337; JAL 22-39, 152-182; JMW 185-188.

Jan. 25: The Karaite Movement and Saadia Gaon. JPJT 337-342, 373-381; URJ 149-17; JMW 233-240, 287-292.

Jan. 27: Jewish Life under Islam: The Genizah Documents and Merchant Activity. JAL 40-53, 64-87, 183-209, 247-251; JMW 293-296.

Feb. 1: The Jews in Muslim Spain I: Social and Political Life. JPJT 342-348; JAL 53-63, 210-230; JMW 297f.

Feb. 3: The Jews in Muslim Spain II: Creative and Artistic Life. Shalom Spiegel, "On Medieval Hebrew Poetry," in Judah Goldin, The Jewish Expression (on reserve); T. Carmi, The Penguin Book of Hebrew Verse, 221-222, 253-254, 286-287, 316-317, 346-347.

Feb. 8: Achievements in Jewish Philosophy I: Saadia Gaon and Judah Halevi. JPJT 382-392; URJ 135-145, 175-186. Handout material: from Saadia´s Book of Doctrines and Beliefs and Halevi´s Kuzari (also JEPM, 59-63, 68-72).

Feb. 10: Achievements in Jewish Philosophy II: Maimonides. JPJT 393-408; URJ 187-214. Handout material: from Mishneh Torah and Guide of the Perplexed (also JEPM, 9-18, 73-92).

Feb. 15: The Jews in Christian Spain I. JPJT 364-370; URJ
215-   237; JMW 34-40.

Feb. 17: The Jews in Christian Spain II. JPJT 370-372; JMW 51-55, 173-178.

Feb. 22: Jewish Mysticism I. URJ 279-300; JPJT 419-422, 425-450. Handout material from the Zohar.

Feb. 24: Jewish Mysticism II: Lurianic Mysticism. JPJT 454-467; S. Schecter, "Safed in the Sixteenth Century: A City of Light and Mystics," in Goldin, The Jewish Expression. Handout material from Hayim Vital, Tree of life.

Mar. 1: MIDTERM EXAM

Baskin

Mar. 3:	The Jews in Western Europe in the Early Middle Ages. JPJT 350-355; JMW 3-7, 227-232, 349-352, 355-359; JAL 163-164.

Mar. 3: The Jews in Western Europe in the Early Middle Ages. JPJT 350-355; JMW 3-7, 227-232, 349-352, 355-359; JAL 163-164.

Mar. 22: Medieval Christendom and the Jews. HA chs. 1,2; J. Huizinga, The Waning of the Middle Ages chs. 1, 3, 12 (on reserve); JMW 101-114, 353-354.

Mar. 24: Franco-German Jewry before 1100. HA ch. 3; URJ 101-115; JMW 360-363.

Mar. 31: The Crusades and their Aftermath I: External Reactions.JPJT 355-360; HA ch. 4; JMW 115-131, 301f.

Apr. 5: The Crusades and their Aftermath II: Internal Responses. HA ch. 5; JPJT 422-425; URJ 303-313.

Apr. 7: Church, State and Jews 1200-1400.   JPJT 360-364; HA chs. 6,7; JLMA chs. 4, 16, 23.

Apr. 12: Daily Life: Economic Activity and Community Organization.   JMW 28-33, 189-191, 364-365, 373-377; JLMA chs. 1, 2, 3, 11, 12.

Apr. 14: Daily Life: Women and Family.   ·JLMA chs. 7-10; JMW 311-316, 389-393, 443-445.

Apr. 19: Medieval Jewish Creativity. I. Twersky, "The Shulkan Aruch: Enduring Code of Jewish Law," in Goldin, The Jewish Expression; B. Narkiss, Hebrew Illuminated Manuscripts; J. Gutmann, Jewish Manuscript Painting.

Apr. 21: The Jews at the End of the Middle Ages: Expulsions, Population Shifts;the Ghetto.JPJT 348-349, 467-82.

REPORT/PAPER TOPICS

Ritual Murder Accusations in England and France
Jewish Women in the Middle Ages East or West
The Medieval Ethical Will
Medieval Hebrew Poetry ;   Medieval Biblical Exegesis
Jewish Magic and Superstition
The Expulsion from Spain in 1492;   Court Jews
Medieval Responsa Literature
The Zohar, or a specific aspect of Jewish mysticism
Jewish Merchants in the Middle Ages or Jews as Moneylenders
Jewish Urban Life in Cairo/Baghdad/Spain/Germany/England
Jewish-Christian Relations;   Islamic Attitudes towards Judaism
An Aspect of Medieval Jewish Philosophy
Benjamin of Tudela: A Medieval Jewish Traveller

ADDITIONAL READINGS ON JEWISH WOMEN AND FAMILY LIFE

Adler, M.   "The Jewish Woman in Medieval England," M. Adler, The Jews of Medieval England.

Agus, I. A.   The Heroic Ages of Franco-German Jewry,   277-309.

Baskin, J. "Jewish Women in the Middle Ages,"   J. Baskin, ed. Jewish Women: Historical Essays (forthcoming).

Epstein, I. "The Jewish Woman in the Responsa," L. Jung, ed. The Jewish Library. Vol. 3, 123-152.

Falk, Z.   Jewish Matrimonial Law in the Middle Ages.

Friedman, M.   Jewish Polygyny in the Middle Ages.

        Jewish Marriage in Palestine.

Goitein, S. D. A Mediterranean Society. The Family. Vol. 3.

Jordan, W. C. "Jews on Top: Women and the Availability of Consumption Loans in Northern France in the Mid-Thirteenth Century," Journal of Jewish Studies (1978), 39-56.

Marcus, I.   "Mothers, Martyrs, and Moneymakers: Some Jewish Women in Medieval Europe," Conservative Judaism 38 (1986), 34-45.

Melammed, R. L.   "The Sephardi Woman in the Middle Ages," J. Baskin, ed. Jewish Women: Historical Essays (forthcoming).

Metzger, T. and M. Jewish Life in the Middle Ages. Illuminated Hebrew Manuscripts of the Thirteenth to the Sixteenth Centuries.

Noble, S. "The Jewish Woman in Medieval Martyrology," C. Berlin, ed. Studies in Jewish Bibliography. History and Literature in Honor of I. Edward Kiev, 347-355.

Rabinowitz, L. The Social Life of the Jews of Northern France in the XII-XIVth Centuries as reflected in the Rabbinical Literature of the Period.

Taitz, E. "Kol Ishah -- The Voice of the Woman: Where was it heard in Medieval Europe," Conservative Judaism 38 (1986), 46-61.

4

THE DEVELOPMENT OF HUMAN CONSCIOUSNESS AND INTELLIGENCE:
EXPLORATIONS IN HISTORIOGRAPHY AND THE PHILOSOPHY OF HISTORY
Elizabeth A. R. Brown
Brooklyn College

How have human consciousness, perception, and
intelligence developed and changed through the centuries?
What explanations have been and can be offered for the
modifications that have occurred? What relationship exists
between these changes and modifications in human
sensibilities and emotions? These are the chief questions
with which this seminar will be concerned. Particular
attention will be paid to the writings of Michel Foucault,
but, in order to understand and assess his point of view,
the seminar will also study, compare, and analyze the
writings of a number of important thinkers who, since early
modern times, have confronted and wrestled with the problems
he discusses. The stands these thinkers take will be
related to the life histories of the individuals who
developed them and to the milieus in which they were
formulated.

The seminar is planned as an essay in exploration and
investigation, as an opportunity for students and faculty
who are interested in these problems to meet together, read
a body of common texts, and discuss and analyze them.
Scholars working on the problems will be invited to attend
meetings of the seminar to discuss their own work and to
participate in our discussions, and I hope that some of the
authors whose works we are reading will be able to be with
us.

REQUIREMENTS

Each student will be asked to write an essay examining
an idea, a thinker, or a group of thinkers: the essay is
not to exceed ten pages in length and must be prepared in
conformity with the MLA Style Sheet. Students will present,
orally, their initial hypotheses and research designs and,
in the final meetings of the seminar, the results of their
investigations. These presentations and the research paper
will be the most heavily weighted components of the course.
Another important requirement of the course will be that
students read the assigned material in advance of each
seminar and participate in class discussion: for reasons
that will be apparent to anyone surveying the list of
readings, this seminar will not and cannot be a lecture
course, and the quality of the results we achieve will
depend on the participation and cooperation of each member
of the seminar. There will be a take-home final examination

which will count for approximately 25% of the final grade.

Copies of the books and ariticles to be assigned will be available on reserve in the Brooklyn College library, although most of the books are available in paperback and have been ordered through the College Bookstore: assigned articles will be available in xeroxed copies. Many participants will have read one or more of the assigned readings, and I encourage them to re-read them as well as to explore additional material related to the topics of the seminar. If you have not investigated the subjects we will be considering, do not be discouraged, and, above all, do not be overwhelmed by the list of readings, since, as you will see, the core of required readings will be manageable. I hope that you will want to do some of the reading before the seminar begins. Particularly appropriate as background are S. I. Hayakawa, Language in Thought and Action; Myron P. Gilmore, Humanists and Jurists: Six Studies in the Renaissance; James D. Watson, The Double Helix, and Francis Crick, Life Itself: Its Origin and Nature (see also the reveiw of this book by Gunther S. Stent in The New York Review of Books, December 3, 1981, pp. 34-36).

MASTER READING LIST
The asterisked readings will constitute the core reading for the seminar

*The New Science of Giambattista Vico, abridged and tr. from the third edition by T.G. Bergin and M. H. Fisch

Julian Jaynes, The Origin and Consciousness in the Breakdown of the Bicameral Mind, and

for those who have not recently read them, the Iliad and the Odyssey are strongly recommended--either or both.

*Jean Piaget, The Child's Conception of the World, and

*The Moral Judgment of the Child.

*Charles M. Radding, "Evolution of Medieval Mentalities: A Cognitive-Structural Approach," American Historical Review 83 (1978) 577-597, and

*"Superstitions to Science: Nature, Fortune, and the Passing of the Medieval Ordeal," American Historical Review 84 (1979) 945-969.

*F. Edward Cranz, two unpublished papers discusssing the reorientation of thought and consciousness in the Twelfth Century.

*Elizabeth A. R. Brown, Review Essay of R. Howard Bloch, Medieval French Literature and Law (Los Angeles and London, 1977), History and Theory 19 (1980) 319-338, and

*"The Tyranny of a Construct: Feudalism and Historians of Medieval Europe," American Historical Review 79 (1974) 1063-1088, and

"Feudalism Five Years Later," unpublished essay.

*Michel Foucault, The Order of Things: An Archaeology of the Human Science, and

*The Birth of the Clinic: An Archaeology of Medical Perception, and

*Discipline and Punishment: The Birth of the Prison, and

*Madness and Civilization, and

*A History of Sexuality, vol. 1, INTRODUCTION.

MEDIEVAL HISTORIOGRAPHY
*CORE COURSE FOR GRADUATE STUDENTS IN MEDIEVAL HISTORY
G57.2113

Penny Johnson   Office hrs: M 3-5
fall, 1987   T 3-5
                                              Room 513, 19 Univ Pl
                                              998-8619 and 998-8600

The purpose of this course is to introduce major historiographic themes
in medieval history so that the graduate student is familiarized with
basic issues and schools in the field. This course is to be a required
course for all graduate students in medieval history. Although the
reading is heavy on some weeks, it is lighter on others. The average
weekly reading is 286 pages, or if you consider that there is <u>no</u>
reading for our last meeting, it averages out to 264 pages per week.

Sept. 21   <u>INTRODUCTION</u>

Sept. 28   <u>THE PROBLEMS</u> (80 pp.)
     Bernard Bailyn, "The Challenge of Modern Historiography," <u>AHR</u>
        87 (1982), 1-24.
     Theodore Rabb, "Coherence, Synthesis, and Quality in History" <u>The
        Journal of Interdisciplinary History</u> 12 (1981), 315-332.
     Gertrude Himmelfarb, "Denigrating the Rule of Reason," <u>Harper's</u>
        268 (1984), 84-90.
     John Van Engen, "The Christian Middle Ages as an Historiographical
        Problem" <u>AHR</u> 91 (1986), 519-552.

Oct. 5   <u>TRANSITION FROM ANTIQUITY</u>
     Peter Brown, <u>The Cult of the Saints: Its Rise and Function in
        Latin Christianity</u> (1981).
     Robin Lane Fox, <u>Pagans and Christians</u> (1986).

Oct. 12   <u>THE BARBARIANS</u> (242 pp.)
     J. Wallace-Hadrill, <u>The Barbarian West: The Early Middle Ages</u>
        (1962). OUT OF PRINT. READ IN BOBST ON RESERVE.
     H. Wolfram, "The Shaping of the Early Medieval Kingdoms," <u>Viator</u>
        1 (1970), 1-20.
     G. B. Ladner, "On Roman Attitudes Toward Barbarians in Late
        Antiquity," <u>Viator</u> 7 (1976), 1-26.
     E. A. Thompson, "Barbarian Invaders and Roman Collaborators,"
        <u>Florilegium</u>, 2 (1980), 71-88.
     Walter Goffart, "Rome, Constantinople, and the Barbarians,"
        <u>AHR</u> 86 (1981), 273-306.

Oct. 19   <u>PIRENNE THESIS</u> (280 pp.)
     Henri Pirenne, <u>Medieval Cities</u> (orig. pub. 1925)
     <u>Problems in European Civilization: The Pirenne Thesis</u> ed. Alfred F.
        Havighurst (1958)   Introduction.
     P. Grierson, "Commerce in the Dark Ages: A Critique of the
        Evidence," <u>Transactions of the Royal Historical Society, Fifth
        Series</u> 9 (1959), 123-140.
     K. F. Morrison, "Numismatics and Carolingian Trade: A Critique of
        the Evidence," <u>Speculum</u> 38 (1963), 403-432.

Oct. 26 THE MIND AND MØNEY ØF THE MIDDLE AGES (301 pp.)
   Lynn White, "The Expansion of Technology 500-1500," in Fontana
      Economic History of Europe ed. Carlo Cipolla (1972), 143-74.
   Georges Duby, The Early Growth of the European Economy: Warriors
      and Peasants from the Seventh to the Twelfth Centuries (1974).

Nov. 2 "FEUDALISM" (390 pp.)
   Joseph Strayer, "Feudalism in Western Europe," Lordship and
      Community in Medieval Europe ed. Fredric Cheyette (1968).
   Elizabeth Brown, "The Tyranny of a Construct: Feudalism and
      Historians of Medieval Europe," AHR 79 (1974), 1063-1088.
   Georges Duby, The Three Ørders: Feudal Society Imagined (1980).

Nov. 9 TWELFTH-CENTURY RENAISSANCE (225 pp.)
   Robert Lopez, "Still Another Renaissance?" AHR 57 (1951),
      1-21.
   Colin Morris, The Discovery of the Individual, 1050-1200
      (1972), reprt. (1988).
   Charles M. Radding, "The Evolution of Medieval Mentalities: A
      Cognitive-Structural Approach," AHR 83 (1978), 577-597.
   Caroline Bynum, "Did the Twelfth Century Discover the Individual?"
      Journal of Ecclesiastical History 31 (1980), 1-17.

Nov. 16 SEXUAL BEHAVIØR AND CELERICAL RESPØNSES (334 pp.)
   John Boswell, Christianity, Social Tolerance, and Homosexuality:
      Gay People in Western Europe from the Beginning of the Christian
      Era to the Fourteenth Century (1980).
   Xeroxed reviews of Boswell.

Nov. 23 HERESY AND DISSENT (368 pp.)
   Christopher Brooke, "Heresy and Religious Sentiment, 1000-1250,"
      Bulletin of the Institute of Historical Research 41 (1968),
      115-131.
         pgs. 88-151 of Brian Stock, The Implications of Literacy
      Written Language and Models of Interpretation in the Eleventh
      and Twelfth Centuries (1983).
   R. I. Moore, The Ørigins of European Dissent (1985).

Nov. 30 WØMEN IN THE MIDDLE AGES (216 pp.)
   David Herlihy, "Life Expectancies for Women in Medieval Society,"
      The Role of Woman in the Middle Ages ed. Rosmarie Morewedge
      (1975), 1-20.
   R. Abels and E. Harrison, "The Participation of Women in
      Languedocian Catharism," Mediaeval Studies 41 (1979), 215-251.
   Vern Bullough, "Female Longevity and Diet," Speculum 55 (1980),
      317-325.
   Caroline Bynum, "Fast, Feast, and Flesh: The Religious Significance
      of Food to Medieval Women," Representations 11 (1985), 1-25.
   Women in Medieval History and Historiography ed. Susan Stuard
      (1987).

Dec. 7 <u>THE CRUSADES</u> (378 pp.)
Giles Constable, "The Second Crusade as Seen by Contemporaries,"
    <u>Traditio</u> 9 (1953), 213-279.
R. W. Southern, <u>Western Views of Islam in the Middle Ages</u>
    (1980). ØUT ØF PRINT. READ IN BØBST ØN RESERVE.
Benjamin Kedar, <u>Crusade and Mission: European Approaches toward the
    Muslims</u> (1984).

Dec. 14 <u>THE LATE MIDDLE AGES: APEX ØR DISINTEGRATIØN?</u> (346 pp.)
Johan Huizinga, <u>The Waning of the Middle Ages</u> (first pub. 1924)
        Chap. 11 of: Edward P. Cheyney, <u>The Dawn of a New Era:
    1250-1453</u> (1936)

Jan. 11 CØNCLUSIØNS

INSTRUCTØR'S EXPECTATIØNS:

    This is a colloquium in which reading, discussion, and analysis of
historical problems lie at the core of the course. The reading is
often heavy and needs to be done if the class meetings are to prove
valuable. Class members need to contribute ideas and interpretations
in class.
    WEEKLY JØURNALS: Each week class members will be responsible for
writing and handing in a response journal to that week's reading.
These are not formal papers but are vehicles for your ideas and
reactions. Individuals may experiment with different formats. What
has worked quite well before is to write a brief thesis statement for
each work and then spend a few paragraphs on the interpretation of the
works as they impinge on each other. However, any organization is
acceptable if it deals with all the works read for the particular
week. Some people may want to raise questions, disagree or agree with
authors, and produce what will be a dialogue with the reading. There
is no fixed length, but I suspect that about two to three pages will
suffice for most weeks. *NB: There will be NØ extensions for these
journals. They are due in class the evening of the discussion.
    ØNE WRITE-ØFF: Each student can available him/herself of one
unprepared class meeting. In other words, the reading is not done and
no paper is handed in. Please advise me at the beginning of class when
taking the write-off.
    ARTICLES: Are all on reserve in Bobst under my name. They are
also available in a packet in my box in the department (in lounge to
the right of my office.) These may be read <u>in the department</u> or
briefly removed   When you remove an article, please sign
it out on the sheet and sign it back in when you return it.
    BØØKS: Are available for purchase at the NYU Book Center. They
are also on reserve in Bobst Library under the authors' names. In
several cases, there are also copies still on the shelves at Bobst
which can be checked out by students.

SEMINAR IN MEDIEVAL EUROPE

HISTORY 724   JOHN A. NICHOLS
SPRING 1984   SLIPPERY ROCK UNIVERSITY

I. TEXTBOOK:

    Norman F. Cantor and Michael S. Werthman (eds.), Medieval Society 400-
1450 (New York: Thomas Crowell, 1972).

II. COURSE SCOPE:

        The intention of this seminar is to offer a survey of the institutional
    and cultural developments in Europe from 400 to 1450 by means of selective
    readings on persons and events in the medieval civilization. Ideally the
    student should already have had some introduction to this time in history
    thanks to a Western Civilization survey course, but some association with
    the discipline of history and a desire to learn would be sufficient pre-
    requisites for the student to comprehend the material covered in this upper
    division graduate course.

III. GRADING:

        There will be no examinations in this class. Rather than conduct the
    class on a normal lecture/test/research paper method, I want to introduce you
    to the medieval civilization by way of a reading seminar. As a consequence,
    your final grade will be the average of grades given for short papers written
    every other week for the duration of the semester, oral reports and class par-
    ticipation based on common reading assignments.

IV. INDIVIDUAL ASSIGNMENTS:

        Every other week each student will be assigned an individual assignment
    which relates to the common reading material in the textbook. The assignments
    will be chosen by all students in turn so that everyone will have read approx-
    imately the same number of pages of reading and have the opportunity to select
    preferential assignments. Once the assignment is read the student will report
    on that assignment orally to the class per questions posed by the instructor.

        In addition the student will prepare a three to five page typed paper
    answering the following questions for each individual reading assignment:

    1) What is the major aim, theme, or intent of the author?

    2) What is the nature of the material (give a brief synopsis of the assigned
       pages)?

    3) Was the presentation clear and organized?

    4) Was the conclusion acceptable given the material?

    5) What relationship, if any, did the assignment have to the common reading?

V. CLASS SCHEDULE:

January 18	– Course Introduction
January 25	– Lecture/Carolingian Prelude, pp. 4-32
February 1	– Reports/Written Assignment #1
February 8	– Lecture/Feudal World, pp. 33-82
February 15	– Reports/Written Assignment #2
February 22	– Lecture/Christian Society, pp. 84-122
February 29	– Reports/Written Assignment #3
March 14	– Lecture/Commerce & Urban, pp. 124-165
March 21	– Reports/Written Assignment #4
April 4	– Lecture/Byzantine, pp. 167-201
April 11	– Reports/Written Assignments #5
April 18	– Lecture/Church & State, pp. 203-229
April 25	– Reports/Written Assignments #6
May 2	– Lecture/Science & Technology, pp. 230-258
May 9	– Reports/Written Assignment #7

VI. BREAKDOWN OF GRADES:

The seven written reports will represent 42% of your final grade or 6% per report. The seven oral reports will represent 42% of your final grade or 6% per report. The class discussion from the common reading assignments will represent 16% of your final grade.

VII. ATTENDANCE:

Since sixty percent of your final grade is based on class participation and oral reports, it is necessary for each student to attend every class meeting. If an absence occurs the student will receive no credit for participation unless an individual makeup is scheduled with the instructor.

VIII. EXTRA CREDIT:

Slippery Rock University, along with other Universities, is sponsoring a Conference on Medieval and Renaissance Cultures on April 6 and 7 at Duquesne University in Pittsburgh. Students may add 10 points (10% of the final grade) to their final average by attending either one day or both days of the Conference, listening to the major papers presented by the speakers, and writing a three to five page typed paper answering the five questions as posed above in IV except instead of relating the talk to a common reading, relate the talk or talks to the Conference theme: The Courtly Tradition. The program for the Conference will be distributed in class when they become available.

IX. OFFICE HOURS:

Office: Room 212-K, SWCB
Hours: 10:30-11:30 M,W,F
       2:15- 3:15 T, Th

In addition, I will be pleased to meet you by appointment; see me at the break, after class or call (412) 794-7189, 794-7317 for an appropriate day and time.

X. COURSE OBJECTIVES:

The hope of organizing the course in the above way is to familiarize the student with the major themes of the Middle Ages, to expose the student to the diversities of opinion about events which transpired during that era in history, to develop a critical manner of evaluating secondary material, to improve the student's written and oral presentations, to acquaint the student with the major scholars and works of this field of study, and last, but not least, to satisfy those requirements each of you may have in taking this course.

SEMINAR IN MEDIEVAL EUROPE

(Carolingian Prelude)

UNIT I   HISTORY 724
JOHN A. NICHOLS   SPRING 1984

COMMON READING:

Robert Lopez, "The Carolingian Prelude" in Medieval Society (New York:
Thomas Y. Crowell, 1972), pp. 4-32.

INDIVIDUAL ASSIGNMENTS:

Pierre Riche, "Cults and Culture" in Daily Life in the World of Charlemagne trans. by Jo Ann McNamara (Phila.: Univ. of Pennsylvania Press, 1978),
pp. 181-229.   49

Peter Lasko, "The Frankish Church" in Kingdom of the Franks (New York:
McGraw, 1971), pp. 71-129.   59

Lynn White, "Stirrup, Mounted Shock Combat, Feudalism, and Chivalry"
in Medieval Technology and Social Change (Oxford: University Press, 1962),
pp. 1-38.   39

Suzanne Wemple, "Carolingian Marriages" in Women in Frankish Society
(Phila.: University Press, 1981), pp. 75-123.   49

Peter Munz, "King, Government, and Army" in Life in the Age of Charlemagne (New York: Capicorn Books, 1971), pp. 40-79.   40

Archibald Lewis, "The Carolingian Era, 781 to 840," in Emerging Medieval
Europe (New York: Knopf, 1967), pp. 76-109.   34

Eleanor Duckett, "Saints Boniface, Lull, and Leoba" in Wandering Saints
of the Early Middle Ages (New York: Norton, 1964), pp. 193-228.   36

QUESTIONS TO CONSIDER:

1. What are the important facts in your assigned reading?

2. In what way, if any, does your assignment relate to the common reading?

3. Did you find any differences between the facts or interpretations of
    your reading with the common reading?

SEMINAR IN MEDIEVAL EUROPE

(The Feudal World)

UNIT II   HISTORY 724
JOHN A. NICHOLS   SPRING 1984

COMMON READING:

   Marc Block, "The Feudal World" in Medieval Society (New York: Thomas Crowell,
1972), pp. 33-82.

INDIVIDUAL ASSIGNMENTS:

   C. Stephen Jaeger "The Courtier Bishop in Vitae from the Tenth to the
Twelfth Century" Speculum 58 (April 1983), 291-325.   35

   Norman Cantor and Michael S. Werthman, "The Dimensions of Popular Religious
Life" in Popular Culture (New York: Macmillan, 1968), pp. 100-121.   22

   Eileen Power, "The Peasant Bodo" in Medieval People (New York: Barnes and
Noble, 1924), pp. 18-38.   21

   Ralph Turner, "The Judges of King John: Their Background and Training"
Speculum 51 (July 1976), 447-461.   15

   Eileen Power, "The Working Woman" in Medieval Women (Cambridge: University Press, 1975), pp. 53-75.   23

   Joseph and Frances Gies, "Small and Big Business" Life in a Medieval City
(New York: Apollo, 1973), pp. 76-108.   33

   Michael Mitterauer and Reinhard Sieder, "The Young in the Family" The
European Family (Chicago: Univ. Press, 1982), pp. 93-117.   25

INSTRUCTIONS:

   1. After reading your assignment, create a medieval character that you
      can tell the class about.

   2. Your character should have a name, dates of birth and death, place
      of inhabitation, responsibilities, obligations, and life-style as
      seen in your reading.

   3. You will report your assignment using the first person single
      pronoun and the present verb tense to give a feeling of who you
      are and what your life is like.

   4. Details are important as is your ability to answer questions at
      reports end.

SEMINAR IN MEDIEVAL EUROPE

(Persons in the English Aristocracy)

UNIT III   HISTORY 724
JOHN A. NICHOLS   SPRING 1984

COMMON READING:

Richard W. Southern, "The Bonds of Christian Society" in Medieval Society,
pp. 84-112.

INDIVIDUAL READING:

David C. Douglas, William the Conqueror (Berkeley: Univ. of Calif. Press,
1964), pp. 15-30, 181-209, 247-264.   60

Edward J. Kealey, Roger of Salisbury (Berkeley: Univ. of Calif. Press,
1972), pp. 1-81.   80

R.H.C. Davis, King Stephen 1135-1154 (Berkeley: Univ. of Calif. Press,
1967), pp. 1-55.   55

W.L. Warren, Henry II (Berkeley: Univ. of Calif. Press, 1973), pp. 54-
149.   95

William W. Kibler, Eleanor of Aquitaine (Austin: Univ. of Texas Press,
1976), pp. 9-24.   13

David Knowles, Thomas Becket (Stanford: Standford Univ. Press, 1971),
pp. 1-20, 30-70, 135-155.   80

Sidney Painter, William Marshall (Baltimore: John Hopkin's Press, 1933),
pp. 1-81.   80

INSTRUCTIONS:

1. Introduce your person to the class with a brief summary of their life
    as given in your assignment.

2. Report on the personality of your character: strengths, weaknesses, etc.
    by using appropriate illustrations/examples.

3. How did your individual become who they became: education, family,
    friends, chance.

4. Judge your person's impact on their own time period, as well as for
    future generations.

SEMINAR IN MEDIEVAL EUROPE

(Medieval Cities)

UNIT IV   HISTORY 725
JOHN A. NICHOLS   SPRING 1984

COMMON READING:

   Henri Pirenne, "The Impact of Commerce and Urbanization", in Medieval
Society (New York: Thomas Crowell, 1972), pp. 124-166.

INDIVIDUAL ASSIGNMENTS:

   Timothy Baker, Medieval London (New York: Praeger Pub., 1970),
pp. 27-49.   · 23

   Michael Winch, "Bruges", in Introducting Belgium (London: Methuen,
1964), pp. 25-64.   35

   Glanville Downey, Constantinople (Norman, Okla.: Oklahoma Press, 1960),
pp. 14-42 and Dean Miller, Imperial Constantinople (New York: John Wiley,
1969), pp. 43-77.   62

   Margaret Lebarge, "Paris: The King's Capitol", in Saint Louis
(London: Eyre and Spottiswoode, 1968), pp. 155-178.   23

   Philip Strait, Cologne in the Twelfth Century (Gainesville, Florida
Univ., 1974), pp. 3-43.   40

   John Davis, Venice (New York: Newsweek, 1973), pp. 14-47.   33

QUESTIONS TO CONSIDER:

   1. Describe your city with reference to demographic data, physical
       appearance, noted buildings and/or structures, and time period
       your reading relates to.

   2. Describe the major economic characteristics of your city, how
       money was made, who made it, major goods produced in the city,
       traded by the city, or imported to the city.

   3. Who were the persons with the wealth/power/influence? Who were the
       persons with the skills/trades? Who were the persons with the poorest/
       worst chance for economic/social success?

   4. What importance did your city have on the economic/political/social/
       intellectual history of medieval Europe?

SEMINAR IN MEDIEVAL EUROPE

(Heritage of Byzantium)

UNIT V   HISTORY 725
JOHN A. NICHOLS   SPRING 1984

COMMON READING:

Deno Geanakoplos, "The Heritage of Byzantium," in Medieval Society
(New York: Thomas Crowell, 1972), pp. 167-201.

INDIVIDUAL ASSIGNMENTS:

Philip Whitting, "Justinian and his Successors" in Byzantium
(New York: New York University Press, 1971), pp. 17-35.   18

Charles Diehl, "Theodora" in Byzantine Empresses (New York:
Alfred Knopf, 1963), pp. 44-64.   20

Peter Arnott, "The Church . . . Missionaries and Monks" in The
Byzantines (New York: St. Martin's, 1973), pp. 137-185.   48

Joan M. Hussey, "Learning and Literature" in The Byzantine World
(London: Hutchinson Univ. Library, 1961), pp. 145-155.   11

Anna Comnena, The Alexiad (Baltimore Penguin Books, 1969), pp.
frontpiece and 11-21, 73-101, 505-515.   49

Philip Sherrard, "A Glittering Culture" in Byzantium (New York
Time-Life, 1966), pp. 134-159.   25

DISCUSSION BY YOU:

1. Report on your reading assignment by giving the important
    information found therein.

2. How, if at all, does your assignment relate to the common
    reading?

3. What is the heritage of Byzantium as found in your assign-
    ment?

SEMINAR IN MEDIEVAL EUROPE

(Medieval Religious Life)

UNIT VI   HISTORY 724
JOHN A. NICHOLS   SPRING 1984

COMMON READING:

   Friedrick Heer, "Church and State," in Medieval Society (New York:
Thomas Crowell, 1972), pp. 203-229.

INDIVIDUAL ASSIGNMENTS:

   Wolfgang Braunfels, "The Beginnings" in Monasteries of Western Europe
(Princeton: University Press, 1972), pp. 9-36.   27

   Louis J. Lekai, The Cistercians (Kent: Kent State Press, 1977),
pp. 1-51.   51

   David Knowles, "The Charterhouse of Witham," in Monastic Order in
England (Cambridge: University Press, 1966), pp. 375-391.   17

   Richard Southern, "The Friars," in Western Society and Church in
Middle Ages (New York: Penguin, 1970), pp. 272-299.   27

   Brenda M. Bolton, "Mulieres Sanctae," in Women in Medieval Society
(Phila.: Penn. Press, 1976), pp. 141-158.   17

POINTS TO CONSIDER:

   1. Describe your assignment with reference to the important facts, names,
       dates, etc.

   2. What contributions did the religious orders make to the medieval
       church in particular and medieval society in general?

SEMINAR IN MEDIEVAL EUROPE

(Science and Technology)

UNIT VII   HISTORY 725
JOHN A. NICHOLS   SPRING 1984

COMMON READING:

    A.C. Crombie, "Medieval Science and Technology" in Medieval Society
(New York: Thomas Crowell, 1972), pp. 230-258.

INDIVIDUAL ASSIGNMENTS:

    Charles H. Gibbs-Smith, The Bayeux Tapestry (London: Phaidon, 1972),
pp. 4-15, plus figures, 52 slides, 1 tray.
                                                         30

    Allan Temko, Notre Dame of Paris (New York: The Viking Press, 1952),
pp. 3-14, 114-153, ____ slides.
                                                         52

    Hans Jantzen, "The Exterior of Cathedrals" High Gothic (Hamburg:
Minerva Press, 1962), pp. 98-156, ____ slides.
                                                         58

    Ronald Sheridan and Anne Ross, Gargoyles and Grotesques (Boston:
Graphic Society, 1975), pp. 11-22, plus figures, 12 slides.
                                                         31

    June Osborne, Stained Glass in England (London: Frederick Muller,
1981), pp. 7-41 and James R. Johnson, The Radiance of Chartres (New
York: Random House, 1965), pp. 67-79, ____ slides, 1 tray.
                                                         48

INSTRUCTIONS:

1. You will receive two grades for this assignment.

2. Your first will be a summary of your individual reading with
   the focus on the technique and meaning behind what they did
   rather than exactly what they did.

3. The second grade will be your discussion of the slides given
   to you using the individual reading assignments as your guide.

   a. You may use other books to help with your description,
      other slides too.

   b. You need not use all the slides I gave you, pick the ones
      you want to talk about and give them to me before your oral
      report.

   c. I want a concise, creative 5 to 10 minute description not a
      dissertation.

BEGINNING AND ORGANIZING RESEARCH TOPICS IN WOMEN'S STUDIES
Elizabeth Petroff
University of Massachusetts

Phase One: Topic and primary sources. Documents.

Step 1: Acquire a small notebook to carry with you in which you will write down everything you look up, take notes on readings, etc. Later you will transfer this information to notecards, outlines. etc.

Step 2: Identify your topic. Examples of topics:

a. an individual woman, eg. Margery Kempe of Lynn, England, wrote 1st autobiography in English.

b. a movement founded by women or participated in by women collectively, eg. beguines in Belgium in 12th century, Marie d'Oignies and her followers in 12th century France.

c. a critical problem in interpretation, eg. literacy of women especially nuns, in the 13th century the role of women in the Christianization of Roman culture in the 4th century. Define for yourself the poles of the argument: women were highly educated/women were almost illiterate; women's influence in converting Rome was indispensible/negligible. Keep your eyes open for evidence used to support these positions.

A topic is elastic—you can shrink or expand it depending on how much information you learn is available. Limits in time, geography, numbers of people, etc.

Step 3: Learn where the primary sources are for your topic. Identify area or type.

a. biography
b. literature
c. history of religion
d. social history
e. arts

Step 4: Check out bibliographies that will give names and locations of collections of primary sources or documents. Begin with Bibliographies on bibliographies, and Paetow, Guide to the Study of Medieval History.

a. biography—start with Dictionary of Christian Biography and Dictionary of Saintly Women. Other collections, esp. hagiographical, in Paetow.

b. literature. Consult Fisher, The Medieval Literature of Western Europe. Fisher is organized according to national literature; useful to get an overview of how a writer fits into general literary picture.

c. history of religion. Consult Paetow, Eckenstein, Women Under Monasticism.

d. social history. Consult Paetow.

e. arts. Check art and architecture section in reference room.

Step 5: Getting your hands on the primary sources.

a. After you have identified the editions of primary sources you want, consult the card catalog.
b. Go to National Union Catalog. Look up volume you want. This is a catalog of all printed books that exist somewhere in libraries in the US; below each entry for a book, there is a code which tells you which US libraries own the book. This is what you need to order the book through interlibrary loan. If the book is relatively near, and you think you can go to the library to use it, ask the reference librarian for a letter of reference to that library. This will introduce you as a serious student and will simplify using their resources.

Phase Two: Secondary Sources. Locating, reading, assessing scholarship; building a useful bibliography.

Step 1: back to the bibliographies to locate journals in your field, recent monographs and books on you topic, and so on.

Basic categories of bibliographies:

a. medieval. International Medieval Bibliography, Quarterly Checklist of Medievalia, International Guide to Medieval Studies. Journals: Medieval Studies, Speculum, Viator, Medium Aevum.
b. Women's Studies annual bibliographies.
c. literature. Modern Language Association Annual Bibliography.
d. religion. Index to Religious Literature. Journals of religious orders, Church History.

Step 2: Getting Started on Your Reading.

By now you should know four or five journals that publish in your topic area, and you will have a short list of books and articles that deal with your topic in some way, often rather peripherally. Now—work backwards chronologically, from most recent publications to older ones, and beginning with articles, then going to books. Begin with articles because they are more up-to-date, get published much faster then books, smaller journals will have more recent material and will take more risks in what they publish than will large respectable journals. Your real bibliography begins in the footnotes to interesting articles and books. One or two good recent articles will give you clues concerning debates on your topic, will summarize available evidence and how that evidence has been interpreted. Articles can tell you what is worth reading in books written decades ago, and will prepare you for the bias in a particular scholar's work.

Step 3: Recording Your Progress. Write down everthing you encounter, even dead ends, in your notebook. You may need this information to retrace your steps. Do not worry about organizing your notebook--it's just a catch-all.

Notecards: I put bibliography on notecards, and I try to use different size cards for books and articles, and different colors for different topics.

Notes on Reading: summaries of articles can go on a large notecard or on a separate piece of paper. What you want is something you can file and find later. File folders for general categories are useful at this point. So are xeroxes of articles if you can afford them.

Step 4: Evaluating Your Information.

a. historical/biographical data: dates, countries, history of person or movement. Where does this historical/biographical evidence come from? Reliable source?
b. sources for further information?
c. How is information used? Basis of argument? Do different scholars interpret same bit of evidence differently? How can you make an argument?

Professor Gabrielle Spiegel
University of Maryland

HISTORICAL WRITING IN THE MIDDLE AGES

This course is an undergraduate seminar. No one actually reads all
These texts, but we do cover quite a few in the first part of the
course, and then each student writes a fairly lengthy paper on a single
text selected from the genres outlined in the syllabus. Each student
presents his/her paper to the class and all students are responsible for
reading each other's papers, which are handed out the week before any
given presentation.

Week I: Introduction: Principles of Greek and Roman Historiography

> read: Collingwood, _The Idea of History_

Week II: The Bible: The Historicity of Sacred Life

> read: _New Testament:_

> > The Gospel according to St. Matthew

> > St. Paul, I Corinthians

> > Collingwood, The Idea of History, pt. II, pp. 46-56

> > Erich Auerbach, "The Arrest of Peter Valomeres," in _Mimesis,_
> > pp. 50-76

Week III: History as Ancilla to Christian Apologetics: The Chronology of
Sacred Life

> read: Eusebius, _The History of the Church from Christ to Constantine_
> Bks. 1-3; pp. 31-153; Bks. 8-10, pp. 327 -414

Week IV: God and His Nation Elect: The Ecclesiastical Histories of Western
European Peoples

> read: Bede, A History of the English Church and People

> > or

> > Gregory of Tours, _History of the Franks_

> > or

> > Paul the Deacon, _History of the Lombards_

Part Two: Evolution of Historical Genres

Biography in the Classical Style:

     Einhard, The Life of Charlemagne

Biography in the Christian Style:

     Gesta Stephani,The Deeds of Stephen, King of England,
         ed. K.R. Potter (Medieval Texts, 1955)

     Helgaud, Life of Robert the Pious, trans. into French by R.-H. Bautier

History as Epic:

     The Song of Roland

     Snorri Sturluson, Heimskringla: History of the Kings of Norway

     The Song of Igor's Campaign

     Guillaume d'Orange, The Coronation of Louis

History and Romance:

     Wace, Roman de Rou,

     Geoffrey of Monmouth, History of the Kings of Britain [as a source
         of later romance themes, rather than a romance histroy]

     Gaimar, L'Estoire des Engles in Rolls Series, vol 91 (Part two
         contains an English translation)

Chronicles of the Crusades:

     Villehardouin, Conquest of Constantinople

     Joinville, The Life of Louis IX

     Both of the above texts can be found in English in: Chronicles of
         the Crusade (Penguin)

Chronicles of the Crusades cont.

Odo of Deuil, De Profectione Ludovici Septimi in Orientem
Engl. Translation Virginia Berry [Columbia Records of
Civilization]

History and Politics in the 12th Century: The Dignity of the Secular World:

Otto of Freising, The Deeds of Frederick Barbarosa

Ordericus Vitalis, The Ecclesiastical History of England trans.
Majorie Chibnall

Suger, Life of Louis the Fat (transcript available from me; also
available in French)

William of Malmesbury, Historia Novella (New History) trans. K.R. Potter

Nelson, 1955

William of Newburgh, The History of William of Newburgh trans. Appleby

Hagiography in a Secular Mode:

The Chronicle of Jocelyn of Brakelond concerning the acts of Samson
Abbot of Bury St. Edmunds, trans. Butler, 1949

Daniel Walter, The Life of Ailred of Rievaulx, trans. Powicke,
1950

Adam of Eynsham, The Life of Saint Hugh of Lincoln, trans. Doule
and Farmer, 2 vols. 1961-2

Autobiography:

Abelard, Historia Calamitatum The Story of Abelard's Adversities
trans. Muckle

Christina of Maryate, The Life of Christina of Markyate, trans.
C.H. Talbot, 1959 [not exactly an autobiography, but useful
in comparison with Abelard, as in Hanning, The Individual
in 12th Century Romance]

Guibert de Nogent, Self and Society in medieval France, the Memoires
of Abbot Guibert de Nogent, trans. J. Benton

About the editor

Penelope D. Johnson is a graduate of Yale College and received her M.Phil. and Ph.D. from Yale University. She is an Associate Professor of History at New York University where she teaches courses in Medieval History and the History of Women. Her publications include <u>Prayer, Patronage, and Power: The Abbey of la Trinité, Vendôme, 1032-1187</u> (N.Y., 1981), "Finding Their Place: The Rich Roles of Religious Women in the Middle Ages," forthcoming in <u>The Struggles of Eve</u>, and articles published in <u>Revue bénédictine</u>, <u>The Dictionary of Christian Spirituality</u>, <u>Bulletin de la société, archéologique, scientifique et littéraire du Vendômois</u>, <u>Augustinian Studies</u> and forthcoming in the proceedings of the fifteen annual Sewanee Medieval Colloquium, <u>Thought</u>, <u>The Journal of Medieval History</u>, and the Actes du IIe Colloque International du CERCOR. She is currently writing a monograph on monastic women in France during the central Middle Ages.